# Reading, Gender and Identity in Seventeenth-Century England

New Historical PERSPECTIVES

*New Historical Perspectives* is an open access book series for early career scholars, commissioned, edited and published by the Royal Historical Society and the University of London Press in association with the Institute of Historical Research. Submissions are encouraged relating to all historical periods and subjects. Books in the series are overseen by an expert editorial board to ensure the highest standards of peer-reviewed scholarship, and extensive support and feedback for authors is provided.

The series is supported by the Economic History Society.



ISSN 3049-5091 (Print)
ISSN 3049-5105 (Online)

INSTITUTE OF HISTORICAL RESEARCH | SCHOOL OF ADVANCED STUDY UNIVERSITY OF LONDON

ECONOMIC HISTORY SOCIETY

# Reading, Gender and Identity in Seventeenth-Century England

Hannah Jeans

UNIVERSITY OF LONDON PRESS

Available to purchase in print or download
for free at https://uolpress.co.uk

First published 2025 by
University of London Press
Senate House, Malet St, London WC1E 7HU



A CIP catalogue record for this book is available from The British Library.

ISBN 978-1-915249-40-1 (hardback)
ISBN 978-1-915249-41-8 (paperback)
ISBN 978-1 -915249-43-2 (.epub)
ISBN 978-1 -915249-42-5 (.pdf)
ISBN 978-1-913739-11-9 (.html)

DOI https://doi.org/10.14296/xisg9568

Cover image: *Woman Reading*, Rembrandt van Rijn, 1634. Clarence Buckingham Collection. Art Institute of Chicago. CCO Public Domain.

Cover design for University of London Press by Nicky Borowiec.
Book design by Nigel French.
Text set by Westchester Publishing Services UK in
Meta Serif and Meta, designed by Erik Spiekermann.

# Contents

# List of figures

# Acknowledgements

I have been very lucky to be at home in the University of York's History department since I started my undergraduate degree, and the many people who have supported and encouraged me over the years since then are innumerable. Conversations with students have often been invaluable, giving me a new perspective on my work even if they may not have realised it. I would like to thank my friends and colleagues at York who have helped this book along, or even just distracted me at opportune times, including (but not limited to) Venus Bivar, Lawrence Black, Simon Ditchfield, Natasha Glaisyer, Sarah Griffin, Sarah Hall, Eliza Hartrich, Edd Mair, Emma Marshall, Emilie Murphy, Helen Smith, Lizzy Spencer, Sophie Weeks and Sam Wetherell. Mark Jenner has been a constant source of support since my undergraduate days, and this book would in no way exist without him. He has been the best mentor I could have asked for, and I am very grateful.

This book could also not have happened without the support, financial and otherwise, of many people and institutions beyond York. I am grateful to the White Rose College of the Arts and Humanities for the PhD funding, and to the Beinecke Rare Book and Manuscript Library, the William Andrews Clark Memorial Library and the Durham Residential Research Library for fellowships that allowed me access to so many wonderful sources. Staff at all three institutions went above and beyond in helping me while I was there. I would also like to thank Alex Barber, Martine van Elk, Amanda Herbert, Kathryn James, Philip Palmer, Jason Peacey and Heather Wolfe for useful conversations and advice. Thanks are also due to staff at the Bodleian Library, the British Library, Cumbria Record Office, Cambridge University Library, Derbyshire Record Office, the Folger Shakespeare Library, the Henry E. Huntington Library, Hertfordshire Archives and Local Studies, Trinity and Magdalene Colleges in Cambridge, Ushaw College, West Yorkshire Archive Service and York Minster Library.

I am grateful to Peter Lang and *Huntington Library Quarterly* for permission to reproduce some work. Portions of Chapter 1 were previously published in *Women in Print 2: Production, Distribution and Consumption*, ed. Caroline Archer-Parré, Christine Moog and John Hinks (Peter Lang, 2022; permission conveyed through Copyright Clearance Center, Inc.) and portions of Chapter 3 were previously published as 'Women and Manuscript News Culture in Early Modern England', *Huntington Library Quarterly* 86 (winter 2023; reprinted with the permission of the Henry E. Huntington Library). The *New Historical Perspectives* team were fantastic, including

Emma Gallon, Sarah Longair and Elizabeth Hurren, and the feedback from Karin Bowie, Ian Forrest, the anonymous readers of the proposal and particularly the participants in the author workshop – Heather Shore, Marcus Nevitt and Michelle O'Callaghan – was invaluable. Any errors are my own.

I would like to thank my friends Roisin Jacklin, Fiona Milne, Harrie Neal and Tom Sissons, my parents and the rest of my family for their support. My grandfather Arthur died not long before this book was finished, and this is for him.

# Introduction

Reading was a highly contentious pastime for women in the early modern period. It was frequently used by writers of contemporary conduct literature to demonstrate the character of a woman, be that good or bad. Women themselves also used reading to signify aspects of their own identities. This book will consider attitudes to women's reading both within early modern gender discourse and from women readers themselves, examining the relationship between identity and reading habits. I will explore how women interacted with different types of books, their methods and experiences of reading, and their representation thereof. There has been a great deal of important work done on women's reading in the early modern period, and this book will develop that discussion by looking across the whole of the seventeenth century and thinking about many different readers – those well known and those almost lost to the historical record.[1]

This book argues that reading was a way of performing and representing identity, particularly, but not solely, gender identity. Women were negotiating gender norms whether reading within or without the bounds of what was deemed acceptable for their sex. Many theorists suggest that we should see gender as performative, something one enacts. Judith Butler, for example, has argued that 'there is no gender identity behind the expressions of gender . . . identity is performatively constituted by the very "expressions" that are said to be its results'.[2] If gender is something that is enacted, then the act of reading becomes a performance of gender. By reading certain books, in light of cultural conventions dictating their acceptability (or lack thereof) for women, individuals could signal their relationship to gender norms. This can be further refined: perhaps one reads as (or like) an aristocratic woman, with the reading experience being determined by both gender and socio-economic position. Perhaps one even read as/like a white woman, reacting to and signalling cultural codes around race that were developing in this period.[3] In examining the role of reading in the performance and creation of identity, we can shed greater light on how early modern women understood gender and how they negotiated and constructed their own identities.

The process of identity creation through reading is complex and ever-changing. Kate Flint has cautioned against seeing the identity of the reader as formed before the act of reading. She argues that reading could play a part in 'the continuing formation of the subject'.[4] I would add to this that identity formation could happen in the act of *representing* reading. When women wrote about their reading habits, they interacted with various gender norms and prescriptions, whether consciously or unconsciously. This reveals a great deal about how they constructed their individual feminine identity and is rarely discussed by scholars of early modern reading. Letters, diaries and other personal writings from the seventeenth century frequently contained mentions of reading, some more detailed than others, but this facet of the early modern reading experience and its connection to an individual's sense of self has been largely overlooked.

I am looking at reading and writing about reading as a process of self-fashioning that was often continual and changeable. The identity that was produced in the performance of representing reading habits is one that was affected by the time, place and conditions of the reading and/or writing experience. Moreover, it was sociable, formed by relationships with and influences from other readers. As will be seen throughout the book, readers were often interacting with other readers and writers, and this interaction was a key part of identity formation. This builds on Julie Crawford's argument that communities were central to literary production. Crawford reminds us that the coteries and the literature they produced were not 'merely affirmative; they were dialogic, contentious, even confrontational'.[5] Representations of reading were relational, formed by ideas about religion, politics and society, and creating identities that might be influenced by or in opposition to certain prevailing ideas, social groupings or individuals.

Much of this identity construction, whether in autobiography, memoirs, letters, diaries or other forms of 'life-writing', was in conversation with the cultural conventions surrounding women's reading (as outlined above) but did not always replicate them.[6] While women may have drawn on ideals of femininity to construct an identity for themselves, this was not simply a case of conformity to a dominant gender ideology. Instead, they used writing as a way of negotiating, or even rejecting, such norms, and the characters that emerged were hugely complex and individual. This can be applied to other forms of writing, beyond the obvious examples of 'life-writing' that usually make up the autobiographical canon. Annotating the margins of books or writing dedicatory inscriptions on flyleaves or notes in commonplace books or recipe books can all also be seen as acts of identity construction and articulation.[7] This was a semi-public form of recording one's reading habits and – crucially – responses to reading material. Moreover, the repeated nature of reading that can often be seen in annotation, and the effect annotation had on future readings, adds another, temporal dimension to identity construction. In examining the varied ways in which women chose to represent their reading habits, we can learn a great deal about how they negotiated identity. How they viewed themselves or wanted others to view them can be explored through their reading.

The field of women's reading has grown exponentially in recent years, with many excellent works looking at the reading habits and practices of individual women in seventeenth-century England.[8] These have tended to focus on case studies, but taken as a corpus the sheer breadth and depth of these works attests to the hugely varied reading experiences open to early modern women. The recent book *Women's Bookscapes in Early Modern England*, for example, uses a range of case studies to consider women's various reading experiences and interactions with the book, considering reading habits, libraries and collecting practices.[9] The collection *Reading Women* takes a similar approach, although this time with a transatlantic scope.[10] Articles by scholars such as Heidi Brayman and Mary Ellen Lamb have highlighted the reading practices and experiences of women such as Anne Clifford, Frances Egerton and Margaret Hoby.[11]

I draw on many of these case studies, but also bring in a much broader range of readers to build up a picture of reading across a whole century. By considering readers both known and unknown, comparing prolific reading figures such as Lady Anne Clifford to women whose identity is indiscernible beyond a signature, a much more comprehensive of women's reading habits will emerge. Such attention to the grand sweep of women's reading is well deserved; we now recognise that women were frequently avid readers, but confining our studies to individual cases, valuable though they may be, does not allow us to think about change over time or situate those case studies in a more macro context.[12] Both Heidi Brayman and Edith Snook have written broader histories of women's reading; although they both have a different focus to the one taken here, they have been immensely useful when building my own study of women readers. Brayman focused more on the specific practices and materiality of reading, and explicitly rejects using the notion of 'genre' as an organising category.[13] While her objection to the category is valid (she points out that early modern readers rarely organised their books by genre, and uses the layout of the Countess of Bridgewater's book list as a guiding principle for her sample), genre was often at the heart of early modern perceptions of reading.[14] As will be seen below, the question of the type of book was integral to the reception of women readers: a good book could confirm their piety or femininity; while a bad one could damn them as immoral or salacious. Meanwhile, Edith Snook has examined the representations and cultural politics of reading in women's writing, looking at both sixteenth- and seventeenth-century examples.[15] My work sits between Snook and Brayman: I am looking at both the practices and representations of reading, although I am focusing more on how women represented reading in their life-writing, whereas Snook considers more 'literary' texts that were either intended for publication or simply were not solely about an individual's life.

The role of reading in identity construction has been considered before, but not in such depth. Scholars such as Mary Ellen Lamb have discussed how Anne Clifford used her books to support her social status and inheritance rights, but again, this has not been broadened out to think about how women generally used their books to understand, negotiate and display their identities.[16] The clear gendering of reading in the early modern period has often been mentioned but little attention has been paid to exactly how that informed and influenced women's actual reading habits (or failed to do so). This book therefore will consider firstly how women's reading was viewed in the early modern period, then examine how women themselves represented their reading habits, to give us a much greater understanding of the process of women's identity formation in the seventeenth century, and how that interacted with established gender norms.

## Cultural discourses of women's reading

Reading is intrinsically connected to the culture in which it takes place. Women's reading habits (as well as men's) were shaped by contemporary cultural beliefs and conventions. Cultural discourses surrounding proper gendered behaviour were present in many forms of early modern media, with representations of femininity present in art, literature and theatre.[17] Instructional and conduct literature gave perhaps the clearest prescriptions for how men and women should behave, setting out guidelines for how to demonstrate qualities appropriate to one's gender and class.[18] Conduct texts aimed at a female readership became increasingly common as the seventeenth century progressed and women's literacy rates rose.[19] There were certain commonalities in the ideals of feminine behaviour, with emphasis often placed on women's chastity, modesty and piety.[20]

Conduct literature discussed women's reading habits at length, but primarily focused on two main types of text: romantic fiction and religious or devotional texts.[21] These represented the perceived dichotomy of female nature; being either transgressively sexual or deeply pious. Conduct literature gave women rules for behaviour that would reflect their inner 'goodness'; reading was one of many habits that was either encouraged or warned against, depending on the book. The centrality of a book's content was made clear in Jacques du Bosc's *The Excellent Woman*, a French conduct book from the mid-seventeenth century that was translated into English and became very popular. In the preface to the book, having extolled the benefits and virtues of reading, du Bosc offered a note of caution:

> since all Books are not excellent, and there are many which truly deserve to be brought to no light but by the fire; the printing of which should rather have been hindred than the reading them: It must be acknowledged that there is no less difficulty in choosing good Books to employ us when we are alone, than to choose good Wits for our entertainment in company. So that if any find they must not rely upon themselves in this matter for the making of a good choice, they ought at least to follow the counsel of the most knowing and most vertuous, for fear that in reading they may happen to infect the Mind or debauch the Conscience.[22]

These fears about reading were based in a belief that reading was transformative and had a powerful effect on the individual. As Adrian Johns has shown, there was a common belief that 'if one wished to retain reliability and independence of mind, then one must be careful of what, and how, one read'.[23] Johns gives many examples of early modern readers being harmed, sometimes irreparably, by reading, particularly reading done during childhood. Reading the wrong book (particularly romances) or reading in the wrong way could have deep and long-lasting physiological effects.[24] Johns describes the story of the natural philosopher Robert Boyle, who had been recommended romances as a boy to ease his melancholy. He tried to counter the influence of these books later in life, disciplining his thinking by reading algebra, but found that his mind often wandered and indulged in romantic imaginings. As Johns noted, 'the effects of reading those romances had proved permanent, and Boyle simply had to live with them'.[25] Given the potential to cause damage, it is no wonder that writers of advice books were often preoccupied with reading.

This image of romances having almost addictive properties is present in many conduct books, stretching back to the influential and enduringly popular sixteenth-century work on female education by Juan Luis Vives.[26] Vives specifically included a chapter on what books should and should not be read, warning against romances and some Greek poetry. He wrote that a woman:

> should avoid these books as she would a viper or a scorpion. And if a woman is so enthralled by the reading of these books that she will not put them down, they should not only be wrested from her hands, but if she shows unwillingness to peruse better books, her parents or friends should see to it that she read no books at all and become unaccustomed to the reading of literature.[27]

The compulsion to read literature that Vives deemed unsuitable was so strong that he advised that no reading at all was better than reading the wrong material. There is also a clear element of community control here: a woman's friends and family were tasked with checking her reading habits. There is no doubt an underlying implication that women were weak-willed, but as in the case of Robert Boyle, this did affect men as well – reading was potentially highly dangerous and had to be carefully controlled.

The direct opposite of romance reading, which could have a highly negative effect on the individual, was religious reading. Absorbing devotional texts improved a person's mind and body (acting both spiritually and physiologically) and was an essential part of early modern piety. The dichotomy between religious and romance reading is perhaps made most clear in the 'conversion narratives' employed by several seventeenth-century conduct book writers, in which they imagine a youthful infatuation with romances being swept away by proper religious devotion once the reader had realised the error of their ways.[28] For example, Richard Allestree declared that once women found piety, the 'devout temper of her mind will by a holy *leger-demain* shuffle the Romances out of her hand and substitute the Oracles of Truth; will not let her dream away her time in phantastic scenes, and elaborate nothing, but promt her to give all diligence to make her Calling and Election sure'.[29] Conversion, therefore, would quite literally push romances away with a 'holy' sleight of hand and substitute proper, devotional reading.

Richard Baxter also employed this conversion narrative in his funeral sermon for his wife, Margaret. He said of Margaret that:

> In her vain youth, *Pride*, and *Romances*, and *Company* suitable thereto, did take her up . . . But in a little time she heard and understood what those better things were which she had thought must be attained . . . Whereupon she presently fell to self-judging, and to frequent prayer, and reading, and serious thoughts of her present state, and her salvation.[30]

There is a clear suggestion here that reading romances translates into other bad behaviour: Margaret not only read the wrong books but she kept 'company suitable thereto'. However, she was saved from her youthful folly and became a model of an ideal pious woman. In setting up this narrative Baxter and Allestree were showing that women could redeem themselves through practising proper behaviours – through praying regularly and reading religious texts.

There has been a tendency to stress that women's reading was curtailed and limited by the culture in which they lived.[31] Kevin Sharpe and Steven Zwicker have argued that 'for most literate women the experience of the book was confined to spiritual genres and to household manuals, to books of housewifery, herbals, and cookery books'.[32] However, not only does this drastically underestimate the wide literary tastes of women, and the ways in which reading in many forms was part of their daily lives, it also overlooks something that has been commonplace in studies of male reading habits in the early modern period. There has long been a recognition that reading was above all meant to be *useful*, that men undertook to read books that informed either their intellect, general knowledge or daily lives. As T. A. Birrell wrote,

> the contents of the 17th-century gentleman's library was of course predominantly utilitarian: he bought the books he needed. As a landowner and magistrate he needed books on law. As a patron of church livings he needed books on theology . . . even the acquisition of literature, belles lettres, was partly utilitarian. It was justified as a mixture of the *utile* and the *dulce*.[33]

Household manuals, cookery books and spiritual genres would have been essential to women's daily lives – they were useful texts, and not necessarily evidence of limitation.

This focus on use has often been framed in terms of 'active' reading, which naturally invites the inverse of 'passive' reading. Active reading has been a mainstay of historical studies of reading habits ever since Lisa Jardine and Anthony Grafton's influential study of Gabriel Harvey, the Elizabethan scholar.[34] Many studies of early modern marginalia have since taken this concept of active reading as the norm.[35] It has become a standard by which to measure the habits of all readers. This is not to lay the blame at the feet of Jardine and Grafton, who made the social boundaries of their work very clear, but suggesting that some reading is active implies that there is a passive form of reading as well. This has frequently been attached to women's reading, or to genres that are usually associated with women. Romances, plays and other forms of fiction are often referred to as 'light reading'.[36] There is an unspoken assumption that reading that elicits an emotional response cannot also be critical. However, as Frances Teague has pointed out, 'some early modern readers found delight in books, but their pleasure was never frivolous enjoyment. Even when indulging in a romance, a woman was unlikely to read quickly or mindlessly'.[37] This is problematic itself, however, still aligning enjoyment with frivolity and an implied lack of intellectual rationality. As many feminist theorists have pointed out, Western epistemology positions rationality and emotion as binary opposites. Writers such as Alison Jaggar have challenged the concept of male rationality, arguing for a more feminist epistemology. Jaggar noted how 'within western philosophical tradition, emotions usually have been considered as potentially or actually subversive of knowledge'.[38] She posits that emotions function as a way of actively engaging with or constructing the world, rather than uncontrollable impulses that are a passive response to events or objects around us. Thus, an emotional reaction can be just as 'active' as an intellectual one, allowing the reader to develop their understanding and knowledge of the world through their reading.

It is necessary therefore to move away from the active/passive binary when approaching early modern reading. Emotional responses to reading can have just as tangible an effect on the individual as intellectual ones, nor are they 'passive'. 'Activity' has been imbued with certain assumptions and connotations that privilege specific types of activity, which has in turn led to a misinterpretation of many people's reading experiences in the early modern period. Reading for spiritual nourishment or to strengthen social bonds was as important as for scholarly endeavour.

## Finding women readers

The 'woman reader' was diverse. However, exploring all the multifaceted ways in which people, and specifically women, in the early modern period experienced reading would be outside the scope of this book.[39] I am focusing on a select group of women: those who tended to leave written traces of their reading, in the form of letters, diaries, notebooks or annotations. These women were from the upper ranks of society, demonstrated by their literacy and education levels, and their purchasing power. These categories were all central to their identities, and it is important to remember therefore that this book is only considering a certain type of femininity, one which was defined as much by class/wealth as by gender.

It is crucial to recognise how archives themselves have worked to perpetuate these categories. The nature of reading itself is one barrier to finding traces of it in the archive, and this is compounded when looking at the reading of marginalised groups.[40] The paucity of evidence for early modern women readers means that such a picture has to be built up from often fragmentary sources: a passing mention of reading or books in a letter or diary, as part of a list in an inventory or a scribbled name or comment in the margins. Finding these references can be challenging, involving extensive archival work and use of online and printed resources. Some of this can prove fruitless, but there is more evidence than is often assumed, if you know how and where to look for it.

There is, first and foremost, a great deal of serendipity involved in this process. Browsing through letters, online catalogues or printed contemporary texts can result in a day with no concrete findings, as is of course commonplace in historical research, but can also end with exciting results, or at least a mention here or there of reading. Primarily, my evidence has come from four main source bases: annotated books (often books inscribed with women's names), commonplace books or other manuscript compilations, letter collections and women's diaries, memoirs or similar autobiographical writings. All of these come with their own difficulties in terms of identification. The organisation of the historical record and its focus on 'significant' figures and events has often resulted in women's records being subsumed and hidden. As Georgianna Ziegler has pointed out, 'even if you look in the places where you would expect to find traces of [women], they have often remained invisible through omission'.[41] At a time when new forms of recording and digitisation offer novel ways of presenting, sorting and analysing the historical record, it is important to reflect on the ways in which technologies enable and prevent research into early modern women.

One of the best and most tangible sources for reading are annotations and marginalia in books – they demonstrate (to varying degrees, depending on the note) a clear interaction with the book or text. There are some online resources for finding annotated books, although by and large these have prioritised male authors and annotators. The Annotated Books Online project is a resource for those interested in early modern reading habits, and involves the collaboration of a number of British, European and American libraries to digitise various annotated books in their collections.[42] However, the majority of annotators have been early modern male intellectuals. The 'highlights' page lists annotators such as Martin Luther, Isaac Newton, Michel de Montaigne, Gabriel Harvey and Erasmus of Rotterdam. This is an extremely valuable resource, allowing remote access to the extensive annotations of figures like Harvey. However, it is partial at best, and searching for readers with names such as 'Elizabeth', 'Anne', 'Mary' or 'Sarah' currently produces no results.

The problem with online collections of this kind is that they are, in general, focused on figures who are the most well known and who fit into grand historical narratives, and this usually results in a largely male source base. This is, of course, due to a desire to make the databases appeal to a wide audience, but it is reflective of a larger issue within the study of history and literature that prioritises work according to a standard of scholarly engagement, often implicitly male, that would have been institutionally inaccessible to most of contemporary society.

The very fact of using annotations as a way into exploring reading contributes to the narrow subject base, as this form of engagement with text generally, for the early modern period, privileges male readers who were more likely to be able to write.[43] Ownership inscriptions are good indicators of women's interaction with books, if not definitive evidence of reading. In order to find these inscriptions, searching rare book catalogues with the term 'her book' often proves fruitful. This can be combined with a common contemporary woman's name to narrow results, although this does of course result in a tendency to focus on readers with certain names.[44] Using popular women's names in conjunction with the term 'commonplace book' also reveals sources. Most online catalogues do not offer gender-specific searching, so using gendered terms or names is usually the best way to navigate results. The use of names, as an alternative to sex-specific searching, is no doubt useful, but it does come with its own methodological implications. Searching by name serves to individuate provenance, prioritising the individual over the collective category. The 'woman reader' therefore becomes a collection of readers named Elizabeth, Mary or Anne. Sex-specific searching would provide an alternative to this, allowing one to utilise the category of 'woman' or 'man' effectively in archival research, although this of course comes with its own methodological issues.

In recent years, however, there has been an effort to increase the visibility of women's annotations, with social media playing an important role. Scholars on social media frequently share images of female ownership inscriptions in early modern books, using the hashtag #HerBook.[45] This can be a useful tool for sourcing and sharing instances of female autograph inscriptions which are often left out of catalogue copy notes. Moreover, there are now several websites dedicated to highlighting female book ownership. The blog 'Early Modern Female Book Ownership' provides an extremely useful repository of books signed by women, searchable by genre and century.[46] This has allowed women's book ownership to be much more widely available, including books that may be housed in private collections or where the inscription is not included in the catalogue record. It has been invaluable for my own research. Similarly, the Clark Library has digitised over 250 of its rare books bearing manuscript annotations, creating a database that can be refined by genre, subject and decade, although this does not necessarily illuminate women's inscription practices.[47]

Some projects focus on specific individuals, such as Sarah Lindenbaum's work on Frances Wolfreston, one of the seventeenth-century female book collectors best known to modern scholars.[48] Lindenbaum has been working on recovering more of Wolfreston's books, adding to those identified by Paul Morgan in the 1980s, and Arnold Hunt, who added twenty-nine books to Morgan's tally.[49] Over 230 of Wolfreston's books have been identified, a marked increase from the 103 Morgan had found in 1989. Lindenbaum has a blog dedicated to Wolfreston and the reconstruction of her library, and she uses this to crowd-source books bearing Wolfreston's distinctive mark.[50] This method of gathering evidence is particularly useful given the often fragmentary nature of sources for women's reading, and the financial and geographical challenges one might face in visiting multiple archives on an international scale.[51]

In this book I will present a picture of women's reading habits that would not be possible without the many resources that other scholars have painstakingly created. I want to highlight the breadth and depth of women's reading habits. Each chapter of this book will consider a different type of reading and the associated reading experiences of women. Religion and romance, as the types of literature most often linked to women, will be discussed first, but I will also explore how women consumed more political and philosophical or scientific texts in Chapters 3 and 4. Finally, Chapter 5 will think more broadly about how women interacted with books beyond simply reading print; how they used books for multiple ends and how they might reread manuscript material as well as printed text. This will demonstrate the many and varied genres that women read, and the ways in which they read them, all of which helped to create a sense of identity.

The organising principle behind the book is types of reading and types of books. This maps very imperfectly onto literary genre, particularly when considering categories of knowledge such as 'the news' or philosophy and science, which were at best porous categories in the early modern period. 'Genre' itself is a relatively modern term; before the nineteenth century, terms such as 'kinds' or 'species' were instead used to classify literary texts.[52] However, early modern thinkers were clearly concerned about the types of text that people were consuming and this concern was often influenced by a person's gender, as is demonstrated by the preoccupation with 'good' or 'bad' books in conduct literature. This book is not about 'genre' per se, but about the different categories of knowledge and types of text that allowed women to advertise, negotiate and fashion different parts of their identities – be that in terms of their politics, intellectualism, relationships or religious belief.

Ultimately, I am considering the category of the 'woman reader' itself. While this figure is taken as a starting point for this book, it is important to remember the ways in which this category can be complicated, and move beyond a simple sex-based analysis. The developments and reading experiences outlined here should not stand for all women, but rather a group of wealthy, educated white women who were able to read and write. The reading habits of other sections of society, both men and women, were very different again, and there is not the space to explore that here. Gerald MacLean has argued that Frances Wolfreston's reading indicates that she did not 'see herself in any normative social roles prescribed for women . . . Wolfreston neither reads nor writes simply as a daughter, or a wife, or a mother, or an object of sexual fantasy', but rather as a political and social agent.[53] These should not be seen as contradictory positions: women readers read as individuals, and were women. This book will pay attention to the gendered aspects of women's identity, but also argue that the ways in which they read, and their reading materials, were formed and influenced by their social situation, politics and religion, as well as their gender.

## Notes

1. A select few includes Heidi Brayman Hackel, *Reading Material in Early Modern England: Print, Gender, and Literacy* (Cambridge: Cambridge University Press, 2005); Leah Knight, Micheline White and Elizabeth Sauer, ed., *Women's Bookscapes in Early Modern England: Reading, Ownership, Circulation* (Ann Arbor, MI: University of Michigan Press, 2018); and Edith Snook, *Women, Reading and the Cultural Politics of Early Modern England* (Aldershot: Ashgate, 2005).

2. Judith Butler, *Gender Trouble: Feminism and the Subversion of Identity* (London: Routledge, 1990), 34.

3. See, for example, Kimberly Poitevin, 'Inventing Whiteness: Cosmetics, Race, and Women in Early Modern England', *Journal for Early Modern Cultural Studies* 11, no. 1 (2011): 59–89. I am grateful to Martine van Elk for initially raising this question of whiteness and reading.

4. Kate Flint, *The Woman Reader 1837–1914* (Oxford: Oxford University Press, 1993), 40–41.

5. Julie Crawford, *Mediatrix: Women, Politics, and Literary Production in Early Modern England* (Oxford: Oxford University Press, 2014), 7.

6. There has been a great deal of valuable work on early modern women's autobiography that has informed my approach here. Some selected works include Sharon Cadman Seelig, *Autobiography and Gender in Early Modern Literature: Reading Women's Lives, 1600–1680* (Cambridge: Cambridge University Press, 2006); Henk Dragstra, Sheila Otway and Helen Wilcox, ed., *Betraying Our Selves: Forms of Self-Representation in Early Modern English Texts* (Basingstoke: Macmillan, 2000); Elspeth Graham, Hilary Hinds, Elaine Hobby and Helen Wilcox, ed., *Her Own Life: Autobiographical Writings by Seventeenth-Century Englishwomen* (London: Routledge, 1989); Julie A. Eckerle and Michelle M. Dowd, ed., *Genre and Women's Life Writing in Early Modern England* (Aldershot: Ashgate, 2007); Hero Chalmers, '"The Person I Am, Or What They Made Me to Be": The Construction of the Feminine Subject in the Autobiographies of Mary Carleton', in *Women, Texts and Histories 1575–1760*, ed. Clare Brant and Diane Purkiss (London: Routledge, 1992), 164–194; and Julie A. Eckerle, *Romancing the Self in Early Modern Englishwomen's Life Writing* (Farnham: Ashgate, 2013).

7. Scholars such as Natalie Zemon Davis, Juliet Fleming and Jason Scott-Warren have explored this in relation to early modern inscription practices and gift-giving, marking out the pages of books as a space for expressing one's sociable and relational identity. See Natalie Zemon Davis, 'Beyond the Market: Books as Gifts in Sixteenth-Century France – The Prothero Lecture', *Transactions of the Royal Historical Society* 33 (1983): 69–88; Juliet Fleming, *Graffiti and the Writing Arts of Early Modern England* (Philadelphia, PA: University of Pennsylvania Press, 2001); Jason Scott-Warren, 'Reading Graffiti in the Early Modern Book', *Huntington Library Quarterly* 73, no. 3 (2010): 363–381. Similarly, scholars such as Julie Eckerle have examined how women used their reading of certain genres to align themselves with various characteristics and modes of behaviour – see Eckerle, *Romancing the Self.*

8. Some key work on women's reading in the early modern period includes Suzanne Hull, *Chaste, Silent, and Obedient: English Books for Women, 1475–1640* (San Marino, CA: Huntington Library, 1988); Brayman Hackel, *Reading Material in Early Modern England*; Heidi Brayman Hackel and Catherine E. Kelly, ed., *Reading Women: Literacy, Authorship, and Culture in the Atlantic World, 1500–1800* (Philadelphia, PA: University of Pennsylvania Press, 2008); Carol M. Meale and Julia Boffey, 'Gentlewomen's Reading', in *The Cambridge History of the Book in Britain. Volume 3: 1400–1557*, ed. Lotte Hellinga and J. B. Trapp (Cambridge: Cambridge University Press, 1999), 526–540; Knight, White and Sauer, ed., *Women's Bookscapes in Early Modern England*; Jacqueline Pearson, 'Women Reading, Reading Women', in *Women and Literature in Britain, 1500–1700*, ed. Helen Wilcox (Cambridge: Cambridge University Press, 1996), 80–99; Snook, *Women, Reading and the Cultural Politics of Early Modern England.*

9. Knight, White and Sauer, ed., *Women's Bookscapes in Early Modern England.*

10. Brayman Hackel and Kelly, ed., *Reading Women: Literacy, Authorship, and Culture in the Atlantic World, 1500–1800* (Philadelphia, PA: University of Pennsylvania Press, 2008).

11. Heidi Brayman Hackel, 'The Countess of Bridgewater's London Library', in *Books and Readers in Early Modern England*, ed. Jennifer Anderson and Elizabeth Sauer (Philadelphia, PA: University of Pennsylvania Press, 2002), 138–159; Brayman Hackel, 'Turning to Her "Best Companion[s]": Lady Anne Clifford as Reader, Annotator and Book Collector', in *Lady Anne Clifford: Culture, Patronage and Gender in 17th-Century Britain*, ed. Karen Hearn and Lyn Hulse (Leeds: Yorkshire Archaeological Society, 2009), 99–108; Mary Ellen Lamb, 'The Agency of the Split Subject: Lady Anne Clifford and the Uses of Reading', *English Literary Renaissance* 22 (1992): 347–368; Mary Ellen Lamb, 'The Sociality of Margaret Hoby's Reading Practices and the Representation of Reformation Interiority', *Critical Survey* 12, no. 2 (2000): 17–32.

12. There has been a great deal of excellent work on reading habits in the early modern period taking this macro lens, although many of them often focus on or privilege male readers, or ignore the gendered aspect of reading. See, for example, Guglielmo Cavallo and Roger Chartier, ed., *A History of Reading in the West*, trans. Lydia G. Cochrane (Cambridge: Polity Press, 1999); Roger Chartier, *The Order of Books: Readers, Authors and Libraries in Europe between the Fourteenth and the Eighteenth Centuries*, trans. Lydia G. Cochrane (Cambridge: Polity Press, 1994); James Raven, Helen Small and Naomi Tadmor, ed., *The Practice and Representation of Reading in England* (Cambridge: Cambridge University Press, 2010); Alberto Manguel, *A History of Reading* (London: Flamingo, 1997); and Robert Darnton, 'First Steps towards a History of Reading', *Australian Journal of French Studies* 23 (1986): 5–30. For general studies of reading in the early modern period, see Jennifer Anderson and Elizabeth Sauer, ed., *Books and Readers in Early Modern England: Material Studies* (Philadelphia, PA: University of Pennsylvania Press, 2002); John N. King, ed., *Tudor Books and Readers: Materiality and the Construction of Meaning* (Cambridge: Cambridge University Press, 2010); Eugene R. Kintgen, *Reading in Tudor*

*England* (Pittsburgh, PA: University of Pittsburgh Press, 1996); H. S. Bennett, *English Books and Readers, 1475–1557: Being a Study in the History of the Book Trade from Caxton to the Incorporation of the Stationers' Company* (Cambridge: Cambridge University Press, 1952); H. S. Bennett, *English Books and Readers, 1558–1603: Being a Study in the History of the Book Trade in the Reign of Elizabeth I* (Cambridge: Cambridge University Press, 1965); H. S. Bennett, *English Books and Readers, 1603–1640: Being a Study in the History of the Book Trade in the Reigns of James I and Charles I* (Cambridge: Cambridge University Press, 1970).

13. Brayman Hackel, *Reading Material in Early Modern England.*

14. Brayman Hackel, *Reading Material in Early Modern England*, 14.

15. Snook, *Women, Reading, and the Cultural Politics of Early Modern England.*

16. Lamb, 'The Agency of the Split Subject'.

17. Jessica Murphy has done an extensive study of the representation of 'virtuous women', taking into account various genres of early modern literature and how they relate to the prescriptions for gendered behaviour set out in conduct books. See Jessica C. Murphy, *Virtuous Necessity: Conduct Literature and the Making of the Virtuous Woman in Early Modern England* (Ann Arbor, MI: University of Michigan Press, 2015). Also see Jacques Carré, 'Communication et Rapports Sociaux dans les Traités de Savoir-Vivre Britanniques (XVIIe–XVIIIe siècle)', in *Pour une Histoire des Traités de Savoir-Vivre en Europe*, ed. Alain Montandon (Clermont-Ferrand: Associations des Publications de la Faculté des Lettres et Sciences Humaines de Clermont-Ferrand, 1994), 269–300.

18. These texts were usually aimed at a middle- and upper-class audience, inculcating the values of polite society. See Robert Shoemaker, *Gender in English Society, 1650–1850: The Emergence of Separate Spheres?* (London: Longman, 1998), 22.

19. Shoemaker, *Gender in English Society, 1650–1850*, 22.

20. Shoemaker, *Gender in English Society, 1650–1850*, 23.

21. Sasha Roberts has discussed the 'restricted range of texts' with which women were identified in the seventeenth century; see Sasha Roberts, 'Reading in Early Modern England: Contexts and Problems', *Critical Survey* 12, no. 2 (2000): 3.

22. Jacques du Bosc, *The Excellent Woman Described by Her True Characters and Their Opposites* (London: Printed for Joseph Watts, [1692]), 5–6. Huntington Library, RB 344780.

23. Adrian Johns, *The Nature of the Book: Print and Knowledge in the Making* (Chicago, IL: University of Chicago Press, 1998), 382.

24. Johns notes that this was not a gender-specific process; it 'transcended place, time, sex, and social rank' (Johns, *The Nature of the Book*, 383).

25. Johns, *The Nature of the Book*, 381.

26. Nine English editions of Vives' text had been published by 1600, and the book maintained its popularity for decades. See Ursula Potter, 'Elizabeth Drama and *The Instruction of a Christian Woman by Juan Luis Vives*', in *What Nature Does Not Teach: Didactic Literature in the Medieval and Early Modern Periods*, ed. Juanita Feros Ruys (Turnhout: Brepols Publishers, 2008), 263.

27. Juan Luis Vives, *The Education of a Christian Woman: A Sixteenth-Century Manual*, ed. and trans. Charles Fantazzi (Chicago, IL: University of Chicago Press, 2000), 78.

28. The conversion narrative was a common rhetorical tool in the Puritan literary tradition, used sporadically in the sixteenth century and reaching a height of popularity in the mid-seventeenth century. It was not only used in reference to women's reading – men certainly recorded 'conversions' of their reading habits as

well – but it was frequently used to depict the frivolity of girlhood versus the (hopeful) piety of women. See D. Bruce Hindmarsh, *The Evangelical Conversion Narrative: Spiritual Autobiography in Early Modern England* (Oxford: Oxford University Press, 2005); Kathleen Lynch, *Protestant Autobiography in the Seventeenth-Century Anglophone World* (Oxford: Oxford University Press, 2012); Abigail Shinn, *Conversion Narratives in Early Modern England: Tables of Turning* (London: Palgrave Macmillan, 2018).

29. Richard Allestree, *The Ladies Calling. In Two Parts. By the Author of the Whole Duty of Man, The Causes of the Decay of Christian Piety, and the Gentlemans Calling* (Oxford: Printed at the Theater, 1673), 115.

30. Richard Baxter, *A Breviate of the Life of Margaret, The Daughter of* Francis Charlton, *of* Apply *in* Shropshire, *Esq; And Wife of* Richard Baxter (London: Printed for B. Simmons, 1681), 4.

31. Mary Ellen Lamb, for example, has argued that portrayals or constructions of women readers in contemporary culture often restricted women's access to certain genres. See Mary Ellen Lamb, 'Constructions of Women Readers', in *Teaching Tudor and Stuart Women Writers*, ed. Susanne Woods and Margaret P. Hannay (New York: The Modern Language Association of America, 2000), 23–34.

32. Kevin Sharpe and Steven N. Zwicker, 'Introduction: Discovering the Renaissance Reader', in *Reading, Society and Politics in Early Modern England*, ed. Kevin Sharpe and Steven N. Zwicker (Cambridge: Cambridge University Press, 2003), 13.

33. T. A. Birrell, 'Reading as a Pastime: The Place of Light Literature in Some Gentlemen's Libraries of the 17th Century', in *Property of a Gentleman: The Formation, Organisation and Dispersal of the Private Library 1620–1920*, ed. Robin Myers and Michael Harris (Winchester: St Paul's Bibliographies, 1991), 114.

34. Lisa Jardine and Anthony Grafton, '"Studied for Action": How Gabriel Harvey Read His Livy', *Past & Present* 129 (1990): 30–78.

35. The relevance of marginalia to both reading and writing studies has been explored in a recent edited collection, which considers annotations in the context of materiality (specifically the history of the book), identity and reading. See Katherine Acheson, ed., *Early Modern English Marginalia* (Abingdon: Routledge, 2019).

36. Birrell, 'Reading as a Pastime', 123.

37. Frances Teague, 'Judith Shakespeare Reading', *Shakespeare Quarterly* 47, no. 4 (1996): 366.

38. Alison M. Jaggar, 'Love and Knowledge: Emotion in Feminist Epistemology', in *Gender/Body/Knowledge: Feminist Reconstructions of Being and Knowing*, ed. Alison M. Jaggar and Susan Bordo (New Brunswick, NJ: Rutgers University Press, 1990), 145.

39. For work on reading lower down the social scale, see, for example, Margaret Spufford, *Small Books and Pleasant Histories: Popular Fiction and Its Readership in Seventeenth-Century England* (London: Methuen & Co., 1981) and Adam Fox, *Oral and Literate Culture in England, 1500–1700* (Oxford: Oxford University Press, 2000).

40. It has long been recognised that archives are, in the words of Rodney Carter, 'spaces of power'. Rodney G. S. Carter, 'Of Things Said and Unsaid: Power, Archival Silences, and Power in Silence', *Archivaria* 61 (2006): 216. There has been a great deal of recent work on the 'silence' of the archives, a term used to signify the gaps in what is recorded and made available to archive users. See, for example, David Thomas, Simon Fowler and Valerie Johnson, *The Silence of the Archive* (London: Facet Publishing, 2017); Marlene Manoff, 'Mapping Archival Silence: Technology and the Historical Record', in *Engaging with Records and Archives: Histories and Theories*, ed. Fiorella Foscarini, Heather MacNeil, Bonnie Mac and Gillian Oliver (London: Facet Publishing, 2016), 63–82; Antoinette Burton, *Dwelling in the Archive:*

*Women Writing House, Home, and History in Late Colonial India* (Oxford: Oxford University Press, 2003); Marisa J. Fuentes, *Dispossessed Lives: Enslaved Women, Violence, and the Archive* (Philadelphia, PA: University of Pennsylvania Press, 2016); Kirsty Reid and Fiona Paisley, ed., *Sources and Methods in Histories of Colonialism: Approaching the Imperial Archive* (Abingdon: Routledge, 2017); Renée Romkins and Antia Wiersma, ed., *Gender and Archiving: Past, Present, Future* (Amsterdam: Verloren, 2017); and Randall C. Jimerson, *Archives Power: Memory, Accountability, and Social Justice* (Chicago, IL: Society of American Archivists, 2009).

41. Georgianna Ziegler, 'Lost in the Archives? Searching for Records of Early Modern Women', in *Teaching Tudor and Stuart Women Writers*, ed. Susanne Woods and Margaret P. Hannay (New York: The Modern Language Association, 2000), 316.

42. Annotated Books Online: A Digital Archive of Early Modern Books, accessed June 23, 2023, www.annotatedbooksonline.com.

43. Keith Thomas, 'The Meaning of Literacy in Early Modern England', in *The Written Word: Literacy in Transition*, ed. Gerd Baumann (Oxford: Clarendon Press, 1986), 103. Thomas posits a complex and nuanced view of literacy, arguing for different levels of literacy. In his model, literacy could be split into the ability to read simple print (in which he also makes a distinction between reading black-letter and roman type); reading manuscript text and the ability to write; and being able to read and write in Latin and Greek, which tended to be the preserve of the (male) intellectual elite. Men were far more likely to attain the higher levels of literacy, and therefore more likely to be able to write extensive notes on their books – women may have owned and been able to read books, but did not necessarily have the ability to write more than their name. For more on literacy, see David Cressy, *Literacy and the Social Order: Reading and Writing in Tudor and Stuart England* (Cambridge: Cambridge University Press, 1980). Anne Laurence has suggested that by the 1720s, 25 per cent of women were fully literate, meaning they could both read and write – see Anne Laurence, *Women in England 1500–1760: A Social History* (New York: St. Martin's Press, 1994), 166. For more recent work on literacy, see Mark Hailwood, 'Rethinking Literacy in Rural England, 1550–1700', *Past & Present* 260, no. 1 (2023): 38–70.

44. I am very grateful to Georgianna Ziegler for suggesting this method of searching the Folger's archives, and her guidance on approaching finding women in their collections.

45. '#HerBook', Twitter, accessed June 23, 2023, https://twitter.com/search?q=%23herbook&src=typed_query. For more examples of scholars' use of X, see Sjoerd Levelt, 'Early Modern Marginalia and #earlymoderntwitter', in *Early Modern English Marginalia*, ed. Katherine Acheson (Abingdon: Routledge, 2019), 234–256. The phrase 'her book' has garnered increasing attention in recent years, as studies of women's book ownership and reading grow. The Rare Book Working Group at Princeton University Library ran a workshop on the topic of 'her book' in October 2018, examining ownership inscriptions in the library's holdings. See Eric White, 'Rare Book Working Group Examines "Her Book"', *Notabilia*, October 29, 2018, accessed June 23, 2023, https://blogs.princeton.edu/notabilia/2018/10/29/rare-book-working-group-examines-her-book.

46. *Early Modern Female Book Ownership: #HerBook*, accessed June 23, 2023, https://earlymodernfemalebookownership.wordpress.com. Similarly, the Early Modern Women's Marginalia blog is an extremely useful repository – *Early Modern Women's Marginalia*, accessed August 12, 2024, https://earlymodernwomensmarginalia.cems.anu.edu.au.

47. 'Early Modern Annotated Books from UCLA's Clark Library', *Calisphere: University of California*, accessed June 23, 2023, https://calisphere.org/collections/26771.

48. There has been a great deal of excellent work on Frances Wolfreston in recent years. See, for example, Sarah Lindenbaum, 'Memorializing the Everyday: The Evidence of the Final Decade of Frances Wolfreston's Life', *The Seventeenth Century* 37, no. 3 (2022): 449–476 and Lori Humphrey Newcomb, 'Frances Wolfreston's Annotations as Labours of Love', in *Women's Labour and the History of the Book in Early Modern England*, ed. Valerie Wayne (London: The Arden Shakespeare, 2020), 243–266.

49. Paul Morgan, 'Frances Wolfreston and "Hor Bouks": A Seventeenth-Century Woman Book Collector', *The Library* 6th Series 11, no. 3 (1989): 197–219; Arnold Hunt, 'Libraries in the Archives: Researching Provenance in the British Library', in *Libraries within the Library: The Origins of the British Library's Printed Collections*, ed. Giles Mandelbrote and Barry Taylor (London: The British Library, 2009), 363–384.

50. Sarah Lindenbaum, 'About', *Frances Wolfreston Hor Bouks*, December 2, 2018, accessed June 23, 2023, https://franceswolfrestonhorbouks.com.

51. Lindenbaum has detailed her findings in her recent book chapter; see Sarah Lindenbaum, 'Hiding in Plain Sight: How Electronic Records Can Lead Us to Early Modern Women Readers', in Knight, White and Sauer, ed., *Women's Bookscapes in Early Modern England*, 193–213.

52. Ralph Cohen, 'History and Genre', in *Genre Theory and Historical Change: Theoretical Essays of Ralph Cohen*, ed. John L. Rowlett (Charlottesville, VA: University of Virginia Press, 2017), 85.

53. Gerald MacLean, 'Literacy, Class, and Gender in Restoration England', *Text* 7 (1994): 309.

Chapter 1

# 'She much delighted in that holy Book': women's religious reading habits

Religious texts were the most commonly recorded reading material of early modern women. Not only was devotional literature central to the forms of femininity constructed by advice book writers (as discussed in the Introduction); it was also, from the evidence we have of book ownership and reading habits, the most popular type of text that women consumed in the seventeenth century.[1] Most book lists and inventories include devotional or religious texts, and often they only record such books. This may be partly an attempt at identity construction, with women making a conscious decision not to include other genres in their inventories (if they were compiled by the woman herself), even if they may have owned those books. However, this does not diminish the popularity of religious texts, and given the clear preponderance of this type of reading, considering how women reacted to and represented these texts allows us to gain a greater understanding of their experience and ideas about identity and gender.

The identities that emerge in this chapter have several facets. They firstly are not static – they are often made through a continual practice of self-making, which happens both through repeated reading of religious texts and through the recording of that reading. Religious reading was meant to be habitual in the early modern period, and the temporal aspect to reading (both in terms of how it structured one's day and how it was repeated over time) is frequently highlighted by readers and writers. Secondly, the self-fashioning that happens through religious reading is rarely isolated; it is produced through conversation and/or disputation with other readers. Thirdly, the early modern pious woman may have drawn on the language of spiritual devotion used in conduct literature, but she was also highly political, using religious reading as a way of indicating her religio-political opinions.[2]

What will become clear is the extent to which the distinction between spiritual devotion, which was often framed at the time as feminine and domestic, and theological 'disputes' that were highly politicised in the early modern period, is often blurred. Crawford has discussed the historiographical tendency to see women's spiritual reading as conforming to female subordination and the domestic sphere, and argues that this is a 'mischaracterisation of the nature of such reading'.[3] As she suggests, early modern religion could be deeply political and controversial, and cannot be seen as 'confined' to the domestic world.[4] The women in this chapter engaged in religio-political debates at the same time as they situated themselves in a familial, domestic and devotional space, often using the same texts to do both things. This self-fashioning then is complex; it both responds to and accepts contemporary ideals of femininity and pushes against them.

The first two aspects of identity that could be fashioned through religious reading were clearly emphasised in contemporary writing about women readers. Conduct book writers and the writers of funeral sermons both made clear the importance of the repeated, habitual practice of religious reading, and of how women should engage in conversation with others as part of this practice – although, as will be seen below, they did not think that disputation was appropriate.[5] In this chapter I will outline some of the contemporary ideas surrounding religious reading, then examine how women themselves interpreted these ideas. They took on and affirmed some of the prescriptions for religious reading habits, but often underpinned their devotion with political ideas and theological disputes.

Religious devotion was perhaps the most important part of being a good woman in the seventeenth century. Reading the Bible and other devotional books was presented as one of the main practices and ways of displaying this devotion, alongside prayer. William Gouge, the Puritan clergyman and author, outlined that a woman's devotional practice should take the form of

> holy and religious exercises in the house, as reading the word, praier, catechising, and such like; which being the spirituall food of the soule are to be euery day, as our bodily food, prouided and vsed. An husband as a master of a family must provide these for the good of his whole

> house; but as an husband, in speciall for the good of his wife: for to his wife, as well as to the whole house he is a King, a Priest, and a Prophet.[6]

Reading therefore was figured as spiritual nourishment and presented as a key part of a woman's 'religious exercises', which were often a regimented programme of prayer, reading and religious conversation. The role of the husband was presented in religious terms (he is a 'priest' to his wife). Similarly, it is evident from the work of another Puritan preacher, William Whately, that religious reading should be an important part of the marital relationship.[7] He argued that husbands and wives should 'reade the Word of God together', reinforcing each other's devotion.[8]

Religious reading for women was strictly defined, however, with some books seen as more appropriate than others, depending on the context for the reading. Whately, for example, gave advice on which texts women should read, proposing that

> women of Quality (who are presumed to want neither Parts nor lesure for it) would a little look into the inside of the Religion they profess; if it be a true one, 'twill bear the inspection, truth never shunning the light; if it be not, the discovery cannot be too early. And indeed among the many remarkable impresses of truth our Church bears, this is one, that she does not blindfold her Proselites, leaves them the use of their discerning Faculty, and does not by obtruding upon them an implicit belief, force them to lay down their Reason when they take up their Faith. And now why should not Ladies spend a few of their many idle hours in this inquisition, I mean not to embark them in a maze of controversies, but only to discern those plain grounds of Truth on which our Church builds; which if well digested, will prove a better amulet against delusion then the reading whole Tomes of Disputations, more apt to distract then fortify their understandings.[9]

Women were encouraged to read some theological tracts and treatises, as enquiry and discovery in Whately's view was permitted by the church to a certain extent. Reading theology was seen as an appropriate use of 'idle time', but only in order to better understand scripture, not to delve into religious controversies. Whately did not think that women should read too deeply into theology, specifically cautioning against 'Tomes of Disputations', which could lead them astray.[10] This reflects the common fear during the early modern period about the dangers of individual interpretation of scripture.[11] The clergy in particular wanted to ensure that lay reading was still governed by expert exegesis. A key term in the passage above is the address to 'women of Quality'. There was a distinct social hierarchy in the prescriptions set out by Whately and Gouge, who focused their advice on women of a certain rank. They were speaking to upper-middle-class and gentry women, mainly married, who had the education to be able to read, the authority within the household to direct devotion, and the leisure time to dedicate to scriptural study.

While the conduct books made the importance of reading religious texts very clear, they were not the only genre to do so. The connection between religious reading and gender was repeatedly emphasised in funeral sermons for women in the seventeenth century. Funeral sermons began to be preached by clergymen following the Reformation.[12] The inclusion of biographical details, focusing on the piety and good deeds of the individual, became common in the late sixteenth and seventeenth centuries and was generally regarded within the Church of England as 'a vehicle of salutary instruction for the living'.[13] Only a fraction were published, although this became increasingly common over the course of the seventeenth century, peaking in the late Stuart period.[14] Such sermons most frequently commemorated the lives of the gentry men and women, but often did so in different ways. As Femke Molekamp has noted, 'while commemorations of deceased men in early modern funeral sermons tended to laud public virtues, it was far more common for the eulogies of women to index the personal piety and devotional conduct of the woman in the sphere of the home'.[15] They therefore worked in tandem with conduct literature to emphasise proper feminine behaviour.

It was important that this devotional conduct was habitual; temporality was crucial to funeral sermons' portrayal of devotional reading. They often noted the frequency and attention with which women read in order to demonstrate the subject's piety, thereby making reading an important part of a woman's duties as a wife and mother. A model for ideal feminine behaviour was created, in which literacy and the practice thereof played a crucial part. But when discussing reading, funeral sermons created a hierarchy of literature, in which religious reading was the only type that was truly praiseworthy. Admittedly, they were intended to highlight the piety of the deceased, but this focus on women's devotional literacy gives an indication of the behavioural norms attached to femininity, and as such they can be used to further explore representations of gender and religious reading.

In the funeral sermon for Lady Frances Hobart, wife of Sir John Hobart of Chapelfield House in Norfolk, John Collinges gave a detailed description of her daily routine, highlighting the central place of devotion and reading:

> [F]rom the time she rose till Seven of the Clock, she spent her time in the private Devotions and retirements of her Closet; then she came out

> to the more publick duties of the family, which she never missed, and seldom was but first in the room in Prayer, *Reading the Scriptures*, Expounding, one or more of these Exercises (as opportunity served) and some discourses afterward she then usually spent more than an hour, the rest of her time till Noon was spent in her Chamber in dressing, or in her Closet, reading, looking over Accounts, &c. Sometimes for half an hour she walked. Then she came out again to Prayer in her Family, in which, and in Dinner, and following Discourses she usually spent two hours, and sometimes exercised her self for half an hour afterward. Her afternoon was spent in *reading*, or making Visits chiefly to such Christians, as she had an Interest in; or sometimes in spinning or sowing with her Maids. About Six she again came to her Family-duties: in which, at Supper, and discourses after it, she ordinarily spent three hours, and then withdrew to her Closet, for many years together there she abode *reading* and praying till Twelve or One of the Clock: till at last with no ordinary difficulty, she was perswaded by her learned Physitian to abate an hour or two of that excess, for her health sake.[16]

This passage makes clear the importance of reading in the day of a pious household. Reading is mentioned alongside prayer and discussion as part of the practice of religion.[17] The emphasis on Hobart's devotional habits serves to make her an exemplary figure. She was following the recommendations given for leading a pious life, which emphasised the importance of both private and communal religious observances in the family. She rose early, and took part in devotions both alone and with her family several times a day. Reading was a significant part of her activities, whether alone or in company, or as part of devotion or household management.

These themes come up again and again in funeral sermons. Elizabeth Hoyle, wife of Thomas Hoyle, the alderman of York, was described in 1644 as a 'constant dayly reader of Gods Word'.[18] A year later, Samuel Ainsworth similarly praised Dorothy Hanbury, the Northamptonshire gentlewoman, for being 'much acquainted with the duties of Religion . . . she spent much time every day in reading the Scriptures, and the pious books of godly men'.[19] This reading was moreover often referred to as a 'duty', and her regularity and consistency of practice were praised. Women were portrayed as reproaching themselves when they were unable to carry out this spiritual task, as in the case of the Warwick gentlewoman Cicely Puckering:

> she made conscience of the duties of religion . . . She was frequent in reading the Scriptures, and desirous to heare them read, when she could not reade her selfe, (because of the soreness of her eyes) and yet she thought her selfe too blame, because she read no more.[20]

Devotional reading relied not only on daily use of books but also on re-reading. Timothy Rogers said of Elizabeth Dunton that she 'took a great Delight in reading Mr. *Howes Blessedness of the Righteous*, and she read it six times over', referring to the first major theological work by Presbyterian minister John Howe, published in 1668.[21] This repeated reading could be quite regimented, with women creating timetables for their study of religious texts.

Frances Hobart, according to Collinges,

> was rarely to be found alone without her Bible before her, she had drawn up for her self a method for reading the Scripture (to which she was very strict) so as every year she read over the *Psalms* Twelve times, the *New Testament thrice*, and the other parts of *the Old Testament once* . . . Besides this, that she might want no satisfaction to any doubt arising upon her reading the Scripture, she had furnished her self with a large Library of English Divines, which cost her not much less than 100 *l.* of which she made a daily use.[22]

This detailed account, alongside the earlier passage from Collinges' sermon, gives us a picture of Hobart's devotional reading as repetitive and habitual; a practice around which her daily *and* yearly routine were structured.

The practice of re-reading was central to the absorption of religious texts, and specifically the Bible, as Isaac Ambrose's sermon for Margaret Houghton, a Lancashire gentlewoman, made clear:

> of all books for constant use and practice she preferred the Bible, telling me often that other Books had their use and delight; till with often reading they became more ordinary, and then they seemed to lose of their former lustre, glory, and excellency; but the Bible was in her often-reading ever fresh, and green, and new.[23]

This reading was presented as something almost natural, particularly with the language of the Bible being 'fresh' and 'green'; the Bible was the only book that could be returned to so frequently, as it was the only one that would be continually enjoyed by the reader – it was evergreen in its attractions.[24] It was important that the duty of devotion was represented as something that a good woman would undertake gladly, and not resent, thus creating a model for a woman's both outward and inward devotion. This transformative potential of reading was thought to happen through extended study from an early age, as George Savile suggested much later in the century: 'Few things are well learnt, but by early *Precepts*: Those well infus'd, make them *Natural*; and we are never sure of retaining what is valuable, till by a continued *Habit* we have made it a Piece of us.'[25]

John Evelyn echoed this advice in his direction that his daughter Mary should 'reade The holy Bible one Chapter & psal: Morning & Evening, getting some practical texts by heart; which will both furnish you for prayer, and Life'.[26] Repetition was seen as part of learning in early modern Europe. It was an integral part of education, particularly religious education (both Catholic and Protestant) which was based on rote learning, and thought to help develop one's memory.[27] The routine of reading was central to achieving the appropriate spiritual effect; in order to make a person truly godly, the study of devotional texts had to be habitual.

Even Lady Anne Clifford, who was an especially active intellectual and political reader, was commemorated in this way. Edward Rainbowe, the Bishop of Carlisle, in his funeral sermon for Clifford in 1676 declared that she 'much delighted in that holy Book'.[28] Rainbowe made sure to emphasise that despite Clifford's wide reading habits, the Bible held a particular importance for her. Having discussed Clifford's reading habits, emphasising both her exemplary piety and femininity, but also her intellectual and aristocratic identity, the sermon went on to say that, besides reading the Bible herself, 'she usually heard a large portion of Scripture read every day, as much as one of the Gospels read every week. So that let her Body be fed never so sparingly, her Soul was nourished with *sound words*, the words of Faith, which must needs give her a growth in Grace, and make a sincere heart'.[29] Religious reading was framed as emotionally stimulating, and as sustenance or nourishment, affecting Clifford internally.[30] The repeated and affective practice of reading as a part of devotion was key to the representation of Clifford as a woman. Rainbowe was using her reading to create a certain image of her for his audience and for posterity.

The identity of the imagined woman religious reader was therefore very clear. Reading was one of several devotional practices that structured her life, and she used it to develop a properly pious form of femininity, which affirmed her religious identity but was quite divorced from the political nature of religion in this period. The influence of these portrayals of women readers, however, needs to be examined. To what extent did they internalise the ideas that were put forward in conduct books and funeral sermons? This rest of this chapter explores women's own representations of their religious reading, and the ways in which they used devotional or theological texts to negotiate and signal their own identities.

## Her Bible: women's religious books

Religious reading material was, as conduct book writers wanted to emphasise, the most popular type of literature for early modern book owners.

The most common books referred to among inventories of women's goods are Bibles or books of common prayer, with little other information given, such as in the case of Francis Pawley, whose 1681 inventory includes 'one old bible'.[31] Similarly, the inventory of Katherine Perceval (née Southwell), recorded, 'I ffrench Comon prayer booke' held in a 'Black Leather Trunk', but no other books.[32] Frequently this is the only reference to be found to books owned by women. Some, however, left much longer book lists, and even these tend to reveal a majority of religious literature. In 1647, when Lady Margaret Heath died, an inventory of the over eighty books kept in her closet was produced.[33] At least fifty-eight texts out of the eighty listed can be categorised as religious, including scripture, devotional literature and theological treatises. Heath's reading tastes do not appear to have been sectarian – the list includes works by Puritan, Protestant, Jesuit and Catholic authors. The mainstays of seventeenth-century religious polemic, such as Bishop Hall and William Gouge, are there, but there are also works by Jeremias Drexel and St Francis de Sales.[34] The inclusion of these books in the collection shows a desire to develop knowledge of other denominational positions. Heath's husband, Sir Robert Heath, was a Royalist judge who is known to have been intolerant of other religions, having supported the persecution of Catholics.[35] Perhaps Heath was using these books to shore up her own contradictory religious beliefs; or perhaps she genuinely disagreed with her husband's position.

Alongside book lists, annotations or marginalia are one of the best records we have of women's literary consumption – better, in fact, as they often give the most tangible evidence we have of actual reading, as opposed to just owning. Sometimes women's annotations are extensive, providing notes on the text and their own interpretations, or even adding details about their lives outside of the book, as in the case of Susanna Beckwith, discussed in this chapter. More common, however, are lone autograph inscriptions, where a woman has written her name in the book and not much else. This certainly indicates an ownership claim; whether it is a sign of reading, we do not know. These inscriptions are still useful when thinking about the interplay between books and identity, however. Rebecca Laroche has examined women's signatures in printed medical texts, arguing that a woman's signature 'claimed her ownership of an expensive volume and the knowledge that it held'.[36] Laroche focused specifically on medical knowledge, and the way women's signatures acted as a claim to this knowledge, allowing them to mark out an area of intellectual authority. She has argued that this was in some ways a subversion of patriarchal authority, as these printed volumes tended to speak broadly to male medical practitioners, with select entries aimed at gentlewomen readers – but by inscribing their name at the beginning of the volume, women were staking a claim to all the knowledge contained therein, not simply that which was deemed acceptable for them.[37]

The act of writing a name in a book, whether to indicate ownership, to stake a knowledge claim, or simply as a form of writing practice, reveals various relationships with a book, either as an object or as a source of information and ideas (or both). These inscriptions tell us not only about this relationship but also about interpersonal relationships in which books become an actor; for example, in the case of gift inscriptions, or in competing ownership claims. They also demonstrate some aspect of performative self-fashioning, as women laid claim to the positions, beliefs or opinions held within the books.

Dedications, therefore, were both performative and performed.[38] Women signing religious texts, be they devotional or theological, demonstrates a lot about how they wanted to situate themselves in a world where religion was highly contested and central to most people's lives. The margins and title pages of books can be seen as an at least semi-public space; Jason Scott-Warren suggests that all annotations are to an extent 'outward-facing' and that books were therefore 'adjuncts to everyday sociability'.[39] Signatures, particularly those which are accompanied by longer inscriptions, or where more than one person has left their mark, are indicators of social relationships, intended for an audience of some kind, and the margins of a book become a space in which a person can present themselves to that audience. Therefore, in Scott-Warren's words, 'the sociable space of the book is a place for marking yourself out', and as books were passed between family, friends and acquaintances, 'aspects of communal life – the negotiation of relationships, the debating of reputations – rubbed off on them'.[40] The identity produced through inscription and annotation is therefore often sociable or relational.

This is particularly evident in early modern Bibles, which were often repositories of annotations by both men and women.[41] The sixteenth-century introduction of the Geneva Bible, with its reading aids, contributed to the developing practice of writing on scripture.[42] The printed marginalia and glosses that were included in the Geneva Bible encouraged private reading practices and, as Femke Molekamp has argued, it 'was a book which owners regularly styled to conform to their tastes and needs'.[43] One particularly good example is the Bible of Susanna Beckwith, now held in the British Library.[44] Biographical details about Beckwith are scant; what we know of her comes from her annotations on her family Bible. Given her level of literacy and the dates of her annotations (which were largely made in the 1610s and 1620s), she was probably a Jacobean woman of the gentry or similar social rank. Beckwith wrote extensively in her Bible, not only inscribing her name and dedicating it to her daughter but also adding family memoranda and some notes on the text.[45] Her annotations give an insight into the place of the book within the family, its use for devotional and theological matters, the practical lessons Beckwith gained from reading and the relationship between reading and the passage of time within a religious household.

Beckwith established her ownership of the book by inscribing her name and initials at several points throughout the text. These appear to bear no relation to the adjacent passages, and it is not clear why Beckwith chose to inscribe her name within the body of the text rather than on or near the title page or end pages, as was more common for such inscriptions. Moreover, she wrote a dedication in the book, addressed to her daughter, which was again, unusually, placed within the main body of the text. At the end of the Apocrypha, Beckwith wrote:

> Susanna Beckwith my deare childe I leaue the this booke as the best Jewell I haue, Reade it with a zealous harte to understand truly, and apply all thou readest either to confirme thy faith, or to increase thy Repentance: Bee not ouercombd with evill: but ouer come evell with goodnese: Bee not wearie of well doing for in due season, thou shalt reape iff thou fainte not. Bee not high minded, but make thy selfe equale unto them of the lower sorte. Now our Lord Jesus Christ himselfe, and god euen our father, which hath loued us, and hath giuen us euerlasting consolation and good hope through grace: comfort thy harte, and stablish therin euerie good word, and worke: to the praise of god, and patient waiting for our Sauiour Christ his coming: come, Lord Jesus, come quickly, for thy servant cometh I ame willing, help my unwillinges 5:23.[46]

This dedication is revealing in the advice given about reading and the relationship with religion that is suggested. Beckwith referred to the Bible as 'the best Jewell I haue'. The spiritual value of the scripture has also been given material value, in the object of the book, and this reference gives an indication of the way in which such books might have been treated within households such as Beckwith's.[47] Beckwith was advising her daughter how to read the book to get the most spiritual benefit from it, creating a conversation between mother, daughter and the text. She was using the book to give advice for her daughter's conduct in life, with the reading of the scripture as a way into this.

Beckwith's reading of the Bible was 'extensive'; it relied on interactions with and input from other texts to produce the best understanding.[48] The question of how to read the book was obviously an important one to Beckwith. On the page facing the translator's address to Queen Elizabeth, she entered a poem beginning with the lines

Heere is the well where waters flow,
To quench our heat of sinne,
Heere is the tree, wheer truth doth grow,
To lead our lines therein.[49]

This verse, comprising seven stanzas in Beckwith's version, was commonly printed in editions of the Geneva Bible after 1578.[50] It was usually placed immediately after the title page, in a similar position to where Beckwith has chosen to write it out. There are some small differences in her version: for example, where she used the word 'well' in the first line, this was traditionally 'spring' in the printed versions. She also swapped two lines from the sixth stanza. The original version read:

Pray still in faith, with this respect,
To fructify therein,
That knowledge may bring this effect,
To mortify thy sin.[51]

However, Beckwith's version became:

Pray still in faith, with this respect
to mortifie thy sinne
that knowledge may bringe god effort
to frutifie therein.[52]

Beckwith's addition of this verse shows her awareness of theological paratexts, specifically other printed versions of the scripture. The verse was not printed in the 1597 edition Beckwith owned, despite being included in other editions from the same year.[53] Whatever the reason for its exclusion, Beckwith's use of this verse demonstrates an awareness of other versions of the Bible beyond her own copy. The mistakes in the manuscript verse, moreover, imply either that she was writing it from memory or at least not copying it line for line from an original, or possibly not reading the original very carefully.

Furthermore, this addition indicates an ability and willingness to adapt a text to give an improved reading experience – evidently, she felt a need to include this verse for future readers, either herself or others in her family. The poem includes the lines:

Reade not this booke in any case
but with a single eye
Reade not, but first desire Gods grace
to understande thereby.[54]

The fact that the verse specifically deals with reading advice shows the way in which she was shaping and controlling the reading experience;

presumably the advice contained therein was meant to be followed when dealing with the text. This is backed up by its similarity to the dedication to her daughter; Beckwith emphasised the need to read scripture in a certain way, both to herself and any potential readers, and very specifically to her daughter.

There is more evidence of the ability to extract and adapt devotional material in Beckwith's marginal annotations. Beneath I Samuel 25:29, Beckwith wrote:

> Wisdome openeth the mouth
> of the dumbe, and maketh the
> tongues of babes eloquent.[55]

This is a line from the Apocrypha: the Wisdom of Solomon 10:21. The chapter of Samuel, beside which Beckwith wrote this extract, tells the story of the relationships between David, Abigail and Nabal. It is unclear exactly why Beckwith felt this verse was relevant to the chapter, if that was why she wrote it there. It may be that she had heard a sermon or read commentary connecting the two, or that she personally felt that the sentiment was appropriate. Whatever the reason, it demonstrates her capacity to assess scripture and make connections, and to shape the reading experience through the margins of her Bible.[56]

There is one other occasion where she added verse to a chapter of the Bible, in the form of a short prayer by John Norden. Underneath Isaiah 66, she wrote:

> Doe nothinge but see first thou craue,
> Aide from the Lord good end to haue;
> Soe shalt thou haue success alwayes,
> As thou shalt wish and happie dayes.[57]

This prayer was entitled by Norden 'a praier for the helpe and assistance of God in all our doings, and that we doe nothing but in his feare and due obedience', and appears in the collection of his prayers, *A Pensive Mans Practise*.[58] This was a very popular book in the Elizabethan and Jacobean period, going through multiple editions and contributing to a form of 'household Protestantism'.[59] Mary Hampson Patterson argues that Norden probably used the Geneva Bible for most of his scriptural references, which may be why Beckwith transcribed it into her copy.[60] Isaiah 66 tells of God's gifts to his followers and punishment for those who disavow him, a sentiment that seems to be echoed by Norden's prayer. This demonstrates Beckwith's 'extensive' and 'active' reading, drawing together different texts to provide context for or to interpret the scripture. These three verse annotations are all written in the same style, likely with the same pen.

The two latter stanzas also have decorative detail surrounding them. They are all neater and perhaps more carefully written than the rest of Beckwith's notes, which have slightly thicker pen strokes and darker ink, and which display less care taken over the form of the letters and the placing on the page. This may be due to the difference in content. Beckwith's other notes were more personal in tone, either relating to her family or making short notes indicating the usefulness of certain passages. This more practical, familiar and quotidian use of the Bible appears not to have warranted such careful annotation as the paratextual devotional additions.

Beckwith's reading was a temporal and repeated practice, integrated into the structure of daily life in the household.[61] Throughout the Psalms, she wrote notations marking when different entries should be read, heard or used in worship. Next to around sixty Psalms, Beckwith has written either 'Mor' (or 'Morn') or 'Even', signifying whether they were to be used in the morning or the evening. This follows the pattern recommended by the Book of Common Prayer, which allocated Psalms for morning and evening prayer.[62] This demonstrates the practical use of the Bible within the household, and the fact that devotion was reliant on habitual and repeated readings of the text. The Psalms would be returned to frequently, and the reading of them both shaped and was shaped by the practice and timetable of devotion in the Beckwith household.

There is another temporal aspect to her annotations, one less connected to devotion. Beckwith recorded the birth dates of her children in the margins of her Bible (specifically the books of Genesis, Exodus and Isaiah), revealing its use as a family memorandum as well as a book of devotion. The entries are in roughly chronological order, except for two instances where the children are recorded in books of the Bible from which they got their names (Matthew and Ester, her third son and third daughter). However, there is a missing entry. Beckwith made note of how many sons or daughters she had in each annotation; for example, the entry 'William Beckwith the fifth sone of Susanna Beckwith was born the 7 February Anno Dm 1623' in the margins of Isaiah 66.[63] However, the birth of her second daughter was not noted, indicating that perhaps she died in infancy or before birth. The other notable absence is that of Beckwith's husband; he was never mentioned, not even to note their marriage. Instead, maternal relationships took precedence in this book, from the dedication to her daughter to the records of her children's births. Annotations show the Bible being passed between generations of women. One hand, not the main annotator, noted above the printer's address that the book was 'Given to me by my deare Grandemother M[rs] Susanna Beckwith', indicating another instance of gift-giving beyond that of the inscription addressing Beckwith's eldest daughter.[64] Through these annotations, Beckwith was centring herself in a familial structure and using the Bible to mark the passage of time throughout her life.

Beckwith's use of her Bible extended far beyond the devotional, allowing her to create a sense of familial identity but also to understand the domestic and political world around her. There is evidence of Beckwith using the text in her own daily life, for example when she wrote beside the first few lines of Isaiah 44, 'are a comfort to your servants'.[65] The chapter is speaking to Jacob, referring to him repeatedly as 'my servant' and outlining God's blessings to him. She was taking passages from scripture and making them applicable to her daily life, and the annotation makes it clear that she wanted a reminder of the lesson, either for her future self or for other readers. This is a very practical use of marginalia, one which she repeated to varying degrees throughout the text. She did not always make her interpretation of verses clear, but her desire to note and return to passages is evident. By the side of several verses and printed annotations Beckwith wrote 'nota', indicating her intention to remember particular sections. On one page, she wrote this three times, beside printed marginal annotations that instruct the reader on how to view misfortune and welcome it as a test from God.

Beckwith's reading blended the political and the personal.[66] Beckwith wrote 'nota' beside an annotation to I Kings 6, which reads, 'There is nothing harder for them, that are in authoritie, then to bridle their affections, & folow good counsel.'[67] There are many possible reasons for this note but, as we know that Beckwith wrote at least some of her annotations in the 1620s, she could have been thinking about George Villiers, first Duke of Buckingham, the controversial favourite of both James I and Charles I.[68] It is difficult to know when Beckwith wrote most of her annotations, but her notes regarding the birth of children give at least approximate dates, placing some of her readings in the 1610s and 1620s (her eldest child was born in 1613; her youngest in 1623). Buckingham was embroiled in scandal in the early 1620s, with his brothers and his mentor, Sir Francis Bacon, being accused of abuse of monopolies and accepting bribes, respectively. He was also involved in negotiations for Prince Charles' marriage, played a key role in the escalating conflict with Spain and was blamed for various failed expeditions to Cadiz and the Palatinate. In 1626 Parliament began impeachment proceedings against Buckingham, accusing him of nepotism and holding too many offices, amongst other things, but Charles I dissolved Parliament before the motion could pass through the House of Lords. Buckingham's influence over both James and Charles was deeply suspect in the eyes of the populace, and it is not hard to see how the passage warning authority figures to be careful with their affections and 'folow good counsel' could apply to the situation.

If this was Beckwith's thinking, this annotation is clear evidence of her engagement with contemporary politics, and active use of her reading in order to understand the wider world around her.[69] The passage in the Bible related to crises she observed in the political world, and she was able to make links and apply her reading to broad real-world concerns. This complicates the domestic image of the family Bible, demonstrating multiple readings and uses of the text, depending on the reader's focus at the time of reading.

Beckwith's Bible, therefore, reveals the various ways in which she read and used the book. It functioned as a memorandum, noting the important household events such as the births of her children; as a spiritual comfort and guide; as a treasured material object; and as a dispenser of more practical advice for daily life, such as interactions with servants. This in turn suggests different levels and types of reading. The activity described in Beckwith's note to her daughter, where she instructed her to 'Reade it with a zealous harte to understand truly', indicates a different engagement with the text than might occur in the reading of the marginalia about Beckwith's family. The Bible moreover situated women, particularly Beckwith, within her family. The heartfelt address to her daughter and the references to her other children portray Beckwith as an exemplary pious mother, according to contemporary ideals of femininity, which suggested that a woman's primary duties were to take care of her children and watch over household devotion. If we follow the idea that annotations provide a space to mark out identity, as was discussed earlier, then we can see Beckwith's positioning of herself more clearly. Through these marginal notes, Beckwith portrayed herself as embodying commendable feminine traits, underlining her piety and constructing an identity both for herself and for any other potential readers of the text.

Books also functioned as important objects in relationships beyond close family circles. Giving or receiving books could serve to make political alliances or intellectual connections, securing a person's place in a more formalised network of acquaintances. Anne Sadleir (née Coke), literary patron and daughter of the jurist Sir Edward Coke, wrote on the flyleaf of her thirteenth-century Apocalypse manuscript when trusting it to the care of a Bishop, and thereafter Cambridge University.[70] She made reference to the political and religious upheavals of the time:

> I commit this booke to the custodie of the Right Reverend Father in god, Raffe lo: Bishop of Exon; when times are better settled (which god hasten) it is with my other booke and my coines, given to Trinitie Colledge Librarie in Cambridge, god in his good time, restore her with her sister Oxford to there pristine happines, the vulgar People to there former

> obedience, and god bless, and restore Charles the second, and make him like his most glorious Father Amen.[71]

This inscription is dated below 'August the 20$^{tie}$ 1649'. Sadleir's Royalist position and view on the Civil War conflict is made clear, and the fact that she chose to write this so explicitly indicates a desire on her part to advertise her views to future readers. This is different from inscriptions on books that were so often aimed at family members or friends; Sadleir knew that this manuscript was going to Cambridge University, and therefore to an unknown audience. Her declaration of ownership, patronage and political opinion therefore gave her a position of authority and suggests a desire to make her ownership and beliefs known to posterity. Sadleir's inscription made her political and social identity very public, difficult to hide from view or detach from the book itself.[72]

Other inscriptions can reveal women's engagement with theological issues, showing their understanding of and position within the politicised religious climate of the seventeenth century. This demonstrates a direct counter to Whately's instructions that they should not read 'Tomes of Disputations' – clearly, women were reading religious texts in order to enter into contemporary debates. Margaret Hoby, a devout Protestant and member of the Elizabethan gentry, left behind evidence of her reading habits in both her diary and various books owned by her.[73] Three theological polemics belonging to Hoby are now kept in York Minster Library, and various levels of marginalia can be found in the texts. These annotations have often been attributed to Hoby, notably by Andrew Cambers.[74] However, the annotations are in a neat secretary hand, which looks very different to the italic hand in which Hoby's diary is written. It is not necessarily possible to prove that Hoby did not write the annotations, but it seems unlikely – more probable is that they were written under her instruction by a male servant or secretary, possibly even the family's chaplain, Richard Rhodes. She did annotate some books herself: there are numerous entries in her diary which allude to this practice, such as when she recorded, 'I wrett in my testament some notes.'[75] However, it seems that this does not include the books now often identified as bearing her marginalia.[76] This introduces a complex perspective on the interplay between gender and intellectual authority in annotations. If Hoby was directing the marginalia but not writing them herself, or if the scribe was interpreting her responses to the text, then her analysis of the text is mediated through a male hand. Moreover, it raises questions about the assumptions surrounding marginalia, namely that it was largely a male activity. Even if the writer was male, this does not mean that it was a solely masculine intellectual act of interpretation; instead, the gendered dimensions could have been complicated and multifaceted. If we assume that Hoby's record of writing notes in her 'testament' refers to her directly inscribing them, then perhaps the genre of the book was relevant to the practice of annotation.

Hoby's reading notes demonstrate the extent to which her religious understanding was politically infused. Her copy of John Donne's *Pseudo-Martyr* bears her name on the title page.[77] There is only one marginal note in this book: at the end of the epistle, under the name of John Donne, the scribe has written 'Hangman'.[78] There is no clear explanation for this – whether it indicates Hoby's personal opinion of Donne (in which case it is interesting that she caused it to be signed, and possibly purchased the book) or something else. The lack of annotation in this book has led Cambers to claim that it is hard to know if she actually read it.[79] However, as we have little evidence that she or the scribe habitually wrote extensive notes on all her books, apart from the Bible that is mentioned in the diary, this is perhaps unfounded. Hoby may well have read the book and left it unannotated; or she may have decided against reading it because of its subject matter (which begs the question of why she owned it in the first place). Donne's work contributed to the religious pamphlet wars, arguing that Roman Catholics should take the Oath of Allegiance to King James.[80] Hoby, as a staunch Protestant and known proselytiser, may have objected to Donne's belief that Catholics could take the Oath without converting, accounting for the note in the epistle. Her annotation, therefore, serves to indicate her religio-political identity. Despite her owning a book that could be considered controversial, the one-word notation emphasises her own position, in relation to that of Donne.

The evidence of Hoby's annotation shows her engaging with politicised theological questions and debates. Her marks of ownership of certain Protestant texts set out her religious position clearly. She owned, for example, two books by Philippe du Plessis-Mornay, a French Huguenot writer and politician:[81] *A Treatise of the Church, Wherein are Handled the Principall Questions Mooued in our Time Concerning that Matter*[82] and *Fowre Bookes, of the Institution, Use and Doctrine of the Holy Sacrament of the Eucharist in the Old Church*.[83] Of these, the former only bears her signature on the title page, but the latter is extensively annotated. This difference could be connected to the physicality of the books. Sherman, in his survey of marginalia habits, has demonstrated that larger books were much more likely to be annotated in the early modern period, possibly due to the larger margin size.[84] The copy of *Fowre Bookes* is a folio, whereas *A Treatise of the Church* is a quarto, thus following the pattern identified by Sherman. Both texts were attacks on Catholicism, and were influential in the development of English Protestantism – Du Plessis-Mornay was connected to Philip Sidney and James I, united by a desire to form an international union of Protestants, and many of his works were translated into English.[85] In owning and perhaps reading these books, therefore, Hoby was again indicating her understanding of key religio-political debates of the time, this time on an international scale.

Her method of annotation and the parts of the text she chose to highlight also demonstrate Hoby's desire to mark her theological knowledge and understanding, making this a part of her identity. *Fowre Books* is heavily annotated. Her name and the year 1600 were inscribed on the title page, leading Cambers to suggest that this may be the year she acquired the book.[86] Then, throughout the main body of the text (but excluding the prefatory materials), there are written notes in the same hand. These annotations cover topics such as communion, image worship and the history of the church, and are most copious in the first two books. Around 40 per cent of the pages in books one and two are annotated, compared to 11 per cent in the third book and 6 per cent in the fourth book.[87] The annotations were often used in combination with underlining certain parts of the text; Cambers has suggested that Hoby may have read the book and underlined passages of interest first, then later added (or instructed the scribe to add) the marginal notes.[88] He suggests that these notes may have been used in compiling a commonplace book.[89] Although Hoby's commonplace book has not survived, we do know that she wrote one, as she records it in her diary, therefore this usage is likely.[90] This gives clear evidence of her use of the methods and practices of active reading. However, it could also be, as Smith suggests, that the different forms of marginalia reveal different types of engagement with the book.[91]

The marginalia in Hoby's books function in a variety of ways. The annotations expand on or summarise points of interest in the text or in the printed notes; they act as a textual guide allowing the reader to parse the text more quickly and effectively. One marginal note reads, 'Allegations agaynste images and the Adoringe of them', neatly summarising the lengthy discourse within the main text.[92] Another function of the marginalia appears to be to make note of passages for a specific extra-textual use. For example, one note reads, 'a good place to prove, that the sayntes know nothing done upon earth'.[93] This implies use of the book in non-textual encounters. Julie Crawford has argued this based on Hoby's diary; she suggests that Hoby's reading has a goal and that it was 'deeply imbricated with her religio-political activism in Yorkshire'.[94] Hoby was active in trying to combat recusancy in the region, and Crawford suggests that she often read in order to debate with her Catholic neighbours.[95] Hoby lived in the remote parish of Hackness, a largely Catholic area of the North Riding of Yorkshire. Both she and her husband, Sir Thomas Posthumous Hoby, were known for their zealous Protestantism and disputes with their neighbours.[96] *Fowre Bookes*, a Huguenot religious polemic, therefore may have been used in order to find arguments and evidence for her Protestant beliefs. Moreover, she mentions similar attempts in her diary: in one section, she writes that she 'reed and talked with a yonge papest maide', implying that she was trying to convert her.[97]

Hoby's annotations (whether she was the scribe or not) on books inscribed with her name served to create an identity for herself that was visible to anyone who picked up the texts. She situated herself within a specific religious and political sphere, demonstrating her religious position clearly. Women could use the pages of religious texts to demonstrate their piety, their politics and their theological beliefs, publicly constructing an identity for themselves.

## Theology, devotion and gender

Many self-authored documents, such as letters and diaries, reveal a pattern of repeated reading, showing a clear connection to the patterns laid out in conduct literature and funeral sermons. These texts recounting reading were not passive records. To a greater or lesser extent, they were part of process of self-fashioning. By emphasising the central place of devotional reading in their daily routine, women could underline their conformity to the feminine ideal presented by both conduct book writers and the writers of funeral sermons, and make themselves into godly women. They engaged in a performance of gender, acting out their femininity through repeated reading and the recording thereof.

One of the most common references to reading of any kind in these texts took the form of women noting their daily religious exercises. In these passages, reading was included as one form of devotion, alongside prayer and listening to sermons. This was frequently in list form, in a rote-like expression of religious routine. Hoby's diary exemplifies this. It is the earliest-surviving example of an Englishwoman's diary and is a rich source for scholars of early modern reading. In almost every entry, when Hoby recounted her day, it revolved around prayer, reading and household duties. For example, in the entry for August 3, 1600, she wrote:

> After priuat praers I did read and went about the house, and, after I had broken my fast, I went to the church: when I Came home I praied: after, dined: and then I talked and reed to some good wiffes that was with me: after, I walked with Mr Hoby, and praied, and then I went againe to the church, and, after, I reed of the testement: and then I talked with Mr Rhodes [her private chaplain] and, after, went to

> priuatt examenation and praier, and then to supper: after, to publeck praers, then to priuatt, and lastly to bed.[98]

This was a Sunday, so her religious activities would have taken precedence, but most days followed this same pattern, although on weekdays Hoby did not attend church so often. Reading in one form or another was part of her religious observances. Hoby's diary gives an image of her following the recommendations for a good woman practically to the letter, with her descriptions of her daily routine reflecting that advised in godly advice literature and described in funeral sermons.[99]

The way in which women recorded devotional reading reflected the way in which they read scripture. The method of reading in which texts were read and re-read daily is echoed in the presentation of reading in diaries as part of a catalogue of daily activities. In Hoby's diary, the entries are repetitive, following a similar written structure each time. As Sharon Cadman Seelig has noted, one can practically pick a date at random and find evidence of this routine.[100] For example, the entry from August 29, 1599 was strikingly similar to that of a year later, quoted above. Hoby wrote that

> After priuat praier I reed of the bible and wrought tell dinner time, before which I praied: and, after dinner, I continewed my ordenarie Course of working, reading, and dispossinge of busenes in the House, tell after 5:, at which time I praied, read a sermon, and examened my selfe.[101]

Many of her entries over the first two years of her surviving diary followed this pattern, with little variation. From about mid-1601 this changed, with Hoby providing less and less information in each entry. On April 9, 1601 she simply wrote: 'thes day I Continewed my ordenarie exercises, I praise god, without sicknes or trouble: and so, like wise, the 10 and:11: day'.[102] These 'exercises' were clearly the normal activities she undertook as part of her household routine, as an earlier entry made clear: 'this day, for prainge, readinge, and workinge, I Continewed my ordenarie exercises'.[103] She used the phrase 'my accustomed exercises' often thereafter, demonstrating the repeated and habitual nature of the activities.

This repeated reading was evidently common practice, but the different ways in which it was recorded show slightly different, individual efforts at self-fashioning. Hoby did not give many details about the specific sections of the Bible she read or the pattern of her re-reading. Other women's texts provide a more detailed explanation of what they read and when. Grace Mildmay (1552–1620), the Northamptonshire gentlewoman medical practitioner and memoirist, began her autobiography by declaring:

> I have found by experience [and] I commend unto my children as approved, this to be the best course to set ourselves in from the

> beginning unto the end of our lives. That is to say: first to begin with the scriptures to read them with all diligence and humility, as a disciple, continually every day in some measure until we have gone through the whole book of God from the first of Genesis unto the last of the Revelation and then begin again and so over and over without weariness.[104]

Mildmay's recommendation to her children reflected the ideal that women should try to meet. She very clearly set out a course of reading that ran from Genesis to Revelation and then started again, whereas Hoby never revealed how she read, not specifying the individual passages or whether she read the text continuously from beginning to end. Instead she wrote, much more vaguely, 'I reed of the bible'.

Sarah Cowper (1644–1720), the diarist and pious Anglican, also noted her repeated reading practices in one of her religious miscellanies:

> In the month of May 1700, I began to read two Chapters a Day in the Holy Bible, one out of the Old, and one out of the New Testament taking Notes and Observations entirely from my own Memory and Meditation, without looking into the interpretation of others, or any comentator whatsoever. This I say because mistakes or Errours there found, may be imputed to my own weakness and Ignorance, to which indeed they will wholly belong.[105]

The structured and habitual nature of her reading was strikingly similar to that of Hoby and Mildmay, despite Cowper writing nearly 100 years later. However, many of Cowper's specific methods of reading were different. Cowper read the Old and the New Testament simultaneously, taking notes as she went. Hoby and Mildmay both mentioned note-taking as a tool to reading and comprehension, although Cowper was much clearer about the specifics of this practice. Cowper's reading curriculum, however, bears resemblance to Frances Hobart's reading, as described by Collinges, when she set out to read the New Testament, Old Testament and the Psalms a certain number of times a year. Cowper's record of her reading was not as repetitive as Hoby's, but this reference to the pattern of her reading life reveals the similarities. Godly women diarists and autobiographers may not always have chosen to outline their routine in the detail Hoby did, but they probably still followed, or aspired to follow, similar devotional patterns.

This sets the practice of devotional reading apart from that of other printed books. Repeated use of religious texts was envisioned as a lifetime effort, even if in reality the dedication to this task may have varied over time. Reading was not seen as an activity for its own sake, or even on its own: it was part of a series of habitual devotional behaviours. This complicates our idea of how women read in the early modern period, and suggests that perhaps we should be distinguishing between different types of reading that are practised for different genres, something which is rarely considered in studies of early modern reading habits.

The self-fashioning of women readers could take different forms. Hoby's diary reveals a process of self-making and self-accounting, which continually created the self as she wrote. As Seelig has argued, 'Hoby's is a spiritual diary, not in the sense of recording the content of her spiritual exercises but rather their very existence. In other words, it was a form of self-monitoring, of record keeping undertaken apparently as a spur to devotional observance.'[106] Hoby was hard on herself when she did not live up to the task she had set herself. On one occasion she noted her failure to read, and condemned herself for it: 'nothinge reading nor profiting my selfe or any, the Lord pardon my ommitiones and Commitions, and giue me his spiritt to be wacthfull to redeme the time'.[107] Hoby was participating in a form of self-fashioning whereby the presentation of the self and of identity was continually developing, and was formed by the act of writing about reading on a regular basis. Mildmay's autobiography, however, reveals a different construction of identity. She wrote it between 1617 and 1620, when she died at age sixty-eight. The document was therefore looking back at her life, and she used reading and writing as a way of crafting a pious identity for herself, shaping the 'self' within the text into a certain form.

This self-construction was not a purely private exercise. These texts were also modes of self-presentation in which women crafted an identity for others, and with others. Reading was often done in company. Anne Clifford, for example, wrote in her diary in 1624 that 'Mr Grasty said Common Prayers and read a Chapter and sung a Psalm in my chamber to mee and my family (as usually is done upon Sundays)'.[108] Not only was reading tied to the structure of her week here (it is 'usually' done on a Sunday) but the importance of communal reading was also made clear. Clifford's aural reading was aided by 'Mr Grasty', the local parson, and his reading was heard by both Clifford and her family, demonstrating the shared nature of the family's devotions.

Similarly, Hoby's diary reveals that reading was an important component of her relationships with local women and members of her household, including her chaplain Richard Rhodes.[109] Mary Ellen Lamb has characterised Hoby's reading practices as essentially relational.[110] As Lamb has argued, 'the centrality of her chaplain Mr. Rhodes to her reading, and even to her writing of her diary, breaks down any simple binary between communal and private reading'.[111] Hoby's diary roughly corresponds with the period of Rhodes' residence in her household, and begins to lose direction after he left, becoming sparser from mid-1601.[112] Hoby's reliance on this communal mode of reading and interpretation was central to her portrayal of her devotion. Hoby's accounting and presentation of herself was not solely for her, but also for Rhodes. The expectation of him as an audience no doubt directly influenced the identity she was fashioning.

So far, we have focused on women writing about devotional reading, usually the reading of scripture. This could be presented firmly within the private sphere, divorced from the world of politics and sectarian conflict. Rainbowe created this distinction in Clifford's funeral sermon, separating devotion or spiritual reading from controversial religious polemic. He did, however, acknowledge that 'Authors of several kinds of Learning, some of *Controversies* very abstruse, were not unknown unto her [Clifford]. She much commended one Book, *William Barklay's Dispute* with *Bellarmine*, both, as she knew, of the *Popish perswasion*, but the former less *Papal*'.[113] This refers to the dispute between the Italian Jesuit Cardinal Robert Bellarmine and Scottish Catholic William Barclay concerning the Oath of Allegiance and the temporal power of the papacy.[114] There was a distinction made between the two texts, suggesting that Barclay was 'less Papal' than Bellarmine. Clifford read several Catholic texts, including François de Sales' *Introduction to a Devout Life*.[115] Leah Knight has argued that this was evidence of her critical reading, and 'her willingness to read works infused with risk and challenge might confirm the untroubled state of her faith'.[116] In the sermon Rainbowe ended with Clifford's pious devotional reading and made it clear that this is the most praiseworthy aspect of her conduct. However, despite the rhetorical privileging of devotional literature, there is in fact plenty of evidence of gentry women reading these other types of religious texts, usually theological or polemical. They were used by women to engage with the important debates of their day and to understand the intense and at times violent political climate.[117]

Not all women read against the grain of their faith, as Clifford did, but there is evidence of them using their reading very deliberately in order to engage in theological debate. Many books mentioned in Margaret Hoby's diary underlined the nature of her religious persuasion and demonstrated her connection with the religio-political culture of the Elizabethan period (as mentioned in the previous section). She both used books, particularly records of books in her diary, to demonstrate her allegiances and read in order to form and support her ideas. In one passage she recorded: 'I kept Companie with Mr Hoby who reed a whill of Cartwrights book to me.'[118] According to Hoby's editor, this was likely to be Thomas Cartwright, the religious controversialist who was involved in the Presbyterian attack on the Elizabethan church in the 1570s and advocated a parliamentarist mixed constitution.[119] While this conflict occurred several years before Hoby's diary was written, it nevertheless demonstrates the intertwining of religion and politics in the period. Through her reading, therefore, Hoby carefully constructed her religious position as a devout Protestant in Catholic Yorkshire, as well as emphasising her devotion and piety, and used her books as tools in theological debate.

Again, this reading and performance of identity was sociable and relational. Hoby's main source of theological discussions and biblical exegesis probably came from Rhodes, her chaplain. The relationship between Puritan clergy and lay women was common in seventeenth-century England. Diane Willen has argued that women 'were much more likely than men to develop strong, perhaps intense, and long-lasting relationships with their clergy'.[120] She goes on to suggest that 'emotionally or intellectually satisfying relationships with clergy were one of the few legitimate male-female friendships open to respectable married women'.[121] Willen has noted that the relationship between the clergy and these godly women was reciprocal, and that the women did not always defer to male clerical authority, using the examples of Joan Barrington, Brilliana Harley and Mary Vere.[122] Similarly, Peter Lake has examined the relationship between Jane Ratcliffe and John Ley, the Chester widow and cleric who engaged in what Lake calls a 'genuinely reciprocal' intellectual exchange.[123]

The role of men in women's religious lives becomes clear when they discussed theology. Debates around theology were almost always presented as an exchange with a male figure. Clifford, for example, related an instance when 'My Lord found me reading with Mr Ran & told me it would hinder his Study, so as I must leave off reading the Old Testament till I can get somebody to read it with me. This day I made an end of reading Deuteronomy.'[124] This passage not only made it clear that her husband's reading takes precedence over hers but also that she needed help to read certain sections of the Bible, but not others. Barbara Lewalski has pointed out that we cannot tell who decided that, as a woman, Clifford should not read unaided; or whether indeed it was Clifford herself who wanted the benefit of an expert.[125] However, it does indicate the culture of biblical exegesis that was a significant part of religious reading and that this often relied on a male figure of authority.

Elizabeth Delaval, the memoirist, also made this point when discussing how and when she read scripture:

> I will also when I have an opertunity of doing it ever red along with the scripture the paraphrase of that learned good man Doctor Hamond, or

> some other learn'd pious man of our church, rather then trust to my own interpretations.[126]

Delaval was referring to Henry Hammond's *A Paraphrase and Annotation upon All the Books of the New Testament* and *A Paraphrase and Annotation upon the Books of the Psalms*, published in the 1650s.[127] Hammond, the clergyman and Anglican divine, was a leading figure in the Anglican Moralism that developed during the mid-seventeenth century and set out to define a Church of England theology.[128] This movement emphasised human responsibility and moral duty; it was staunchly Royalist and dedicated to the Book of Common Prayer.[129] Delaval clearly valued his interpretation above her own, and implied that to truly understand scripture it was necessary to read one of the many paraphrases or works of biblical exegesis being published in the seventeenth century. She created a hierarchy of readers, with the 'learn'd pious m[e]n of our church' at the top. This is in contrast with the later example of Cowper who declared that she would follow only her own interpretation of scripture, although she did suggest that the absence of exegesis might lead her to make interpretative errors.

The practice of discussion between men and women becomes even clearer in some women's correspondence. Some women, such as Anne Sadleir, showed a clear willingness to participate in theological debate, mediated through reading. This may have been a product of the Civil War era. While there is evidence of women engaging in these issues pre-1640, for example with Hoby entering into disputes with her neighbours, the range of topics and intensity of debate were probably a product of the 1640s, and would continue into the 1690s with the Rage of Party.[130] Sadleir corresponded at length with male intellectuals and relatives about thorny theological issues, but showed none of the hesitancy about expressing her own opinion and position that we see in diaries and remembrances. Whereas godly women's diaries and autobiographies highlighted certain qualities, women such as Sadleir used very different textual techniques in debating theology. She used her reading, both of letters and of printed texts, to form and back up her own ideas, often in opposition to her male correspondents. This was a different form of self-fashioning, not accounting to God or another reader but instead forming an identity in opposition to others.

Sadleir's letters show her negotiating complex religious issues. She was not using her religious reading as evidence of her personal, feminine piety but rather to support her theological position. This becomes clear in an exchange with her Catholic nephew, Herbert Aston, in which she engaged in a debate with him partially through reference to her reading:

> this advantage I must tell you our Religion have over yours . . . wee have the liberty to read all bookes as well as yours thou you must read none of ours, but you must confess it as a sinn, and I have read most of all yours that I could git, and I thank allmighty god they have bin soe far from converting me, that they have more confermed me in my owne sum I have read that I must tell you I stand Amased at, one of them is called the flowers of the English saints, which I take to be but the Romances of those times.[131]

Sadleir's conception of Protestantism as a religion of reading was clearly key to her religious identity, and is a remarkable insight into her relationship to her faith. The letter was part of an ongoing debate between Sadleir and her nephew. Aston wrote to Sadleir, presumably in response to the above (although the letter is undated, and is placed earlier in the letterbook):

> the Protestants liberty of reading all bookes & further freedome of being their owne carvers & directors in spirituall matters & our restraint I confess, but y^e advantage by it I cannot yeald to, y^e effects of it in our litle kingdome are sad proofes of the contrary.[132]

This discussion is reminiscent of Hoby's attempts to convert her Catholic neighbours. Sadleir emphasised that she had done her research on Catholicism, as was permitted by her religion (in direct contrast to Aston's religion, which by implication was portrayed as strict and confining). The literate culture of Protestantism was made clear, and Sadleir stated that despite reading so many Catholic texts ('most of all yours that I could git'), she found this only served to confirm her own beliefs. It is particularly interesting that she used the term 'Romances' when describing Jerome Porter's 'the flowers of the English saints'.[133] Considering the cultural condemnation of romances (see Chapter 2), this was at best dismissive, and portrayed the Catholic culture of saints as fanciful and a fiction, implying that Aston was foolish to have been taken in by it. Sadleir's efforts to read Catholic texts show her intellectual and theological curiosity, but she used the books as a way of criticising Aston and his religion, as well as affirming her own beliefs. Aston's response, however, made the political nature of the discussion clear. His reference to the Civil War, and the apportioning of blame to Protestant 'liberty of reading . . . and further freedome', was a sharp rebuke to Sadleir's claims and demonstrates the political underpinning of their theological discussion. Both used reading as a way of framing their dialogue and supporting their views, and Sadleir showed no reticence in debating such thorny issues.

Sadleir clearly read biblical exegesis and theological texts widely. She listed some of her preferred religious texts in another, undated letter, saying:

> I have given over reading many bookes . . . those that I now read, besides the Bible, are first the late Kings Booke: Hookers Ecclesiasticall Politie: Reverend Bish: Andrews sermons, *with his other devine meditations:* D^r Jer: Taylors works, and D^r: Tho: Jacksone upon the creed: sum of these my dear father was a great admirer of and would often call them the glorious lights of the church of England.[134]

She was writing here to Roger Williams, the founder of the colony of Rhode Island. Williams had been a protégé of Sadleir's father before leaving for the New World in 1631. He was respected for his godliness in New World Puritan circles, but was controversial for his support for separation from the Church of England.[135] Sadleir was evidently familiar with an impressive range of religious and theological texts, and the writers that Sadleir mentioned, which she called 'the glorious lights of the church of England', demonstrate her Royalist Anglicanism.[136] The 'late Kings Booke' was *Eikon Basilike*, supposedly Charles I's spiritual autobiography, which perpetuated the cult of Charles as a martyr.[137] Richard Hooker was considered to be one of the 'founding fathers' of Anglicanism after the 1660, and his *Ecclesiastical Polity* was seen by many as a statement of reformed orthodoxy in England.[138] Thomas Jackson's commentary on the Apostle's creed, in Sarah Hutton's words, 'amounts to a learned defence of the Church of England'.[139] Lancelot Andrewes, the Jacobean Bishop of Winchester, moreover, was an affirmed anti-Puritan and a proponent of the divine right of kings, which no doubt clashed with Williams' ideas for the separation of church and state.[140] Sadleir's letter, then, did not shy away from their theological differences. Indeed, she ends this passage by saying that 'these lights shall be my guide, I wish they may be yours'. Many of the books mentioned here and later in their letters were published in the late 1640s, making it probable that the correspondence dates from the late 1640s or early 1650s.

In the two letters examined here Sadleir entered into a lively and sometimes playful debate with Williams about religion. This was often enacted, as in the passage above, through the recommendation or discussion of books she had read. Williams evidently sent her suggestions for reading material, which she did usually engage with, but rarely liked. In one instance Williams recommended Jeremy Taylor's *A Discourse on the Liberty of Prophesying*, published in 1647, to which Sadleir cuttingly responded:

> I have also read Taylors book of the liberty of protesting though it please not me yet I am sure it does you or els I you not have wrot to me to have read it, I say it and you would make a good fire.[141]

Taylor was an Anglican writer, but the *Liberty of Prophesying* was a call for religious toleration, something for which Williams was known.[142] Sadleir made it clear that she did not object to all of Taylor's works, who was included in her list of the 'glorious lights of the church of England', quoted above. She suggested that Williams consider Taylor's other books, writing 'have you sene his devine institution of the office ministeriall, I assure you that is both worth your reading and practice'.[143] She read critically and selectively, although her suggestion that Taylor's call for toleration should be burnt was an extreme (and witty) dismissal.

They also discussed Milton, with whom Williams was friends. Sadleir gave her opinion of Milton in no uncertain terms:

> for meltons [Milton's] book that you desire I should read if I be not mistakn, that is he that has wrot a book of the lawfulnes of devorce, and if report sais true he had at that time two or thre wives living, this perhaps were good Doctrine in new England, but it is most abominable in old England, for his book that he wrot against the late King that you would have me read, you should have taken notice of gods judgment upon him who stroke him with blindnes, and as I have heard he was faine to have the helpe of one Andrew Marvell or els he could not have finished that most accurssed Libell, god has begun his judgment upon him here, his punishment will be here after in hell.[144]

In taking such a hard line on Milton, apparently without having read the book suggested to her (it is unclear which text Sadleir was referencing), Sadleir was aligning herself with one side of the cultural debate surrounding Milton's tracts on divorce, which had been condemned by the church establishment and Parliament.[145] Sadleir also mentioned Milton's 'book that he wrot against the late King', which could either mean *Eikonoklastes*, his defence of regicide written in response to *Eikon Basilike* (which she listed as one of her guiding 'lights'), or his *The Tenure of Kings and Magistrates*.[146] She implied that he was struck blind by God in punishment for his writings, and suggested that he was not even capable of finishing the text without Marvell's help.[147] Her criticism of Milton was damning and unforgiving, writing that he would be punished for his 'Libell' in hell as well as by blindness during his life. By responding in this way, she both underlined her religious and social sensibilities, a significant part of her identity construction, and affirmed her own knowledge and authority.

Sadleir also kept Williams up to date with interpretations of political events, again largely through reading recommendations. This appears to have been part of their religious debates, as was implied in this same letter:

> for the bloud you mention, which has bin shed in these times which you would father upon the late king, there is a booke called the Historie of independencie, a booke worth your reading, that will tell you by whom all this Christian bloud has bin shed, if you cannot git that there is a sermon in print of one Paul Knells the text the first of amos verse that 2 that will informe you.[148]

Here Sadleir was referring to Clement Walker's *History of Independency*, first published in 1648, which attacked the New Model Army and their parliamentary allies for obstructing a settlement with the king.[149] Walker, though by no means a staunch Royalist, was heavily critical of the increasing divisions between the Presbyterians and the Independents, and wrote numerous pamphlets attacking parliamentary radicals.[150] Some of his works were reprinted during the Restoration as part of his *The Compleat History of Independency*.[151] Paul Knell, whose sermon she recommended, was a Church of England minister and a Royalist. The connection between religion and politics is inescapable here. Sadleir's religious and political reading were used in tandem in order to understand the Civil War. Although the letter is undated, it is clear that the conflict was, if not ongoing, then still a hugely pertinent issue, again making it likely that they were corresponding sometime around 1650. Sadleir represented both her political and religious position to Williams through the books she recommended.

Sadleir's references to her reading, then, did not serve to indicate traditional femininity. Instead, she linked her piety to a more intellectual endeavour, demonstrating her broad literary education as a way to justify her position in the debate with her nephew and with Williams. While not constructing a character in the same way as one would when writing a memoir, nevertheless Sadleir was creating a persona for herself, one which was linked to her devotion and religious affiliation, but not necessarily her femininity. She, moreover, used her reading, still often religious in nature, to engage in debates about the political state of affairs. Sadleir's letters demonstrate the close intertwining of these complex issues in the mid-seventeenth century, and the ways in which women negotiated contemporary debates through reading and letter-writing.

## Conclusion

Religious writings, whether devotional or theological, were used and represented in a number of different ways in early modern women's letters, meditations and spiritual diaries. Women could choose to echo the language of advice literature and funeral sermons, emphasising their practices of re-reading scripture and the ways in which it moved them. This created an image of exemplary feminine piety, and helped to situate the woman in her role within the devout Protestant household. That is not to say, however, that this reading was indeed 'confining' women to a world of conventional spirituality and domesticity. Instead, that was merely how they chose to represent themselves. They made a choice to use devotional literature and their recorded responses to it to demonstrate their feminine identity.

This is often seen in their personal devotional writings, and is partly due to the nature of that form of autobiography. Spiritual diaries, like that of Margaret Hoby, were used as a record of piety. The idea of recording one's life and devotions for future use by the writer, or for posterity, had a clear effect on the ways in which these women presented themselves. They conformed to the conventions of the genre, and this was central to their portrayal of their identity. This was still a choice, however, and makes clear the ways in which women negotiated and constructed their own gender identity within the text.

Some women's letters, however, particularly from the mid-seventeenth century, give the lie to the idea of devotion and religious reading being 'confined' to the domestic sphere. Here, women were fully engaged with the socio-political consequences of their religion. Sadleir was not afraid to enter into complex theological debates with her male friends and relatives, and used her reading to support her position. Her religio-political reading became a marker of her identity, intellectually, politically and religiously. It was not, however, a mark of her conformity to traditional, pious femininity. While Sadleir clearly was deeply religious, she did not feel the need to emphasise her adherence to contemporary constructions surrounding gendered reading and behaviour. While this is, of course, partly due to the nature of epistolary exchange and the subjects about which she was writing, it demonstrates the multiplicity of ways in which women could use their religious reading. Women did not only conform to the duties and prescriptions laid out in advice literature, but chose for themselves how to present their identity, dependent on the context in which they were writing.

Finally, the identities that were being created through women's religious reading were multiple and continual; they were created through the process of repeated reading, and were often influenced by others, be they family members, clergy, friends or neighbours. The use of religious reading to structure time allowed for a continual process of self-fashioning and reaffirming of identity, a process that was frequently done in company.

## Notes

1. See the 'Her Bible' section of this chapter for more information.

2. Both Sasha Roberts and Julie Crawford have emphasised the need to see religion and politics as intertwined for women readers and writers in this period, just as they were for men. Roberts has argued that 'it is not enough to characterise women's reading of religious texts as conventionally pious and conformist: the complexities of religious change, sectarianism, and conflict in the early modern period require a much more nuanced approach' and Crawford concludes, through studying Margaret Hoby's diary, that 'recording one's reading was a way of registering and affirming religious and political alliances'. See Sasha Roberts, 'Reading in Early Modern England: Contexts and Problems', *Critical Survey* 12, no. 2 (2000): 4; Julie Crawford, 'Reconsidering Early Modern Women's Reading, or, How Margaret Hoby Read Her De Mornay', *The Huntington Library Quarterly* 73, no. 2 (2010): 223.

3. Crawford, 'Reconsidering Early Modern Women's Reading', 205.

4. Crawford, 'Reconsidering Early Modern Women's Reading', 206.

5. The oral nature of reading is important, particularly but not solely in a religious context. Jennifer Richards, for example, has argued that 'script and print *depend* on the physical voice for their meaning'. I do not propose to discuss orality too much here, as it has been so well demonstrated by Richards, but it is clearly a very important part of religious reading practice. See Jennifer Richards, *Voices and Books in the English Renaissance: A New History of Reading* (Oxford: Oxford University Press, 2019), 18.

6. William Gouge, *Of Domesticall Duties Eight Treatises* (London: printed by Iohn Haviland for William Bladen, 1622), 397.

7. For more on the marital relationship, see Adrian Wilson, *Ritual and Conflict: The Social Relations of Childbirth in Early Modern England* (Farnham: Ashgate, 2013). For more on Whately himself, see Jacqueline Eales, 'Gender Construction in Early Modern England and the Conduct Books of William Whately (1583–1639)', *Studies in Church History* 34 (1998): 163–174.

8. William Whately, *A Bride-Bush, Or A Wedding Sermon: Compendiously Describing the Duties of Married Persons: By performing whereof, Marriage shall be to them a great Helpe, which now finde it a little Hell* (Printed at London by William Iaggard, for Nicholas Bourne, 1617), 10.

9. Whately, *A Bride-Bush*, 35.

10. Women were often not taught the skill of 'reason', or disputation, which was a mainstay of humanist education. Aysha Pollnitz has explored the way in which early modern princes were educated, and how royal women were often at a disadvantage in terms of their ability to construct arguments. See Aysha Pollnitz, *Princely Education in Early Modern Britian* (Cambridge: Cambridge University Press, 2015).

11. As Kate Narveson has shown, 'Bible reading helped to usher in a transitional world in which the growing availability of printed resources was in tension with the sense that lay people should turn for answers to the authority of learned men'. Kate

Narveson, *Bible Readers and Lay Writers in Early Modern England: Gender and Self-Definition in an Emergent Writing Culture* (Aldershot: Ashgate, 2012), 28.

12. Ralph Houlbrooke, *Death, Religion and the Family in England, 1480–1750* (Oxford: Clarendon Press, 1998), 295.

13. Houlbrooke, *Death, Religion and the Family*, 297; Joris van Eijnatten, ed., *Preaching, Sermon and Cultural Change in the Long Eighteenth Century* (Leiden: Brill, 2009).

14. Houlbrooke, *Death, Religion and the Family*, 298.

15. Femke Molekamp, 'Seventeenth-Century Funeral Sermons and Exemplary Female Devotion: Gendered Spaces and Histories', *Renaissance and Reformation/ Renaissance et Réforme* 35, no. 1, Special issue: Gendering Time and Space in Early Modern England (2012): 44.

16. John Collinges, *Par Nobile. Two Treatises. The one, concerning the Excellent Woman, Evincing a person Fearing the Lord, to be the most Excellent Person: Discoursed more privately upon the Death of the Right Honourable, the Lady Frances Hobart, late of Norwich, from Pro.31.29,30,31. The other, Discovering a Fountain of Comfort and Satisfaction, to persons walking with God, yet living and dying without sensible Consolations: discovered, from Psal. 17. 15. at the Funerals of the Right Honourable, the Lady Katharine Courten, preached at Blicklin, in the County of Norfolk, March 27. 1652. With the Narratives of the holy Lives and Deaths of those two Noble Sisters* (London: Printed in the Year 1669), 25. RB 441734, Henry E. Huntington Library, San Marino. My italics.

17. Andrew Cambers has noted the importance of reading and discussion combined in a godly household, arguing that religious reading was often a communal practice that involved reading aloud and subsequent discussion (referred to sometimes by contemporaries as 'expounding'). Andrew Cambers, *Godly Reading: Print, Manuscript and Puritanism in England, 1580–1720* (Cambridge: Cambridge University Press, 2011), 89.

18. John Birchall, *The Non-Pareil, Or, the Vertuous Daughter Surmounting all her Sisters: Described, In a Funerall Sermon upon the Death of that vertuous Lady,* Elizabeth Hoyle, *late wife of the Worshipfull* Thomas Hoyle, *Alderman of the City of* Yorke (York: Printed by *Tho: Bro[. . .]*, 1644), 12.

19. Samuel Ainsworth, *A Sermon Preached at the Funerall of that religious Gentlewoman M[is]* Dorothy Hanbury, *Wife to* Edward Hanbury *Esq. living at Kelmarsh in Northampton-shire: Who dyed the 12. day of* June, *and was buried at Navesby in Northampton-shire* July *13. Anno Dom.* 1642 (London: Printed by Richard Cotes, for Stephen Bowtell, 1645), 28.

20. John Bryan, *The Vertuous Daughter. A Sermon Preached at Saint Maries in Warwicke at the Funerall of the most vertuous and truely religious young Gentlewoman, Mistresse Cicely Puckering, Daughter and Co-heire to the right Worshipfull, Sir Thomas Puckering, Knight and Baronet, the fourteenth day of Aprill, 1636* (London: Printed by *Thomas Harper*, for *Lawrence Chapman*, 1636), 16.

21. Timothy Rogers, *The Character of a Good Woman, Both in a Single and Marry'd State. In a Funeral Discourse on Prov. 31. 10. Who can find a vertuous Woman? For her Price is far above Rubies. Occasion'd by the Decease of Mrs. Elizabeth Dunton, Who Died May 28. 1697. With an Account of Her Life and Death; and part of the Diary writ with her own Hand: With a Preface, containing a Brief History of several Excellent Women* (London: Printed for John Harris, 1697), 130. RB 231012, Huntington Library, San Marino. Also see John Howe, *The Blessednesse of the Righteous, Discoursed from Psal. 17, 15* (London: Printed by Sarah Griffin, for Samuel Thompson, 1668).

22. Collinges, *Par Nobile. Two Treatises*, 26–27.

23. Isaac Ambrose, *Redeeming the Time. A Sermon Preached at Preston in Lansashire, January 4th 1657, at the Funeral of the Honourable Lady, the Lady Margaret Houghton.*

*Revised, and, somewhat Enlarged; and, at the importunity of some Friends, now published* (London: Printed for Rowland Reynolds, 1674), 14.

24. For more on re-reading, see Chapter 5.

25. George Savile, Marquis of Halifax, *The Lady's New-year's Gift: Or, Advice to a Daughter, Under these following Heads: Viz. Religion, Husband, House, Family and Children, Behaviour and Conversation, Friendships, Censure, Vanity and Affectation, Pride, Diversions* (London: Printed for Matth. Gilliflower and James Partridge, 1692), 5, RB 329955, Huntington Library.

26. John Evelyn, 'Directions for the Employment of Your Time [to Mary Evelyn]', [early 1680s?], Evelyn Papers, Vol. CCLXXIII. F38r, Add MS 78440, British Library.

27. R. A. Houston, *Literacy in Early Modern Europe: Culture and Education 1500–1800* (London: Routledge, 2002), 61–62. For more on memory in the early modern period, see Andrew Hiscock, *Reading Memory in Early Modern Literature* (Cambridge: Cambridge University Press, 2011). For more on the concept of repetition in early modern Europe, see Lorna Clymer, ed., *Ritual, Routine, and Regime: Repetition in Early Modern British and European Cultures* (Toronto: University of Toronto Press in association with the UCLA Center for Seventeenth- and Eighteenth-Century Studies and the William Andrews Clark Memorial Library, 2006).

28. Edward Rainbowe, Lord Bishop of Carlisle, *A Sermon Preached At the Funeral of the Right Honorable Anne Countess of* Pembroke, Dorset, *and* Montgomery, *Who died* March *22. 1675/6, and was Interred* April *the 14th following at* Appleby *in* Westmoreland. *With Some Remarks on the Life of that Eminent Lady* (London: Printed for *R. Royston*, Bookseller to his most Excellent-Majesty, and *H. Broom*, 1677), 61.

29. Rainbowe, *A Sermon Preached*, 62.

30. This idea of nourishment is not one that will be considered at length here, but for more on the relationship between food and reading, see Jason Scott-Warren and Andrew Elder Zurcher, ed., *Text, Food and the Early Modern Reader: Eating Words* (Abingdon: Routledge, 2019).

31. Francis Pawley, of Broomfield, county Kent: Inventory of her goods: 1681, Add Ch 44538, British Library.

32. Egmont Papers Vol. XXIII, Katherine Perceval, née Southwell; wife of Sir J Perceval, 1st Baronet: Correspondence, etc., with her brother, Sir R. Southwell: 1659–1686, Add MS 46942, f167v, British Library. There is of course a difference between post-mortem inventories such as Pawley's and book lists made by the women themselves, and there are various factors which might have affected the inclusion or exclusion of certain books. It is possible, for example, that Perceval's book might have been packed for travelling, given the location of a 'Black Leather Trunk'. Nevertheless, devotional literature was prominent in inventories and lists compiled both post-mortem and while alive.

33. The catalogue displays a range of genres and lists the volumes by size. 'An Inventory of Bookes in the Lady Heaths closet', Heath and Verney Papers. Vol. VI (ff. 229). Miscellaneous inventories and accompts 1599–1799, Egerton MS 2983, f79r, British Library.

34. The Protestant reception of de Sales' *Introduction to a Devout Life* has been discussed in Mary Hardy, 'The Seventeenth-Century English and Scottish Reception of Francis de Sales' *An Introduction to a Devout Life*', *British Catholic History* 33, no. 2 (2016): 228–258.

35. Paul E. Kopperman, *Sir Robert Heath, 1575–1649: Window on an Age* (Woodbridge: Boydell Press for the Royal Historical Society, 1989).

36. Rebecca Laroche, '"To take in hand the practice of phisick": Early Modern Women's Signatures in Print Medical Texts', in *New Ways of Looking at Old Texts, IV,*

ed. Michael Denbo (Tempe, AZ: Arizona Center for Medieval and Renaissance Studies, 2008), 271.

37. Laroche, 'To take in hand the practice of phisick', 274.

38. Jason Scott-Warren, *Sir John Harington and the Book as Gift* (Oxford: Oxford University Press, 2001), 2.

39. Jason Scott-Warren has suggested that 'graffiti' might be a good term for these autograph inscriptions, arguing that 'many early modern books are "tagged" and "pieced" as the average wall in a European capital city'. Jason Scott-Warren, 'Reading Graffiti in the Early Modern Book', *Huntington Library Quarterly* 73, no. 3 (2010): 368, 377–379. He is developing Juliet Fleming's work on early modern graffiti, which argues that the act of writing on walls 'appears against the grid of what we understand to be the difference between public and private'. See Juliet Fleming, *Graffiti and the Writing Arts of Early Modern England* (Philadelphia, PA: University of Pennsylvania Press, 2001), 33. Katherine Acheson has also recently drawn on Fleming's work in her study of marginal notes and space, arguing that marginalia 'allowed women to enter forbidden spaces and extend their selves within those worlds'. See Katherine Acheson, 'The Occupations of the Margins: Writing, Space, and Early Modern Women', in *Early Modern English Marginalia*, ed. Katherine Acheson (Abingdon: Routledge, 2019), 87.

40. Scott-Warren, 'Reading Graffiti in the Early Modern Book', 381, 379.

41. William Sherman has surveyed annotations on Bibles at the Huntington Library, noting that about one in five Bibles and prayer books in the collection contained significant marginalia. He listed eight different types of annotation commonly found in Bibles, although none of these included family notes of the kind explored here. See William H. Sherman, *Used Books: Marking Readers in Renaissance England* (Philadelphia, PA: University of Pennsylvania Press, 2008), 73, 80, 83.

42. Femke Molekamp, 'The Making of the Geneva Bible: Histories of Translation and Reading', *AHRC Translating Cultures*, accessed June 24, 2019, http://translatingcultures.org.uk/awards/fellowship-awards/the-making-of-the-geneva-bible-histories-of-translation-and-reading.

43. Femke Molekamp, '"Of the Incomparable treasure of the Holy Scriptures": The Geneva Bible in the Early Modern Household', in *Literature and Popular Culture in Early Modern England*, ed. Matthew Dimmock and Andrew Hadfield (Farnham: Ashgate, 2009), 135.

44. I have not found other women's Bibles bearing the same level of annotations as Beckwith's, although this is not to say that they do not exist. This is probably more a case of women's annotations rarely being recorded in archive catalogues.

45. *The Bible. That is, the Holy Scriptures Conteined in the Olde and New Testament. Translated according to the Ebrew and Greeke, and conferred with the best transla-ons in diuers languages. With most profitable annotations vpon all the hard places, and other things of great importance, as may appeare in the Epistle to the Reader* (Imprinted at London by the Deputies of Christopher Barker, Printer to the Queenes most excellent Maiestie. Anno Domini 1597), 464.c.5.(1.), British Library.

46. 2 Macc. 464.c.5.(1.), British Library.

47. The centrality of the Bible and reading to the godly community has been demonstrated by many scholars, including Andrew Cambers and Michelle Wolfe. See, for example, Andrew Cambers and Michelle Wolfe, 'Reading, Family Religion, and Evangelical Identity in Late Stuart England', *The Historical Journal* 47, no. 4 (2004): 875–896. The Bible would hold a special position both spiritually and materially in the godly household due to the importance of reading.

48. The idea of 'extensive reading' was developed by Rolf Engelsing, the German historian who argued for a 'reading revolution' in the early modern period.

Engelsing's work has not been translated into English, but has been influential on many studies of reading since. See, for example, Ian Jackson, 'Approaches to the History of Readers and Reading in Eighteenth-Century Britain', *The Historical Journal* 47, no. 4 (2004): 1041–1054.

49. 464.c.5.(1.), British Library.

50. The Geneva Bible was the preferred Bible of English Puritans. It included extensive marginal notes to aid comprehension and the reading experience. See, for example, Christopher Durston and Jacqueline Eales, ed., *The Culture of English Puritanism, 1560–1700* (London: Palgrave Macmillan, 1996). It was never officially sanctioned by the state in England, but was popular across the country. See Dan G. Danner, 'The Contribution of the Geneva Bible of 1560 to the English Protestant Tradition', *The Sixteenth Century Journal* 12, no. 3 (1981): 5–18.

51. *The Bible translated according to the Ebrew and Greeke, and conferred with the best translations in diuers languages; with most profitable annotationsvpon all the hard places, and other things of great importance, as may appeare in the epistle to the reader; and also a most profitable concordance for the readie finding out of any thing in the same conteined* (Imprinted at London by the Deputies of Christopher Barker, Printer to the Queenes most excellent Maiestie, 1599). The verse is normally entitled 'Of the Incomparable Treasure of the Holy Scripture'.

52. 464.c.5.(1.), British Library.

53. STC (2nd ed.), 2168. For more about the editions of the Geneva Bible, see Maurice S. Betteridge, 'The Bitter Notes: The Geneva Bible and Its Annotators', *The Sixteenth Century Journal* 14, no. 1 (1983): 41–62.

54. 464.c.5.(1.), British Library.

55. 1 Sam. 25:29, 464.c.5.(1.), British Library.

56. For more on readers of the Geneva Bible, see Michael Jensen, '"Simply" Reading the Geneva Bible: The Geneva Bible and Its Readers', *Literature and Theology* 9, no. 1 (1995): 30–45.

57. Isa. 66, 464.c.5.(1.), British Library.

58. John Norden, *A Pensive Mans Practise verie profitable for all persons* (London: Printed by William Hall for Richard Bradocke, 1610), 87. I am very grateful to Michelle O'Callaghan for identifying this poem via the Folger First Lines Index.

59. Mary Hampson Patterson, *Domesticating the Reformation: Protestant Best Sellers, Private Devotion, and the Revolution of English Piety* (Madison, WI: Fairleigh Dickinson University Presses, 2007), 158–161. Patterson has argued that Norden expected a 'fairly intense cerebral involvement' from the reader and that he was 'preoccupied with a piety that is very personal and internal in nature' (p. 159).

60. Patterson, *Domesticating the Reformation*, 167–168.

61. Tara Hamling and Catherine Richardson have demonstrated how prayer was integral to household routine in the early modern period, particularly in the morning, where 'routine activities in the early morning, from first waking until after dressing, were supposed to be accompanied and punctuated by a series of pious meditations as well as formal prayer'. See Hamling and Richardson, *A Day at Home in Early Modern England: Material Culture and Domestic Life, 1500–1700* (New Haven, CT: Yale University Press, 2017), 44.

62. John E. Booty, ed., *The Book of Common Prayer: The Elizabethan Prayer Book* (Charlottesville, VA: Published for the Folger Shakespeare Library by the University of Virginia Press, 2005), 24. Many thanks to Dr John Hinks for suggesting this.

63. Isa. 66, 464.c.5.(1.), British Library.

64. 464.c.5.(1.), British Library.

65. Isa. 44, 464.c.5.(1.), British Library.

66. For reflections and debates on the political nature of the Geneva Bible, see Tom Furniss, 'Reading the Geneva Bible: Notes towards an English Revolution?', *Prose Studies* 31, no. 1 (2009): 1–21; Richard L. Greaves, 'The Nature and Intellectual Milieu of the Political Principles in the Geneva Bible Marginalia', *Journal of Church and State* 22, no. 2 (1980): 233–249.

67. 1 Kings 6, 464.c.5.(1.), British Library.

68. For Buckingham's life, see Roger Lockyer, *Buckingham: The Life and Political Career of George Villiers, First Duke of Buckingham, 1592–1628* (London: Routledge, 1981).

69. This is similar to Kevin Sharpe's hypothesis regarding William Drake's reading habits: see Sharpe, *Reading Revolutions: The Politics of Reading in Early Modern England* (New Haven, CT: Yale University Press, 2000).

70. For more on Sadleir's reading and book collection, see Arnold Hunt, 'The Books, Manuscripts and Literary Patronage of Mrs Anne Sadleir (1585–1670)', in *Early Modern Women's Manuscript Writing: Selected Papers from the Trinity/Trent Colloquium*, ed. Victoria E. Burke and Jonathan Gibson (Aldershot: Ashgate, 2004), 205–236.

71. The Trinity Apocalypse, R.16.2, Trinity College, Cambridge.

72. Natalie Zemon Davis has argued that the book as a patronage gift had an advantage over many other items, as the original owner's message could not be so easily lost or divorced from the object. She writes that, '[i]n the book, everything could be made explicit and the dedications themselves could draw heavily on the language of gifts and responsibilities'. Natalie Zemon Davis, 'Beyond the Market: Books as Gifts in Sixteenth-Century France – The Prothero Lecture', *Transactions of the Royal Historical Society* 33 (1983): 79.

73. Claire Cross has noted the impressive scope of Hoby's theological study, arguing that it 'must have outpaced all but the most dedicated of Protestant ministers'. See Claire Cross, 'The Religious Life of Women in Sixteenth-Century Yorkshire', *Studies in Church History* 27, Women in the Church (1990): 323.

74. See Andrew Cambers, 'Readers' Marks and Religious Practice: Margaret Hoby's Marginalia', in *Tudor Books and Readers: Materiality and the Construction of Meaning*, ed. John N. King (Cambridge: Cambridge University Press, 2010), 211–231.

75. Margaret Hoby, *The Diary of Lady Margaret Hoby*, ed. Dorothy M. Meads (London: George Routledge & Sons, 1930), 107.

76. Helen Smith, noting that the annotations were not in Hoby's hand, has nonetheless identified other markings in the books that could be attributed to Hoby herself. These include various dots and trefoils, which marked passages that could have been of particular interest to Hoby. See Helen Smith, *'Grossly Material Things': Women and Book Production in Early Modern England* (Oxford: Oxford University Press, 2012), 186.

77. John Donne, *Pseudo-Martyr. Wherein Out of Certaine Propositions and Gradations, This Conclusion is Evicted. That Those Which Are of the Romane Religion in This Kingdome, May and Ought to Take the Oath of Allegiance* (London: Printed by *W. Stansby* for *Walter Burre*, 1610). Hackness 57, York Minster Library, York.

78. Donne, *Pseudo-Martyr.*

79. Cambers, 'Readers' Marks and Religious Practice', 220.

80. Olga Valbuena, 'Casuistry, Martyrdom, and the Allegiance Controversy in Donne's "Pseudo-Martyr"', *Religion and Literature* 32, no. 2, Faith and Faction: Religious Heterodoxy in the English Renaissance (2000): 49–80. For more on the

Oath of Allegiance, see Marcy L. North, 'Anonymity's Subject: James I and the Debate over the Oath of Allegiance', *New Literary History* 33, no. 2, Anonymity (2002): 215–232; Conal Condren, *Argument and Authority in Early Modern England: The Presupposition of Oaths and Offices* (Cambridge: Cambridge University Press, 2006).

81. For more on Mornay, see Arthur L. Herman, 'Protestant Churches in a Catholic Kingdom: Political Assemblies in the Thought of Philippe Duplessis-Mornay', *The Sixteenth-Century Journal* 21, no. 4 (1990): 543–557.

82. Philip of Mornai, *A Treatise of the Church, Wherein are Handled the Principall Questions Mooued in our Time Concerning that Matter* (Imprinted at London by L. S. for George Potter, 1606). Hackness 66, York Minster Library.

83. Philip of Mornai, *Fowre Bookes, of the Institution, Use and Doctrine of the Holy Sacrament of the Eucharist in the Old Church. As Likewise, How, When, And by what Degrees the Masse if Brought in, in place thereof* (London: Printed by Iohn Windet, for I. B. T. M. and W. P., 1600). Hackness 47, York Minster Library.

84. Sherman, *Used Books*, 19–20.

85. Mark Greengrass, 'Philippe Duplessis-Mornay, Jacques VI et Ier, et la réunion de christianisme 1603–1619', *Albineana* 18 (2006): 423–461; Jaime Goodrich, *Faithful Translators: Authorship, Gender and Religion in Early Modern England* (Evanston, IL: Northwestern University Press, 2014).

86. Cambers, 'Readers' Marks and Religious Practice', 220.

87. Exact figures: Book One is annotated on 39.4 per cent of its pages; Book Two 40.7 per cent; Book Three 11.1 per cent; and Book Four 6.4 per cent.

88. Cambers, 'Readers' Marks and Religious Practice', 228.

89. Cambers, 'Readers' Marks and Religious Practice', 228.

90. Hoby, *The Diary of Lady Margaret Hoby*, 67.

91. Smith, *'Grossly Material Things'*.

92. Mornai, *Fowre Bookes*, 129.

93. Mornai, *Fowre Bookes*, 305.

94. Crawford, 'Reconsidering Early Modern Women's Reading', 194.

95. For more on neighbourly relationship, parish politics and religion, see Naomi Tadmor, *The Social Universe of the English Bible: Scripture, Society, and Culture in Early Modern England* (Cambridge: Cambridge University Press, 2010); Keith Wrightson, 'The Politics of the Parish in Early Modern England', in *The Experience of Authority in Early Modern England*, ed. Paul Griffiths, Adam Fox and Steve Hindle (London: Palgrave Macmillan, 1996), 10–46.

96. Felicity Heal, 'Reputation and Honour in Court and Country: Lady Elizabeth Russell and Sir Thomas Hoby', *Transactions of the Royal Historical Society* 6 (1996): 163. For more on Thomas Hoby, see G. C. F. Forster, 'Faction and County Government in Early Stuart Yorkshire', *Northern History* 11, no. 1 (1976): 70–86.

97. Hoby, *The Diary of Lady Margaret Hoby*, 105. For work on the Bible as a conversion tool overseas in the early modern period, see Helen Smith, '"Wilt thou not read me, Atheist?": The Bible and Conversion', in *The Oxford Handbook of the Bible in Early Modern England, c. 1530–1700*, ed. Kevin Killeen, Helen Smith and Rachel Willie (Oxford: Oxford University Press, 2015), 351–366.

98. Hoby, *The Diary of Lady Margaret Hoby*, 136.

99. While Hoby's diary was written before most of the conduct literature and funeral sermons surveyed here, it is clear that she was part of this conversation about godly reading and women that was developing during the early modern period, and uses remarkably similar language and tropes.

100. Sharon Cadman Seelig, *Autobiography and Gender in Early Modern Literature: Reading Women's Lives, 1600–1680* (Cambridge: Cambridge University Press, 2006), 16.

101. Hoby, *The Diary of Lady Margaret Hoby*, 67.

102. Hoby, *The Diary of Lady Margaret Hoby*, 168.

103. Hoby, *The Diary of Lady Margaret Hoby*, 166.

104. Linda Pollock, ed., *With Faith and Physic: The Life of a Tudor Gentlewoman, Lady Grace Mildmay, 1552–1620* (London: Collins & Brown, 1993), 23. Women were not the only ones to practise this ordered, habitual method of reading scripture. Nehemiah Wallington, for example, recorded reading a chapter of the Bible every night. See Nehemiah Wallington, *The Notebooks of Nehemiah Wallington, 1618–1654: A Selection*, ed. David Booy (Aldershot: Ashgate, 2007), 267, 272.

105. Sarah Cowper, *Miscellany*, D/EP F44, 87, Hertfordshire Local Studies and Archives, Hertford.

106. Sharon Cadman Seelig, *Autobiography and Gender in Early Modern Literature: Reading Women's Lives, 1600–1680* (Cambridge: Cambridge University Press, 2006), 16.

107. Hoby, *The Diary of Lady Margaret Hoby*, 69–70.

108. Anne Clifford, *The Diaries of Lady Anne Clifford*, ed. D. J. H. Clifford (Stroud: Sutton Publishing, 1990), 265.

109. Mary Ellen Lamb, 'The Sociality of Margaret Hoby's Reading Practices and the Representation of Reformation Interiority', *Critical Survey* 12, no. 2 (2000): 17–32.

110. Lamb, 'The Sociality of Margaret Hoby's Reading Practices', 28.

111. Lamb, 'The Sociality of Margaret Hoby's Reading Practices', 18.

112. Scholars have begun to question the 'privileging of the individualistic male self over the relational model more common to women' in the historiography of early modern autobiographical writings. See Lamb, 'The Sociality of Margaret Hoby's Reading Practices', 28.

113. Rainbowe, *A Sermon Preached*, 39.

114. Bernard Bourdin, *The Theological-Political Origins of the Modern State: The Controversy between James I of England and Cardinal Bellarmine*, trans. Susan Pickford (Washington, DC: The Catholic University of America Press, 2010), 135. William Barclay was the father of John Barclay, author of *Argenis*, which Clifford read and annotated – see Chapter 2.

115. Leah Knight, 'Reading across Borders: Anne Clifford's "Popish" Books', *Journal of the Canadian Historical Association* 25, no. 2 (2014): 27–56.

116. Knight, 'Reading across Borders', 46.

117. Lucy Hutchinson is well known for her religio-political writings in the mid-seventeenth century, and demonstrates the political nature of religious reading very well. Elizabeth Scott-Baumann has argued that Hutchinson's *Order and Disorder* encourages a 'kind of politicised reading of the Bible'. See Scott-Baumann, 'Lucy Hutchinson, the Bible and *Order and Disorder*', in *The Intellectual Culture of Puritan Women, 1558–1680*, ed. Johanna Harris and Elizabeth Scott-Baumann (Basingstoke: Palgrave Macmillan, 2011), 176–189.

118. Hoby, *The Diary of Lady Margaret Hoby*, 97.

119. Hoby, *The Diary of Lady Margaret Hoby*, 260 (note 284); Patrick Collinson, 'Cartwright, Thomas', *Oxford Dictionary of National Biography*, 2004, accessed September 12, 2023, www.oxforddnb.com/view/article/4820?docPos=1. For more on Thomas Cartwright, see Stephen A. Chavura, 'Mixed Constitutionalism and

Parliamentarianism in Elizabethan England: The Case of Thomas Cartwright', *History of European Ideas* 41, no. 3 (2015): 318–337.

120. Diane Willen, 'Godly Women in Early Modern England: Puritanism and Gender', *Journal of Ecclesiastical History* 43, no. 4 (1992): 570. Willen builds on the work of scholars such as Patrick Collinson, who studied the place of women in early modern Protestantism, but convincingly argues that they did not pay enough attention to the ways in which gender operated in (female) lay and (male) clerical relationships. See Patrick Collinson, 'The Role of Women in the English Reformation Illustrated by the Life and Friendships of Anne Locke', *Studies in Church History* 2 (1965): 258–272.

121. Willen, 'Godly Women in Early Modern England', 570–571.

122. Willen, 'Godly Women in Early Modern England.' For more on Barrington and Harley, see Chapter 3.

123. Peter Lake, 'Feminine Piety and Personal Potency: The "Emancipation" of Mrs Jane Ratcliffe', *The Seventeenth Century* 2, no. 2 (1987): 154.

124. Clifford, *The Diaries of Lady Anne Clifford*, 52.

125. Barbara Kiefer Lewalski, *Writing Women in Jacobean England* (Cambridge, MA: Harvard University Press, 1993), 150. Evidently, Clifford's husband also wanted this communal reading, although the gendered authority was no doubt different in that interaction.

126. Elizabeth Delaval, *The Meditations of Lady Elizabeth Delaval, Written Between 1662 and 1671*, ed. Douglas G. Greene (Gateshead: Printed for the Surtees Society by Northumberland Press, 1978), 117.

127. Henry Hammond, *A Paraphrase, and Annotations Upon all the Books of the New Testament: Briefly explaining all the difficult places thereof* (London: Printed by *J. Flesher* for *Richard Royston*, 1653); Henry Hammond, *A Paraphrase and Annotations Upon the Books of the Psalms: Briefly Explaining the Difficulties thereof* (London: Printed by *R. Norton*, for *Richard Royston*, 1659).

128. Michael McGiffert, 'Henry Hammond and Covenant Theology', *Church History* 74, no. 2 (2005): 255–285.

129. Neil Lettinga, 'Covenant Theory Turned Upside Down: Henry Hammond and Caroline Anglican Moralism: 1643–1660', *Sixteenth-Century Journal* 24, no. 3 (1993): 653–669. For more on Moralism, see C. FitzSimons Allison, *The Rise of Moralism: The Proclamation of the Gospel from Hooker to Baxter* (London: SPCK, 1966).

130. Dorothy Moore's letters are another good example of this – she often discussed matters of church and state with her male correspondents. See Lynette Hunter, ed., *The Letters of Dorothy Moore, 1612–64: The Friendships, Marriage and Intellectual Life of a Seventeenth-Century Woman* (Aldershot: Ashgate, 2004). Carol Pal has examined how the writings of Moore and other contemporary female intellectuals was influenced by the Civil War period and the influx of radical Protestant ideas from the Netherlands. See Pal, *Republic of Women: Rethinking the Republic of Letters in the Seventeenth Century* (Cambridge: Cambridge University Press, 2012).

131. Anne Sadleir to Herbert Aston, March 20, 1663, R.5.5. f10, Trinity College, Cambridge.

132. Herbert Aston to Anne Sadleir, March 31 [no year], R.5.5. f6, Trinity College.

133. This is almost certainly the 1632 book on English saints by Father Jerome Porter, a Benedictine monk. See Jerome Porter, *The Flowers of the Liues of the Most Renowned Saincts of the Three Kingdoms England Scotland, and Ireland Written and collected out of the best authours and manuscripts of our nation, and distributed according to their feasts in the calendar* (Printed at Doway, 1632).

134. Anne Sadleir to Roger Williams, undated, R.5.5. f35, Trinity College.

135. Timothy L. Hall, *Separating Church and State: Roger Williams and Religious Liberty* (Urbana, IL: University of Illinois Press, 1998).

136. Many other women, including Elizabeth Delaval and Anne Halkett, recorded reading some or all of these texts. See Julie A. Eckerle, *Romancing the Self in Early Modern Englishwomen's Life Writing* (Farnham: Ashgate, 2013), 28–29.

137. Robert Wilcher, 'What Was the King's Book For? The Evolution of *Eikon Basilike*', *The Yearbook of English Studies* 21 (1991): 218–228.

138. Peter Lake, 'Business as Usual? The Immediate Reception of Hooker's *Ecclesiastical Polity*', *The Journal of Ecclesiastical History* 52, no. 3 (2001): 456–486.

139. Sarah Hutton, 'Thomas Jackson, Oxford Platonist, and William Twisse, Aristotelian', *Journal of the History of Ideas* 39, no. 4 (1978): 637.

140. Jonathan McGovern, 'The Political Sermons of Lancelot Andrewes', *The Seventeenth Century* 34, no. 1 (2019): 3–25.

141. Anne Sadleir to Roger Williams, undated, R.5.5. f36, Trinity College.

142. John D. Schaeffer, 'Tropical Latitude: Prophecy, Orality, and the Rhetoric of Tolerance in Jeremy Taylor's *The Liberty of Prophesying*', *Studies in Philology* 101, no. 4 (2004): 454–470. See Jeremy Taylor, *Theologia eklektike. A Discourse of the Liberty of Prophesying. Shewing the unreasonableness of prescribing to other mens faith, and the iniquity of persecuting differing opinions* (London: Printed for R. Royston, at the Angel in Ivie-Lane, 1647).

143. Anne Sadleir to Roger Williams, undated, R.5.5. f36, Trinity College.

144. Sadleir to Williams, undated, R.5.5. f36, Trinity College.

145. Diane K. McColley, 'Milton and the Sexes', in *The Cambridge Companion to Milton*, ed. Dennis Danielson (Cambridge: Cambridge University Press, 1999), 181. It is likely from the wording that Sadleir was referring to Milton's *Doctrine and the Discipline of Divorce*, first published in 1643.

146. John Milton, *Eikonoklastes. In answer to a book intitl'd Eikon basilike, the portrature of His Sacred Majesty in his solitudes and sufferings* (London: Printed by T. N., 1650); John Milton, *The Tenure of Kings and Magistrates: Proving, that is it Lawfull, and hath been held so through all Ages, for any, who have the Power, to call to account a Tyrant, or wicked King, and after due conviction, to depose, and put him to death; if the ordinary Magistrate have neglected, or deny'd to doe it* (London: Printed by Matthew Simmons, 1649). I am grateful to Marcus Nevitt for this second identification.

147. Nigel Smith has argued that this claim was 'groundless, a post-regicide slur, and possibly a confusion of Marvell and Milton's collaboration in 1653 or 1654'. See Nigel Smith, *Andrew Marvell: The Chameleon* (New Haven, CT: Yale University Press, 2010), 106.

148. Anne Sadleir to Roger Williams, undated, R.5.5. f36, Trinity College.

149. Clement Walker, *Anarchia Anglicana: Or, the History of Independency. With observations historicall and politicque upon this present Parliament, begun Anno 16. Caroli Primi* ([London, s.n.], 1648).

150. David Underdown, 'Walker, Clement', *Oxford Dictionary of National Biography*, 2004, accessed September 12, 2023, www.oxforddnb.com/view/10.1093/ref:odnb/9780198614128.001.0001/odnb-9780198614128-e-28473?rskey=nCQKGq&result=1.

151. Royce MacGillivray, *Restoration Historians and the English Civil War* (The Hague: Martinus Nijhoff, 1974).

## Chapter 2

# 'Reading unprofitable romances': gender, identity and the romance genre

John Evelyn, when he made a record of his daughter Mary's books and papers after her death in 1685, included in the list 'A parchment booke w$^{th}$ some loose papers in it containing collections out of History, divinity &c: by way of comonplace, w$^{th}$ descriptions out of Romances.'[1] The use of the phrase 'by way of commonplace' to describe the manuscript indicates an intriguing way of reading and responding to romances, one that many might not connect with the romance genre. Mary clearly not only read romances but deemed them worthy of extracting and collecting excerpts from her books in the same way that humanist scholars did to aid their learning. Commonplace books usually have been seen as central to humanist pedagogy, designed as collections of excerpts for education and emulation.[2] For Mary Evelyn, then, to collect passages from romances, alongside extracts from works of history and divinity, 'by way of commonplace', suggests that she read all three genres in the same active way, using a method usually associated with scholarly endeavour. Mary appears to have been a frequent reader of romances. In a letter to her, Evelyn referenced her enjoyment of the genre but cautioned her against too much credulity: 'if you looke for perfection, and all things agreable to the *Idias* you reade of in *Romances*, or indeede, Conceive to be in nature: Let me tell you, there is no such thing'.[3] Despite this warning, she still decided to include extracts from romances alongside quotes from devotional and historical works.

This is in distinct opposition to the way that romances were usually portrayed in early modern rhetoric, and indeed in more recent scholarship.

John Evelyn's intimation that romances did not contain any lessons for life draws on a more commonly discussed view of romances, which saw them as devoid of intellectual value and instead representative of passive, leisure reading. Conduct books that gave advice and prescriptions for women readers tended to warn against reading romances, fearing the effect they may have on young, impressionable women.

This chapter begins by outlining this cultural rhetoric surrounding the romance genre, and then explores how women actually read such books, and how they responded to the gendered discussions of the genre. I argue that women were clearly aware of the disapproval surrounding female romance reading, but that this did not mean that they avoided reading romances, or even castigated themselves for doing so. While some did repent their romance reading, others acknowledged their consumption and even enjoyment of their books, pushing back against constructed gender ideals. Representing romance reading was often central to a construction of some form of feminine identity, in conversation with but not dictated by contemporary cultural conventions. Moreover, women often explicitly denied the 'frivolous' nature of romance reading, challenging the active/passive reading binary that has so often been used in scholarship. Women read these books for many reasons, but their very use of romance in their construction of femininity shows that they were not reading passively or uncritically, even if they were enjoying their texts. They frequently seemed to find 'profit' in their reading, despite the common view of the genre as 'unprofitable'.

There are plenty of examples of 'active' reading practices applied to romances, such as Mary Evelyn's habit of excerpting them. Other women wrote on their books, using marginalia and annotations as part of their reading, and clearly displaying the fact that they read the genre. Women such as Anne Clifford and Frances Wolfreston, both well known to the history of reading, annotated their romance books in some way. The first section of this chapter, therefore, will look at several instances of physical evidence of women's romances reading, using marginalia and autograph signatures to explore how women might have used their romance books. In the second section, I explore how ideas of gender and identity, and the relationship between reading and women's textual constructions of femininity, were represented in women's 'life-writing'.[4] I consider this through the lens of four seventeenth-century women who wrote about their experiences of reading romantic fiction. These women, Elizabeth Delaval, Dorothy Osborne, Elizabeth Isham and Mary Hatton Helsby, all recorded different responses to the genre, but all used romances to signify some aspect of their identity or specifically their femininity as articulated in their personal writings.

In the early modern period, as the romance genre increased in popularity, so did its connection to women.[5] The binary between women's devotional and recreational reading habits that was common in seventeenth-century advice literature became a mainstay of contemporary discussions about gender. However, it was not unique to the seventeenth century. These conversations surrounding women and reading, particularly romance literature and fiction, have continued to this day. The rhetoric surrounding seventeenth-century prose romances, eighteenth-century novels and even modern 'chick lit', whose covers are adorned with pictures of handbags and shoes, attests to the endurance of the tropes of dangerous or frivolous women's reading.[6] This language has also been reproduced in historiography about seventeenth-century literature, in various ways and with varying levels of intent. As this chapter will show, underlying many scholarly studies of women's reading is the assumption that romances constituted frivolous reading and were intrinsically connected to a woman's desire for romantic love.

The connection between passivity and recreational reading is reinforced by many of the longer-term narratives in the history of reading. Many scholars have identified a move from intensive reading to extensive reading in the long eighteenth century and often connected it to the rising popularity of prose fiction. This model was first put forward by Rolf Engelsing and has been repeated so often as to become a scholarly commonplace.[7] Intensive reading involved memorisation, repetition and in-depth focus on a particular text, often the Bible. Extensive reading, by contrast, was a practice that is much more identifiably modern, involving the reading of multiple different genres and books with little re-reading or close attention paid to the text. This is commonly discussed with reference to the practice of reading novels and deeply embedded with ideas of gender and class, with the implicit (or sometimes explicit) non-intellectualism of the practice. Similarly, Steven Zwicker's claim that the 'site' and 'gender' of reading changed in the early modern period from the 'masculine world of the humanist schoolroom' to the 'leisured boudoir of the novel reader' underlines this narrative.[8] Zwicker argues that the latter was 'intent less on the production of learning than on the generation of feeling and opinion', making the contrast between masculine intellectualism and feminine emotion explicit.[9] Women readers have not usually been seen as participants in the reading practices of the male intellectual elite, apart from in very exceptional cases.

However, the idea that women did not read romances in a way that could be considered intellectual or active is not borne out by the evidence. Alongside Evelyn's record of Mary keeping extracts from romances, Josephine A. Roberts has described Lady Katherine Manners' (1603–1649) notebook, in which she copied out several passages from Sidney's *Arcadia*, narrating significant parts of the romance, alongside excerpts from historical and religious sources.[10] Roberts suggests that Manners 'copied the passages probably for writing practice, since she occasionally re-copied the excerpts two or more times'.[11] This may well be true, but it does show that women used romances not solely as pleasurable pastimes.[12] Manners may have felt a particular connection to those passages, or had other, less functional reasons for excerpting them. Whatever her motivation, the fact that Manners chose to include a work of romance in a commonplace book is significant, as such manuscripts are often held up as clear evidence of intensive reading practices.

The emotional aspect of reading is important in this active/passive narrative. In exploring the transition, Rebecca Tierney-Hynes has examined the implications of the concepts of intensive and extensive. She argued that 'when we examine theories, rather than practices, of reading, we find that in fact seventeenth- and eighteenth-century theorists aligned "intensive" with critical, distant reading, and "extensive" with absorptive, seductive and unreflective reading'.[13] The alignment of 'absorptive' and 'unreflective', in opposition to 'critical', is key to the gendered distinctions between types of reading. Fears about romance reading often centred on the emotional response readers may have had, with that response being framed as at best unthinking, and at worst an incitement of base urges. Questions of *how* people read, therefore, have been almost inextricably tied to gender. Moreover, the genre itself of romance was imbued in the early modern period with a range of gendered ideas, focusing on the dangers of the supposed passivity and emotionality of its readers. In order to explore how women responded to these ideas, we must first examine the representation of romance reading in advice literature.

Richard Allestree, the Church of England clergyman and Royalist, repeatedly discussed the dangers of romance reading in his book *A Ladies Calling*:

> There is another thing to which some devote a very considerable part of their time, and that is the reading Romances, which seems now to be thought the peculiar and only becoming study of young Ladies . . . I fear they often leave ill impressions behind them. Those amorous passions, which 'tis their design to paint to the utmost life, are apt to insinuate themselves into their unwary readers, and by an unhappy inversion, a copy shall produce an original.[14]

Young women here are portrayed as easily influenced by their reading material, fitting into the idea of the inherent weakness of female nature. There is an implication of irrationality and impressionability in this depiction, assuming that women were prone to copying what Allestree saw as the deeply problematic behaviour displayed in romantic fiction. The act of reading had an explicit effect on behaviour and character; it is portrayed as transformative in some way for the impressionable young woman, in the way described by Johns, discussed in the Introduction.[15] The reader is 'unwary' (the implication being that they were passive), and Allestree very specifically stated that romance reading was the 'peculiar . . . study of young Ladies'.

Female sexuality was a preoccupation of many writers of conduct books, with a binary created between passive, idealised femininity and a transgressive, threatening sexual nature.[16] The poet and writer Nicholas Breton made the distinction between the manifestations of femininity and the perceived dangerous nature of transgressively sexual women clear when outlining the characters of 'A good Wife' and 'A wanton Woman'. The former, he said, was 'a care of necessity, and a course of Thrift, a booke of Huswifery, and a mirror of modestie. In summe, she is Gods blessing, and Mans happinesse, Earths honour, and Heauens creature',[17] while the latter was 'a spice of madnesse, a sparke of mischiefe, a tutch of poyson, and a feare of destruction'.[18] The fact that Breton referred to a good wife as a 'booke of Huswifery' indicates that these types of books were seen as embodying and reflecting certain feminine virtues.

This manifestation of sexuality was often explicitly connected to romance reading. Richard Brathwaite was the Kendal-born author of the conduct manual *The English Gentlewoman* (1631), which is often said to be the first conduct book specifically aimed at women.[19] Books and reading were central to his construction of an ideal gentlewoman, provided they were the right books.[20] Brathwaite claimed that '*Books* treating of light subiects, are Nurseries of wantonnesse . . . *Venus* and *Adonis* are vnfitting Consorts for a Ladies bosome'.[21] The term 'wanton' is a common one when referring to the reading of such texts, and recalls Breton's use of the term for a threateningly sexual woman. Some writers made this connection an explicitly physiological one, such as Nicholas Culpeper, the well-known physician and herbalist, in his chapter 'Of the Frenzie of the Womb'.[22] According to Culpeper, this condition 'is a great and foul Symptome of the womb; both in Virgins and Widdows, and such as have known man'.[23] He went on to outline the symptoms and causes, declaring that 'the outward Causes, are hot meats spiced, strong wine, and the like, that heat the privities, idleness, pleasure, and dancing, and *reading of bawdy Histories*'.[24] A person's choice of reading matter was seen as symptomatic of a medicalised, uncontrolled sexuality.[25]

Despite the ubiquity of these gendered concerns about reading, however, there were some representations of romance reading as socially acceptable for women. These were admittedly few, but those that did exist appeared in the mid-seventeenth century onwards and focused on the potential beneficial influences they might have on a woman's character.[26] Hannah Woolley, for example, argued for some benefits to romance reading, despite her exhortations to women to read theological and devotion materials:

> Some may imagin, that to read Romances after such practical Books of Divinity, will not only be a vain thing, but will absolutely overthrow that fabrick I endeavoured to erect: I am of a contrary opinion, and do believe such Romances which treat of generosity, gallantry, and virtue, as *Cassandra, Clelia, Grand Cyrus, Cleopatra, Parthenessa,* not omitting Sir *Philip Sydney's* Arcadia, are Books altogether worthy of their Observation. There are few Ladies mention'd therein, but are character'd what they ought to be; the magnanimity, virtue, gallantry, patience, constancy, and courage of the men, might intitle them worthy Husbands to the most deserving of the female sex.[27]

Woolley rejected the binary created by so many religious and secular conduct writers between devotional and romantic literature. The concept of romantic reading being transformative, as seen in Allestree's work, was still present, but she turned the idea on its head and instead saw these books as having the potential to improve women's characters by presenting exemplary figures in the text. She connected the romance genre to the qualities of 'generosity, gallantry and virtue', reminiscent of the chivalric tradition, and argued that it presented female characters that were patient, constant and courageous. Lori Humphrey Newcomb has suggested that empathetic reading habits were increasingly accepted towards the end of the seventeenth century, suggesting a development in the idea of reading for profit. While originally 'profit' tended to be framed in intellectual or ethical terms, Newcomb argues that by the later seventeenth century 'profit' could be more emotional, intertwined with the idea of reading for pleasure.[28] The idea of pleasurable profit cannot be seen in Woolley's work, but this recognition of the potential beneficial effects of an empathetic reading of romance is an early stage of that development. Woolley did, however, recognise the dangers of other types of reading in her section 'Of wanton Songs and idle Ballads', in which she also discussed poetry and plays along with the eponymous genres:

> Ladies, accuse me not of too much severity, in endeavouring to take away this too much accustomed delight in singing wanton, though witty Sonnets: I say excuse me rather, since I aim at nothing more than your welfare. I know your inclinations as you are young and youthful, tend

> rather to these things, than what is more serious; and are apt to read those Books which rather corrupt and deprave good manners than teach them.[29]

Woolley therefore set up a distinction between various genres in which romances actually depicted idealised models of female – and male – behaviour, while certain songs and ballads were the more problematic genre.[30] She did not deny that books had the power to corrupt, but she chose not to replicate the common association between this corruption and romantic fiction. Her more positive view of romance reading was echoed by other polemicists in the later seventeenth century, notably Judith Drake who believed that romances had some practical benefit in teaching women 'words and sense', and indeed suggested that they contributed to women maturing faster than men.[31] However, this was a minority opinion amongst conduct book writers. The trope of romances representing and encouraging female corruption, whether in terms of sexual behaviour or lack of devotion, was common and has endured to the modern day.

## Writing on romance books: women's annotations and inscriptions

Despite this cultural opprobrium surrounding the genre, women in the seventeenth century frequently did read and enjoy romances. Much of the evidence we have for this comes from records of ownership, particularly the book inventories and library catalogues of noblewomen. Frances Stanley Egerton, the Countess of Bridgewater, had several romances and works of literary fiction in her library.[32] The catalogue was compiled in 1627, with additions into the early 1630s, and attests to the range of genres enjoyed by the countess. Works such as folios of Mary Wroth's *Urania*; John Barclay's *Argenis*; *Les Amours de Clidamant et Marilinde* by Nicolas des Escuteaux (1570–1628); and *L'Astrée* by Honoré d'Urfé (a hugely popular work both in France and abroad),[33] all well-known seventeenth-century romances, are present in the library.[34] The book list of the Countess of Carlisle, Lady Anne Howard (née de Vere Capell), also included several romances and poems, such as *Le Grand Cyrus* by Madeleine de Scudéry and an unidentified 'Comicall Romance'.[35] Similarly, David McKitterick has noted the presence of contemporary romances in Elizabeth Puckering's library, arguing that her partiality for the romance genre 'ran true to what was widely considered female taste'.[36] Women also inscribed romances with their names or annotated the margins.[37] While most of these examples can only ever give hard evidence of ownership, Anne Clifford's annotations in particular make it clear that she read and enjoyed romances.[38]

Clifford left evidence of her reading through annotations on many of her books, either written in her own hand or by a scribe, and in *The Great Picture*, a triptych, commissioned by Clifford and showing her and her family at different stages of her life, always surrounded by books.[39] The middle panel, showing Anne aged fifteen, depicts her surrounded by books including works by Chaucer, Spenser and Ovid, *Don Quixote*, and Philip Sidney's *Arcadia*.[40] The last of these, *The Countess of Pembroke's Arcadia* by Sir Philip Sidney, published in 1590, was annotated by Clifford. It is one of two romance books annotated by her, the other being John Barclay's *Argenis*, although she was a prolific annotator of books of numerous genres. Clifford's annotations reveal the careful and attentive ways in which she read and re-read them. Both *Argenis* and *Arcadia* have been portrayed by Paul Salzman as comments on contemporary politics.[41] Salzman argues that *Arcadia*, which was very popular in the seventeenth century, was read during the reign of King James I as 'a dark commentary on monarchical power and its abuse'.[42] This was largely allegorical, but *Argenis* represented a more direct comment on recent history and contemporary politics: in Salzman's words, it 'offers an elaborate and detailed depiction of specific historical circumstances . . . but also a sophisticated series of meditations on current political issues'.[43]

Clifford's copy of Barclay's *Argenis* is now held at the Huntington Library, and reveals a great deal about how Clifford read and her opinions on her reading.[44] On the blank page facing the title page, there is a manuscript note reading, 'I began to reade this booke to yo^r Ladiship the xvi^th day of Jannary: 1625: and ended it the xxv^th of the same moneth.'[45] The volume is heavily annotated, both by Clifford and the unnamed scribe, probably indicating multiple readings on Clifford's part. Clifford's own annotations tend to be shorter, and either summarise sections of the text – for example, writing, 'The strange discovery of the Poysoned Braselet' beside the relevant text – or make personal comment on the writing – she wrote, 'An exelent Chap:' several times in the margins.[46] The scribe's hand sometimes followed this pattern but also copied out certain underlined passages and wrote 'note' in the margins next to select sections.

The scribe's annotations indicate sections that were of particular interest to Clifford, and could be quite political in nature. For example, next to a passage stating that 'good Subjects should not exact such security; neither would they so often seeke it, if it were at any time safe. But they give their aydes, and obey or refuse the Kings commands, more like fellowes, then Subjects', the scribe has written 'to bee noted'.[47] On the same page, the word 'note' has been inscribed in the margins next to a sentence declaring, '[f]or as the hatred is most deadly, which is heated with controversies between severall religions; we must justly feare'.[48] Both of these passages could be taken as a comment on the religious and political climate of the mid-1620s, which saw the beginnings of the unrest that would eventually lead to the English Civil War. The second passage, certainly, warns starkly against religious factionalism and the 'hatred' that can emerge out of clashes between different religious sects. The first passage criticises subjects who have given aid to their ruler and then demand thanks, setting themselves as equals to the monarch. The paragraph goes on to accuse people acting in this way of making 'themselves Iudges of the gods, and of their Princes; and measure what duety they owe to either, not by Religion, but according to their owne dispositions'.[49] This clearly emphasises the role of the king above his people, possibly reflecting Clifford's political preoccupations at a time when the relationship between the King and Parliament (the representatives of the people) was under strain. Clifford herself underlined a passage saying, 'So that most often the pampred fatnes of the people, and the apprehension of too much liberty, are greater enemies to the peace of the Common-wealth, than the sharpe rigor of Princes who have shewed greater severity', and wrote in the margins, 'The pampred fatnes of the people.'[50] This is quite clearly criticising the danger of allowing people 'too much liberty' for fear that this will disrupt the peace, and favours a king ruling harshly over the people holding too much power. These annotations suggest a preoccupation with the conflict between the people and the Crown, indicating Clifford's own Royalist leanings in the unrest to come.

Clifford's other annotated volumes include political works, such as Anthony Weldon's indictment of James I (with whom Clifford had clashed over her inheritance claims), *The Court and Character of King James* and *A Mirour for Magistrates*, a collection of poems published in 1559 written from the perspective of various statesmen warning about the abuse of power.[51] Both contain annotations that are often quite personal, drawing on her own political and familial experiences to understand the text.[52] Some scholars have viewed the annotations of these political and romance texts through different lenses. Brayman Hackel has argued that, despite the topical nature of Barclay's *Argenis*, Clifford's reading of the text, attested to by the annotations, was 'ultimately personal and idiosyncratic' and more interested in the 'narrative and philosophical elements of the romance' than its political implications.[53] However, I would argue that, with her personal comments on political texts and political readings of romances, Clifford's personal and political interests and opinions were often intertwined, and cannot be so easily delineated. Her marginalia give us an insight into those opinions. She certainly was not reading uncritically, frivolously or in order to 'dream away her time in phantastic scenes', as Allestree warned of romance readers. She read in order to find support and justification for her political views, and her annotations demonstrate her active engagement with that reading material, be it romances or political polemics.

Unfortunately, it is rare to find many examples of women annotating romance texts in the way that Clifford did, but there are certainly examples of women inscribing their names or short dedications on such books. In writing their names on romance books, women were making a potentially controversial statement, given the widespread disapproval of the genre. This may or may not have been intentional, or it may indicate that lack of influence that the cultural rhetoric surrounding romances had on actual readers.

Women may not have set out to make a subversive statement when inscribing their romance books, but some clearly did want to advertise either ownership or readership (or both).[54] An English translation of Vital d'Audiguier's *Histoire Trage-Comique de Nostre Temps* (1635), for example, was signed by several women, including Margaret Corbyn, who used the blank page of the flyleaf to experiment with various different spellings of her name.[55] She also added to one signature the words 'hir booke', and further down the page, in a neater hand, wrote 'Margrit Corbyn Eius Liber'. This Latin formulation, meaning 'her book', was unusual for women autographers, being much more common amongst scholarly men, who signed their book in this way or with the words 'ex libris' and then their name. As discussed above, romances were generally seen as being read for pleasure and having little or no educational value. Latin inscriptions, however, were more often found on scholarly works, and so Corbyn's use of the phrase, indicating her education, potentially subverted these ideas about the romance genre.

Most women did not follow Corbyn's use of Latin, but they did still use their signatures to make their ownership of the books clear. A copy of Jean Desmarets de Saint-Sorlin's *Ariana* was signed by two related women: on the front flyleaf are the signatures of 'M$^{rs}$ Margret Carpenter har Booke Marche' and 'Elizabeth Carpenter', along with further pen trials of Elizabeth's name.[56] The pen trials may indicate that Elizabeth's signature was motivated by writing practice rather than any particular relationship to the book, but Margaret obviously wanted to lay claim to the text itself. Some romances even bear multiple signatures from the same person, such as a copy of M. Le Roy Gomberville's *The History of Polexander* which has the signature of Anne Townshend on both the title page and the first page of text. The former is followed by 'her boke', clearly claiming ownership of the text itself and indicating this was not simply writing practice.[57]

The fact that women, even in the few examples mentioned here, signed and annotated their romance books indicates that perhaps the general condemnation of the genre by advice literature was not adhered to very strictly by the female reading public. Evidently, some women did not feel the need to hide their romance reading, and indeed advertised it to anyone who happened to come across their book. Moreover, they clearly were not reading romances passively, as most seventeenth-century advice literature feared. Clifford gives a valuable example of a woman who read her romances carefully, partly through a political lens.

## Romances and femininity in women's life-writing

While the annotations on romance literature suggest that the rhetoric surrounding it did not necessarily influence women's choice to read the genre, the gendered assumptions and tropes underlying romance reading can be explored further by looking at how women write about romance reading. Because of the highly gendered nature of the conversation about the romance genre, the ways in which women represented the act of reading romantic fiction in their life-writings can demonstrate how individuals negotiated and constructed their own gender identity in life-writings. Using these sources does not, of course, reveal a lived experience of gender and identity, one that we might call 'real', while cognisant of the many problems associated with such a term. Instead, they provide a resource for looking at how women perceived themselves and wanted to be perceived by others. Scholars of seventeenth-century women's autobiography have argued that 'it is necessary to make choices and therefore exclusions in writing a life, so the act of writing involves a patterning and thus an interpretation'.[58] Therefore, when writing any form of autobiographical text, the author makes a choice to include certain aspects of their lived experience. Writing about reading romances reveals a particularly deliberate choice, given the contemporary controversy around the genre. Women, in recording their reading of and reaction to romantic fiction, were engaged in an explicit effort of textual self-construction, one which reveals their negotiation of early modern gender norms.

The uses to which women put romance reading in their own writings have been acknowledged in the last decade or so by some scholars, notably Ramona Wray and Julie Eckerle. Wray, examining Mary Rich's autobiography and diary, has demonstrated the extent to which contemporary women's reading of romances can be seen in their writings, even if they did not explicitly record it.[59] The spiritual motivations and methods behind women's life-writing have been well explored in modern scholarship, but the secular influences less so.[60] The ideas put forward by conduct literature, even if not followed in practice, did have an effect on the wider cultural conversation surrounding gender. It is therefore useful to look at how women both replicated and rejected those ideals, and used them in the construction of their own character. Writing about reading romances had the potential to be quite a subversive act, challenging the norms of femininity and appropriate literary activity. However, some women used the acknowledgement of their romance reading to demonstrate their conforming or more traditionally feminine behaviour, by showing that they understood the error of their ways and had reformed.

The women discussed here by no means amount to a complete list of every woman who registered reading a romance. However, these four can be set apart from their contemporaries due to the detail they gave about their romance reading habits. Their discussions of romance all appeared in different forms of life-writing: Elizabeth Delaval and Elizabeth Isham wrote spiritual autobiographies, while Dorothy Osborne and Mary Hatton Helsby left evidence of romance reading in letters. Their works largely date from the mid-seventeenth century: Isham was writing in the 1630s and Delaval in the 1670s, but Osborne and Hatton Helsby's letters both date from the 1650s. The timespan of this study does reflect the increasing popularity of the romance genre from the mid-seventeenth century onwards, but also the continuing influence of the rhetorical framing of romances from early seventeenth-century Puritan advice books, which emphasised the dangers of the genre. Taken together, the texts surveyed here demonstrate the range of reactions women could have to the romance genre, and reflect the influence (or lack thereof) of advice literature on the construction of feminine identity.

Lady Elizabeth Delaval (née Livingston) was an English noblewoman, who is known both for her memoirs and meditations and her involvement in the Pewter Pot plot of 1689, when a warrant was issued for her arrest for carrying correspondence from the exiled court of James II.[61] She married Sir Robert Delaval, heir of Sir Ralph Delaval, in 1670, although the marriage was not a happy one and they had no children.[62] Her *Meditations*, written between 1662 and 1671, record her early life, and give an insight into her reading habits. According to Delaval, she wrote the meditations between the ages of fourteen and twenty, and collected them together at twenty.[63] She used the memoir form to reflect on her youth, and ultimately to affirm her devotion and piety. The text is set out in the form of meditations, but largely contains autobiographical reflections on her life, returning repeatedly to repent her actions as a young girl. Despite Delaval's manuscript providing extensive evidence, she has been given little critical attention by scholars of early modern reading.[64]

Reading was important for Delaval's personal story. She replicated common tropes of advice literature, such as the moral and highly gendered distinction between romance reading and religious reading. She charted her transition from the former to the latter in terms of the development of her spiritual wellbeing and increased piety. This is strikingly similar to the conversion trope used in some seventeenth-century advice literature, such as that of Richard Baxter or Richard Allestree. It is also reminiscent of Catholic conversion tales such as that of Teresa of Avila, who framed her life before her conversion as a series of failings, saved only by God's grace.[65] Avila recorded reading chivalric romances with her mother as a girl. She portrayed this pastime as dangerous for her younger self, impeding her piety. However, she did not condemn her mother for her reading choices, instead suggesting that it was a necessary escape from her difficult life.[66] This fits with the impression given in advice literature, discussed above, that romances were most harmful when read by young women, often teenagers, who were at their most impressionable.

Delaval recorded reading celebrated seventeenth-century French romances when she was about ten years old, including Madeleine de Scudéry's *Artamènes, ou, Le Grand Cyrus* and *Cassandra* by Gautier de Costes, seigneur de la Calprenède.[67] De Scudéry's text was first translated into English in 1653, and Calprenède's in 1652, so Delaval was reading them several years after the translation (she was born in 1649). She wrote, 'I was but some few month's past ten year's old before I had red severall great volum's of [romances]: all Cassander, the Grand Cyrus, Cleopatra and Astrea.'[68] Both De Scudéry and Calprenède were very popular in mid-seventeenth-century England.[69] Delaval's record of them situates her within the mid-century romance market, demonstrating her interest in the staples of the genre.

She introduced a social and religious dimension to her representation of romances by blaming her literary habits on a family servant, Mistress Carter, who looked after Delaval as a young girl. Delaval accused Carter of encouraging a taste for romantic fiction and persuading her to neglect her religious devotions, saying that she 'had so fill'd my head with foly's that . . . what I red was alltogether romances'.[70] She connected this to Carter's Presbyterianism, claiming,

> I was not quite 6 month's past 10 yeare old when Mris. Carter begun most pernicesouly to insinuate Presbiterian princeples into me, in

> some interval's of time when she did not talke to me of love and fary tales; so that had I not been deliver'd soon out of her hand's without doubt I shou'd have had the great misfortune of being bred up a Presbiterian.[71]

This provides a connection between Delaval's reading of romances and religious dissent, adding another dimension to the idea of the conversion narrative and the religious rhetoric surrounding romance literature. Outlining Carter's Presbyterianism allowed Delaval (an Anglican) to attribute her youthful behaviour to indoctrination, and emphasises the connection between romantic fiction and immorality. If taken as similar sins, then the implication is that reading romances is going against God, rather than simply an enjoyable leisure pursuit. This is, moreover, an unusual image of Presbyterianism, considering the general godly attitude towards romances. Perhaps Delaval was insinuating that Carter was undisciplined, unbiblical and lower class, as part of a general criticism of her religion. Carter's social status is important; as Lori Humphrey Newcomb has demonstrated, 'a class line was drawn between elite and popular romance forms, between credulous and knowing versions of female readers'.[72] Carter here represents the former; a maidservant misusing her leisure time and tempting Delaval into unserious, credulous romance reading.

These early reading habits were presented as dangerous or foolish pastimes in comparison to the religious education she should have been developing: at one point she said, 'thus vainely pass'd the blosome time of my life, which shou'd have been spent in laying a good foundation of what is to be learnt in such book's as teach's us heavenly wisdom'.[73] Once again, books and reading were the key to her character, as they could either provide spirituality and morality or lead one into temptation and sin; they were used to represent the two possible paths for Delaval to take. She went on to emphasise this link between romance reading and an avoidance of devotion, saying:

> nothing seem'd to me so grieveous as to spend time in the learning of my duty in reading thy holy word and in praying to thee, nothing so pleasant as the waisting of my houer's in foleish devertisment's and in reading unprofitable romances.[74]

Significant in this passage is the term 'unprofitable'; romantic fiction was seen as carrying no lessons for spiritual, intellectual or moral improvement, and thus was not a productive use of women's time. This replicates common narratives in advice literature, discussed above, which castigated women for passing time reading romances rather than scripture.

However, Delaval realised her errors and much of the rest of the first half of the *Meditations* is concerned with repudiating her early sins and reading habits. She wrote:

> When we are past our childish age and can attend to what we do without a perpetuall wandering fancy tis folly to spend our time any longer in reading ill chosen boock's, such as romances are, which serve onely to please our fancy not to guide our judgement, and to make our minutes passe away (tis said by some) less tediously then they wou'd do, were we otherwise imploy'd.[75]

Romances therefore were simply pleasurable, used to 'please out fancy not to guide our judgement'. Although she admitted the attraction of this, as it made time pass quickly, she argued that it was 'folly' to spend time reading the genre. Delaval became a devout woman, stressing that, 'When some other duty dos not take up my time, I will not only read every day in my closet alone or to my servants in the gospels, but also in the Psalmes.'[76] This meditation was written several years after the two quoted above, demonstrating Delaval's continuing preoccupation with her reformation. It is worth noting that Delaval made it clear that religious reading is not simply an adherence to her duty; rather, she charted her emotional development and reaction, coming to actively prefer devotional texts – at one point in the text she mentioned how she now 'delights' in 'holy books'. Her 'conversion' was now complete and was evidenced through her reading habits.

In Delaval's dichotomy between romance reading and religious reading, she did not see them as genres that can be read in tandem, but condemned romance reading completely. Her reformation and later preference for devotional literature thus affirms her pious character all the more by constructing it in opposition to her youthful transgressions. Through this representation of her reading habits, Delaval aligned herself with a certain kind of ideal femininity, and situated herself firmly within the domestic sphere of adulthood and proper devotion. She portrayed herself as taking on the role of the pious wife, as outlined by Gouge and Whately, in reading scripture to her servants and spending her days in spiritual reflection. The fact that her religious leanings were very different to the Puritanism of Gouge and Whately indicates the extent to which this idea of a gendered asceticism permeated throughout early modern society. The attitudes displayed by Gouge, Whately, Baxter and Allestree, and replicated by Delaval, attest to the strength of the concern surrounding female reading, from all religious groups. However, Delaval has also made a choice to use reading as a way of constructing her femininity within the text. This is not evidence of her submissiveness to contemporary gender prescriptions, but rather of the agency she had in taking those prescriptions and conventions and using them to present her character in a certain way.

This replication of the cultural controversy surrounding romance reading, however, was not employed in all women's life-writing. Instead, many women openly enjoyed or at least engaged with romances. Even godly women discussed reading romances, demonstrating the extent to which the stereotype of Puritan culture needs to be complicated. Elizabeth Isham (1608–1654), the Northamptonshire diarist, recorded romance reading in her *Booke of Rememberance*, an autobiography written in about 1639.[77] In her autobiography, Isham took a very different position to that of Delaval regarding romantic fiction. Although the manuscript was primarily concerned with demonstrating her spirituality, she also revealed a wide range of reading habits and took a much more nuanced view than Delaval of non-devotional genres.[78] In one section she wrote:

> my friends thinking that the Booke of Marters made me mallancoly though I found no hearm it did my brother lent me Sir phillips sidnes Booke (and after Spencer) which I hard much comended by some. and others againe discomended the reading of such Bookes of love. but I found no such hurt.[79]

Isham's construction of romantic fiction here, particularly in relation to religious reading, demonstrates the complexity of the cultural reaction to romances. She noted that her friends and brother recommended reading romances and poetry – in this case, Sidney's *Arcadia* and Spenser's *The Faerie Queene* – as an antidote to the melancholy they thought the Book of Martyrs provoked in her.[80] This is an inverse of the usual contemporary narrative of religious reading being an antidote to melancholy or other ills brought on by reading. She even repeatedly emphasised that she found no 'hearm' or 'hurt' in reading romances, distancing herself from the critiques of the genre.

Isham struggled with her mental health, and books often provided a comfort for her, as well as provoking melancholy. Anne Cotterill has noted that books were generally brought into the household by men (and indeed were usually written by men), and argues that they 'came to represent a prop of masculine strength of mind and body, a calming and clarifying power that Isham found women so often required'.[81] She frequently used scripture for comfort, and was deeply religious.[82] However, it is notable that she recorded romances possibly having a similarly salutary effect (although she did not confirm that *Arcadia* helped her; rather that her friends believed it might). In using them for comfort, and openly admitting to reading them, she clearly defied the binary constructed by godly advice literature between romance and religious literature.

In the passage above, Isham acknowledged the divisions within the rhetoric surrounding romantic fiction, but affirmed that she did not find it damaging or problematic.[83] Indeed, she recorded in a note in the margins that she continued to read Sidney's book 'for the most part on evenings'.[84] Reading the romance clearly became part of her everyday routine, as she read it repeatedly at a specific point during the day, and Isham's acceptance of the gender, and rejection of the fears surrounding romantic fiction, is particularly notable when situated in the wider field of autobiographical writings, which rarely discussed romances.[85] Isham treated romances like other books, and clearly did not accept the warnings of godly advice writings.

The generic expectations of godly or spiritual autobiography meant that romance reading was not always recorded, even if it may have occurred. In letters, however, audience and conventions were different, and as such they sometimes contained extensive discussions of romance reading. Although there has been plenty of work demonstrating that early modern letters were not private, and that there was an assumption that the audience would extend beyond the recipient, there was still an arguably different readership, one which was more fleeting and less intergenerational than memoirs or spiritual autobiographies, and therefore there was less concern about constructing a character for posterity or exemplification.[86] Letters often function as more of a conversation, rather than a record of events, so the construction of character occurs in a different way.

When gentry women did mention their reading of prose romance in letters, therefore, they rarely condemned the genre in the way that Delaval did. Women's analyses of their reading were not always aligned so clearly to contemporary moralistic mores, and cannot be so easily divided into either finding pleasure in romances or finding them corrupting and immoral. Women (perhaps less pious women than Delaval) recorded complex critiques or praise of romantic fiction, reflecting highly individual and personal responses, and often emphasising the 'profit' they gained from their reading. As Eckerle has noted, 'although references to romance reading frequently acknowledge pleasure, they not surprisingly emphasise moral, emotional, and intellectual engagement even more'.[87] Women in the seventeenth century clearly read their romances carefully, and with a critical eye. They assessed the plots, characters and themes, and discussed their reading with others.

This discussion, certainly in epistolary form, appears to have largely been a heterosocial interaction. I have found no letters between women that contain extensive discussion of romances. There is some evidence, such as that of Dorothy Osborne explored below, of women sharing books with other women. However, most of the evidence of in-depth discussion appears between men and women, often those either engaged or married. Elizabeth Pepys, the wife of the diarist Samuel Pepys, for example, is known to have enjoyed Madeleine de Scudéry's *Le Grand Cyrus* (1649–1653), and wanted to talk about it with her husband.[88] Kate Loveman has argued that 'discussing the ideas in a heroic romance was a means for men and women to establish shared understandings on a variety of issues related to conduct (especially conduct in love), to advertise them as discerning, sensitive readers, and to exchange tacit compliments'.[89] While we need to be wary of attributing romantic endeavour as a motive for women's engagement with romances, it is true that many of the discussions of the genre come from letters between suitors or spouses. Two of the best-known examples of women discussing romances with their fiancés are the letters of Mary Hatton (later Helsby) and Dorothy Osborne.

Mary Hatton, whose letters are held in the Folger Shakespeare Library, demonstrated a critical reading of romantic fiction, and did not conceal the fact that she had read them. Little is known about Hatton but her letters to her fiancé, Randolph Helsby (of the Helsby family based in Cheshire), in the early 1650s, have survived. They show the pair exchanging books frequently, including romances.[90] In one letter, Hatton wrote this commentary:

> I do not methinks approve of stories of romance all so alike that they seem as if I had read y$^{e}$ same one hundred times, besides that how vain it was (for him which writt it) to make ye yong gentle woman run awaie wth a sweet hearte (her younger of manie years) when all were agreed upon ye matche save only his more sober unkle. Tis as olde as Helsby towre but this, and this is in deede some thing very freshe & newe as such a youthe could make itt. If you have not read itt I would advise you sadly if by my commendations you would waste a candell over itt. I had rather do some thing of more use than he that writ it by turning m wheel without a stop till some other had read throu itt in my stead. But it hath little bits in itt that shewe he could not with carefulness & practise be without much commendation. I do scorne & disdaine these scribling pass times & nought else can I learne from manie of them.[91]

As Emily Griffiths Jones suggests, this could seem like a commonplace indictment of romantic fiction, with Hatton even asserting her femininity by saying that she would prefer to be spinning than reading the book in question.[92] However, this is a more complex critique. Hatton here was engaging with the characters, and contending with the authority of the writer and their motivations. She did criticise romances, and drew on some of the rhetoric dismissing them as a misuse of leisure time, but her letters did not reflect the moral condemnation of conduct book writers.

Her criticism stemmed from what she personally found lacking in romantic fiction; she was reading in order to learn something, but her expectations were thwarted. She called the texts 'scribling pass times' and declared 'nought else can I learne from manie of them', quite clearly setting up an active/passive divide. This suggests that, even if she was not ultimately rewarded for her pains, she read romances with the aim of reading providing some sort of transformative experience, with the absorption of a lesson.

Her reading was also relational. As Paul Trolander has suggested, Hatton was using books and reading to find common ground with Randolph Helsby, solidifying social bonds through shared experiences or views. He has claimed that her 'strong condemnation of the entire genre' was a way of testing her future husband. Trolander argues that Hatton

> suggested that such texts took away from time that might be used to cultivate more socially appropriate beliefs and practices. To differ with such views might be possible, but in the context of courtship, such censure was a line drawn in the sand. If Helsby was morally challenged, uncritical, and a time-waster, he was surely not the man for Mary.[93]

In fact, Hatton did not roundly condemn all romantic fiction, nor did she suggest that there was nothing worthy of praise to be found in the stories. She seems to argue that it is the unnamed author's failings that are the problem, not the genre of romance. If he had more 'carefulness and practise', she wrote, then he would be commendable as a writer, and she can already discern hints of this in the text. Unfortunately, it is unclear to which author or text she was referring specifically. Her letters demonstrate a familiarity with the genre as a whole, implying that she did generally enjoy reading such books. In an earlier letter she wrote, 'I am reading of your newe booke of Mr Spenser w$^{ch}$ I like well. I do believe his poetry for excellency is as abundently great & in as handsome & pretty language as many of the beste in the worlde.'[94] She clearly enjoyed Spenser, admiring his use of language, although it is difficult to tell which of Spenser's works she read.[95] Poetry was often condemned alongside romances in seventeenth-century advice literature, but Hatton clearly had no qualms about reading either genre. Her letters reveal her discerning taste; she did not see the poetry and romances as irretrievably bad or immoral, but was critical of stories that did not have much literary merit.

In Dorothy Osborne's letters to her suitor, William Temple, she provided a similarly nuanced, although much more positive, critique of romances. Osborne (1627–1695) was a Royalist, daughter of the lieutenant-governor of Jersey, who played a part in arranging the marriage of William of Orange and Mary, the daughter of James, Duke of York. She is best known today as a letter-writer, particularly her letters to Temple that survive for the period 1652–1654.[96] Her letters are a valuable resource for examining the complexity of women's responses to the romance genre. Osborne read many of the same texts as Delaval, including various works by French author Madeleine de Scudéry, but, unlike Delaval, she did not openly repent her reading. She frequently recommended romances that she read to Temple, and discussed her opinions of the stories and their authors with him, just as Mary Hatton and Randolph Helsby shared their impressions and recommendations of reading. In one instance, she sent him several volumes of the romance *Cleopatra*, by French author Gautier de Costes:

> since you are at Leasure to consider the moone you may bee enough to reade Cleopatra, therefore I have sent you three Tomes. When you have done with those you shall have the rest, and I beleeve they will please, there is a story of Artemise that I will recomende to you, her disposition I like extreamly, it has a great deal of Gratitude int, and if you meet with one Brittomart pray send mee word how you like him.[97]

Contrary to many conceptions about the genre, there is little evidence in Osborne's letters that women were the primary readers of romance. At one point Osborne suggested that Temple won't have time for reading, writing, 'what an asse I am to think you can bee idle enough at London to reade Romances'.[98] However, the implication here is that a lack of free time is the only thing preventing him, not a dislike or disapproval of the genre. Instead, she exchanged books with him frequently, and they discussed what they both read in detail.

Apart from the exchange of romances between the couple, the habit of sharing books with a wider circle of friends and acquaintances is made clear in the letters, with Osborne often asking Temple to send books back to her so she could pass them on to others. She wrote at one point:

> If you have done with the first Part of Cyrus I should bee glad Mr Hollingsworth had it, because I mentioned some such thing in my Last to my Lady, but there is noe hast of restoreing the other unlesse she should send to mee for it which I beleeve she will not. I have a third Tome heer against you have done with the second, and to Encourage you let mee assure you that the more you read of them you will like them still better.[99]

Mr Hollingsworth appears to have been a retainer of the Lady mentioned, rather than a reader himself. It is likely that he was going to pass the book on to Lady Diana Rich, with whom Osborne often exchanged books.

Osborne emphasised her emotional, affective reading experiences. This was often something feared in anti-romance invectives: that women would feel too much for the characters of romance and that this was an uncritical response that could produce ill effects. However, Osborne shows no concern about her response to the text. When discussing *Artamène, ou Le Grand Cyrus*, the ten-part historical romance by Madeleine de Scudéry telling the story of the lovers Cyrus and Mandane, who were repeatedly kept apart, Osborne wrote of one character, 'i'le swear I cryed for her when I read it first tough shee were an imaginary person'.[100] She clearly felt a deep connection to the characters in books; as Trolander has pointed out, she 'referred to [prose romances'] characters as real individuals . . . Indeed, her vouching for such friends as Lady Diana Rich was often done in terms similar to vouching for characters in Le Caprenède's *Cléopâtre*'.[101] He suggests that this was born of a desire to see Temple 'come to know and like them as people' and part of Osborne's effort to strengthen the affective bonds with her intended.[102]

It is possible to glean many details about Osborne's reading habits and preferences from her letters, often connecting to wider developments within the prose romance genre. She enjoyed De Scudéry's books, which were the most popular romantic texts of the mid-seventeenth century.[103] De Scudéry published under her brother's name throughout her life, and Osborne clearly believed that Georges was the author, although she does note certain rumours about Madeleine's role in the authorship (and her apparently unfortunate appearance):

> They say the Gentelman that writes this Romance has a Sister that lives with him as Mayde and she furnishes him with all the litle Story's that come between soe that hee only Contrives the maine designe and when hee wants somthing to Entertaine his company withal hee call's to her for it. Shee has an Exelent fancy sure, and a great deal of witt, but I am sorry to tell it you, they say tis the most ilfavourd Creatur that ever was borne, and it is often soe, how seldome doe wee see a person Exelent in any thing but they have some great deffect with it that pulls them low enough to make them Equall with Other People, and there is Justice in't.[104]

Osborne has often been known for her criticism of Margaret Cavendish, of whom she commented that 'there are many soberer People in Bedlam' and wrote 'the poore woman is a litle distracted, she could never bee soe rediculous else as to venture at writeing book's'.[105] This criticism of women writers has been discussed many times, and, as Carrie Hintz has noted, 'cast within the study of seventeenth-century women writers as the conservative counterpart to the daring polymath Cavendish, Osborne has been viewed by feminist scholars primarily as the voice of repression and of scorn'.[106] However, her assessment of De Scudéry tempers this; she did not seem to condemn her for writing, although she did imply that it had caused her to become an 'ilfavourd Creatur'. There is, however, a clear recognition of De Scudéry's literary talents. Again, Osborne was able to assess the literary merit of a text despite potential controversy surrounding its publication, genre and author, displaying her critical reading faculties.

Osborne had a preference for French romances, and usually read the texts in the original language.[107] When she did read in English, she often provided acerbic critiques of the translators and translations:

> I have noe Patience neither for these Translatours of Romances. I mett with Polexandre and L'Illustre Bassa, both soe disguised that I who am theire old acquaintance hardly knew them, besydes that they were still soe much french in words and Phrases that twas imposible for one that understood not french to make any thing of them.[108]

She went on to take further issue with the translation of *L'Illustre Bassa*, another work of De Scudéry, criticising the writing style and speech:

> Another fault I finde too in the stile, tis affected. Ambition'd is a great word with him, and ignore; my concerne, or of great concern, is it seem's properer then concernment; and though hee makes his People say fine handsome things to one another yet they are not Easy and Naïve like the french, and there is a little harshnesse in most of the discourses that one would take to bee the fault of the Translatour rather then of an Author.[109]

This was probably referring to the translation undertaken by Henry Cogan, which was first printed in 1652.[110] This was two years before the letter was written, indicating that Osborne kept up to date with new publications. She clearly read with a very sharp critical eye, focusing on details of the text, such as the specific language and phrasing used in the translation.

It has become commonplace for scholars looking at Osborne to attribute her feelings for the characters and her enjoyment of romances to her frustrated courtship with Temple. Their families would not allow them to marry for various political and financial reasons. According to James How, Osborne's letters 'become a sustained attempt to open up a new form of imaginary social space in which she could be alone with Temple'.[111] Similarly, Femke Molekamp has argued that 'Osborne weaves her reading of romances into her letters to engage an affective reading process serving as an outlet for the sorrows of the romantic trials which she and Temple endure, and to associate their courtship with the turn from anguish to regeneration usual to the structure of romance'.[112] Hintz sees the exchange about romantic between Osborne and Temple as an attempt on her part to mould their future relationship, arguing that 'romances were another venue for Osborne to exert control over Temple's opinions, but also to inculcate him into the process of openly discussing relationships and comportment with her'.[113]

This focus on the relationship between Osborne and Temple has led scholars to argue that Osborne saw herself in romances. Helen Wilcox and Sheila Ottway have argued that Osborne's imaginative world, informed by the romance genre, allowed her an alternative to reality, and that 'she envisages Temple and herself as the archetypal star-crossed lovers of fictional romance'.[114] This presumes that Osborne was using reading as a form of escapism rather than to understand the world around her. This buys into the rhetoric linking romantic fiction, pleasure and women. Suggesting that romances provided Osborne with the opportunity to escape the world detaches her reading from any real-world or potentially useful (itself a loaded term) implications. Moreover, it connotes a certain kind of reading, which only results in personal pleasure, rather than improved understanding.

There is some evidence of Osborne's escapist reading of works other than romantic fiction, for example when Osborne compared herself and Temple to Baucis and Philemon, a charitable old married couple who appear in Ovid's *Metamorphoses*:

> Doe you remember Arme and the little house there [?] shall we goe thither [?] that's next to being out of the worlde[.] there wee might live like Baucis and Philemon, grow old together in our litle Cottage and for our Charrity to some shipwrakt stranger obtaine the blessing of dyeing both at the same time. How idly I talk tis because the Storry pleases mee, none in Ovide soe much. I remember I cryed when I read it, mee thought they were the perfectest Characters of a con[ten]ted marriage where Piety and Live were all theire wealth and in their poverty feasted the Gods where rich men shutt them out.[115]

She clearly was attracted to this romantic vision of married life, and it is hard to dispute that she was using this story to outline a future for herself and Temple. However, the causal link scholars have found between Osborne's romance reading and her own romantic life is problematic. It echoes the fears that many conduct book writers had about women admiring and imitating the behaviour of romantic heroines. Moreover, perhaps the clearest problem with this approach is the way that it centres on Osborne and Temple's courtship as the most important facet of her epistolary self-presentation. Seeing Osborne's literary motivations and preferences as being solely due to her desire to create an imaginary world where she could live out a successful courtship is reductive, not allowing her an identity outside of her romantic relationship. Furthermore, it is not borne out by Osborne's writings. In one passage, she described a story in *Parthenissa*, the serially published 1650s prose romance by Roger Boyle, first Earl of Orrery, saying of the female protagonist:

> She was in a besieged Towne, and perswaded all those of her Sexe to goe out with her to the Enemy (which were a barbarous People) and dye by theire swords, that the provision of the Towne might last the longer for such as were able to doe service in deffending it. But how angry I was to see him spoile this againe, by bringing out a letter this woman left behind her for the Governour of the Towne, where she discovers a passion for him and makes that the reason why she did it. I confesse I have noe patience for our faiseurs de Romance, when they make women court.[116]

Osborne's larger point was that it was improper for women to actively court, but there is perhaps another point underlying this about women's actions not being motivated by men. It may be that, instead of using romances to live out her fantasy of a courtship with Temple, Osborne found models for female behaviour within them. Her annoyance at Boyle's character motivations reflects her frustration in trying to find roles in fiction that she could empathise with and emulate. Her display of these emotions in her letters to Temple shows a complex character construction, one which did not necessarily conform to contemporary feminine ideals, but which was nevertheless engaged with concepts of femininity.

This link between women writing about romance and their own romantic lives is apparent in other scholarly works examining the early modern period. Raymond Anselment made a similar suggestion about writing choices being motivated by personal romantic relationships when he said of Elizabeth Delaval: '[her] meditations become more specifically personal as she responds to the frustrations of romance and the disillusionment of marriage'.[117] This is not to suggest that personal tribulations and romantic feelings would not have had any effect on women's reading and interpretation, but rather that we do women in the past a disservice by considering romance, courtship and relationships with the men in their lives as the sole motivation behind their reading and writing. Instead, they had much more complex, individual responses to texts, born of various personal circumstances and preferences, which informed both what they read and how they wrote about their reading habits. Moreover, their reading was not driven by escapist fantasy, but was both critical and emotional, allowing them to find 'profit' in the stories.

## Conclusion

In their records of romance reading, then, the women surveyed here reveal a range of reading practices. They were not simply reading for fun, or in a way that implies seduction or addiction to the genre, with little regard for intellectualism. Instead, they read carefully and critically, analysing language and character construction. Some were also looking to find lessons in romances concerning their behaviour in society. This prefigures the suggestions of advice writers such as Hannah Woolley and Judith Drake who believed that romances could be beneficial in teaching women proper behaviour and conversation. While they may have been frustrated in this aim, as Mary Hatton Helsby was, they nevertheless were approaching the genre with a critical and intellectual eye. This, however, did not lessen the enjoyment they often record taking from the books. To create a distinction between emotional and rational reading, as both contemporary and scholarly accounts often do, does not take into account the complexity of the reading experience.

The differing approaches to romance reading of the women surveyed here exemplify the complexity of the relationship between gender and reading in the early modern period. On the one hand, we have Elizabeth Delaval, following strict gender conventions about proper feminine behaviour and reading habits. She also replicated the anxiety felt about the adverse effects of romances on young female readers. On the other, Dorothy Osborne openly enjoyed reading romances, and appeared to feel no inhibitions about admitting this. Osborne may have felt freer to express her literary preferences, in writing letters to personal acquaintances – although there is, of course, no guarantee that she envisaged her letters as private between her and Temple; indeed, it is likely she knew that they would be read more widely, as letters were often shared between family members and friends. She clearly made a very different choice to Delaval with regards to representing her reading habits, and thus aligned herself with a different manifestation of early modern femininity, more complex than the dichotomous idealised or sexually transgressive female readers constructed by contemporary gender norms.

This way of using romantic fiction appears to have emerged in the middle of the century. Osborne and Hatton were writing in the early 1650s; Delaval in the 1670s. This ties in with the increasing popularity of the prose romance in the mid-seventeenth century, when the genre proliferated, largely due to an influx of French texts. This is also the point at which Newcomb identifies a class split in the idea of women reading romances; in the mid-seventeenth century it became more acceptable for upper-class women to read these texts, but the dangers associated with romances became attached specifically to lower-class women.[118] That is not to say that women were not reading romances before the 1650s; evidence from Elizabeth Isham, writing in the 1630s, and Anne Clifford demonstrates the presence of romances on women's bookshelves throughout the seventeenth century. Perhaps it is simply that by the middle of the century gentry and noblewomen were able to present their romance reading as more 'serious' and were more likely to use romances in their efforts at textual self-construction.

Whatever the prescriptive conventions and moralistic conversation surrounding romance reading in the seventeenth century, put forward mainly in advice literature, it is clear that it was not unusual for women to read romances.[119] While we can make suppositions about the popularity of romantic fiction, however, it remains clear that this was an area of debate for many early modern men and women, and therefore the ways in which women choose to represent their romance reading become highly significant. This agency should not be forgotten in modern discussions of seventeenth-century women romance readers. It is simplistic to portray them as engaging in a frivolous pastime or assume that their reading choices and opinions were governed by their relationships with the men in their lives.

Instead, they responded in highly individual ways and used romance reading in their construction of their own identity. Some, such as Delaval, chose to replicate tropes and narratives found in advice literature, emphasising their exemplary pious femininity and engaging in an act of self-justification. Some engaged in literary critiques, but this clearly came from familiarity with the genre. Others, such as Dorothy Osborne, Anne Clifford and Elizabeth Isham, took pleasure in their reading. Osborne in particular was keen to discuss it with others, and felt a deep, personal connection to the characters. Reading romantic fiction, and discussing it with others, provided a way for women to explore their lives and themselves. They used and adapted the genre to their own ends through interpretation and discussion.

## Notes

1. Mary Evelyn, daughter of John Evelyn the diarist: Correspondence and papers: [1675]–1685, Evelyn Papers Vol. CCLXXIII, Add MS 78440, f46r, British Library, London. Mary Evelyn was known for her literary talents and interests: see Gillian Darley, *John Evelyn: Living for Ingenuity* (New Haven, CT: Yale University Press, 2006), 264.

2. Ann Blair has argued that 'humanists advocated the careful study of models of ancient rhetoric, notably by copying out the best passages from one's reading in a

notebook, where they could be retrieved for emulation and citation'. Ann M. Blair, *Too Much to Know: Managing Scholarly Information before the Modern Age* (New Haven, CT: Yale University Press, 2010), 69.

3. Douglas D. C. Chambers and David Galbraith, ed., *The Letterbooks of John Evelyn* (Toronto: University of Toronto Press, 2014), 688.

4. As Julie Eckerle has noted, women's 'life-writing' (by which she terms diaries, memoirs, meditations, letters and other autobiographical texts) gives us a good insight into women's reading of romances, although only a few explained their thoughts about the genre in detail. See Julie A. Eckerle, *Romancing the Self in Early Modern Englishwomen's Life Writing* (Farnham: Ashgate, 2013), 51–52.

5. See, for example, Steve Mentz, *Romance for Sale in Early Modern England: The Rise of Prose Fiction* (Aldershot: Ashgate, 2006).

6. For more on the genre of chick lit, see Suzanne Ferriss and Mallory Young, ed., *Chick Lit: The New Woman's Fiction* (London: Routledge, 2006); Lynne Pearce, 'Popular Romance and its Readers', in *A Companion to Romance: From Classical to Contemporary*, ed. Corinne Saunders (Oxford: Blackwell Publishing, 2004), 521–538.

7. Dorinda Outram, *The Enlightenment* (Cambridge: Cambridge University Press, 2005), 16.

8. Steven N. Zwicker, 'The Constitution of Opinion and the Pacification of Reading', in *Reading, Society and Politics in Early Modern England*, ed. Kevin Sharpe and Steven N. Zwicker (Cambridge: Cambridge University Press, 2003), 311.

9. Zwicker, 'The Constitution of Opinion', 311.

10. Josephine A. Roberts, 'Extracts from *Arcadia* in the Manuscript Notebook of Lady Katherine Manners', *Notes and Queries* 28, no. 1 (1981): 35–36.

11. Roberts, 'Extracts from *Arcadia*', 35.

12. Admittedly, *Arcadia* was recognised at the time for its poetry and innovative style, so perhaps has a slightly different impact than other romance works, but Manners' use of it alongside religious sources in particular is notable. See Gavin Alexander, 'Sir Philip Sidney's *Arcadia*', in *The Oxford Handbook of English Prose, 1500–1640*, ed. Andrew Hadfield (Oxford: Oxford University Press, 2023), 219–234. However, it has been argued that *Arcadia* was classed very differently when read by male versus female readers – Mary Ellen Lamb has argued that men read it as a 'serious work' but that women readers of *Arcadia* were generally represented as 'culpably frivolous and dangerously sexual'. See Mary Ellen Lamb, *Gender and Authorship in the Sidney Circle* (Madison, WI: University of Wisconsin Press, 1990), 112.

13. Rebecca Tierney-Hynes, *Novel Minds: Philosophers and Romance Readers, 1680–1740* (Basingstoke: Palgrave Macmillan, 2012), 4.

14. Richard Allestree, *The Ladies Calling. In Two Parts. By the Author of the Whole Duty of Man, The Causes of the Decay of Christian Piety, and the Gentlemans Calling* (Oxford: Printed at the Theater, 1673), 151.

15. Adrian Johns, *The Nature of the Book: Print and Knowledge in the Making* (Chicago, IL: University of Chicago Press, 1998).

16. Laura Gowing has pointed out that in the early modern period, lust was seen as a natural (and sinful) part of female nature, whereas chastity was something they should aspire to. See Laura Gowing, *Gender Relations in Early Modern England* (Harlow: Pearson, 2012), 17.

17. Nicholas Breton, *The Good and the Badde, Or Descriptions of the Worthies, and Unworthies of this Age. Where the Best may see their Graces, and the Worst discerne their Baseness* (London: Printed by George Purslowe for Iohn Budge, 1616), 30.

18. Breton, *The Good and the Badde*, 28.

19. Anthony Fletcher, *Gender, Sex and Subordination in England, 1500–1800* (New Haven, CT: Yale University Press, 1995), 380.

20. Elaine Leong has noted Brathwaite's prescriptions for reading, paying particular attention to *how* he directs women to read herbals. See Elaine Leong, '"Herbals she Peruseth": Reading Medicine in Early Modern England', *Renaissance Studies* 28, no. 4 (2014): 556–578.

21. Richard Brathwaite, *The English Gentlewoman, drawne out to the full body: Expressing What Habilliments doe best attire her, What Ornaments doe best adorne her, What Complements doe best accomplish her* (London: Printed by B. Alsop and T Fawcet, for Michael Sparke, dwelling in Greene Arbor, 1631), 139.

22. The womb was often described in emotional terms in the early modern period and could be constructed as a malevolent force. Various conditions, including the 'frenzy' of the womb, were thought to be caused by excess seed or fluid and connected to lust and hysteria. See Amy Kenny, *Humoral Wombs on the Shakespearean Stage* (London: Palgrave Macmillan, 2019).

23. Nicholas Culpeper, *Culpeper's Directory for Mid Wives: Or, a Guide for Women. The Second Part* (London: Printed by *Peter Cole*, 1662), 115.

24. Culpeper, *Culpeper's Directory for Mid Wives*, 116. My italics.

25. The physiological effects of reading are a very fruitful line of enquiry, and were central to early modern concerns surrounding reading. For more on this, see Johns, *The Nature of the Book*.

26. Lori Humphrey Newcomb has demonstrated the changing attitudes towards romance reading for both men and women, arguing the mid-seventeenth century onwards saw increasing appreciation of the genre, connected to the rise and respectability of leisure reading practices. See Lori Humphrey Newcomb, 'Gendering Prose Romance in Renaissance England', in *A Companion to Romance: From Classical to Contemporary*, ed. Corinne Saunders (Oxford: Blackwell Publishing, 2004), 121–139.

27. Hannah Woolley, *The Gentlewomans Companion; O, A Guide to the Female Sex: Containing Directions of Behaviour, in all Places, Companies, Relations, and Conditions, from their Childhood down to Old Age: Viz. As, Children to Parents. Scholars to Governours. Single to Servants. Virgins to Suitors. Married to Husbands. Huswifes to the House. Mistresses to the Servants. Mothers to Children. Widows to the World. Prudent to all. With Letters and Discourses upon all Occasions. Whereunto is added, A Guide for Cook-Maids, Dairy-Maids, Chamber-Maids, and all others that go to Service. The whole being an exact Rule for the Female Sex in General* (London: Printed by A. Maxwell for Dorman Nowman, 1673), 9.

28. Newcomb, 'Gendering Prose Romance', 137.

29. Woolley, *The Gentlewomans Companion*, 77.

30. For more on women, reading and ballads, see Sandra Clark, 'The Broadside Ballad and the Woman's Voice', in *Debating Gender in Early Modern England 1500–1700*, ed. Cristina Malcolmson and Mihoko Suzuki (Basingstoke: Palgrave Macmillan, 2002), 103–120.

31. [Judith Drake], *An Essay in Defence of the Female Sex. In which are inserted the Characters of A Pedant, A Squire, A Beau, A Vertuoso, A Poetaster, A City-Critick &c. In a Letter to a Lady, Written by a Lady* (London: Printed for A. Roper and E. Wilkinson, and R. Clavel, 1696), 57.

32. Heidi Brayman Hackel has reproduced the countess' library catalogue, which is held in the Huntington Library. See Brayman Hackel, 'The Countess of Bridgewater's London Library', in *Books and Readers in Early Modern England:*

*Material Studies*, ed. Jennifer Anderson and Elizabeth Sauer (Philadelphia, PA: University of Pennsylvania Press, 2002), 138–159.

33. Louise K. Horowitz, 'Pastoral Fiction', in *A New History of French Literature*, ed. Denis Hollier (Cambridge, MA: Harvard University Press, 1994), 261–262.

34. Brayman Hackel, 'The Countess of Bridgewater's London Library', 147–154.

35. Hannah Jane DeGroff, 'Textual Networks and the Country House: The 3rd Earl of Carlisle at Castle Howard' (PhD thesis, University of York, 2012). DeGroff has very usefully transcribed the book list, entitled 'My Laydes Books at Noward August 31: 1693' – see pages 206–209.

36. David McKitterick, 'Women and Their Books in Seventeenth-Century England: The Case of Elizabeth Puckering', *The Library* 1, Seventh Series (2000): 376.

37. There are many reasons why these signatures may have been inscribed. They cannot be taken as definite evidence of readership. Sometimes the names written on the flyleaves of books are obviously pen trials, and there is no evidence that the woman then went on to read the book she had just signed. Instead, it may have simply been the use of a blank page that was immediately at hand. In this case, women tend to practise writing their name several times over, at different points on the page, without any clear acknowledgement of the book itself. However, the common occurrence of the phrase 'her book' indicates a different intention behind the inscription. These appear to be signs of book ownership, possibly distinguishing the text from others in the household, or providing a record if it was lent to someone.

38. Brayman Hackel speculates about the question of readership in her study of Frances Stanley Egerton's books, noting that they do not contain marginalia or other signs of reading. She asks, 'What are we to make of this absence? Did Lady Bridgewater merely possess her books as objects of status? Were they read aloud to her? Did she read them without marking in them? If so, another series of questions arises about why she did not mark her books as an active reader: did she not consider herself a serious reader? Did she not re-read her books? Or did she, like her daughter-in-law, read them and make notes elsewhere?' Brayman Hackel, 'The Countess of Bridgewater's London Library', 145–146.

39. There have been several articles dedicated to Clifford's reading and annotating of specific books, including, most recently, Georgianna Ziegler, 'Lady Anne Clifford Reads John Selden', in *Early Modern English Marginalia*, ed. Katherine Acheson (Abingdon: Routledge, 2019), 134–154.

40. Edith Snook, *Women, Reading, and the Cultural Politics of Early Modern England* (Aldershot: Ashgate, 2005), 1.

41. Paul Salzman, 'Royalist Epic and Romance', in *The Cambridge Companion to Writing of the English Revolution*, ed. N. H. Keeble (Cambridge: Cambridge University Press, 2001), 215–232. The exact nature of the political commentary in *Arcadia* has been debated, but Fred Schurink used various readers marks in a copy of *Arcadia* housed at the Folger Shakespeare Library to examine its politics. See Fred Schurink, '"Like a Hand in the Margine of a Booke": William Blount's Marginalia and the Politics of Sidney's *Arcadia*', *Review of English Studies* 59, no. 238 (2008): 1–24.

42. Salzman, 'Royalist Epic and Romance', 221.

43. Salzman, 'Royalist Epic and Romance', 222.

44. For more on Barclay's text, see Helen Moore, 'Romance: *Amadis de Gaule* and John Barclay's *Argenis*', in *The Oxford Handbook of English Prose, 1500–1640*, ed. Andrew Hadfield (Oxford: Oxford University Press, 2013), 59–76.

45. John Barclay, *Barclay his Argenis: Or, The Loves of Poliarchus and Argenis: Faithfully translated out of Latine into English, By Kingesmill Long, Gent.* (London: Printed by G. P. for Henry Seile, 1625). RB 97024, Henry E. Huntington Library, San

Marino. As Brayman points out, the dates recorded mean that Clifford and the scribe, most likely a member of her household, read the book 'at the fairly voracious pace of forty folio pages a day'. According to Brayman, it would take a modern reader two and a half hours to read forty pages aloud, without interruption, giving a useful insight into the amount of time Clifford spent on oral reading and the 'seriousness with which some, albeit quirky, book owners treated their reading of prose fiction'. Heidi Brayman Hackel, 'Lady Anne Clifford as Reader, Annotator and Book Collector', in *Lady Anne Clifford: Culture, Patronage and Gender in 17th-Century Britain*, ed. Karen Hearn and Lyn Hulse (Leeds: Yorkshire Archaeological Society, 2009), 106.

46. E.g. Barclay, *Argenis*, 97, 246.

47. Barclay, *Argenis*, 78.

48. Barclay, *Argenis*, 78.

49. Barclay, *Argenis*, 78.

50. Barclay, *Argenis*, 305.

51. Harriet Archer and Andrew Hadfield, ed., *A Mirror for Magistrates in Context: Literature, History and Politics in Early Modern England* (Cambridge: Cambridge University Press, 2016). See Chapter 5 for a more detailed discussion of these texts.

52. See, for example, Stephen Orgel, 'Marginal Maternity: Reading Lady Anne Clifford's *A Mirror for Magistrates*', in *Printing and Parenting in Early Modern England*, ed. Douglas A. Brooks (Aldershot: Ashgate, 2003), 267–289.

53. Brayman Hackel, 'Lady Anne Clifford as Reader', 108.

54. While signatures may not prove readership, they do at least point to an interaction with books and manuscripts, and the importance of them as material objects. The act of writing a name in a book, whether to indicate ownership, stake a knowledge claim or simply as a form of writing practice, reveals various relationships with a book, either as an object or as a source of information and ideas (or both). These inscriptions tell us not only about this relationship but also about interpersonal relationships in which books become an actor; for example, in the case of gift inscriptions, or in competing ownership claims.

55. Vital d'Audiguier, *A Tragi-Comicall History of Our Times, Under the Borrowed Names of Lisander and Calista* (London: Printed by R. Y. for G. Lathum, 1635), STC 907 (copy 1), Folger Shakespeare Library, Washington, DC.

56. Jean Desmarets de Saint-Sorlin, *Ariana. In Two Parts. As it was translated out of the French, and presented to my Lord Chamberlaine* (London: Printed by John Dawson for Thomas Walkley, 1641). Hfc31 010, Beinecke Library, New Haven.

57. M. Le Roy Gomberville, *The History of Polexander: in Five Bookes. Done into English by William Browne, Gent. For the Right Honourable Philip, Earle of Pembroke and Montgomery, &c.* (London: Printed by Tho: Harper, for Thomas Walkley, 1647). RB 113855, Huntington Library.

58. Elspeth Graham, Hilary Hinds, Elaine Hobby and Helen Wilcox, 'Introduction', in *Her Own Life: Autobiographical Writings by Seventeenth-Century Englishwomen*, ed. Elspeth Graham, Hilary Hinds, Elaine Hobby and Helen Wilcox (London: Routledge, 1989), 17.

59. She argues that 'Rich's personal experience is transformed, through the writing act, into a romantic paradigm . . . [her] indebtedness to romantic motifs and structures is everywhere apparent'. Wray suggests that this use of romance motifs was done in order to give Rich power over her situation, and to reset a reality in which her husband was violent and abusive, to one in which she enjoyed a happy marriage and over which she had some control. Ramona Wray, 'Recovering the Reading of Renaissance Englishwomen: Deployments of Autobiography', *Critical*

*Survey* 12, no. 2 (2000): 36, 40. Similarly, Eckerle has argued that that 'despite a critical assumption that early modern Englishwomen's life writing was predominantly spiritual in nature, the romance genre exerted a powerful and pervasive pressure on women's life writing – and self-formation – during this time'. Eckerle, *Romancing the Self*, 4.

60. Eckerle has found evidence of women strategically repurposing the romantic genre, and argues that romantic fiction gave women 'an imaginative and narrative landscape within which to explore and represent personal experience'. Eckerle, *Romancing the Self*, 20.

61. Margaret J. M. Ezell, 'Delaval, Elizabeth', *Oxford Dictionary of National Biography*, 2004, accessed September 19, 2023, www-oxforddnb-com.libproxy.york.ac.uk/display/10.1093/ref:odnb/9780198614128.001.0001/odnb-9780198614128-e-68215?rskey=LKNd5H&result=1.

62. Elizabeth Delaval, *The Meditations of Lady Elizabeth Delaval, Written Between 1662 and 1671*, ed. Douglas G. Greene (Gateshead: The Surtees Society, Northumberland Press Limited, 1978), 11–12.

63. Delaval, *The Meditations of Lady Elizabeth Delaval*, 26.

64. Margaret Ezell has explored the ways in which Delaval's manuscript exposes the difficulty of defining genre in the early modern period; she argues that Delaval used conventions of romance fiction rather than spiritual meditations, and that, as Delaval did not title her work, the classification of 'meditation' has been imposed by later editors. However, Ezell does not specifically consider Delaval's reading habits, but rather how contemporary prose fiction influenced her writing style and her presentation of personal relationships within the manuscript. Margaret J. M. Ezell, 'Elizabeth Delaval's Spiritual Heroine: Thoughts on Redefining Manuscript Texts by Early Women Writers', in *English Manuscript Studies, Volume 3*, ed. Peter Beal and Jeremy Griffiths (London: The British Library, 1992), 223.

65. Joseph F. Chorpenning, 'Santa Teresa's *Libro de la Vida* as Romance: Narrative Movements and Heroic Quest', *Revista Canadiense de Estudios Hispánicos* 14, no. 1 (1989): 52.

66. Jennifer R. Goodman, '"That wommen holde in ful greet reverence": Mothers and Daughters Reading Chivalric Romances', in *Women, the Book and the Worldly: Selected Proceedings of the St Hilda's Conference, 1993, Volume II*, ed. Lesley Smith and Jane H. M. Taylor (Cambridge: D.S. Brewer, 1995), 28–29.

67. These books are also mentioned by Dorothy Osborne – see below.

68. Delaval, *The Meditations of Lady Elizabeth Delaval*, 32.

69. Alice Eardley has argued that the publication of these aforementioned works, alongside De Scudéry's *Ibrahim* and *Clélie*, was part of an attempt by the publisher Humphrey Moseley to foster a market for heroic romances in the 1650s. Eardley has also argued that these books had a broad middle-class readership, contrary to some modern scholarship that has claimed they had a mainly aristocratic audience in England. See Alice Eardley, 'Marketing Aspiration: Fact, Fiction, and the Publication of French Romance in Mid-Seventeenth-Century England', in *Seventeenth-Century Fiction: Text and Transmission*, ed. Jacqueline Gomski and Isabelle Moreau (Oxford: Oxford University Press, 2016), 130–142.

70. Delaval, *The Meditations of Lady Elizabeth Delaval*, 32.

71. Delaval, *The Meditations of Lady Elizabeth Delaval*, 33. This would have been in 1659, during the Interregnum, when her Royalist parents were still in exile on the continent.

72. Newcomb, 'Gendering Prose Romance', 134.

73. Delaval, *The Meditations of Lady Elizabeth Delaval*, 32.

74. Delaval, *The Meditations of Lady Elizabeth Delaval*, 62.

75. Delaval, *The Meditations of Lady Elizabeth Delaval*, 45.

76. Delaval, *The Meditations of Lady Elizabeth Delaval*, 117.

77. As Julie Eckerle has noted, Isham's text is 'one of the earliest female-authored prose narratives about the self' and 'provides extraordinary insight into her own reading and writing habits'. Julie A. Eckerle, 'Coming to Knowledge: Elizabeth Isham's Autobiography and the Self-Construction of an Intellectual Woman', *a/b: Auto/Biography Studies* 25, no. 1 (2010): 97.

78. Isaac Stephens has pointed out Isham's apparent rejection of some strictures for women's reading, noting that she also read Ovid's *Metamorphoses*. See Isaac Stephens, *The Gentlewoman's Remembrance: Patriarchy, Piety, and Singlehood in Early Stuart England* (Manchester: Manchester University Press, 2016), 156.

79. Elizabeth Isham, *Book of Rememberance*, f26r, accessed August 30, 2023, http://web.warwick.ac.uk/english/perdita/Isham/bor_p26r.htm.

80. For more on Isham's mental health, see Erin Sullivan, *Beyond Melancholy: Sadness and Selfhood in Renaissance England* (Oxford: Oxford University Press, 2016), 133–139.

81. Anne Cotterill, 'Fit Words at the "pitts brinke": The Achievement of Elizabeth Isham', *Huntington Library Quarterly* 73, no. 2 (2010): 229.

82. Isaac Stephens has described her text as an 'intense form of puritan life-writing'. Isaac Stephens, '"My Cheefest Work": The Making of the Spiritual Autobiography of Elizabeth Isham', *Midland History* 34, no. 2 (2009): 195.

83. Erica Longfellow has argued that Isham 'displayed little awareness of gendered restrictions on women's intellectual activity', attributing this partly to the fact that she did not record reading any advice literature aimed at women (although this not only underestimates the pervasiveness of gender norms but also assumes that Isham recorded every item she read). See Erica Longfellow, '"Take unto ye words": Elizabeth Isham's "Booke of Rememberance" and Puritan Cultural Forms', in *The Intellectual Culture of Puritan Women, 1558–1680*, ed. Johanna Harris and Elizabeth Scott-Baumann (Basingstoke: Palgrave Macmillan, 2011), 125.

84. Isham, *Book of Rememberance*, f26r.

85. Memoirists and diarists such as Margaret Hoby, Grace Mildmay, Ann Fanshawe and Anne Halkett all discussed their reading habits, but did not make mention of romantic fiction. See Margaret Hoby, *The Diary of Lady Margaret Hoby*, edited by Dorothy M. Meads (London: Routledge, 1930); Linda Pollock, ed., *With Faith and Physic: The Life of a Tudor Gentlewoman, Lady Grace Mildmay, 1552–1620* (London: Collins & Brown, 1993); John Loftis, ed., *The Memoirs of Anne, Lady Halkett and Ann, Lady Fanshawe* (Oxford: Clarendon Press, 1979). Eckerle has argued that both Anne Halkett and Ann Fanshawe draw heavily on the themes of romances in their autobiographies, demonstrating their influence even if they do not necessarily record reading them. See Eckerle, *Romancing the Self*.

86. See, for example, James Daybell, *The Material Letter in Early Modern England: Manuscript Letters and the Cultures and Practices of Letter-Writing, 1512–1635* (Basingstoke: Palgrave Macmillan, 2012).

87. Eckerle, *Romancing the Self*, 51.

88. Eckerle, *Romancing the Self*, 52. Samuel Pepys also bought Elizabeth a copy of De Scudéry's *Ibrahim, ou L'illustre Bassa* in 1668. See Gesa Stedman, *Cultural Exchange in Seventeenth-Century France and England* (Abingdon: Routledge, 2016), 94.

89. Kate Loveman, *Samuel Pepys and His Books: Reading, Newsgathering, and Sociability, 1660–1703* (Oxford: Oxford University Press, 2015), 151.

90. Sara Heller Mendelson, 'The Weightiest Business: Marriage in an Upper-Gentry Family in Seventeenth-Century England', *Past & Present* 85 (1979): 130 (note 26).

91. Mary Hatton Helsby, *Autograph letters signed from Mary Hatton Helsby to various recipients [manuscript], 1651–1668*. X.d.493, (6), Folger Shakespeare Library.

92. Emily Griffiths Jones, 'Romance, Narrative Vision, and Elect Community in Seventeenth-Century England' (PhD thesis, Boston University, 2014), 22.

93. Paul Trolander, *Literary Sociability in Early Modern England: The Epistolary Record* (Newark, DE: University of Delaware Press, 2014), 165.

94. Mary Hatton to Randolph Helsby, March 27, 1654. X.d.493 (4).

95. The phrase 'newe booke' may mean that it was new to Helsby, but it may also mean that it was newly published. If this is the case, it was likely the edition of Spenser's pastoral *Shepherds Calendar*, written in both Latin and English and printed in 1653. Edmund Spenser, *Calendarium pastorale, sive Æglogæ duodecim, totidem anni mensibus accommodatæ. Anglicè olim scriptæ ab Edmundo Spensero anglorum poetarum principe: nunc autem eleganti Latino carmine donatæ a Theodoro Bathurst, aulæ Pembrokianæ apud Cantabrigienses aliquando socio* (Londini: impensis M[ercy]. M[eighen]. T[homas]. C[ollins]. & G. Bedell, 1653).

96. Osborne has often been commended for her writing style, with scholars such as Sheila Ottway suggesting that they read like an epistolary novel when taken in sequence. See Sheila Ottway, 'Dorothy Osborne's Love Letters: Novelistic Glimmerings and the Ovidian Self', *Prose Studies* 19, no. 2 (1996): 149–159. Ottway recognises that 'Osborne clearly would never have thought that her own letters constituted literature, but considered as a whole, the sequence of her love letters to Temple form a coherent narrative with its own momentum and sense of direction' (p. 151).

97. Letter 10, March 1653. Dorothy Osborne, *Dorothy Osborne: Letters to Sir William Temple*, ed. Kenneth Parker (London: Penguin Books, 1987), 59–60.

98. Letter 9, February 1653. Osborne, *Dorothy Osborne: Letters to Sir William Temple*, 57.

99. Letter 27, June 1653. Osborne, *Dorothy Osborne: Letters to Sir William Temple*, 97.

100. Letter 39, September 1653. Osborne, *Dorothy Osborne: Letters to Sir William Temple*, 125.

101. Trolander, *Literary Sociability*, 164.

102. Trolander, *Literary Sociability*, 164.

103. Jane Donawerth, ed., *Rhetorical Theory by Women before 1900: An Anthology* (Lanham, MD: Rowman and Littlefield, 2002), 82. De Scudéry also published various essays and drew on classical authors to develop a theory of rhetoric and composition. She hosted a weekly salon at her house and was connected to women such as Mme. de Sévigné and Mme. de Lafayette. According to Nathalie Grande, she departed from the heroic romances of Calprenède and Gomberville, instead employing a classical aesthetic, aiming to both instruct and please her readers. See Nathalie Grande, 'Quand le Roman Oeuvre en Moraliste: Madeleine de Scudéry et Clélie', *Dalhousie French Studies* 27: Réflexions sur le genre moraliste au dix-septième siècle (1994): 31–49.

104. Letter 40, September 1653. Osborne, *Dorothy Osborne: Letters to Sir William Temple*, 128.

105. Letter 20, May 1653; Letter 19, April 1653. Osborne, *Dorothy Osborne: Letters to Sir William Temple*, 75–79.

106. Carrie Hintz, *An Audience of One: Dorothy Osborne's Letters to Sir William Temple, 1652–1654* (Toronto: University of Toronto Press, 2005), 3.

107. As Kenneth Parker has pointed out, her letters 'corroborate the opinion, developed in our time, that the chief fictive prose form was that of the French romance'. Osborne, *Dorothy Osborne: Letters to Sir William Temple*, 37.

108. Letter 41, September 1653. Osborne, *Dorothy Osborne: Letters to Sir William Temple*, 131.

109. Letter 59, February 1654. Osborne, *Dorothy Osborne: Letters to Sir William Temple*, 180.

110. Madeleine de Scudéry, *Ibrahim, or, the Illustrious Bassa. An Excellent New Romance. The Whole Work, In Foure Parts. Written in French by Monsieur de Scudery, and Now Englished by Henry Cogan, Gent* (London: Printed for Humphry Moseley, *William Bentley*, and *Thomas Heath*, 1652).

111. James How, *Epistolary Spaces: English Letter Writing from the Foundation of the Post Office to Richardson's* Clarissa (Aldershot: Ashgate, 2003), 41.

112. Femke Molekamp, 'Therapies for Melancholy and Inordinate Passion in the Letters of Dorothy Osborne to Sir William Temple (1652–1654)', *The Seventeenth Century* 29, no. 3 (2014): 262.

113. Hintz, *An Audience of One*, 64.

114. Helen Wilcox and Sheila Ottway, 'Women's Histories', in *The Cambridge Companion to Writing of the English Revolution*, ed. N. H. Keeble (Cambridge: Cambridge University Press, 2001), 157.

115. Letter 54, January 1654. Osborne, *Dorothy Osborne: Letters to Sir William Temple*, 164–165. Sasha Roberts has suggested that Ovid, although in the canon of respected literature, was often seen as dangerous to 'vulnerable readers' – i.e. women – because of the work's amorous nature. See Sasha Roberts, *Reading Shakespeare's Poems in Early Modern England* (Basingstoke: Palgrave Macmillan, 2003), 21.

116. Letter 59, February 1654. Osborne, *Dorothy Osborne: Letters to Sir William Temple*, 179–180.

117. Raymond Anselment, 'Feminine Self-Reflection and the Seventeenth-Century Occasional Meditation', *The Seventeenth Century* 26, no. 1 (2011): 72.

118. Newcomb, 'Gendering Prose Romance', 134–135.

119. As Eckerle has suggested, 'romance had a firm place in early modern aristocratic life, offering an entertaining and pleasant way to pass the time, providing fodder for conversation, stimulating women's intellect and creativity, and – perhaps most importantly, if somewhat paradoxically – contributing to the impression of good breeding among elite women, for whom the genre had powerful courtly associations'. Eckerle, *Romancing the Self*, 53.

Chapter 3

# 'I harde yow once saye yow loved forryne newes': women news readers

Women in the history of news reading and consumption are generally conspicuous only by their absence. Kate Loveman and David Randall have demonstrated the importance of news reading to a seventeenth-century gentleman's identity, examining the importance of news to masculinity, but the same is rarely done for femininity.[1] Richard Allestree gives perhaps the only mention of news reading in *The Ladies Calling*, asking his readers that 'this Discourse may not be taken only as a Gazet for its newness, & discarded as soon as read', and instead suggesting they return to his book year after year, in order to better absorb its lessons.[2] This shows a general disdain for the fleeting nature of news reading (as printed news is discarded as soon as it is read), but does not appear to be particularly gendered – there is no clear suggestion that news was an inappropriate genre for women readers.[3]

The absence of representations of women reading the news has perhaps led to a misapprehension that they did not do so.[4] In an article about manuscript transmission of the news in the seventeenth century, Ian Atherton suggested that 'it is possible that women may have been less interested in the news. Female correspondents very rarely included even a line of news in their letters, where their male counterparts rarely let a letter pass without some mention of the events of the day'.[5] He does then go on to acknowledge a problem inherent in discussions of early modern news, the 'tendency to call reports from men "news" and those from women "gossip"', and that women had a role in producing, selling, distributing and reading the news, but his statement reflects a common assumption about women's lack of interest in the news; or the fact that there is a lack of evidence for that interest, at least in comparison to male news readers.[6]

However, there is a multitude of evidence that women were dedicated and regular readers of the news in the seventeenth century. They received letters from friends and family detailing current affairs, they subscribed to printed and manuscript news, and they acted as key participants in epistolary news networks, reading and transmitting the news in their correspondence. This chapter will consider the many and varied examples of women reading the news, demonstrating that there is evidence for a keen and continued interest in seventeenth-century current affairs among gentry women. This shows the effort they made to engage with political events both in England and overseas, despite being physically removed from places and institutions of political power, and it was a key way in which they could participate in the political sphere.

Women's interactions with politics have long been recognised in other areas of early modern history. Scholars have shown that women's writing often engaged with 'news-worthy' themes, and that women's political participation often occurred behind the scenes.[7] Women prophets have received attention for their intervention in the public sphere, as have Quaker women, whose effective use of print has been demonstrated by Kate Peters.[8] Historians such as Ann Hughes have examined women's more explicit political participation in the Civil War period, demonstrating the extent to which women had an active role in the conflict, taking part in military operations, defending their homes and influencing the political discussion.[9] Moreover, the political influences and interests in the works of Delarivier Manley, Aphra Behn and Mary Astell, and the political actions of women such as Lucy Hutchinson, Anne Halkett and Ann Fanshawe, have all demonstrated the relationship that women had with politics in the seventeenth century.[10]

These women writers and actors must have acquired their information about contemporary events and politics from somewhere, and it seems a very reasonable assumption that they all consumed the news in some form or other. This may have been through oral networks, but it may also have been in either manuscript or print. Jason Peacey, when looking at the private circulation of printed news, argues convincingly that 'gentry women were enthusiastic readers and distributors of topical material, who gained access to "printed papers" even in remote parts of the country', suggesting that they often received such material from their husbands.[11] This was a significant way in which women accessed information; however, I want to build on this to argue that women not only received their news through the mediation of other family members but were also frequently recipients themselves, and that news reading should be fully integrated into the history of early modern women and politics.

The idea that women were absent from news culture has been challenged by a number of scholars in recent years. Women's roles in the production and distribution of news have been illuminated by scholars such as Paula McDowell, Claire Walker and Marcus Nevitt.[12] Nevitt in particular has recognised that women read newsbooks, citing Lucy Hutchinson and Brilliana Harley in particular, but has otherwise largely focused on women's roles in the production, rather than consumption, of the news.[13] The developing public sphere of the late seventeenth and early eighteenth centuries, where news was consumed and discussed (particularly in coffee houses), has traditionally been seen as masculine, both rhetorically and in terms of physical space.[14] However, this model has been increasingly complicated by historians who have argued that women could and did participate in coffee-house culture.[15] There is increasing recognition that women were interested in the news, and were able to be active participants in many areas of seventeenth-century news cultures. This still leaves room, however, for a discussion of women's roles as readers and consumers of the news.[16] Coffee houses are of course an important area of research for exploring early modern women and news culture, but less attention has been paid to how women engaged with the news at home, often far from London. In this chapter, I focus on seventeenth-century women news readers in domestic spaces and consider *how* women read the news.

Determining how people read the news can be challenging, particularly given the general absence of marginalia or other readers' marks from printed news. The lack of annotation of news publications has been commented on by several scholars, with a distinction often drawn between news-reading habits and the 'goal-oriented' reading of other texts.[17] This, however, overlooks the aim of intellectual development; the desire to gain knowledge about the world must have been at least a partial motivator behind news reading, as would, presumably, the desire to be able to discuss current affairs, at least in certain circles. Both of these aims could be considered as examples of 'active' reading. The fact remains, however, that news, whether manuscript or print, rarely bears readers' marks. Perhaps this is more indicative of a lack of repeated reading than anything else. News reading is, by its very nature, immediate and often short-lived: it is unlikely that one would go back to newsletters or newsbooks for multiple readings over a long period of time, as we saw happening with the Bible in Chapter 1.[18]

A much-discussed phenomenon of seventeenth-century news culture is the plurality of texts open to readers. There was, as has been mentioned above, a rise in print news publications in the 1640s and readers had plenty of choice in the news marketplace, at least during periods when the Licensing Act was not in place. One of the most striking things about the scholarship on seventeenth-century news, however, is the division between manuscript and print genres. In the focus on the rise of new genres and the attempt to both trace and complicate the origins of the newspaper, the manuscript transmission of news has often been somewhat separated from print news.[19] It is worth, therefore, considering all the ways in which news was transmitted in the seventeenth century, to examine if women interacted with any forms in particular and how they were approached. From my research, the two forms that emerge most concretely are letters containing news, sent by friends, family or acquaintances; and the manuscript newsletter. The absence of other forms does not necessarily mean that women were not consuming them (there are several references to printed news publications in the sources I discuss here), but rather that we have less evidence thereof. These two genres have often been overlooked by scholars focused on the explosion of print news in the seventeenth century, but there is increasing recognition of their continued importance in the early modern period, despite the influx of new forms of news transmission.

This mix of manuscript and printed sources is important when considering how people read and received the news. As will be demonstrated below, there is plenty of evidence that news was gathered from a multiplicity of sources, both manuscript and print.[20] King has discussed the interplay between different forms of communication in the news marketplace of the late seventeenth century, arguing that 'written and printed media worked in tandem and in addition to the traditional oral circulation of news, offering users a range of communicative options rather than replacing or overriding each other', in a form of 'extensive' reading.[21] In gathering knowledge about current affairs, seventeenth-century readers, both male and female, relied on a variety of different sources to keep them informed, using both manuscript and print throughout the seventeenth century.

Women received the news in letters from friends and family, and in formalised documents such as newsletters, newsbooks and corantos. I will explore examples of letters sent to and from women such as Joan Barrington, Elizabeth Mordaunt and Jane Cornwallis Bacon, to consider the ways in which women participated in epistolary news networks among friends and families, and manuscript newsletters sent to women such as Anne Pole and Barbara Clopton, which demonstrate women's interest in serial news consumption. What emerges is a picture of reading in which gentry women consumed the news in print and manuscript form, often absorbing multiple accounts of the same event or using different publications to acquire knowledge of different events. This does not appear to be markedly different from the way in which men read the news, challenging the traditional divisions that have been put in place between male and female participation in the public news sphere.

Women's reading as a form of political participation has often been overlooked. Kevin Sharpe and Steven Zwicker have argued for viewing 'reading as political experience and performance'.[22] They also connected this political reading to questions of identity, suggesting that the process of reading was one of identity creation (be that political or religious identity), concluding that 'we are what we read'.[23] This, surely, is an important form of political engagement. We do not always know for certain that women read the news that they received, but, as Amanda Vickery has argued, 'possessions [are] crucial props in self-fashioning'.[24] Therefore, in receiving the news, whether through personal letter, newsbook or manuscript newsletter, these women were creating an identity for themselves, something which is in itself a form of political activity.

The examples of news reading considered here fall roughly into three chronological periods, corresponding with periods of change in news culture more generally. The late 1620s and early 1630s, with the rise of corantos and serials, is the context for the news reading of figures such as Joan Barrington and Jane Cornwallis Bacon, who received news from their friends and family. Brilliana Harley, Elizabeth Mordaunt and Mary Hatton Helsby were reading the news in the context of the Civil War and Restoration, when a significant number of new printed forms were available to the reading public. Barbara Clopton and Anne Pole were receiving newsletters in the 1680s and 1690s, when news saw another spike alongside the context of the Glorious Revolution and the Rage of Party. These are all recognised as significant moments in the development of printed news, while the evidence collected here is largely manuscript, in the form of personal letters or scribal newsletters. However, there is evidence throughout that these women were reading printed news forms as well, demonstrating the significance of the rise of the news genre not only for the male public sphere but also for women, who often lived at a remove from the political centre of the country.

## Letters of news

There are numerous examples of women discussing news in epistolary form throughout the seventeenth century.[25] This correspondence is often with male family members or acquaintances, usually based in London and updating their female relatives on the news from the capital. There are, however, also examples of women sharing news in their letters to each other. Letters can also give evidence of other forms of news reading, as newsbooks, corantos and broadsides were often sent by friends and family, alongside letters. The examples gathered here, ranging from the 1620s to the 1690s, demonstrate several women's interest in news reading and participation in seventeenth-century news transmission. The case studies here have been chosen because they explicitly discuss political or international news. Not all women's letters do this (although it appears to be more likely in times of political upheaval or war, as is perhaps unsurprising) and there is certainly room to expand this study by considering a much broader definition of 'news'. However, for the purposes of this chapter I have chosen women who, through their epistolary interactions with friends and family, demonstrated very clearly their appetite for current affairs.

Many women received detailed news in letters from their male family members, often their husbands, sons or sons-in-law, who were in London and could report on events in the capital. The letters sent to Joan Barrington and Jane Cornwallis Bacon (née Meautys, 1580/1–1659), the gentry woman and letter-writer, reveal a great deal about their news-reading habits and interests. Both received letters from a variety of family members and acquaintances, who updated them, often in great detail, on important items of both foreign and domestic news.

Barrington was at the centre of an epistolary network within her family.[26] The family's letters are held in the British Library. Those in the volume edited by Arthur Searle come from the years 1628–1632, when a large number of letters were sent to Barrington after the death of her husband, Sir Francis Barrington.[27] Various family members and acquaintances sent Barrington updates about current affairs, and her interest in the news appears to have been common knowledge, at least within the family. This was in the midst of the Thirty Years' War. Richard Cust has argued that there was a great deal of interest in foreign and domestic news at this time, with the public following the conflict on the continent, the Spanish match and parliamentary politics, citing the fact that there is a 'marked increase in the survival of newsletters and "separates"' after 1620.[28] This increased interest in foreign (mostly continental) news is certainly echoed in Francis Harris' remark to his aunt that 'I harde yow once saye yow loved forryne newes.'[29]

Barrington was clearly also interested in domestic news, however. Her sons often sent her news of Parliament, or other political news from London. On January 28, 1629, her son Robert wrote:

> I cannot now have tyme to relate how many excellent speeches were made both yesterday and this day in the cause of religion and against both popery and arminianisme. We are to goe to the king to morrow to receave his gratious answer upon the petition of both houses for a generall fast, which we make no doubt of being graunted. Forraigne newes I heare none, only there is a speech that the Hollanders have taken more shippes of late and surprized the convoy that as comeing with money to pay the souldiers in the archduchess' country.[30]

This was concerning the ongoing condemnation of Arminianism by Parliament in the 1620s, and the petition for a general fast, which was a common response to outbreaks of disease in England.[31] The whole letter was taken up with political news, with only scant mention of personal matters, or Robert's welfare. These matters would, however, have been personally important to him, as he was describing his professional life. When seen within the context of family intimacy, this complicates the idea of a public/private divide, demonstrating that women often necessarily had close links to political proceedings due to their family members' professional positions. Letters such as these were frequent, often sent every few days, allowing Barrington to stay as up to date as possible with the affairs of the day.

However, her sons often took on a distinct editorial role, seemingly based on what they thought would interest their mother. In one letter from 1630, John Barrington wrote to his mother, 'I heare of no newes in this towne worthy of your knowledge.'[32] This idea of 'no newes' demonstrates the editorial role her correspondents could take. John Barrington clearly put a premium on certain kinds of news, and was discerning in what he sent to his mother. It also indicates the role family members played in deciding what news was relayed to women, and what not to communicate. There is a similar example in 1693, when Margaret Grey received a letter from her son William Grey.[33] William wrote, 'I read over the news[letter] just now but can find nothing worth writing.'[34] Grey appears to have relied on her son to digest the news for her, reading the newsletter and deciding what content may or may not interest his mother. While it is very possible that Grey had other news sources, whether printed or manuscript, the role of male family members in processing and editing news for their female family members is evident.

Jane Cornwallis Bacon similarly received news in various letters from her male family members. Her second husband, Nathaniel Bacon, wrote to her detailing the news of the Thirty Years' War from mainland Europe, in a similar style to manuscript newsletters:

> for news here is very little, but some hopes that the strong report of the King and Prince's death of Polonia may prove untrue, for here has lately arrived a ship out of these countries, which relates no such thing; and besides, the Spanish ambassador has no such intelligence. The report is also of an ambassador out of Spain for the Low Countries, to treat of peace; for whose entertainment there is there great preparation. A confirmation also of the sea fight betwixt the French King and the Rochellers, 6 of the King's ships being sunk, and 3 taken; and also of the other news I last wrote, of another navy of ships is also preparing, the intent unclear, some sat for Spain, the match proceeding according to the common report.[35]

This letter gives a detailed overview of the various events across the continent, referencing the difficulty people had in confirming news reports or reconciling conflicting information. Moreover, it is implied that this is a regular correspondence: Nathaniel Bacon mentioned 'the other news I last wrote', suggesting that this was not a one-off communication, and that he had relayed news to her before.

Bacon's cousin, Thomas Meautys, gave her updates on the news from London, including the events at Parliament and the accompanying political intrigue and manoeuvring. In one letter he wrote, 'our Parliament was this day adjourned till Thursday next. The Upper House is not satisfied with the reasons of the King's detaining my Lord of Arundel from them, and are resolved to press it further'.[36] This refers to Charles I's arrest of Thomas Howard, the Earl of Arundel, after his son eloped in 1626 with Lady Elizabeth Stuart, daughter of the Duke of Lennox and the king's ward. The House of Lords protested his detention as one of their members, and adjourned Parliament until Arundel was released.[37] Meautys later wrote, 'I am the shorter in news, because I understand by your last that you want not our Parliament news from better and readier hands.'[38] She also was clearly able to read in at least two languages, and her family were therefore able to send her additional materials and reports to add to her reading. In June 1628, Meautys wrote, 'the enclosed, for those few words which are in French, and for which you want no interpreter, was the King's answer to our petition; the rest was somewhat which he spoke before and after the answer given'.[39] Bacon's understanding of the news was drawn from multiple places, as she clearly had several news sources in different languages.

She was also apparently concerned with the truthfulness and accuracy of the reports she received, as Sir Ambrose Randolph, a cousin and close friend, at one point wrote to her:

> I knowing your love to the truth of news, rather than first or common report of it, shall, as you wishes me, send you a relation of the King of Sweden's great victory, the 7th September, as it was told by him that brought the news to our King since my coming to town; an Englishman, who the King has now knighted, his name Sir John Castell.[40]

This was the Battle of Breitenfeld, one of King Gustavus Adolphus' most significant victories in the Thirty Years' War, and the rest of the letter is taken up with a very detailed account of the conflict. The similarity to Harris' reference to Barrington's 'love' of the news is striking; both women were keen to keep well informed, and utilised their large network of friends and family to help them do so, despite any physical distance they might have from London political circles.[41] Their news reading broadened their political and cultural horizons, allowing them to intellectually engage with current affairs.[42]

Evidence of extensive reading, mixing both manuscript and print genres, is present in Barrington's family letters. Her correspondents frequently sent her copies of the latest newsbooks, keeping her up to date on events that way. Her son-in-law, William Masham, wrote in 1631: 'we have noe domesticke newes, only some whispers at Parliament. When the booke of newes comes forth I will send it you; as yet I cannot heare of any this weeke'.[43] Masham again, a month later, wrote, 'I have sent you this week's curranto and I hope the next will make things more certaine', after reporting the foreign news in his letter.[44] There also appears to have been an expectation that Barrington would have read English corantos and serials. Given the lack of annotations or other readers' marks on most print news publications, particularly for women, references such as these to the consumption of print news genres are very useful. While there are few sources which give as much evidence for women reading newsbooks and other print publications as the Barrington family letters, such references do crop up in other women's letters from across the seventeenth century. In the 1690s, Elizabeth Packer, a friend of the Evelyn family, wrote in a letter to Mary Evelyn: 'I was told from the publick news letter of the danger M^r [?] had been in but knew not the particulars till y^r letter.'[45] This gives an impression not only of women discussing the current events but also, again, of the mix of manuscript and print transmission of the news.

Brilliana Harley, the parliamentarian and third wife of Sir Robert Harley, is often included in studies of women during the Civil War period for her defence of her family home, Brampton Bryan.[46] She similarly received both letters containing news and other records of current affairs from her family members. In her affectionate correspondence with her son, Edward (Ned) Harley, she frequently refers to texts sent to her by either him or her husband. He sent her copies of various declarations and Acts of Parliament to keep her up to date with news from the capital. On one occasion, she wrote to her son, 'I thanke you for the acts of parlament, and for doctor Dowing booke.'[47] This probably refers to Calybute Downing, a clergyman and author who wrote several tracts and sermons in the early 1640s legitimising resistance to the king and promoting Presbyterianism.[48] Harley displayed a keen interest in following current affairs, and implied a reliance on her correspondents for this information gathering: in another letter to her son, she wrote, 'your letter by the post and by the carrier are both very wellcome to me; for besides the knowledge you giue me of the publicke affaires, the assurance of your health is very deare to me'.[49] Harley here distinguishes between different types of news, public and personal, but suggests they are both of value to her; there is no suggestion that one is more appropriate to her.

While the majority of these letters communicating news to women appear to be from male correspondents, there is some evidence of women passing and discussing news with other women.[50] On one occasion, Judith Barrington, Joan Barrington's daughter-in-law, added in a postscript to her letter, 'I have made bould to send you the booke of news.'[51] It is not clear whether this phrasing indicates some sort of transgressive element to Judith sending the newsbook or whether it might simply be a form of social politeness between mother-in-law and daughter-in-law.[52] Judith was not the only woman to send news to Joan. Joan St John, Barrington's granddaughter, wrote to pass on news from her husband, acting as a conduit for the information, writing, 'my husband comands me to tel you there shal be a parlament; you may beleve it for it cam from my Lord Treseure who told it my Lord Bedford of a sertain. Whither it be cause of joy or sorow, the sucses will shew'.[53] She added, later in the letter, 'I have sent you the book of nus with a map which is new printed.'[54] Barrington's female correspondents may have talked about news less than their male counterparts, but they did still participate in this exchange of news.[55] This disparity is perhaps due to situational constraints. Barrington's male family members primarily sent her news they came across through their acquaintances, or which they witnessed themselves; perhaps the infrequency of news in women's letters is more indicative of the fact that they could not participate in the political sphere in the same way than it is of lack of interest in the news.

Some women clearly also played important roles in transmitting the news, taking their place in extended epistolary news networks between friends and family. Anne Finch, wife of the Earl of Nottingham and daughter of Christopher, Viscount Hatton (1632–1706), relayed news to her father based on news that she herself had received and read.[56] For example, she wrote him an account of the Battle of Steenkerque, fought on August 3, 1692, as part of the Nine Years' War:

> This morning came the Flanders letters that were written Tuesday last w$^{ch}$ bring a fuller account of the battle then anny we had before for now every body has had time to writte to there friends. The Duke of Ormond is not killed but slightly wounded and a prisoner and the Duke of At Albans not mention so I suppose not killed, & by the Imagination of the man y$^{t}$ came from the Duke of Wirtennberg several other officers were killed w$^{ch}$ now prove to be alive for there is not one Collonel killed some slightly wounded but none dangerously escept Comte Solmes and they doe not say if he be dead.[57]

Finch here showed a familiarity with the conflict on the continent that implies regular news reading, and we can speculate that her information came from a newsbook or newsletter. This communication to her father puts her in a position of knowledge and authority: he would have to trust her interpretation and re-telling of events, particularly if he received no other news source.

Mary Hatton Helsby displayed a similar interest in and willingness to discuss the news when writing to her father, Peter Hatton, in 1660. Her letter contains an insightful analysis of the contemporary political situation during the Restoration, as Charles II and Royalist courtiers returned to England from the continent, and the resulting fears about the influence of European Catholicism. The letter is worth quoting at length:

> It will be a gaine full thing me thinks for the countrey when all is settled, but there be some that fear that the manner of ye new Court will be full of the outlandishe breeding of so many in forreine parts for all these years among popishe people. Tis certaine that some do think religion the the [sic] only medicine for ye times we have had after so much bleeding, & to stay any more of such breakings forth out of the body politicke. But methinks too many doctors will be as bad as too few; but tis so easie in seasons of tryall to make ye people beleive in the pleasant doctoring of them that thinke their churche is every thing & the people nothing, which is true enough perhapps of all those that followe such beliefe. I fear me we have much yet to go through if they aim at this, namely, that the popes men shall helpe ye King to governe. Tis not a comfortable thought for any but expecially for ye ffamilyes of those men them selves in after times, who then may live to curse their own fathers & helpe more than any freshe risings & warrings through out ye land.[58]

Hatton Helsby showed no reticence about expressing her opinion here, and she was evidently very well informed about the political upheaval. Her predictions about the future of the country reflect a confidence perhaps born of familiarity with the conflict, perhaps gained through reading newsletters or newsbooks. She was obviously very comfortable about expressing her opinions with such authority to her father, and there is no hint that this was a subject that was unsuitable for her.

This type of communication did not only happen within families. A letter from Jael Boscawen (née Godolphin) to John Evelyn in 1685 demonstrates her role in passing news along:

> I imagine when y$^{u}$ see a letter from me, y$^{u}$ will expect newes, w$^{ch}$ is y$^{e}$ chief reason I have not write to y$^{u}$ sooner, having soe little of any certainty besides what y$^{u}$ will see in y$^{e}$ Gasette perhaps as soon as y$^{u}$ have this, w$^{ch}$ is y$^{t}$ S$^{r}$ John Cochran & his son are both taken in Scotland & Argyle beheaded, y$^{e}$ Rebells in y$^{e}$ west pop up and down in y$^{e}$ close countrey between Bridgewater & Taunton, they plunderd Wells last week, & there was great suspitions that they intended to march towards Exter, where y$^{e}$ Duke of Albemarle is w$^{th}$ y$^{e}$ Malitia of Devonshire, & likewise my Lord of Bathe w$^{th}$ some of his new raised men.[59]

This addresses the Argyll rebellion, led by Scottish lords against James II and VII, which took place shortly before the Monmouth rebellion.[60] Not only does Boscawen clearly play a role in sending him news that the *Gazette* is lacking, but this also appears to have been a standing arrangement, as she references him expecting to receive news from her. Boscawen obviously read the *Gazette*, but combined it with other sources, likely both print and manuscript, to get a fuller picture of events. Moreover, the fact that she was loath to simply repeat what was reported in the *Gazette* implies a certain authority, and suggests that Evelyn saw her (or she saw herself) as a useful source of news in her own right.

Often these communications indicate some sort of political involvement or action on a woman's part. Elizabeth, Lady Mordaunt (née Carey) played her part in an extended news network, as the letterbook of her husband, John Viscount Mordaunt, makes clear.[61] She received and wrote many letters from her husband, other members of her family and various friends and acquaintances, which often consist of in-depth discussions of Royalist affairs in the late 1650s. Mordaunt was deeply involved in the Royalist cause and with her husband's efforts to set up a Presbyterian–Royalist alliance. She often gave advice to her correspondents, and was a key participant in the transmission of news within the network.[62]

Her correspondents often asked her to pass along information or instructions to others. Nicholas Armorer, a Royalist conspirator, for example, wrote to her in October 1659 with news from Bordeaux, and a request for her to pass on news to another correspondent, Colonel Newgent, in his stead:

> I should have writ to Collonel Newgent this day, but I must loose my occasion of going if I doe. Pray, Madame be pleased to send to let him know if he receives no orders from the duke of Yorke, then he has no other thing to doe but to keep his friends right, and to strengthen them as much as may be, untill such time as he have orders from the person most concerned, which he will have with all imaginable speede.[63]

Armorer's letter demonstrates his trust in Mordaunt, allowing her to speak and even give strategic orders on his behalf. There are many such letters within the collection demonstrating Mordaunt's influence: she corresponded in French with General Schomberg, who was the Duke of Schomberg and a marshal of France, and received several letters from Charles II. Her husband clearly relied on her, at one point writing:

> I have so very much to discourse, that you must not chide me if I give you general orders what to doe. In the first place, keep up the designe of Dunkirk. Assure Count Schomburg the warr is begun, and both armies upon their march, Lambert conducts this, and this day we heare nothing but drums and trumpets. 4 regiments march from hence to joyne with the others in Lincolnshire. Monck is come into England with 15 regiments, 9 of foot, 4 of horse, and 2 of dragoons, he has taken Carlisle and Berwick, and marches to Newcastle. I feare Lambert will be too soone distroyed. And if the King loose this opportunity, he will loose both his reputation, and his crown's.[64]

The importance of Mordaunt's role in this communication network is evident, both from the breadth of her correspondence and from the in-depth strategic and political discussions in which she engaged. However, as with many of the women mentioned here, these discussions largely took place in letters from men; there are a few letters between Mordaunt and other women, but these do not contain similar discussions of politics or current affairs.

Mordaunt, Hatton Helsby, Finch and others clearly participated in these epistolary discussions of the news with authority, despite many historiographical claims that women's reading habits, and indeed their lives, were confined to matters of religion and the home. There does not appear to be any hesitation on the part of the women surveyed here to read or report the news, and their male correspondents do not display any condemnation of their interest. Just as the gendered nature of the space of the public sphere has been questioned, so too should the gendering of the genre of news that is so key to the separate-spheres model. By looking at readers, as well as producers, of the news, we can complicate ideas about who could participate in early modern politics.

## Manuscript newsletters

Women received the news from more formalised sources, as well as relying on private correspondence. Manuscript newsletters were a popular form of news communication in the seventeenth century and continued in popularity into the eighteenth century, despite the rise of printed news forms. There are not many clear examples of women receiving such newsletters, but there are certain significant collections that attest to women's engagement with and consumption of newsletters as both a conduit of information and a commercial product. I will discuss two such collections here: a small group of letters sent to Barbara Clopton in 1688–1689 and the much larger Pole newsletter collection (c. 1690–1710).

The Beinecke Library holds a letterbook of newsletters to Lady Clopton from 1688 to 1689, imparting information about the ongoing Glorious Revolution.[65] Barbara Clopton was the daughter of the Royalist Edward Walker, Garter King of Arms from 1645 to 1677 and wife of Sir John Clopton.[66] There is no address on the newsletters but they were probably sent to the family seat of Clopton House, near Stratford-upon-Avon. It appears that these newsletters were commissioned specifically to follow the political events surrounding the revolution, as they only cover a short period of time. On the last letter in the volume Clopton's husband, John, has written: 'News lett.$^{rs}$ $^{my}$ wife had of M$^{r}$ Hamon from K. James his goeing away.'[67] This note makes Lady Clopton's ownership of the newsletters clear, independent of her husband. It also underlines her interest in politics and contemporary news. They give the impression of Clopton having a specific interest in a moment of history, rather than a general desire to stay up to date with current affairs, but her ownership of them (and therefore the information they contained) is emphasised, and hints at a deeper awareness of the significance of the period. The letters are almost completely focused on the progress of the Glorious Revolution; they do not include any international news, and few domestic matters unrelated to the political upheaval are mentioned. They do not seem to favour either the Jacobite or the Williamite cause, but go into detail about the negotiations and political manoeuvrings surrounding William and Mary taking the throne.

The Pole newsletter collection, also held partially at the Beinecke Library, is one of the largest extant newsletter collections belonging to an early modern woman.[68] Between 1690 and 1710, Anne Pole of Radbourne, Derbyshire, received hundreds of manuscript newsletters from London. Pole lived in the hamlet of Radbourne, a few miles away from Derby. She was born Anne Newdigate, daughter of Sir Richard Newdigate, the politically and religiously moderate lawyer and landowner.[69] In 1650, she married Sir German Pole (1626–1683) and lived at the Pole family seat of Radbourne Hall until her death in 1710. German was admitted to Gray's Inn in 1647 and acted as patron for his father-in-law when Newdigate became a serjeant-at-law in 1654.[70] German went on to become High Sheriff of Derbyshire in 1679.[71] After German died in 1683 without issue, the estate passed to Samuel Pole, his closest male relative. Anne remained at Radbourne for the rest of her life, and this appears to be when she first subscribed to the newsletters.

Pole's news reading gives us clues as to her place in the family, and her relationships within both her childhood and marital homes. It is not clear how Pole developed her appetite for current affairs. It was, however, a family pursuit. She came from a political family, albeit one that was not always consistent about its allegiances. Her father, Sir Richard Newdigate, first baronet, was a moderate parliamentarian, serving somewhat reluctantly under Cromwell as serjeant-at-law, a position he was persuaded to take by Royalist friends.[72] Pole's brother Richard, the second baronet, was an avid collector and reader of news, something Barber attributes to him spending a great deal of time at the family estate in Warwickshire rather than in London.[73] Newdigate had a short-lived political career in Westminster, but his Whig leanings and his 'tangential' connection to the Rye House Plot in 1683 led to his early retirement from public life, remaining at Arbury Hall almost constantly from 1681 until his death in 1710.[74] A significant collection of manuscript newsletters belonging to the Newdigate family, numbering nearly 4,000 items, is now held in the Folger Shakespeare Library, shows Newdigate's continued passion for the news.[75]

Pole evidently shared her brother's interest. She even received her own newsletters when she was visiting her family at Arbury, despite Richard's own subscription to scribal newsletters.[76] Perhaps she preferred her own particular newsletter, or wanted to ensure she received her news independent of her brother. Pole had to inform the scribe of her change of address, although this information did not always get through in time. On one occasion the scribe added a note, saying, 'Madam. Being absent I rec$^{d}$ your Letter of the 28 yesterday so my Thursdayes Letter went for Radbourn, & my next will goe to Arbury, if I doe not rec$^{d}$ your order to the contrary.'[77] The effort she made to redirect her newsletters, even for a short trip, are one of the best indications that she took an active interest in them and did read them regularly, as it seems unlikely that she would have them sent to Arbury if they were only a status symbol or occasional pursuit.

The siblings were not receiving identical newsletters. For example, on September 1, 1694, when Pole was staying with her brother, they both received letters. They were, however, written by different scribes, and were not replicas of each other. Pole's newsletter, for example, began, 'this afternoon arrived 2 fforeign Mailes with these following paragraphs', and went on to report news from Madrid and Vienna.[78] The letter to Richard, however, began with news from Edinburgh.[79] This is probably because they were receiving newsletters from different providers. Newdigate was receiving newsletters from John Dyer, amongst others, a successful newsletter writer who appealed to Tories and high churchmen, although who nonetheless attracted readers from across the political spectrum.[80] Pole does not appear to have patronised Dyer, although there are similarly tentative glimpses of her political allegiance: from 1695 she subscribed to *The Post Boy*, sent alongside her manuscript newsletters (see below), which was one of the main Tory news publications in a print market dominated by the Whigs.[81]

There are letters to two other of Pole's family members in the collection held at the Clark Library. Three newsletters addressed to German Pole, Anne's husband, are included, dating from the early 1680s. They were sent in 1682 and 1683, just before German's death. There are also thirteen newsletters addressed to Samuel Pole, German's heir, in the Clark Library collection, dating between 1704 and 1706.[82] It is probable, then, that Samuel and Anne Pole were both receiving newsletters at the same time, although there are no extant newsletters addressed to Anne for the same dates as those addressed to Samuel. She did not receive newsletters at the same time as her husband, possibly indicating that they did share the letters, or that her own interest in the news was not sparked until several years after his death.

While there may be relatively few traces of Pole's response to the newsletters, there is some evidence of her life before she was widowed. She and her husband appear to have had a close, loving relationship. She frequently wrote to him when they were apart, always opening her letters with 'Deare love'.[83] On one occasion in 1653 Anne, staying in London at the time, wrote to German, 'I often wish wee were together.'[84] Her letters to him are full of affection, giving him news of the family's health; however, there are no discussions of political matters or national news. Indeed, German's own politics are hard to determine. He was only sixteen when the Civil War broke out and there are no records of him playing a significant part in the conflict, unlike men from neighbouring gentry families such as the (initially) parliamentarian Sir John Gell or the Catholic Royalist Rowland

Eyre.[85] He did later become involved with local politics and governance, however, acting as High Sheriff of Derbyshire. Given their affectionate relationship, and German's evident interest in the news during his lifetime, it is possible that Pole decided to take the newsletters as a reminder of her late husband. However, she did not start receiving them (or did not start preserving them) until eight years after his death. She did not simply continue his subscription but instead took out one of her own, independent of her husband's interests.

This independence is somewhat unusual in the historical record, and underlines the importance of Pole in the history of news reading. Jason Peacey, when looking at the private circulation of printed news, argues convincingly that 'gentry women were enthusiastic readers and distributors of topical material, who gained access to "printed papers" even in remote parts of the country', suggesting that they often received such material from their husbands.[86] This is certainly true of the many letters we saw earlier in the chapter, where women such as Barrington were sent newsbooks by their male relatives, but it does overlook the role they played in transmitting the news. This was a significant way in which women accessed information; however, women not only received their news through the mediation of other family members but could also be recipients in their own right, as in the case of Anne Pole. While it is possible (I would argue probable) that Pole read news received by her father, brother and husband earlier in her life, once she was widowed, she began to subscribe under her own name.

Her widowhood is key to her news reading. Many scholars have seen women 'operating at [their] most independent' following the death of a spouse, as they became legal entities in their own right.[87] Pole did not subscribe to the newsletters until eight years after German's death, when she was living alongside Samuel Pole and his wife (also called Anne, née Mundy), and crucially she took out a subscription in her own name. As a widow, she would have had more leisure time, relieved of her duties in running the household when Samuel took possession of the estate. She was also a more independent figure. The fact that the newsletters address her specifically is significant – these letters, and the information contained within them, belonged to her. Whatever her reasons for subscribing to the newsletters, Pole was surrounded by politically engaged family members. The Newdigates' interest in following the news is well documented, and the Poles were no doubt similarly aware of the need to remain up to date with current affairs. This may also have played into Pole's identity construction: the newsletters represented her social status and her family's values, providing a link to her father, brother and husband.

Newsletters could also provide evidence of social status beyond the family, with the circumstances surrounding their production and their content conferring a level of socio-economic cachet. The business of manuscript newsletter writing was booming by the late seventeenth century. It is difficult to determine how many newsletter writers were operating in this period, as they rarely signed their work, but there was a significant increase in the number of newsletters circulating in the years of the Popish Plot.[88] Joseph Williamson and Henry Muddiman were key figures in the establishment of *The London Gazette*, but were also heavily involved in the lucrative business of the confidential private newsletter.[89] These manuscript newsletters had a large number of subscribers. Among them, according to James Sutherland, were 'peers and members of parliament, postmasters and country booksellers, clergymen and doctors, army officers, merchants, innkeepers and other, mostly living in England, but some in Scotland and Ireland, and even a few abroad'.[90] They were so popular with certain social groups that Sutherland notes that many gentlemen continued receiving manuscript news even after the expansion of the newspaper press under Queen Anne, as they believed they were able to receive some news not permitted in the printed version.[91]

Manuscript newsletters were often perceived to provide news that printed sources could not – even if this is not entirely true, the perception was important. Scholars have posited that their manuscript, epistolary nature kept them from being censored in the same way as the printed press in the earlier seventeenth century, although it is debated how effective and influential these regulations were in the latter half of the century.[92] Alex Barber has noted that 'elite participants read scribal news to attain information about government, court and parliament' that could not be found in many forms of printed news, which had to focus on events abroad due to censorship laws.[93] This was aided by an assumption that they were essentially private documents.[94] The perception of privacy and the subsequent freedom from censorship meant that they were a prized commodity, conferring a specialised knowledge to the subscriber that could not be found elsewhere.

This is particularly evident in the Pole collection through references to printed news publications, often *The London Gazette*, the paper published twice weekly from 1665 by the office of the Secretaries of State.[95] The *Gazette* had a long relationship with manuscript newsletters, as Natasha Glaisyer has demonstrated; it was often sent alongside scribal newsletters and acted as a 'shared point of reference' for many correspondents.[96] The newsletter frequently supplements or corrects the account given in the *Gazette* with its own information, displaying an evident reliance on Pole reading the newspaper as well.[97] Erin Keating has argued that this way of referencing printed publications indicates the position of the manuscript newsletter within the news genre, and the social status of their readers. She has suggested that the newsletter writers 'clearly position their information as supplementary to the public news, as information meant for a more elite class of reader who can be trusted with sensitive details both with respect to the political events outlined in the papers but also with respect to the gossipy anecdotes'.[98] In choosing to subscribe to manuscript news, therefore, Pole was ensuring that she was provided with information only available to a select group. Not only was she making an effort to stay up to date with current affairs, but she was also accessing a level of knowledge not open to most readers of newspapers and pamphlets.

The relationship between Pole and the newsletter writers also underlines the more elitist nature of the newsletters. There were multiple scribes acting at different times, as several different scribal hands appear. The direct communication between them and Pole, although infrequent, was always marked by a level of deference. There was evident concern to keep Pole updated, and to ensure that she was getting a good product for her money. Methods of payment were discussed, showing some of the mechanics behind the newsletter-writing business. In January 1694 one John Sims (the only time that the scribe is named) addressed Pole directly, discussing the terms of his employment in a note added on to the end of the letter:

> Madam I was ordered by M$^{r}$ Smith to send you this Letter allso acq$^{t}$ you that 4$^{l}$ p[er] annum is the price that all men have that desire to live and perform their buisness dillegently I shall continue the Letter unless I receive an order to the contrary pray order y$^{r}$ Letter directed for me to be left at the Widow Humphreys Coffee house in S$^{t}$ Peters alley Cornhill I am y$^{r}$ Ladyshipps most humble servant – John Sims.[99]

This is the only evidence we have in the whole collection as to the writer's identity, and while we do not know anything more about John Sims, it gives an insight into his profession and the cost of doing his job. It seems that the newsletter writer could negotiate directly with individual recipients about his fee, indicating a degree of autonomy, although the reference to Mr Smith suggests that Sims was in someone else's employ. There was clearly no physical space to house the business, but instead payment was sent to a coffee house in Cornhill, a ward in the City of London and a popular location for the city's coffee houses.[100] This indicates the link between coffee houses and scribal newsletters writers, who often had rooms above coffee houses in which to write, allowing them to make use of the gossip and news exchange going on below. In early eighteenth-century slang, newsletter scribes were even referred to as 'coffee-men'.[101]

'Widow Humphreys' was probably one of several women who took over their husband's coffee house after their death, such as in the case of Bowman's coffee house, which Widow Bowman took on in the early 1660s.[102] It was probably a small establishment in comparison to well-known coffee houses such as Bowman's or Garraway's, as there are few references to it in contemporary sources.[103] The price of £4 per annum was around the norm for manuscript newsletters, with Henry Muddiman charging £5 a year for his newsletters.[104] This is certainly more expensive than the price of the *Gazette*, for example, which was sold at around 1d per copy in the mid-1690s.[105]

Most of the scribes addressed Pole directly at some point, primarily regarding postage problems, but also discussing payment (as above) and occasionally offering seasonal greetings, but they always maintained a deferential tone.[106] The newsletter on December 25, 1693 began by saying, 'Madam, I pray yo$^{r}$ Ladysp to excuse the Brevity by reason of the day.'[107] A few days later, he wrote in a note in the bottom left-hand corner of the last page to thank her for his payment: 'Madam I have rec$^{d}$ my quarterage & humbly thank yo$^{r}$ Ladye wishing you a happy new year.'[108] Evidently Pole paid the scribes quarterly, and it appears to have been common practice to write and thank her for the payment. In October 1694 Sim added similarly on the back of the newsletter, 'M$^{dm}$ I received y$^{e}$ mony and return you humble thanks.'[109]

Another writer excused himself for illness at one point, detailing his afflictions in a very apologetic manner:

> Madame? [sic] The sudden Indisposition which this day was seauenni-ght by stoppadge of urine violent ague, a great paine in the side &$^{did}$ put a stop to my duty in serueing you with my letter these holly dayes for which I begg your favourrable excuse, & haveing got God be thanked this day some reliefe I hoape I will recover my strength as to be able to serve you, as formerly if you please.[110]

This and all other direct addresses to Pole make clear the hierarchical relationship between newsletter writer and reader. Pole is clearly in the position of power, with the scribes providing a service for her, and that relationship is reinforced through all their communication to her. Newsletters such as these were more expensive than broadsides or newsbooks, and could be a marker of status. Indeed, Harold Love has suggested that some newsletter writers 'enjoyed circulations that would have justified printing, if it were not necessary to maintain the supposed exclusivity and hence the high price of the product'.[111] The newsletters for Pole, then, could act as a marker of status, something reaffirmed by the relationship between her and the scribes.

The fact that the newsletters were addressed specifically to 'Madam [or Lady] Pole' most clearly highlights her identity as a possessor and reader of the items. As discussed previously in this book, an autograph signature on the title page of a book could function as a claim to the knowledge held within the text.[112] This can be applied to Pole's newsletters. In naming herself as the recipient of the newsletters, she was laying claim to their specialised knowledge, and fashioning an identity for herself that was highly informed and political.

There is a clear expectation in the newsletters that the reader would be knowledgeable about contemporary politics, and that they would have the reading skills and habits necessary to understand events fully. As mentioned above, there was a symbiotic relationship between printed and manuscript news, and the reliance on information provided by the *Gazette* is evident in these newsletters. In many cases, understanding the context of the news presented would have depended on reading multiple news sources. In June 1692, for example, the newsletter writer reported: '[w]ee rec$^{d}$ yesterday 2 fforraine Mailes of the 10$^{th}$ & 12$^{th}$ ins$^{t}$ which give many particulars of the proceeds of the seige of Namour, but I shall give (without whats mentioned in the Gazett) as briefe an acc$^{t}$ as I can'.[113] If the reader of this passage was not familiar with the *Gazette*'s reporting of the siege, then it is unlikely that the newsletter would have made as much sense. There is clearly an underlying assumption that the recipient of the newsletter would also be reading the *Gazette*. Whether Pole did so or not, we do not know, but it seems likely, given the frequency with which the newsletters cross-reference reports from the publication. Indeed, even if she did not originally read the *Gazette*, she may have been encouraged to by the newsletters, in order to follow the stories properly.

This reading is extensive; Joad Raymond has pointed out that this necessity to cross-reference when reading, either with different publications or referring back to previous newsletters to follow the story, relies on the reader actively engaging with the news being presented and having to develop certain reading skills in order to do so.[114] The interested consumer would have to be fully engaged with all forms of the genre and make an effort to keep up to date, varying their reading habits and reading critically and carefully to understand the news fully. This process was streamlined somewhat by Pole's newsletter writers in the second half of the 1690s, when a hybrid print-manuscript newsletter appeared. Most of the newsletters after about 1695 consist of print publications, either *The Post Boy* or *The Post-Man: And the Historical Account, &c*, with manuscript additions.[115] The printed text covers two sides, and the notes are written on the blank back page, sometimes spilling over to the verso of that sheet,

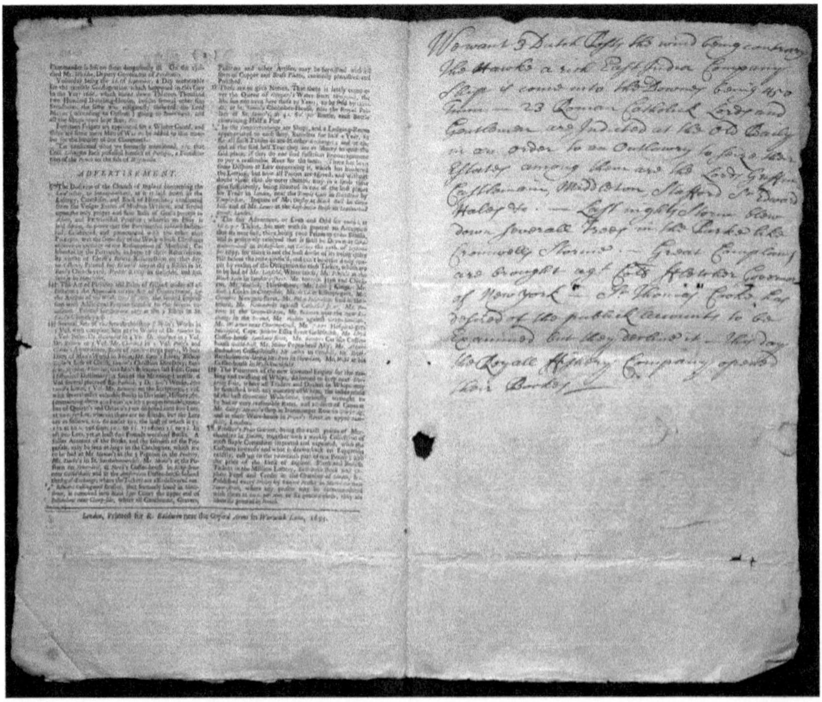

**Figure 3.1:** 31st August–3rd September 1695, box 3, folder 34, MS.1951.021, William Andrews Clark Memorial Library, University of California, Los Angeles.

above the address. The two sections supplement each other: the print publication deals with mostly foreign news, while the manuscript letter generally focuses on domestic events.

The manuscript section, being written after the printed publication, could also provide more up-to-date information. In the manuscript notes on the edition of *The Post Boy* from August 31 to September 3, 1695, the scribe has included an item of news that was not present in the printed sheet (see Figure 3.1). He wrote, '23 Roman Catholick Lords and Gentlemen are Indicted at the Old Baily in an order to an Outlawry to seize their Estates among them are the Lords Griffin Castlemain, Middleton, Stafford S^r Edward Hales &c.'[116] This item of news is then reported in the next edition of *The Post Boy*, covering September 3 to 5, which records:

> Last week at the Sessions held at the *Old-bayley*, there were bills of High Treason found by the Grand Jury against the Earls of *Midleton*, *Stafford*, *Castlemaine*, and the Lord *Griffin*. The Duke of *Berwick* Lieutenant General *Hamilton*, Sir *Edward Hales*, Sir *William Walgrave*, and many others to the number of 23, upon an Account of their being in *France*

> with the late King *James*, and if they do not come back into *England*, and surrender themselves they will be Outlawed, and their Estates confiscated.[117]

Both accounts were referring to a prosecution of Jacobite politicians and courtiers opposed to the Williamite regime. The latter account is more detailed, but it is clear that receiving the newssheet with the manuscript additions could give the reader a much more up-to-date picture of events, which could then be expanded on several days later.

The imagined reader in the newsletters, then, appears to be one with significant reading skills and highly informed about events at home and abroad. There is clearly an assumption of a certain level of knowledge about current affairs, international relations and parliamentary politics. Events are usually reported with little to no explanation of their significance. However, on occasion the writer does provide some explanatory details, for example when discussing the outcome of a court case. He wrote that, 'Mr Croone is now repreived sine die, which is the next door to a Pardon.'[118] *Sine die* is a legal term meaning that no day has been assigned for a hearing, so that the defendant essentially is reprieved through lack of a trial. The writer's explanation shows an awareness that the reader may not have much legal knowledge (*sine die* was a standard term). Conversely, there are other occasions where Latin terms have not been translated, such as when new regulations are introduced for the East India Company. The newsletter reports: '[t]he Regulations, which the K. has made for the E. India Company, are now passed the seales & are in substance the same as were agreed by the H. of Coms & are not for any time of years but Durante Regis Beneplacito'.[119] The writer does not explain the Latin phrase, which means 'for the duration of the king's pleasure', assuming either a level of Latin comprehension or of common political terms. It is not clear if Pole had either, but this level of knowledge was at least assumed by the newsletter writer.

This contrasts to a newsletter from earlier in the seventeenth century, sent to Elizabeth Tollemache, which reveals a very different relationship between scribe and recipient. Tollemache was born Elizabeth Stanhope, daughter of Sir John Stanhope, and married Lionel Tollemache, the MP and Privy Councillor to both James I and Charles I. Their family home was Helmingham Hall in Suffolk. The letter was written in 1619 by one Arthur Grant, whose connection to the family is unclear. He was probably a professional newsletter writer, similar to the scribes who wrote to Pole, but he appears to have had a closer, or more personal, relationship with his reader. Instead of assuming a level of knowledge of the places and events he was describing, Grant wrote Tollemache: 'there is much news abroad but what I send shalbe [sic] true . . . if yo$^{r}$ Ladye$^{sp}$ please to send mee word, of what you doe not understand, because you shall read of strange countres, men and towns I shall in writtinge discribe them'.[120] This concern for Tollemache's comprehension, and the obvious exchange of letters between the two, contrasts with Pole's more detached, business-like interactions with her scribes. Perhaps this suggests that Grant was operating on a smaller scale than the almost mass-produced newsletters that Pole received, something which developed in the later seventeenth century.

In the Pole collection, the writer does occasionally outline hypothetical outcomes of certain events. In February 1691, he wrote that '[t]here is a hott report, that the L$^{d}$ Prestons pardon is passing the seales, which if true, will convince the world, y$^{t}$ he has made a Confession, that deserves the same'.[121] This refers to Richard Graham, Viscount Present, the Jacobite politician due to be executed for treason but whose confession granted him a pardon. On another occasion the writer intimated the potential consequence of the death of the king of Denmark, writing, 'By a Vessell arrived in the North from denmark wee heare y$^{t}$ that King is dead, which if true, & true also, y$^{t}$ his eldest & not second son is in ffrance, some strange things wee may expect to heare upon it.'[122] However, most of the time the consequences of political manoeuvrings or international events are left to the reader's imagination. To discern the significance of these events would rely on a working knowledge of international relations, perhaps one that readers were expected to gain through frequent reading of various news publications.

However, this readerly identity is at odds with the gendered expectations for news readers, which is made obvious through some textual clues. The newsletters appear to have been mass produced to an extent, with a writer creating the same letter for numerous recipients. In the Pole collection the scribes often headed their letters with the word 'S$^{r}$', despite being addressed on the back to 'Madam' or 'Lady Pole'.[123] There are a few newsletters which are headed 'M$^{dm}$' in the Pole collection, but this is relatively rare.[124] The reason for this occasional change is unclear – perhaps the writer simply forgot, most of the time, to use the female address. There is even one occasion where the scribe originally wrote 'S$^{r}$', but then crossed it out and replaced it with 'Madam'.[125] It is evident from this and from the direct messages from the scribe discussed above that they did know they were writing to a woman, but the newsletter writer clearly had a male reader in mind. This suggests either that men made up a significant part of their market or that the ideal audience was thought to be male, irrespective of to whom they were writing. This may have contributed to a general assumption in the historiography that men were the primary readers of newsletters. Most extant large collections of newsletters were addressed to men, although that does not necessarily mean that Pole was unusual in her habits; perhaps many addressed to women were not preserved.[126] Whatever the make-up of their audience, however, the letters are gendered from when they were first written, and in reading them, Pole was subverting expectations.

The newsletters that Anne Pole received would have given her, had she read them diligently, a thorough and detailed knowledge of the political, economic and intellectual developments across early modern Europe, along with a passing familiarity with events in the Americas and the Middle East. She may have been a very well-informed woman, engaged with events far beyond her rural Derbyshire home. She also would have been encouraged to draw on both manuscript and print news sources, reading widely to gain a fuller understanding of events.

The Pole collection is, as stated earlier, unusual in its size and scope, at least for newsletters addressed to a woman in this period. However, we should not assume that she was an outlier among her peers. As demonstrated briefly here, there are other examples of women reading manuscript newsletters, stretching from Elizabeth Tollemache in the early seventeenth century to Barbara Clopton in the 1680s and 1690s. Women in early modern England clearly did and could consume the news, often paying a significant price to receive the more coveted form of the manuscript newsletter. Moreover, their news reading was distinct from the men in their life. Clopton's husband clearly marked her newsletters as 'hers', not his. Pole was receiving her own newsletters at the same time as several male family members were, including her brother and the new owner of Radbourne, Samuel Pole. Pole was choosing to subscribe to newsletters in her own name, despite the fact that others were available in the house at the time. Both women were staking a claim to their own knowledge about current affairs and showing their dedication to following politics.

## Conclusion

We can draw several conclusions about women's news reading from the sources gathered here. Firstly, they were very reliant on manuscript sources, be they scribal newsletters or personal letters containing news. Many clearly supplemented this with printed news media, such as Joan Barrington receiving newsbooks from her friends and family members. However, there is no clear evidence for printed news being their primary source of information. This may be because individuals were less likely to leave evidence of reading printed news, but there are no collections of women's newsbooks comparable to that of Narcissus Luttrell or George Thomason.

Women's news reading, however, relied on networks. These may have been small, professional networks (such as Pole subscribing to her manuscript newsletter), but often they were large, epistolary networks composed of friends and family members. These could form interpretative communities, allowing members to discuss the news at length, as well as giving individuals an editorial role when transmitting information. There was frequently concern for getting the 'truth' of reports and ensuring that they had the most up-to-date and accurate version of events, whether receiving letters or more formalised newsletters. They also received news from multiple sources, relying on a number of informants and types of news media, allowing them to compare, contrast and assess information.

Moreover, news reading could form an important part of a gentlewoman's identity, especially a woman who, like Pole, was socially and financially independent, either in widowhood or having never married. Owning and reading manuscript newsletters, therefore, could allow a woman to highlight certain parts of her character; to demonstrate her independence, her social standing as a member of the gentry and her political allegiances – something which should certainly be considered a political action, if we are to follow Sharpe and Zwicker's suggestion that reading should be seen as political performance.

It is clear, therefore, that more work has to be done to illuminate women's place as consumers of the developing news genre. The assumption that they were not keen news readers overlooks the many women in this chapter who had a clear and demonstrable interest in following the news, and doubtless many more women who are yet to be considered. The examples given here suggest that news reading may have been much more widespread than we have previously acknowledged, even if the archival records are patchy. This will develop not only our view of the news genre but also our understanding of women's participation in early modern politics. News, whether carried in familial letters or in more formalised sources such as newsletters or newsbooks, allowed women to participate in the political sphere, despite often living at some distance from London. Exploring how women consumed the news, and how widespread this practice was, allows us to add another dimension to our understanding of early modern women and politics, showing that even those women who were not openly involved in political matters were far from disinterested in or removed from the early modern political world, but instead viewed it as a crucial part of their identity.

## Notes

1. Kate Loveman, *Samuel Pepys and His Books: Reading, Newsgathering, and Sociability, 1660–1703* (Oxford: Oxford University Press, 2015); David Randall, 'Joseph Mead, Novellante: News, Sociability, and Credibility in Early Stuart England', *Journal of British Studies* 45 (2006): 293–312.

2. Richard Allestree, *The Ladies Calling. In Two Parts. By the Author of the whole Duty of Man, The Causes of the Decay of Christian Piety, and The Gentlemans Calling* (Oxford: Printed at the Theater, 1673), 235.

3. There is a reference in Ben Jonson's poem 'Epigram on the Court Pucell' to the titular women spreading news, framing it as rumour produced by a 'Tribade lust' and written in an 'Epicoene fury'. See Jongsook Lee, 'Who Is Cecilia, What Was She? Cecilia Bulstrode and Jonson's Epideictics', *Journal of English and Germanic Philology* 85, no. 1 (1986): 30. I am grateful to Michelle O'Callaghan for this reference.

4. There have been studies of news readerships and some aspects of news reading, but none have considered women readers in any depth. See, for example, Joad Raymond, *The Invention of the Newspaper: English Newsbooks, 1641–1649* (Oxford: Clarendon Press, 2005); Michael Frearson, 'The Distribution and Readership of London Corantos in the 1620s', in *Serials and Their Readers, 1620–1914*, ed. Robin Myers and Michael Harris (Winchester: St Paul's Bibliographies, 1993), 1–25; Jason Peacey, *Print and Public Politics in the English Revolution* (Cambridge: Cambridge University Press, 2013).

5. Ian Atherton, '"The Itch grown a Disease": Manuscript Transmission of News in the Seventeenth Century', in *News, Newspapers, and Society in Early Modern Britain*, ed. Joad Raymond (London: Frank Cass, 1999), 49.

6. For more on early modern gossip and gender, see Bernard Capp, *When Gossips Meet: Women, Family and Neighbourhood in Early Modern England* (Oxford: Oxford University Press, 2003); Heather Kerr and Claire Walker, ed., *Fama and Her Sisters: Gossip and Rumour in Early Modern Europe* (Turnhout: Brepols, 2015).

7. Elaine Chalus has done valuable work on women's many and varied ways of participating in politics in eighteenth-century England, arguing for a re-framing of the 'political' arena. See, for example, Elaine Chalus, *Elite Women in English Political Life, c.1754–1790* (Oxford: Clarendon Press, 2005).

8. For work on prophecy, see Phyllis Mack, *Visionary Women: Ecstatic Prophecy in Seventeenth-Century England* (Berkeley, CA: University of California Press, 1992); Elaine Hobby, *Virtue of Necessity: English Women's Writing, 1646–1688* (London: Virago, 1988); Diane Watt, *Secretaries of God: Women Prophets in Late Medieval and Early Modern England* (Cambridge: D.S. Brewer, 1998); Manfred Brod, 'Politics and Prophecy in Seventeenth-Century England: The Case of Elizabeth Poole', *Albion* 31, no. 3 (1999): 395–412; Katharine Gillespie, *Domesticity and Dissent in the Seventeenth Century: English Women's Writing and the Public Sphere* (Cambridge: Cambridge University Press, 2004). For work on Quaker women and politics, see Kate Peters, *Print Culture and Early Quakers* (Cambridge: Cambridge University Press, 2005); Catie Gill, *Women in the Seventeenth-Century Quaker Community: A Literary Study of Political Identities, 1650–1700* (Aldershot: Ashgate, 2005).

9. Ann Hughes, *Gender and the English Revolution* (Abingdon: Routledge, 2012).

10. Ruth Herman, *The Business of a Woman: The Political Writings of Delarivier Manley* (Newark, DE: University of Delaware Press, 2003); Derek Hughes and Janet Todd, ed., *The Cambridge Companion to Aphra Behn* (Cambridge: Cambridge University Press, 2004); Jacqueline Broad, *The Philosophy of Mary Astell: An Early Modern Theory of Virtue* (Oxford: Oxford University Press, 2015); Susan Wiseman, *Conspiracy and Virtue: Women, Writing, and Politics in Seventeenth-Century England*

(Oxford: Oxford University Press, 2006); Helen Wilcox, 'Private Writing and Public Function: Autobiographical Texts by Renaissance Englishwomen', in *Gloriana's Face: Women, Public and Private, in the English Renaissance*, ed. S. P. Cerasano and Marion Wynne-Davies (Detroit, MI: Wayne State University Press, 1992), 47–62.

11. Peacey, *Print and Public Politics*, 69.

12. Paula McDowell, *The Women of Grub Street: Press, Politics and Gender in the London Literary Marketplace, 1678–1730* (Oxford: Clarendon, 1998). Claire Walker has done work on the role of nuns in Royalist news networks. See Claire Walker, 'Crumbs of News: Early Modern English Nuns and Royalist Intelligence Networks', *Journal of Medieval and Early Modern Studies* 42, no. 3 (2003): 635–655.

13. See, for example, Marcus Nevitt, 'Women in the Business of Revolutionary News: Elizabeth Alkin, "Parliament Joan", and the Commonwealth Newsbook', in *News, Newspapers, and Society in Early Modern Britain*, ed. Joad Raymond (London: Frank Cass, 1999), 84–108; Marcus Nevitt, *Women and the Pamphlet Culture of Revolutionary England, 1640–1660* (Aldershot: Ashgate, 2006).

14. This was not only true of the late seventeenth and early eighteenth centuries. Ann Hughes has explored the intrinsic association of the public and the masculine in the Civil War period, but notes that their private lives were also key to their political identities. See Ann Hughes, 'Men, the "Public" and the "Private" in the English Revolution', in *The Politics of the Public Sphere in Early Modern England*, ed. Peter Lake and Steven Pincus (Manchester: Manchester University Press, 2007), 191–212.

15. Steven Pincus, '"Coffee Does Politicians Create": Coffeehouses and Restoration Political Culture', *Journal of Modern History* 67, no. 4 (1995): 807–834; Brian Cowen, 'What Was Masculine about the Public Sphere? Gender and the Coffeehouse Milieu in Post-Restoration England', *History Workshop Journal* 51, no. 1 (2001): 127–157.

16. Helen Berry has explored serial publications and the public sphere through examining the *Athenian Mercury*, which appears to have had both male and female readers, and has examined the gendering of that readership. She has also argued that certain women were present in coffee houses, although she noted that they might be there for different reasons to men; notably upper-class women attending social events and women of the lower classes being employed in such establishments. Helen Berry, *Gender, Society and Print Culture in Late-Stuart England* (Aldershot: Ashgate, 2003); Berry, '"Nice and Curious Questions": Coffee Houses and the Representation of Women in John Dunton's *Athenian Mercury*', *The Seventeenth Century* 12, no. 2 (1997): 257–276.

17. Raymond sees it as reflective of a lack of advice on how to read the news; there were books advising how to read and annotate other genres, but this did not exist for news publications, leading him to suggest that a lack of training made people unwilling to annotate their newsbooks and newspapers. He has argued that the method of reading the news was different to the traditional humanist model of active, goal-oriented reading: that people read the news diligently, but without any particular outcome in mind. Joad Raymond, 'Irrational, Impractical and Unprofitable: Reading the News in Seventeenth-Century Britain', in *Reading, Society and Politics in Early Modern England*, ed. Kevin Sharpe and Steven Zwicker (Cambridge: Cambridge University Press, 2003), 204. Atherton, on the other hand, has argued that the lack of annotation was due to the circulation of news publications among friends and family, and an unwillingness to impose one's own interpretation of the news upon subsequent readers. This is not wholly convincing, given early modern readers' complete lack of scruples about annotating other texts that might be passed around family and friends. Atherton, 'The Itch grown a Disease', 51. For recent work on annotation practices, see Katherine Acheson, ed., *Early Modern English Marginalia* (London: Routledge, 2019).

18. There are few examples of news media being collected in the same way that books were in the early modern period, although there are significant exceptions to this in the form of George Thomason and Narcissus Luttrell. For more on contemporary collecting culture, see Marjorie Swann, *Curiosities and Texts: The Culture of Collecting in Early Modern England* (Philadelphia, PA: University of Pennsylvania Press, 2001); Daniela Bleichmar and Peter C. Mancall, ed., *Collecting across Cultures: Material Exchanges in the Early Modern Atlantic World* (Philadelphia, PA: University of Pennsylvania Press, 2011). For more on pamphlet collecting, see Michael Mendle, 'Preserving the Ephemeral: Reading, Collecting, and the Pamphlet Culture of Seventeenth-Century England', in *Books and Readers in Early Modern England: Material Studies*, ed. Jennifer Anderson and Elizabeth Sauer (Philadelphia, PA: University of Pennsylvania Press, 2002), 201–216. For more on news collecting, see Noah Millstone, 'Designed for Collection: Early Modern News and the Production of History', *Media History* 23, no. 2 (2017): 177–198.

19. There has been some excellent work on manuscript news, including Alex W. Barber, '"It is Not Easy What to Say of our Condition, Much Less to Write It": The Continued Importance of Scribal News in the Early 18th Century', *Parliamentary History* 32, no. 2 (2013): 293–316; Rachael Scarborough King, 'All the News That's Fit to Write: The Eighteenth-Century Manuscript Newsletter', in *Travelling Chronicles: News and Newspapers from the Early Modern Period to the Eighteenth Century*, ed. Siv Gøril Brandtzæg, Paul Goring and Christine Watson (Leiden: Brill, 2018), 95–118.

20. Oral transmission of news is also an important facet of this discussion, but not one I plan to explore further here, as I will be focusing on how individuals read the news.

21. Rachael Scarborough King, *Writing to the World: Letters and the Origins of Modern Print Genres* (Baltimore, MD: Johns Hopkins University Press, 2018), 25. This method of reading widely is often explored in relation to the idea of the 'reading revolution' that scholars have outlined for the seventeenth and eighteenth centuries, by which 'intensive', in-depth reading of a small number of (primarily religious) texts was replaced by 'extensive' reading of a broad number of (largely secular) works. This idea was first coined by Rolf Engelsing, but has been repeated, revised and challenged by many scholars since. See, for example, Ian Jackson, 'Approaches to the History of Readers and Reading in Eighteenth-Century Britain', *The Historical Journal* 47, no. 4 (2004): 1041–1054; Reinhard Wittman, 'Was There a Reading Revolution at the End of the Eighteenth Century?', in *A History of Reading in the West*, ed. Guglielmo Cavallo and Roger Chartier, trans. Lydia G. Cochrane (Cambridge: Polity Press, 1999), 284–312. This has not often been considered by historians of early modern news, apart from King and Atherton; Atherton has argued that 'Newsletters had to be read *extensively*. A large volume of news was demanded by the discerning and wise because it was recognized that even the best reports might be uncertain, temporary judgements in need of later confirmation or denial.' Atherton, 'The Itch grown a Disease', 45.

22. Kevin Sharpe and Steven Zwicker, 'Introduction: Discovering the Renaissance Reader', in *Reading, Society and Politics in Early Modern England*, ed. Kevin Sharpe and Steven Zwicker (Cambridge: Cambridge University Press, 2003), 18.

23. Sharpe and Zwicker, 'Introduction', 23.

24. Amanda Vickery, *Behind Closed Doors: At Home in Georgian England* (New Haven, CT: Yale University Press, 2009), ch. 4, accessed December 15, 2020, www-jstor-org.libproxy.york.ac.uk/stable/j.ctt5vkxx9.

25. James Daybell has recognised that 'the treatment of news of all varieties . . . was commonplace in women's letters' in the Tudor period, examining their place in manuscript news networks. James Daybell, *Women Letter-Writers in Tudor England* (Oxford: Oxford University Press, 2006), 152.

26. As Arthur Searle has noted: 'the quantity of letters to Lady Joan Barrington at this period, as well as their content, indicate that she was the focal point of the extended family, the dowager and respected matriarch on a recognisable early seventeenth-century pattern'. Arthur Searle, ed., *Barrington Family Letters, 1628–1632*, Camden Fourth Series Volume 28 (London: The Royal Historical Society, 1983), vii.

27. Searle has focused on this period in order to demonstrate Joan Barrington's place at the centre of an epistolary network, but has included all letters from the collection in chronological order within that date range.

28. Richard Cust, 'News and Politics in Early Seventeenth-Century England', *Past & Present* 112, no. 1 (1986): 69. 'Separates' were a form of manuscript newsletter.

29. Letter 204, October [?] 1631. Searle, *Barrington Family Letters*, 206–207. There is no sense of disapproval in Harris' remark, despite the fact that there was a lot of rhetoric about the problem of people becoming passionate about reading the news in the seventeenth century. Joad Raymond has argued that 'in the increasingly commercialised marketplace of print the mass of injudicious readers threatened to engulf the studied and disciplined few', and that passionate or emotional reactions to the news were seen as disruptive and an 'enemy to reason'. Instead, Harris seems to admire his aunt's taste. See Raymond, 'Irrational, Impractical and Unprofitable', 186, 188.

30. Letter 23, January 28, 1629. Searle, *Barrington Family Letters*, 50–51.

31. Hillel Swartz, 'Arminianism and the English Parliament, 1624–1629', *Journal of British Studies* 12, no. 2 (1973): 41–68; Lori Anne Ferrell, 'Preaching and the English Parliaments in the 1620s', *Parliamentary History* 34, no. 1 (2015): 142–154.

32. Letter 116, February 19, 1630. Searle, *Barrington Family Letters*, 134.

33. Margaret and William Grey's biographies are unclear, although they were ancestors of Sir Charles Grey (1785–1865), a colonial governor in India, whose family papers are held in the Bodleian Library.

34. Letter from William Grey to his mother Margaret Grey, February 23, 1693, Grey Family Correspondence, 1691–1788. MS. Eng. c. 6812, f4r, Bodleian Library, Oxford.

35. Letter 74, October 26, 1624. Joanna Moody, ed., *The Private Correspondence of Jane Lady Cornwallis Bacon, 1613–1644* (London: Associated University Presses, 2003), 122.

36. Letter 105, 1626. Moody, *The Private Correspondence of Jane Lady Cornwallis Bacon*, 148–149.

37. Mark Kishlansky, 'Charles I: A Case of Mistaken Identity', *Past & Present* 189 (2005): 55.

38. Letter 123, April 1628. Moody, *The Private Correspondence of Jane Lady Cornwallis Bacon*, 176.

39. Letter 128, June 11, 1628. Moody, *The Private Correspondence of Jane Lady Cornwallis Bacon*, 181.

40. Letter 169, November 3, 1631. Moody, *The Private Correspondence of Jane Lady Cornwallis Bacon*, 211.

41. Jason Scott-Warren has examined how letters containing news addressed to Thomas Cornwallis allowed him to keep in touch with the wider world, and how news acted as a commodity or gift in such epistles, creating bonds of intimacy between himself and his correspondents. See Jason Scott-Warren, 'News, Sociability, and Bookbuying in Early Modern England: The Letters of Sir Thomas Cornwallis', *The Library* 7th series, 1 (2000): 377–398.

42. Susan Wiseman has done work on how seventeenth-century women engaged with politics through writing. See Wiseman, *Conspiracy and Virtue*. Elizabeth Clarke has also looked at letter-writing as a form of political engagement for women: see

Elizabeth Clarke, 'Beyond Microhistory: The Use of Women's Manuscripts in a Widening Political Arena', in *Women and Politics in Early Modern England, 1450–1700*, ed. James Daybell (Aldershot: Ashgate, 2004), 205–221.

43. Letter 209, October 28, 1631. Searle, *Barrington Family Letters*, 211.

44. Letter 216, November 1631. Searle, *Barrington Family Letters*, 218.

45. Elizabeth Packer to Mary Evelyn, October 21, 1693, Add MS 78436, f83r, British Library, London. The name here is illegible.

46. See, for example, Jacqueline Eales, *Puritans and Roundheads: The Harleys of Brampton Bryan and the Outbreak of the English Civil War* (Cambridge: Cambridge University Press, 1990).

47. Letter 128, Brilliana Harley to Edward Harley, July 16, 1641. Thomas Taylor Lewis, ed., *Letters of the Lady Brilliana Harley, Wife of Sir Robert Harley, of Brampton Bryan, Knight of the Bath* (London: Printed for the Camden Society, 1854), 140.

48. Barbara Donagan, 'Downing, Calybute', *Oxford Dictionary of National Biography*, 2010, accessed May 26, 2019, www.oxforddnb.com/view/10.1093/ref:odnb/9780198614128.001.0001/odnb-9780198614128-e-7980?rskey=45ypi8&result=1.

49. Letter 149, Brilliana Harley to Edward Harley, May 6, 1642. Lewis, *Letters of the Lady Brilliana Harley*, 157.

50. For more on women's letters and female alliances and friendships, see Amanda Herbert, *Female Alliances: Gender, Identity, and Friendship in Early Modern Britain* (New Haven, CT: Yale University Press, 2014).

51. Letter 213, November 5, 1631. Searle, *Barrington Family Letters*, 215.

52. A similar phrase was used by Lady Mary Eden, when she wrote to Barrington, 'I have made bould to send you a token, a payer of gloves to dress you in'. Letter 6, August 13, 1628. Searle, *Barrington Family Letters*, 34.

53. Letter 221, December 1631. Searle, *Barrington Family Letters*, 222. This letter references the uncertainty surrounding Parliament during Charles I's period of personal rule, following the assassination of the Duke of Buckingham in 1628. See Kevin Sharpe, *The Personal Rule of Charles I* (New Haven, CT: Yale University Press, 1992).

54. Letter 221, December 1631. Searle, *Barrington Family Letters*, 223.

55. Of the forty letters sent to Lady Joan Barrington by other women, only six contain items of what we might deem 'political' news – they were much more likely to give information on the health and wellbeing of family and friends.

56. For more on the Hatton family and book collecting, see Nicola Stacey, 'Antiquarian Patronage in the 17th Century: Sir Christopher Hatton's Library at Kirkby Hall', *English Heritage Historical Review* 9, no. 1 (2014): 66–81.

57. Anne Finch to Christopher Hatton, [?] 1692, Add MS 29596, f114r-f114v, British Library.

58. Mary Helsby to Peter Hatton, May 1, 1660, X.d.493 (1), Folger Shakespeare Library, Washington, DC.

59. Jael Boscawen to John Evelyn, July 6, 1685, Evelyn Papers, Vol. CXLII, Add MS 78309, f92r, British Library. Jael's sister-in-law, Margaret Godolphin, was a close friend of Evelyn's.

60. See, for example, A. Kennedy, 'Rebellion, Government and the Scottish Response to Argyll's Rising of 1685', *Journal of Scottish Historical Studies* 36, no. 1 (2016): 40–59.

61. Mary Coate, ed., *The Letter-Book of John Viscount Mordaunt 1658–1660*, Camden Third Series, vol. 66 (London: Offices of the Royal Historical Society, 1945).

62. Nadine Akkerman included a chapter on Elizabeth Mordaunt in her book, examining Mordaunt's political activities. See Nadine Akkerman, *Invisible Agents: Women and Espionage in Seventeenth-Century Britain* (Oxford: Oxford University Press, 2018).

63. Letter 123. Coate, *The Letter-Book of John Viscount Mordaunt*, 91.

64. Letter 123. Coate, *The Letter-Book of John Viscount Mordaunt*, 81. This refers to the army led by General George Monck, Duke of Albemarle, from Scotland into England in support of Charles II.

65. 25 letters of news relative to the abdication of K. James 2 to Lady Clopton, from Mr. Hamon, 1688–1689. Osborn fb210, Beinecke Library.

66. A. M. Mimardière, 'CLOPTON, Sir John (1638–1719), of Clopton, Stratford-on-Avon, Warws', *History of Parliament Online*, accessed June 6, 2021, www.historyofparliamentonline.org/volume/1660-1690/member/clopton-sir-john-1638-1719.

67. Osborn fb210, f358v. Beinecke Library.

68. This collection has been explored by Rachael Scarborough King. King has used Pole as an example of women's participation in a news community; however, I would argue that this moves beyond parliamentary politics, and that a case can be made for women as political actors in a broader sense. King, '"~~Sir~~ Madam": Female Consumers of Parliamentary News in Manuscript Newsletters', *Parliamentary History* 41, no. 1 (2022): 119–134. Also see King, 'The Manuscript Newsletter and the Rise of the Newspaper, 1665–1715', *Huntington Library Quarterly* 79, no. 3 (2016): 411–437; King, *Writing to the World.*

69. The identification of 'Madam Pole' as Anne Newdigate Pole is somewhat speculative, as there were other Anne Poles alive at the time, but given the fact that the newsletters stop almost exactly at the date of her death, and that there is extensive evidence of her visiting the Newdigate seat of Arbury Hall, she seems by far the most likely candidate. For more on the Newdigate family, see Steve Hindle, 'Below Stairs at Arbury Hall: Sir Richard Newdigate and His Household Staff, c.1670–1710', *Historical Research* 85, no. 227 (2012): 71–88; Vivienne Larminie, 'Fighting for Family in a Patronage Society: The Epistolary Armoury of Anne Newdigate (1574–1618)', in *Early Modern Women's Letter-Writing, 1450–1700*, ed. James Daybell (London: Palgrave Macmillan, 2001), 94–108; Larminie, 'Marriage and the Family: The Example of the Seventeenth-Century Newdigates', *Midlands History* 9, no. 1 (1984): 1–22.

70. Joseph Foster, *The Register of Admissions to Gray's Inn, 1521–1889, together with the register of marriages in Gray's Inn Chapel, 165–1754* (London: Hansard Publishing Union, 1889), 243; Vivienne Larminie, 'Newdigate, Sir Richard, first Baronet', *Oxford Dictionary of National Biography*, 2004, accessed December 10, 2020, www-oxforddnb-com.libproxy.york.ac.uk/view/10.1093/ref:odnb/9780198614128.001.0001/odnb-9780198614128-e-20002?rskey=dlDYzJ&result=1.

71. 'A List of the Sheriffs of the several Counties appointed for the Year ensuing', *The London Gazette*, issue 1355, November 11, 1678, 2.

72. Larminie, 'Newdigate, Sir Richard, first Baronet.'

73. Barber, '"It is Not Easy What to Say of our Condition"', 297.

74. Hindle, 'Below Stairs at Arbury Hall', 71.

75. Newdigate family collection of newsletters, Folger.MS.L.c.1-3950, Folger Shakespeare Library, Washington, DC.

76. See, for example, August 28, 1694, box 3, folder 67, OSB MSS 60, James Marshall and Marie-Louise Osborn Collection, Beinecke Library, Yale University.

77. September 2, 1693, box 1, folder 80. MS.1951.021, Clark Library.

78. September 1, 1694, box 3, folder 68, OSB MSS 60, James Marshall and Marie-Louise Osborn Collection, Beinecke Library, Yale University.

79. Newsletter received by Richard Newdigate, Arbury, September 1, 1694. L.c.2366. LUNA: Folger Digital Image Collection.

80. Barber, 'It is Not Easy What to Say of our Condition', 303.

81. Barber, 'It is Not Easy What to Say of our Condition', 299.

82. Box 2, folders 89–98, 106, 112; box 5 folder 9, MS.1951.021, Clark Library.

83. Letters written by Madam Pole. D5557/2/18/1-49, Derbyshire Record Office, Matlock.

84. D5557/1/18/1, Derbyshire Record Office.

85. See, for example, Rosamond Meredith, 'A Derbyshire Family in the Seventeenth Century: The Eyres of Hassop and their Forfeited Estates', *British Catholic History* 8, no. 1 (1965): 12–77. There is relatively little correspondence remaining from the Pole family for the Civil War years. A letter from German to his mother in 1647 only communicates news about friends and family members, not touching on political matters. See D5557/2/4, Derbyshire Record Office.

86. Jason Peacey, *Print and Public Politics*, 69.

87. Sandra Cavallo and Lyndan Warner, 'Introduction', in *Widowhood in Medieval and Early Modern Europe*, ed. Cavallo and Warner (Abingdon: Routledge, 2014), 1.

88. James Sutherland, *The Restoration Newspaper and Its Development* (Cambridge: Cambridge University Press, 1986), 8.

89. Andrew Pettegree, *The Invention of News: How the World Came to Know about Itself* (New Haven, CT: Yale University Press, 2014), 239.

90. Sutherland, *The Restoration Newspaper*, 7.

91. Sutherland, *The Restoration Newspaper*, 8.

92. Sabrina A. Baron, 'The Guises of Dissemination in Early Seventeenth-Century England: News in Manuscript and Print', in *The Politics of Information in Early Modern Europe*, ed. Brendan Dooley and Sabrina A. Baron (London: Routledge, 2001), 47. This suggestion of greater freedom from censorship has been convincingly disputed by King, but the perception of a more exclusive product is the key point here. See King, 'The Manuscript Newsletter and the Rise of the Newspaper', 420.

93. Barber, 'It is Not Easy What to Say of our Condition', 296; Atherton, 'The Itch grown a Disease', 42; Joad Raymond, 'Introduction', in *Making the News: An Anthology of the Newsbooks of Revolutionary England 1641–1660*, ed. Joad Raymond (Witney: The Windrush Press, 1993), 3.

94. Sabrina Baron has suggested that it was possible that newsletters 'could not be divorced from the fact that they were formatted and transmitted in the same way as all letters, making them personal rather than public'. Baron, 'The Guises of Dissemination', 47.

95. Natasha Glaisyer, '"The Most Universal Intelligencers": The Circulation of the *London Gazette* in the 1690s', *Media History* 23, no. 2 (2017): 256.

96. Glaisyer, 'The Most Universal Intelligencers', 262.

97. Glaisyer has noted that this expectation was a common feature in manuscript newsletters. See Glaisyer, 'The Most Universal Intelligencers', 262.

98. Erin M. Keating, 'The Role of Manuscript Newsletters in Charles II's Performance of Power', *Restoration: Studies in English Literary Culture, 1660–1700* 41, no. 2 (2017): 38.

99. January 25, 1693/4, box 3, folder 55, OSB MSS 60, James Marshall and Marie-Louise Osborn Collection, Beinecke Library, Yale University. Pole clearly did not issue any contradictory orders about pay, as Sims continued writing to her until 1695.

100. Brian Cowen, 'The Rise of the Coffeehouse Reconsidered', *The Historical Journal* 47, no. 1 (2004): 33.

101. Barber, 'It is Not Easy What to Say of our Condition', 305.

102. Markman Ellis, *The Coffee House: A Cultural History* (London: Weidenfeld and Nicolson, 2004).

103. Several of the most prominent coffee houses are mentioned in 'Old and New London', including Garraway's and Bowman's, but there is no mention of Widow Humphreys or indeed any other coffee houses in St Peter's Alley. See Walter Thornbury. 'Cornhill, Gracechurch Street, and Fenchurch Street', in *Old and New London: Volume 2* (London: Cassell, Petter & Galpin, 1878), 170–183. *British History Online*, accessed December 16, 2020, www.british-history.ac.uk/old-new-london/vol2/pp170–183. 'Humphrey's Coffee-House' was mentioned in *The Flying Post* in 1697 as a place where people could buy Mr Read's 'Cathartick Pills', which purported to cure a diverse array of ailments – see 'News', *The Flying Post, or the Post-Master*, issue 401, December 7, 1697.

104. Sutherland, *The Restoration Newspaper*, 8.

105. Glaisyer, 'The Most Universal Intelligencers', 265.

106. There are a series of letters in the Clark Library collection from the 1700s that reference ongoing problems with postage, specifically postage charges. See, for example, box 5.

107. December 25, 1693, box 2, folder 46, OSB MSS 60, James Marshall and Marie-Louise Osborn Collection, Beinecke Library, Yale University.

108. December 30, 1693, box 2, folder 46, OSB MSS 60, James Marshall and Marie-Louise Osborn Collection, Beinecke Library, Yale University.

109. October 27, 1694, box 3, folder 71. OSB MSS 60, James Marshall and Marie-Louise Osborn Collection, Beinecke Library, Yale University.

110. January 4, [?], box 2, folder 54, OSB MSS 60, James Marshall and Marie-Louise Osborn Collection, Beinecke Library, Yale University. It is unclear why the writer placed a question mark after the word 'Madame', which heads the letter, but one could speculate that it indicates an uncertainty about the recipient's gender.

111. Harold Love, 'Scribal Publication in Seventeenth-Century England', *Transactions of the Cambridge Bibliographical Society* 9, no. 2 (1987): 141.

112. Rebecca Laroche, '"To take in hand the practice of phisick": Early Modern Women's Signatures in Print Medical Texts', in *New Ways of Looking at Old Texts, IV*, ed. Michael Denbo (Tempe, AZ: Arizona Center for Medieval and Renaissance Studies, 2008), 271.

113. June 7, 1692, box 1, folder 21, OSB MSS 60, James Marshall and Marie-Louise Osborn Collection, Beinecke Library, Yale University.

114. Raymond, 'The Newspaper, Public Opinion, and the Public Sphere', 132.

115. This was an amalgamation of two publications: *The Post Boy, With Foreign and Domestic News*, established in May 1695, and *The Historical Account, &c*, which then became *The Post-Man* in October 1695 after the original print of *The Historical Account* withdrew. See Stanley Morison, *The English Newspaper: Some Account of the Physical Development of Journals Printed in London 1622–1932* (Cambridge: Cambridge University Press, 1932), 57–59.

116. August 31 to September 3, 1695, box 3, folder 34, MS.1951.021, Clark Library.

117. September 3 to 5, 1695, box 3, folder 34, MS.1951.021, Clark Library.

118. Undated, box 1, folder 2, OSB MSS 60, James Marshall and Marie-Louise Osborn Collection, Beinecke Library, Yale University.

119. November 14, 1693, box 2, folder 40, OSB MSS 60, James Marshall and Marie-Louise Osborn Collection, Beinecke Library, Yale University.

120. Arthur Grant, Autograph Letters signed to Elizabeth Tollemache, 1615–1619, Misc Mss, Clark Library.

121. February 28, 1691, box 1, folder 4, OSB MSS 60, James Marshall and Marie-Louise Osborn Collection, Beinecke Library, Yale University.

122. July 21, 1692, box 1, folder 24, OSB MSS 60, James Marshall and Marie-Louise Osborn Collection, Beinecke Library, Yale University.

123. King has observed a similar habit in the Hobson/Newey newsletters, which were sent to either Mrs Hobson or Mrs Newey, but were frequently headed with 'Sir'. King, 'All the News That's Fit to Write', 115; King '~~Sir~~ Madam'.

124. January 1693/4, box 3, folder 55, OSB MSS 60, James Marshall and Marie-Louise Osborn Collection, Beinecke Library, Yale University.

125. December 21 to 24, 1695, box 3, folder 38, MS.1951.021, Clark Library.

126. The Folger finding aid for the Newdigate papers has lists of similarly significant collections of newsletters; of these, the Pole collection is the only one specifically addressed to a woman. However, as demonstrated in this article, there are a number of smaller collections of newsletters addressed to women. See 'Newdigate Family Collection of Newsletters', *Folger Finding Aids*, accessed January 20, 2019, https://findingaids.folger.edu/dfonewdigate.xml.

Chapter 4

# Women reading science and philosophy: medical, culinary and philosophical knowledge

The connections between early modern science and early modern print have attracted a great deal of scholarly attention.[1] Within this, women's reading of scientific or philosophical texts in the seventeenth century has certainly been discussed, but largely in relation to women's writing practices. The reading habits and book collections of well-known philosophers such as Margaret Cavendish and Anne Conway have been carefully examined, often with a view to exploring how they formed their own thoughts and ideas.[2] However, this is once again relatively episodic, focusing on extraordinary women who are known for their scientific endeavour and interest.[3] There have been few considerations of how women generally interacted with the ever-growing genre of scientific literature, although it has been argued that the move away from the primacy of academic institutions in seventeenth-century intellectualism precipitated a rise in women's involvement in science.[4] This chapter will think about how women interacted with and used scientific and philosophical texts in their lives. There are some instances here of women who were clearly reading in order to make a contribution to the intellectual field, but there are also more domestic forms of 'science'. If, as Elaine Leong, amongst others, has suggested, we broaden the scope of what we consider 'scientific', women's understanding of and interactions with science become much clearer.[5]

In doing so, what also becomes clear is the way that women were presenting themselves as diligent, scholarly and experimental readers and writers. They were drawing on some of the most influential and up-to-date ideas about science and philosophy, and constructed themselves as intellectual participants in the debates. They were also using practices associated with scholarly reading to do this, often using annotation and excerpting as part of their reading.[6] This is true whether they were aiming to create a career as an intellectual figure (as Mary Astell did) or were creating recipes to be used in the quotidian life of the household. Lara Dodds has argued that Cavendish's work 'reinsert[ed] experiment into the experience of domestic spaces', showing, as Wendy Wall does, the creation of knowledge that happened within the household.[7] Dodds has convincingly argued that Cavendish's life-writing 'participates in the interrogation of the foundations of modern science and modern subjectivity' – that in exploring the 'self' through textual form and thinking about the nature of experience, life-writing itself functions as a form of scientific endeavour.[8] If we extend this to women's reading practices (which, as I have argued throughout this book, are a way of negotiating and creating a form of selfhood), we can better understand women's participation in early modern science. Reading scientific works (similarly to reading the news, as explored in Chapter 3) was a way for women to have active involvement with early modern science and philosophy, despite the many barriers that excluded them from the institutional spaces of early modern science.

This chapter will deal with examples of both scientific and philosophical reading, viewing them as fundamentally connected disciplines. This follows the argument made by David Marshall Miller and Dana Jalobeanu that 'the emergence of modern philosophy and that of modern science were not separate phenomena, but facets of the same transformations, taking place in the same period, in texts often written by the same authors'.[9] Therefore, a certain blurring of boundaries between the types of knowledge is appropriate – Mary Astell, for example, read Descartes' thoughts on the laws of motion very carefully. This chapter will focus on texts that broadly dealt with questions about how the world worked, including philosophy, natural history, mathematics, medicine and other forms of science.

Despite the fact that women were rarely admitted to scientific institutions, reading scientific and philosophical works was not discouraged for women. As the seventeenth century progressed, more writers perceived a female market for scientific works, and some were published specifically with women readers in mind.[10] John Evelyn, when writing instructions for how his daughter Mary should pass her time in the early 1680s, suggested that after playing her harpsichord she could 'or looke over what you have learn'd of Geometrie &c: that you may have some usefull notions, and not be altogether ignorant how God has by his various providences governed the World, & therefore you may also profitably reade over the English

Histories, consult Herbals, & Natural Histories &c'.[11] The study of science, through multiple disciplines, is presented by Evelyn as a way of better understanding God's world, and therefore important for shaping a young girl's mind.

Conduct book writers also increasingly emphasised the need for women's education in the seventeenth century. This was not always specifically scientific, but there was a growing movement that valued education for women, largely to make them better conversationalists in their interactions with men.[12] A few writers, however – largely women – extolled the importance of scientific education in order for a woman to fulfil her role in the household. In the 1670s, the scholar and teacher Bathsua Makin argued:

> To buy Wooll and Flax, to die Scarlet and Purple, requires skill in Natural Philosophy. To consider a Field, the quantity and quality, requires knowledge in Geometry. To plant a Vineyard, requires understanding in Husbandry: She could not Merchandize, without knowledge in Arithmetick: She could not govern so great a Family well, without knowledge in Politicks and Oeconomicks: She could not look well to the wayes of her Houshold, except she understood Physick and Chirurgery: She could not open her Mouth with Wisdom, and have in her Tongue the Law of kindness, unless she understood Grammar, Rhetorick and Logick.[13]

This passage contains a broad suggested curriculum for women, but it is worth noting that she still connected this education to a woman's role within the household. Makin had a more complex conception of the domestic sphere than many of her male predecessors and contemporaries, and of the various skills needed to fulfil a woman's traditional role.[14] She emphasises the need for a well-rounded scientific education: a woman needed to understand natural history, geometry, mathematics and medicine in order to properly keep a home.

In the 1690s, Mary Astell argued that women (of a certain class) should be taught foreign languages and use that knowledge in order to read philosophy, saying, 'since the *French Tongue* is understood by most Ladies, methinks they may better improve it by the study of Philosophy (as I hear the *French Ladies* do) *Des Cartes, Malebranche,* and others, than by reading idle *Novels and Romances*'.[15] She went on to defend women gaining knowledge, arguing, 'as unnecessary as it is thought for Women to have Knowledge, she who is truly good finds very great use of it, not only in the Conduct of her own Soul but in the management of her Family, in the Conversation of her Neighbours and in all the Concerns of Life'.[16] Astell implicitly acknowledged the potential dangers of women's learning, but argued that as long as they were morally and spiritually good, they would benefit from education; that knowledge acquisition would help them to fulfil their role in life.

Science and philosophy, then, were increasingly becoming acceptable topics of reading for women. In this chapter I explore the extent to which this is reflected in women's actual reading habits. I will demonstrate how scientific reading was not just the preserve of 'extraordinary' women such as Cavendish and Conway, but that many women owned texts that might be deemed scientific in nature. The extent to which they used and engaged with these texts varied, but they were certainly familiar genres, as is demonstrated by contemporary book lists and autograph signatures. I will discuss one woman who was known for her philosophical output – Mary Astell – but I am less interested in how her reading informed her views and more interested in putting her reading first; I explore what we can discover about her reading habits from her annotations and book collection, and how they can show her construction of an intellectual identity.

I will then move on to think about women's scientific manuscripts, namely recipes books and collections of medical receipts. Much of the evidence for women's reading of science and indeed their scientific practice comes from manuscript texts, not printed ones.[17] As with Chapter 3, if we overlook the manuscript nature of women's reading habits, we can only gain a very partial understanding of their participation in seventeenth-century thought. The scientific revolution has often been closely tied to print culture, but women's manuscript books show perhaps the most sustained, widespread and experimental engagement with scientific ideas.[18] They were clearly drawing on printed texts, but also on their own experience and practice to test theories and ideas. In doing so, they marked out a place for themselves as educated experimenters and situated themselves within sociable and intellectual networks.

## Her philosophy: ownership and annotation

Scientific texts were frequently present in book lists and inventories, showing that women were not concealing their reading. Perhaps one of the most famous records of female book ownership, Lady Anne Clifford's *Great Picture* contains depictions of books such as Gerard's *Herbal*, as well as a manuscript volume of 'Alchemist Extractions, of Distillations and excellent Medicines' compiled by Lady Margaret Clifford, Anne's mother.[19] This was not unusual: as mentioned earlier, the majority of seventeenth-century book lists focus on religious or devotional texts, but books such as herbals or medicinal tracts frequently appear.[20] In the catalogue made of Lady

Margaret Heath's library (which we briefly examined in Chapter 1), there are several medical works listed, including 'Gerards Herball in fol. uncolourd', 'Gerards Herball in fol. coloured', 'Woodhalls Chirurgery fol.' and 'Wirtsungs practise of phisick fol.'.[21] Gerard's *Herbal* was an extremely popular book that was often found in women's book lists, although the fact that Heath owned two copies, 'coloured' and 'uncolour'd', is notable. 'Wirtsungs practise of Phisick' was *The General Practice of Physick*, a translation of a text written by German physician Christoph Wirsung.[22] The final title is perhaps more unusual. 'Woodhalls Chirurgery' is probably a book by John Woodall, who was appointed the first surgeon-general of the East India Company in 1613.[23] Woodall published *The Surgions Mate, or A Treatise discovering faithfully and plainely the due contents of the Surgions chest* in 1617, a text that was chiefly aimed at sea surgeons and which reflected Woodall's interest in Paracelsian iatrochemistry.[24] This appears to have much less relevance to Heath's everyday life than Gerard's *Herbal*, indicating that she may have had an interest in surgical method or in Woodall's Paracelsian ideas. It has been recognised that women often had an interest in Paracelsian concepts and alchemy more generally, particularly its ideas about medicine and pharmacology.[25] Alternatively, she may have been given the book or kept it for some reason unrelated to the actual contents; it is very difficult to know the motivations behind book lists, but Heath's ownership of this text does suggest that some women interacted with scientific books that did not have any immediate 'use'.

The inventory of Elizabeth Sleigh's books, also made in 1647, similarly contains a copy of *The General Practice of Physick*, although this one is listed under the name of the translator 'Dr Mosan' (Jacob Mosan). Sleigh's inventory also includes 'Gwillimeau$^{s}$ Childbirth, 4$^{to}$', which refers to Jacques Guillemeau's *Child-birth or, The Happy Delivery of Women*.[26] Elizabeth Freke's book list, created in 1705, includes 'i book of cirgiary by Colebach', 'i Compleatt Herball by Peachy', '2 new books of Cullpepers phisick' and 'i book of the Family Phisition'.[27] She also added 'i abstractt of Gerralds herbal of my wrightine now in the great black trunke', indicating that she also made her own copies or summaries of texts and included them with the rest of her printed books. Some women, however, also read more esoteric scientific works. Heath owned a copy of 'Bacons naturall History' in folio. Freke also included 'i abstract of P Helins geography, quarto' in her inventory. This was probably Peter Heylyn's *Cosmographie*, which had been through seven editions by 1703.[28] This is not necessarily something that would be seen as unusual for women, at least not educated, wealthy women; as mentioned at the start of this chapter, a rounded education in science and philosophy was seen as part of an effort to understand God's works.

There is evidence of women reading or owning scientific texts from inscriptions and marginalia, although again admittedly this is nowhere near as common as religious texts. Nevertheless, there are some good examples of ownership inscriptions. Many of these come without other, more extensive annotations, but there is still an ownership claim at work. A copy of James Hodder's *Arithemetick*, for example, held in the Beinecke Library, bears the signature of 'Miss Elizabeth Bantoft her booke 1668' on the front flyleaf.[29] Bantoft also left a more embellished signature on the following page, with artistic details on the letters, reading, 'Miss Elisab. Bantoft Oct.19.68'. This may have just been a pen trial, but the 'her booke' and the dates on both inscriptions suggest she was making a claim to owning the book itself. Hodder's *Arithemetick* was a very popular text, aimed at introducing readers to mathematics (James Hodder was a mathematician and school teacher).[30] Bantoft then was perhaps interested in furthering her education, or using the book as a reference text – although this is just speculation, as without any further annotations it is hard to tell the extent of her interaction with the text.

The Beinecke also holds a copy of Robert Fage's *Cosmography*, signed on the inside front cover 'Ann Avery her Book 1678', but similarly lacking in any other signs of use.[31] An edition of Philip Barrough's *The Method of Phisicke* in the Huntington Library is the same; it is signed on the title page 'The Lady Bacons booke' but otherwise unannotated.[32] The Wellcome Library's copy of Jane Sharp's *The Midwives Book* has been signed by two women in the same family, in what look like late seventeenth-century hands: one of the front flyleaves bears the signature 'Mary Rowe' with what looks like 'her Book' (although this has been damaged and is not fully legible), while one of the back flyleaves reads 'Abigall Rowe her Book and hand'.[33] This may have been a competing ownership claim or the book may have passed from one woman to another, either as part of inheritance or as a gift. Unfortunately, there are no other details to explain these women's relationship or the extent to which they interacted with the book.

However, certain readers did provide more extensive annotations on their works. This is unusual but invaluable in determining how individual women read their philosophical and scientific works. Mary Astell, who was such a strong proponent of women's education, left a remarkable collection of annotations on her books. Astell's library has recently been uncovered at Magdalene College, Cambridge, and reveals a great deal about her reading habits.[34] She read many texts that were philosophical or scientific in nature, principally from French thinkers such as René Descartes and Nicolas Malebranche. Astell annotated her books to varying extents, but a few texts in her collection bear extensive and highly revealing annotations. Astell is often called a Cartesian and the influence of

Descartes can certainly be seen in her library, which contains many of his publications.[35] However, as Jacqueline Broad has pointed out, she was also influenced by the 'Neoplatonist and Augustinian principles at work in the philosophies of Nicolas Malebranche and John Norris', and was not afraid to read works that disagreed with Cartesian principles.[36] Astell's library and indeed her annotations on her books attest to her broad philosophical interests and influences, and her sense of her place in the intellectual culture of the time.

Astell's reading notes represent her as a reader who was fully participating in the debates and discussions within her books. She constructed an image of a reader who made every effort to understand the nuances of the ideas in the text, cross-referencing and creating systems to parse the text. She is the perfect example of an active and extensive reader, in the scholarly sense of the terms, even working to ensure that she checked the most recent or 'best' editions to be as well informed as possible. This all worked to justify her participation in the intellectual network of philosophers that she was reading – she was an active participant in the debates. Her copy of Descartes' *Les Principes de la Philosophie* is the most heavily annotated in the Magdalene collection. It shows the extent to which she used manuscript notes to structure and understand her reading. The text itself is in French, which Astell learnt as an adult, and her annotations are in a mix of French and English. Astell frequently cross-referenced other texts in her annotations, showing the breadth of her reading and her efforts to understand certain topics. For example, she added a lengthy marginal annotation to her copy of Descartes' *Principes*, which reads:

> Plato whom y$^{e}$ Antients say follow'd Heraclitus in Physic's taught, que nos sens sont fort sujets à se tromper, & qu'il n'y a point dans leur deposition de verité seure. La Vie de Plato par Dacier p.76. He believ'd there was but one world; y$^{t}$ all things were produc'd by their contrarys; yt Beings were produc'd by Motion, wch he calls war, & yt there dissolution was from Rest Ibid La vüë & l'oüye ont ells quelque sorte de verité, & leur deposition est elle fidelle ou le Poëtes ont ils raison de nous chanter que nous n'entendons ni ne voyons rien veritablem$^{t}$. & so says Socrates in Phado p.174 & adds yt if these two senses are neither true nor sure, y$^{e}$ other y$^{t}$ are more feeble must needs be less so.[37]

The printed passage it corresponds to is marked with an '(a)' and is about the senses and how they can be mistaken. Here Astell explicitly mentions two texts, even providing page numbers. The *La Vie de Plato* she mentions was by André Dacier, the French classicist and translator.[38] There is no evidence of Dacier's text in Astell's library at Magdalene, but that does not mean she did not own it; she may also have borrowed the text. The French portion of the annotation was copied directly from Dacier's *Les Oeuvres de Platon*, for which the page reference is correct, but Astell also summarised some of the previous page by mentioning Plato following Heraclitus.[39] We know from a note on the upper pastedown that Astell had used the Descartes text in some way in July 1695 (whether this was the date of purchase, of reading or of annotating is unclear); Dacier's text had been published the previous year, so she was drawing on very up-to-date works in her reading notes.

The second reference she included was also to Dacier's *Platon*, this time the second volume, in which he has translated the *Phaedo*.[40] Again, the French passage is copied directly from Dacier, but this time Astell added a brief translation in her own words, summarising the rest of Socrates' speech. It seems that she must have been reading the Descartes text with Dacier's *Platon* to hand: as the translations are so exact, she must have copied them directly from the text. This is clearly evidence of extensive reading and reading to better understand an issue – Astell was drawing on multiple texts to consider the concept of the senses. She may have had several reasons for writing this down, but it was in all likelihood part of her intellectual process. The marginal notes may have served as a way of thinking through the issues, or may have been intended to help her remember the links she had made at a future date (or both).

There is evidence of Astell reading complementary texts in tandem in order to better understand the ideas. Dacier's *Platon* was clearly an important text to Astell. Intriguingly, she wrote a very similar note to the one above on another book in her collection. On her copy of the first volume of Nicolas Malebranche's *De la Recherche de la Verité*, she wrote, 'Plato taught que nos sens sont fort sujets à se tromper, & qu'il n'y a point dans leur deposition de verité seure en sa vie p76' below 'Chapitre VI'.[41] The chapter itself is about sight and how we can be deceived by our eyes. Astell shortened her annotation from Descartes, but the quote from Dacier is word for word the same as in the other annotation. This appears to suggest that she was reading with a purpose: she was interested in gathering knowledge about the senses and built up that knowledge by cross-referencing several texts.

Astell's commitment to Cartesian ideas is demonstrable in many of her references to other texts. In her copy of the second volume of Malebranche's *De La Recherche de la Verité*, at the end of the table of 'éclairissements' (explanations or glossary), she wrote:

> That Beasts are only machines was Maintain'd by a Spanish Physician Gomesius Pareira who publish'd it at Medina del Campo 1554 in a book

> yt cost him 30 years labour, call'd Antoniana Margarita, He liv'd in y$^{e}$ 1500 not in y$^{e}$ 1200 contrary as l'Abbe Gerard in his Philosophie des Gens de Cour would have it. See La Bête transformée en Machine par J Darmanson 12 1684.[42]

Astell here was engaging with the beast–machine controversy; over whether animals had souls or were simply automata, as proposed by Descartes in his *Discourse on the Method* in 1637.[43] Malebranche was also an animal automatist and *Recherche de la Verité* argued that God provided the intelligence displayed in animals.[44] The Spanish physician is Gómez Pereira, whose work on the nature of animals as machines preceded Descartes by many years.[45] Descartes supposedly denied any familiarity with Pereira's work.[46] Astell appears to be advocating for Pereira's influence, but her broad knowledge of the ideas relevant to Cartesian philosophy comes across clearly; she evidently read very widely and was highly knowledgeable about the development of such ideas. Her particular interest in animal automatism – something which occupied not only Descartes and Malebranche but also John Norris, whose influence on Astell is well documented – is clear from this note, if not from other annotations; she evidently read in depth on the development of the theory.[47]

There is more evidence of Astell's extensive reading habits at the end of her copy of Descartes' *Principes*. On the lower pastedown, for example, she wrote:

> According to M. Halley in Philers.Trans. Sept or Oct 1688 by an experim$^{t}$ mention'd there in 24 hours 6 ounces of water evaporated from a surface of 8 Inches Diameter, & thence he concludes yt 60 square Inches surface furnish in vapours a Cubic Inch of Water. Each square foot half a pint four sq feet a Gallon. A Mile square 6914 Tun, a Degree sq (viz. 69 Miles sq) exhales 33 Millions of Tuns.[48]

She was referring to an article by Edmund Halley in an edition of *Philosophical Transactions*, the journal of the Royal Society. The article was about gravity, something Astell had made lengthy notes on earlier in her Descartes text. Together with Descartes' text, Astell had bound a series of plates (which were often sold separately by booksellers) and many blank pages which she covered with her own copious notes. These relate to various scientific ideas expounded in the text, such as the laws of motion, and there is a long section on gravity.

The fact that she linked to Halley in particular, however, shows another facet of her reading; that she was willing to engage in debates and challenge Cartesian ideas. In the article, Halley quite explicitly criticised Descartes' *Principes*, writing:

> *Des Cartes* his Notion, I must needs confess to be to me Incomprehensible, while he will have the Particles of his *Celestial Matter*, by being reflected on the Surface of the *Earth*, and so ascending therefrom, to drive down into their places those *Terrestrial Bodies* they find above them: This is as near as I can gather the scope of the 20, 21, 22 and 23 *Sections* of the last Book of his *Principia Philosophiae*; yet neither he, nor any of his Followers can shew how a body suspended *in libero aethere*, shall be carried downwards by a continual Impulse tending upwards, and acting upon all its parts equally: And besides the obscurity wherewith he expresses himself particularly, *Sect.* 23 does sufficiently argue according to his own Rules, the confused *Idea* he had of the thing himself.[49]

Astell did not address this criticism; however, the fact that she included a mention of Halley, and particularly an article in which he was so scathing of Cartesian ideas, shows her wide reading. She was evidently willing to read across the philosophical barricades; she did not only read texts that agreed with one another but drew from texts that explicitly disagreed in order to form her own views.

All of the examples above do not show any explicit reference to the links between the texts; rather, we are left to infer them from the placement of the annotation and similarities between the subjects. However, there is one example from Astell's library where she quite clearly made a comparison between two authors. On the upper endpaper of Astell's copy of Malebranche's *Meditations Chrestiennes*, she wrote a note about the work of Sir Francis Bacon:

> so much is the mind of Man dispos'd to love order, y$^{t}$ my Ld Bacon reckons it among his Idola tribus, "y$^{t}$ y$^{e}$ intellect of man has an innate propensity to suppose in things a greater order & equality y$^{n}$ it finds (another of y$^{m}$ is "y$^{t}$ being unable to rest or acquiesce it does always tend further & further) apud y$^{e}$ Reconcile: of Reas. & Relig. P30 How well does y$^{s}$ agree w$^{th}$ Maleb.[50]

Astell was suggesting that Malebranche and Bacon would agree, making links between the two philosophers. Bacon coined the term *Idola Tribus* (Idols of the Tribe) in his *Novum Organum* to describe the idea that humans are often drawn to certain incorrect conclusions about the world. Astell made a very valid link between the two philosophers; they shared ideas about the importance of logic, and Malebranche was influenced by Bacon.[51] Astell was clearly thinking carefully about the ideas presented by various philosophers regarding the human mind and paying attention to the similarities between them.

However, in her annotation Astell was actually quoting from a text written by Sir Robert Boyle, *Some Considerations about the Reconcileableness of Reason and Religion*. Boyle mentions the ideas of 'Verulam'; Bacon was granted a peerage as the Baron of Verulam. Astell quoted directly from Boyle, but she broke the quote up. Boyle's text reads, 'As that the Intellect of Man has an innate Propensity to suppose in things a greater order and equality than it finds, and that being unable to rest or acquiesce, it does alwayes tend further and further', whereas Astell put the second half of this passage in brackets, presenting it as a quote taken from a different section of the book.[52] The fact that she quoted this way, rather than drawing directly on any of Bacon's published writings, indicates that perhaps she did not have them to hand; she may not have read or owned any of Bacon's works (he does not appear in the library she left to Magdalene College).

Astell was also very concerned that she acquired the best edition of her books in order to further her understanding even more. In a number of her texts she wrote notes about different editions, usually on or near the title page. On the title page of Descartes' *Les Meditations Metaphysiques*, she wrote, 'Y$^{e}$ first Edit. was at Paris 1641 y$^{s}$ being y$^{e}$ 2$^{d}$ work he publish'd y$^{e}$ first having for Title Discours de la Methode pour bien conduire sa raison, chercher la verite dan les sciences. Plus la Dioptrique les Meteores & la Geometrie qui sont des essais de cette methode A Leyde, publish'd June 8 1637.'[53] This refers to Descartes' *Discourse on the Method*, originally published in Leiden, alongside essays about the nature of light ('la Dioptrique') and geometry. Astell clearly had a good understanding of Descartes' whole oeuvre, including when each of his texts were published, despite the fact that not all of his works are included in her library. Her note contextualised the book within Descartes' other publications, paying attention to the paratextuality of his work. She also added a note about the translation, writing at the bottom of the title page, 'The Duke De Luines translated the Meditations & Mr Clersehier ye Answers & Objections', giving some provenance for the text.

There is an even longer note about editions in Astell's copy of Malebranche's *Recherche de la Verité*, this time on the verso of the title page:

> This Book was first Printed at Paris 1677 The best edition is the 5$^{th}$ Paris chez Michel David 1700. In wch one many alterations & additions as I have here inserted ym besides new illustrations. The Author in an Advertismt tells il y a plus de vingt-cinq ans que cette ouvrage est compose, & how this agrees wth ye Letters Patents before this Edit. In 1700 dated March 27 1677. The Author tells us ye best

> editions of his works are as follows 1 Conversations Chretiennes, Rouen, 1695 2 Traite de la nature & de la Grace Rotterdam chez R Leers 3 Traite de morale Lyon 1697 4 Meditationes Chretiennes Lyon 1699 5 Responses a M Arnaud Rotterdam six little volumes in different years 6 Entretiens sur la Metaphysiques & sur la Religion Paris 1696 7 Traite de l'Amour de Dieu & la Suite Paris 1699 & he would have ym read in this order.[54]

This passage has several important points. Astell noted that she took 'additions' and 'alterations' from the 'best edition' of *Recherche* and added them into her copy, demonstrating her desire to get the best from her text and reflect the most up-to-date version of Malebranche's ideas. This implies she had perhaps borrowed the edition from 1700, perhaps from a friend or acquaintance; if she owned it, there would be little point in making the alterations to her 1677 copy. She was also obviously interested in Malebranche's editorial comments and his concept of his own oeuvre, as she made a note of his rankings of his own books.

Astell made the effort to acquire these 'best editions' of Malebranche's works, or at least to remind herself of which were the superior copies. She owned the copy of *Traité de la Nature et de la Grace* printed 'chez Rainier Leers' and noted on the title page that 'y$^{s}$ is y$^{e}$ best edition, according to y$^{e}$ Author in his Advertisement to his search after Truth (5$^{th}$ Edit. Paris 1700 w$^{ch}$ is y$^{e}$ best)' (referring back to the 1700 edition of *Recherche*).[55] In her copy of *Traité de Morale*, she wrote 'Lyon 1997' on the title page – this was not that edition, but clearly she wanted to remind herself which one was the best.[56] Similarly, on her copy of Malebranche's *Meditations Chrestiennes*, she wrote at the bottom of the title page: 'best Lyons 1699 Responses a M Arnaud a Rotterdam 6 little volumes in different years', quite clearly harking back to the note on *Recherche*.[57]

Astell's concern for the best editions of her scientific works shows her intellectual rigour; with both Descartes and Malebranche she was clearly interested in the author's work as a whole, and made an effort to think about their conception of their publications as well as to contextualise them. This all added to her reading; she was trying to aim for the best reading experience possible by selecting the 'right' editions or making alterations to her own copies to reflect the most up-to-date version of the author's ideas. She was also situating herself within a network of philosophers, adding her own voice to their debates and theories. All of Astell's annotations show her playing an authoritative, interpretative role as a reader. She did not attempt to argue with or contradict the authors she was reading, but she did signal her own intellectual authority by making links between different theories and texts. She did not show any sense of submitting to the authority of the author; instead, her annotations imply that she was on the same intellectual level, as she added to and contextualised their ideas. The texts she owned show her intellectual priorities; the collection at Magdalene College gives a clear indication of her preference for Descartes and Malebranche, and she was evidently a very dedicated reader.

## Knowledge, science and manuscript recipe books

Alongside the evidence of women's ownership of printed scientific texts, we can learn a great deal about their interaction with scientific ideas through their manuscript books, in particular recipe books. These were extremely common in the seventeenth century, owned and compiled by both men and women. There has been a lot of scholarship on recipe books in recent years, led by historians such as Sara Pennell, Amanda Herbert and Elaine Leong. Many of the recent conversations in this scholarship have revolved around questions of knowledge, authority and female self-representation. They were records of various aspects of the compiler's life and social interactions, as seen through the attributions and markers of social relationships that litter early modern manuscript recipe books.[58] They are therefore a valuable insight into women's conceptions of their own sociable identities. Moreover, Wendy Wall has argued that there was an intellectual authority displayed in recipe books, often overlooked due to their designation as part of domestic culture. She has suggested that recipes allowed people to interact with philosophical questions and humanist thought, as they 'asked readers outside formal sites of education to reflect on how something called "nature" was to be positioned in relation to the artifactual; they demanded that practitioners think about how and when to put natural materials in and out of time and how to evidence "truth"'.[59] Recipe books are therefore a particularly useful way of understanding women's knowledge; we can see the scientific ideas that they were using and absorbing, often through reading practices, and the ways in which they used these ideas to position themselves as intellectual authorities within particular social networks.

Recipe books can and should be considered examples of early modern science and knowledge production. As Elaine Leong has argued, 'household recipe books record not only how householders produced a range of foods and medicines, but also how they investigated and used natural materials and production techniques, how they understood and looked after their bodies in sickness and in health, and how they positioned themselves within their natural environment'.[60] Leong calls recipe books examples of 'household science' and situates them at the centre of everyday knowledge production, demonstrating how people understood not just scientific processes but also social relationships and household management.[61]

This is how I will consider recipe books: as evidence of scientific and domestic knowledge production. However, I am going to particularly think about the readers of recipe books; a lot of work so far has focused on their compilation, but they were also books that were intended to be read. We do not know a great deal about the activity and place of reading recipe books. It is not clear whether they were read in the kitchen, perhaps in the process of cooking, although there are rarely marks of use that would indicate this, such as food stains. This might have meant that they were more commonly used as reference books (or that they had been cleaned by subsequent owners). We also do not know precisely who used them: whether they read by the middle- and upper-class women who compiled them or whether cooks and kitchen maids also read them. We can assume, however, that they were looked over, re-read and filled with recipes copied from other books or scraps of paper, due to the many notations accompanying the recipes.

Recipe books were deeply embedded with a sense of sociability and personal identity. There is a clear sense of female ownership in many recipe books, as they were often inscribed with the formula of a woman's name, followed by some variation on the phrase 'her book'. This is very similar to the way they inscribed other, printed books; they wanted to stake a claim to the text and the book as an object. In the Wellcome Library's collection of recipe books, many bear one or more women's signatures. Searching for the term 'her book' for the years 1600–1699 in the Wellcome Library's digitised collection of recipe books returned eighty-two results (although some were from the same manuscript). This signature is often accompanied by a date, for example in the case of Hannah Bisaker, who signed the manuscript, 'Hannah Bisaker Her Booke The 12$^{th}$ September Anno: 1692'.[62] It is unclear if this refers to the date the manuscript was started, finished or even bought, but in general such inscriptions are clearly by the author of the book, being in the same hand. Such ownership claims are sometimes repeated, such as in Sarah Hudson's receipt book.[63] On the first preliminary page, she wrote, 'Sarah Hudsone hir Booke in y$^{e}$ year of our Lord and Sa[v]ior Jesus Christ 1687/8', then on the second preliminary page, 'Sarah Hudson her book February y$^{e}$ 15$^{th}$ day in y$^{e}$ year of our Lord and Saviour Jesus Christ 1678'. It is unclear why she signed the first page so long after she had signed the second. Underneath the second signature she wrote, 'Sarah hudson god preserue her in all her voiges wheathersoeuer she goetth god preserue & keep her in all parts of y$^{e}$ world whear so euer she goeth & whith whosoeuer she goetth'. Her inscriptions amount to more than simple pen trials; they repeatedly stake her claim to the manuscript.

As well as personal ownership claims, there is frequently evidence of relationships within the pages of recipe books. Wall has argued that 'recipes were transit points that actively created and defined knowledge communities and networks of association'.[64] Gift inscriptions were common in manuscript recipe books, again underlining the part books played in sociable and familial networks.[65] In Lady Frances Catchmay's (d. 1629) recipe book, there is an inscription on the verso of the second preliminary page, reading:

> This Booke with the others of Medicins, preserues and Cookerye, My lady Catchmay lefte with me to be delivered to her Sonne Sir William Catchmay Earnestly desiringe and Chardginge him to lett every one of his Brothers and Sisters to haue true Coppyes of the sayd Bookes, or such parte thereof as any of them doth desire. In witness that this was herrequest, I haue herevnto sett my hand at the delivery of the sayd Bookes. Ed. Bett.[66]

Copies of the book are therefore being passed to both her sons and daughters, despite recipe books being traditionally seen as largely owned and created by women.[67] The fact that Catchmay asked for 'true coppyes' to be made of the book for 'every one' of his siblings indicates the value she placed on it as a bequest.

The similarity in the inscriptions of print and manuscript texts indicates the lack of any real dividing line between the two media in early modern inscription culture. They were inscribed with the same formula, making the same ownership claim. Manuscript recipe books were passed between friends and family, possibly carrying emotional or relational significance within that network, just as printed works were. However, if we follow Laroche's argument that signatures were a way of claiming the knowledge contained within a book, this functioned in a slightly different way in manuscript recipe books. The person who signed the book was usually the compiler, thus the knowledge within the book was already theirs; the signature merely reinforces this. Leong has discussed women's critical reading of print herbals and medicinal texts, and the ways in which they drew on their own knowledge both to read printed texts and compile manuscript books, arguing that they 'fully utilised the offerings coming off the printing presses to extend, confirm and challenge their own medical knowledge'.[68] However, there is more care within manuscript recipe books to provide alternative attribution, ensuring that the signer does not lay claim to all the recipes contained therein.

Attribution was important in seventeenth-century receipt books, as Herbert has discussed when looking at the place of recipe books in early modern female sociable networks.[69] It was common for women to not only sign their books but also note the provenance of individual recipes. For example, Rebecca Winch's receipt book (signed on the front flyleaf 'Rebeckah Winche 1666') contains multiple attributions referencing both acquaintances and well-known authors.[70] Her *aqua mirabilis* recipe has 'Mrs Hobby' written in the margins, while another recipe is entitled 'The Lady Hewets Water'. There is also a recipe for 'Lucatellos Balsom', a common item in seventeenth-century manuscript recipe books and a reference to the physician Matthew Lucatello.[71] Michelle DiMeo has also discussed how attributions can be used to situate women within intellectual networks, and are evidence of knowledge sharing among friends and acquaintances.[72] Providing provenance for recipes and referring to well-known physicians and writers could have been a way of emphasising the compiler's authority, claiming her place within a skilled and knowledgeable community. For the compiler herself, or for other readers (friends, family and servants), her identity, networks and reading habits (if, for example, they borrowed a recipe book from a friend and copied out useful entries) were made clear.

Provenance was not always provided, however, even when it is evident that recipes have been taken from printed sources. Margaret Baker's manuscript,[73] which contains provenance notes of many recipes, also includes some recipes which bear striking similarities to those of Hannah Woolley, printed in *The Accomplish'd Lady's Delight*.[74] For example, Baker's oil of fennel recipe reads, 'Take a Quantity of ffennell between two tyles or plates of iron make them very hotte and presse outt y$^{e}$ licoure; and this oyle is good for the tissicke or dry scabes & for burning or scaldinge',[75] while Hannah Woolley's printed recipe for the same product states, 'Put a quantity of Fennel between two Tile-stones, or Plates of Iron, make them very hot, and press out the Liquor; and this Oyl will keep a great while, for it is good for the Tissick, dry Scab, burning and scalding.'[76] There is, however, no mention of Woolley in Baker's book. These recipes may have been common, but the similarity of language used by both Woolley and Baker implies that Baker was familiar with Woolley's work, rather than just including recipes that were common knowledge. If that is the case, she is therefore assuming Woolley's culinary authority, indicating that the practice of attribution was complex and individual.[77] These practices of transcribing printed medical texts give us an insight into reading practices.[78] Women 'engaged critically and selectively with their texts', showing a complex and nuanced reading practice that did not simply rely on intellectual authority as represented by the printed text, but took into account their own lived experiences.[79]

Alongside reading herbals and printed recipe books, some women's compilations reveal their reading of key texts of the scientific revolution. By blending extracts from scientific texts with medicinal or culinary recipes, they more clearly situate their manuscripts in the world of science, making a clear statement about their intellectual understanding and identity.[80] Anne Wentworth Watson (1629–1695), Baroness Rockingham and daughter of Thomas Wentworth, the first Earl of Strafford, kept a commonplace book that evidences her scientific reading and understanding.[81] This was written entirely in Latin, beginning with Latin phrases, and corrected by another hand. Following this, Watson copied out 'Physiologiae Paripateticae' and 'De Phylosophia Moralis'. The former was a textbook on Aristotelian natural philosophy, published by Johannes Magirus in 1597, and still in use in the seventeenth century. The latter is likely taken from Phillip Melanchthon's *Epitome philosophiae moralis*, first published in 1538, which explored the links between natural philosophy and the laws of God. If Watson herself was the transcriber of these texts (it would appear that, even if she did not write the book herself, she caused it to be written, as her name is written on the front flyleaf in the same hand as the majority of the text), then this reveals a good understanding of Latin and an interest in Aristotelian natural philosophy.

Similarly, Sarah Horsington's manuscript, held in the Clark Library, is a collection of medical, chemical and culinary writings, combining extracts from contemporary scientific texts with recipes and her husband's medical notes (see Figure 4.1).[82] It provides an interesting example of the problems associated with separating commonplace and recipe books in modern scholarship, and demonstrates the ways in which early modern women's knowledge has been treated. Horsington, of whom there appear to be no other extant records, gave the manuscript a title, with its own title page in imitation of print conventions: *Arcana, or, Mysteries in ye theory of physiology and chymistry: being authentick rules, for preparing spagyricall medicaments, for my own observation and satisfaction. Also are manyfold private receipts, and remedies, prescriptions of T: H: M: D: Collected by ye Industry of the transcriber, of this manuscript, uxoris ejus S: H:*. She clearly identifies her role in the compilation of the manuscript, both by the reference to herself as Thomas Horsington's wife ('uxoris ejus') in the title and by inscribing her name on the first page.[83]

Horsington's manuscript has been largely overlooked by scholars.[84] The book contains extracts from learned works alongside recipes, demonstrating the significant overlap of the two forms. There is, moreover, quite

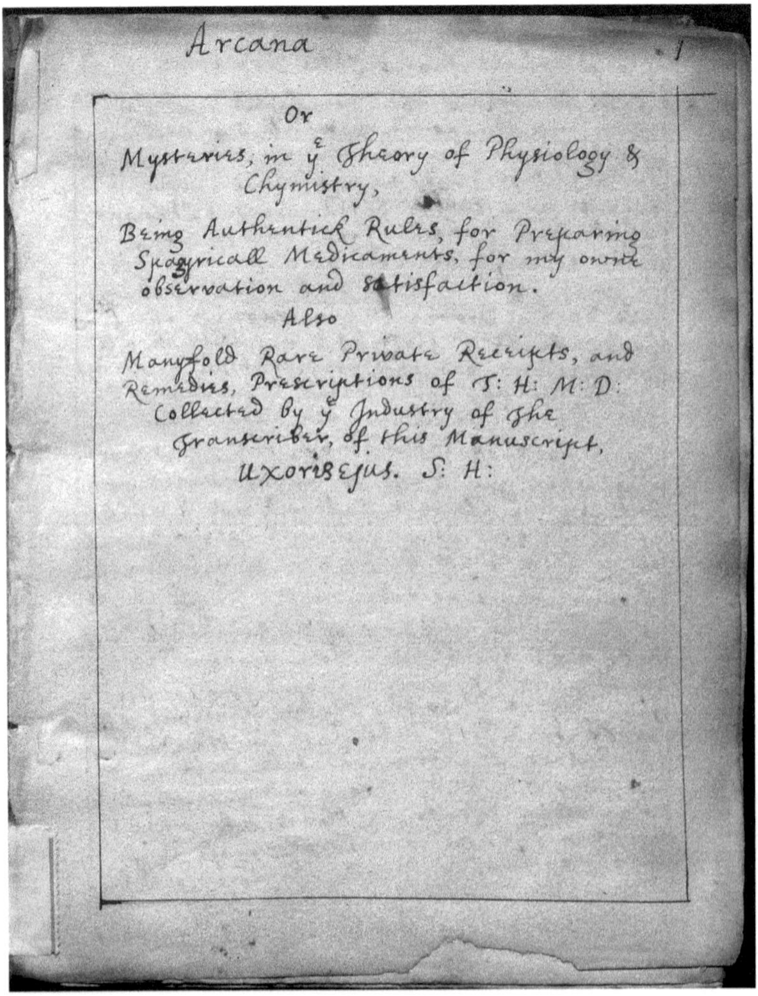
Arcana 1

Or

Mysteries, in ye Theory of Physiology & Chymistry,

Being Authentick Rules, for Preparing Spagyricall Medicaments, for my owne observation and satisfaction.

Also

Manyfold Rare Private Receipts, and Remedies, Prescriptions of T: H: M: D:

Collected by ye Industry of the Transcriber, of this Manuscript, Uxoris ejus. S: H:

**Figure 4.1:** Sarah Horsington, *Arcana*, MS.2009.015, William Andrews Clark Memorial Library, University of California, Los Angeles.

clear evidence of Horsington's personal reading practices in the extracts she has transcribed, particularly those at the beginning and end of the manuscript. Before the title, on the verso of the first page of the manuscript, Horsington wrote out extracts from Robert Boyle's *Some Considerations Touching the Usefulness of Experimental Naturall Philosophy*.[85] She used quite selective quotation, however, in one piece quoting at length from Boyle but removing any sentences dealing with St Augustine. The reason for this is unclear, but it is unlikely that it was simply a mistake: in the last sentence, Horsington accidentally omitted the words 'a provident' (from 'by Solomon God sends the sluggard to schoole to the Ant, to learne a provident Industry'[86]), and made a little mark in the text to indicate missing words, writing them at the end of the quotation. It may have been that some of the passages Boyle quoted from Augustine were in Latin, which Horsington might not have been able to understand. She preceded this extract, the last of three on the page, with a subtitle reading, 'Mr Boyle. speaking of contemplating the works of God', providing some provenance for the text.

From her extracts, we can also see her interaction with printed marginalia. She quoted: 'each page in the Great volume of Nature is full of Real Hieroglyphicks, where (by an inverted way of expression) things stand for words, and their qualities for letters. The heavens declare the glorie of God: Psal: 19'. In the original, this reads: 'each Page in the great Volume of Nature is full of real Hieroglyphicks, where (by an inverted way of Expression) Things stand for Words, and their Qualities for Letters. The Psalmist observes, *That the Heavens declare the glory of God*', with a note in the margins reading 'Psal. 19. 1'.[87] Horsington clearly paraphrased the text, making use of the marginal notation for reference.

The extract in between the two discussed above, which are on consecutive pages, comes from much earlier in Boyle's book, on page 16. Here Boyle was discussing Pliny's writing on insects, but again there is some evidence of Horsington skipping certain sections of the quote. Her manuscript reads:

> Pliny in y^e II book nat: Hist: treating of Insects, transported with an unwonted admiration of the workmanship of Nature rerum artificio: In nothing elsewhere is the workmanship of nature more remarkable then in y^e contexture of these little creatures. & after a wonder, not unworthy of a Philosopher, he concludes Rerum Natura nusquam magis quam in minimis tota est: Nature in Her whole Power is never more wholly seene then in Her smallest works.[88]

In Boyle's text, this section included more Latin text:

> *Pliny* in the eleventh Book of his Natural History, where he treats of Insects, is a little after the entrance, transported with an unwonted admiration of the Workmanship of Nature in them: *Nusquam alibi* (says he) *spectatiore Naturae rerum artificio: In nothing elswhere* (saith he) *is the workmanship of Nature more remarkable then in the contexture of these little Creatures.* And after a Wonder, not unworthy a Philosopher, he concludes, *Rerum Natura nusquam magis quam in minimis tota est: Nature in her whole Power is never more wholly seen then in her smallest Works.*[89]

Horsington therefore missed a few words between 'Nature' and 'rerum', the majority of them Latin. This is common in her manuscript. There are more extracts from Boyle's *Experimental Naturall Philosophy* at the end of the manuscript, on the final two pages. Horsington copied a short passage about a fear of spiders, taken from chapter 16, followed by a longer extract from the very beginning of the book and one short extract in which Boyle quotes Galen.[90] She again quoted very carefully and accurately, but missed out large sections of the text, all of which contained parts in Latin. Indeed, in the passage dealing with Galen, Boyle provided both the Latin original and the English translation, and it is this latter section that Horsington transcribed. While the rest of the manuscript does contain Latin, this may have been from her husband's papers, while the extracts from Boyle were Horsington's own selections. This could reinforce the practice of her re-reading her own commonplace book; there would be little point in fully transcribing passages in Latin if she could not understand them. This might also indicate a mode of reading that passes over Latin script: perhaps when Horsington was reading Boyle, she ignored the Latin passages that she knew she would not understand. She may have had some level of Latin (certainly the Pliny quote includes some phrases), but perhaps not enough for her to pay close attention to transcribing it. This would result in a very different reading experience to those who had the language capabilities to comprehend the entire text.

It is unclear why the section on insects was inserted; whether Horsington felt that it complemented the other quotations or if it is evidence of a disrupted or selective reading process. It may be indicative of re-reading, with Horsington writing out quotes when they struck her as important, if we assume that the transcription took place over an extended period of time. It may also, of course, have been simply a copy of her husband's notes, but the position of the extracts before the title page of the manuscript implies that it could have been a separate endeavour to the transcription of Thomas Horsington's papers. This selective quotation is also evident at the top of the page, where Horsington wrote out Greek script, followed underneath by the words, 'The manyfold wisdome of God'. This is also present in Boyle's text on page 38, with Greek script preceding what is presumably an English translation, reading, 'manifold Wisdom of God'.[91] Perhaps Horsington felt that this was a particularly useful phrase, or was interested in the Greek. In general, there is no obvious reason as to why Horsington chose these extracts in particular to transcribe, but the carefulness with which she copied from the text, and the selectiveness employed within the extracts, indicate a careful and thoughtful reading process.

The extracts are positioned at the beginning and end of the manuscript, with none of the formatting features (such as pagination) of the main body of the text, which she has entitled the *Arcana*. It is possible that she added them later, or perhaps before she compiled the *Arcana*. Whichever it was, the influence of Boyle's *Experimental Naturall Philosophy* is clear, both in the extracts discussed here and in the main body of the text, where she references him several times. Her manuscript is dated 1666, only three years after Boyle published *Experimental Naturall Philosophy*. Horsington, or perhaps her husband, were clearly up to date in the latest scientific thinking: Boyle's work in the 1660s brought him widespread attention, and he was a leading thinker in seventeenth-century mechanical philosophy.[92]

Horsington's ownership of the manuscript itself is evidenced by the inscription on the first page, where she wrote, 'Sarah Horsington Her Manuscript. Bought 21, 10mb$^{r}$ Pretiu[m] 16$^{d}$'.[93] This does, admittedly, imply at least some familiarity with Latin ('pretium' translates as 'price'), but it does not mean that she would have been competent enough to read philosophical arguments in the language. While Horsington may have called herself a 'transcriber', she clearly plays a much more direct authorial role, not simply copying out extracts from Boyle and from her husband's papers but editing and commenting on them. Moreover, the manuscript appears to have been intended for her own use, implying a practice of re-reading and referencing.

A great deal of the rest of the manuscript is given over to receipts of various kinds, culinary, medical and chemical. There is a glossary of chemical symbols and a list of medical terms in Latin, along with comments on the effectiveness and methods of the receipts. Horsington made her ownership of some of the content clear, writing in the title of the work, 'for my own observation and satisfaction'. Evidently this was a manuscript used by Horsington beyond the initial compilation, and perhaps served multiple purposes; it may have been a connection to her husband, as well as a place for her reading notes and attempts to understand and perhaps use Boyle's work, and her inclusion of the extracts served to emphasise her own knowledge and understanding.

## Conclusion

When looked at through the lens of reading, both manuscript and print, women's understanding of and engagement with early modern science and philosophy becomes much more evident to modern observers. Most women may not have accessed the spaces traditionally associated with early modern science, and they may not have always read some of the key scientific texts of the period (works by authors such as Robert Hooke, William Harvey or Isaac Newton, for example, have not appeared in this chapter). However, through their reading they could still engage in practices at the heart of the scientific revolution – observation and experimentation.

Crucially, this is a story of manuscript reading. As I argued in Chapter 3, if we focus on print reading above all else, then we miss a great deal of women's experiences. Relatively few women (although there are some important exceptions here) appear to have read the mainstays of the scientific revolution or were clearly up to date in the latest philosophical or scientific theories. However, they were clearly reading about culinary science and medicine, often evidenced through the compilation of their own recipe books which evidently relied on both experiment and the reading of other people's recipes. That is not to say, however, that women were not interested in reading about the intellectual developments of the seventeenth century. Clearly, they had an interest in philosophy, medicine, physics and chemistry. Astell's reading of Descartes and Malebranche, and Horsington's reading of Boyle, as well as the ways in which they read those texts, demonstrate their extensive knowledge and understanding of contemporary scientific methods, constructing themselves as intellectual figures. Their use in particular of the hallmarks of 'active' reading such as annotation and commonplacing, so often associated with humanist scholars earlier in the period, reinforces this scholarly and intellectual identity.

This is also a story of re-reading. Recipes books, by their very nature, would be read and re-read multiple times, as additions were made and the recipes themselves were used. Astell, Horsington and Wentworth Watson may have made multiple readings of both the printed texts and of their own notes on those texts. As will be explored in the next chapter, this process of re-reading is one we should not ignore or pass over, as it reveals a great deal about not only how women used text but also how they understood themselves and their world.

## Notes

1. Adrian Johns, *The Nature of the Book: Print and Knowledge in the Making* (Chicago, IL: University of Chicago Press, 1998); Rima D. Apple, Gregory J. Downey and Stephen L. Vaughn, eds., *Science in Print: Essays on the History of Science and the Culture of Print* (Madison, WI: University of Wisconsin Press, 2012); Susan Dackerman, ed., *Prints and the Pursuit of Knowledge in Early Modern Europe* (Cambridge, MA: Harvard Art Museums, 2011); Elizabeth L. Eisenstein, *The Printing Revolution in Early Modern Europe* (Cambridge: Cambridge University Press, 1983).

2. See, for example, Sandrine Parageau, 'Auto Didacticism and the Construction of Scientific Discourse in Early Modern England: Margaret Cavendish's and Anne Conway's "Intellectual Bricolage"', in *Women and Science, 17th Century to Present: Pioneers, Activists and Protagonists*, ed. Donna Spalding Andréolle and Véronique Molinari (Newcastle: Cambridge Scholars Publishing, 2011), 3–18.

3. There has been a great deal of important work on the intellectual influences of seventeenth-century women who were known for their participation in scientific or philosophical discussions. The reading materials of Margaret Cavendish, Anne Conway, Mary Astell, Damaris Masham and others have been examined, often as a way of exploring how they formed their own theories and ideas. Elizabeth Spiller, for example, has considered how Cavendish's role as a reader influenced her own theories of reading, as put forward in her published works. Spiller argues that Cavendish gave agency to the role of the reader; that her 'own texts imagine active readers who are not simply necessary to the creation of knowledge but powerful enough to threaten that knowledge'. See Elizabeth Spiller, *Science, Reading and Renaissance Literature: The Art of Making Knowledge, 1580–1670* (Cambridge: Cambridge University Press, 2004); Spiller, 'Reading through Galileo's Telescope: Margaret Cavendish and the Experience of Reading', *Renaissance Quarterly* 53, no. 1 (2000): 192–221.

4. Karen Detlefsen, 'The Rise of a Public Science? Women and Natural Philosophy in the Early Modern Period', in *The Cambridge History of Philosophy of the Scientific Revolution*, ed. David Marshall Miller and Dana Jalobeanu (Cambridge: Cambridge University Press, 2022), 128–145.

5. Elaine Leong, *Recipes and Everyday Knowledge: Medicine, Science and the Household in Early Modern England* (Chicago, IL: University of Chicago Press, 2018).

6. Both writing marginal annotations on books and the practice of creating 'commonplace' books from textual excerpts have been seen as mainstays of humanist education and reading practices. Commonplace books were originally part of humanist pedagogy, wherein a reader would collect short extracts of text under various headings in a manuscript book (such as fortune, virtue, justice, death and life), intended to provide a personal compendium of information to be used later, often in original composition. These compilations were used as part of a young boy's education, and as part of scholarly work. This originated with the Italian *florilegium* in the fifteenth century: excerpting and collecting quotations from classical texts was an important part of their recovery. Italian private schools in the early fifteenth century were key to the development of European classical education, and the use of notebooks for reading notes was a key part of their curriculum. See Ann Moss, *Printed Commonplace-Books and the Structuring of Renaissance Thought* (Oxford: Clarendon, 1996). The form developed, however, and was a popular reading tool across many social groups in the seventeenth century. For work on prolific male commonplacers, such as William Drake and John Dee, see Kevin Sharpe, *Reading Revolutions: The Politics of Reading in Early Modern England* (New Haven, CT: Yale University Press, 2000); William H. Sherman, *John Dee: The Politics of Reading and Writing in the English Renaissance* (Amherst, MA: University of Massachusetts Press, 1995).

7. Lara Dodds, 'Margaret Cavendish's Domestic Experiment', in *Genre and Women's Life Writing in Early Modern England*, ed. Michelle M. Dowd and Julie A. Eckerle (London: Routledge, 2007), 163; Wendy Wall, *Recipes for Thought: Knowledge and Taste in the Early Modern English Kitchen* (Philadelphia, PA: University of Pennsylvania Press, 2016).

8. Dodds, 'Margaret Cavendish's Domestic Experiment', 164.

9. David Marshall Miller and Dana Jalobeanu, 'The Disciplinary Revolutions of Early Modern Philosophy and Science', in *The Cambridge History of Philosophy of the*

*Scientific Revolution*, ed. David Marshall Miller and Dana Jalobeanu (Cambridge: Cambridge University Press, 2022), 1–12.

**10.** Patricia Phillips, *The Scientific Lady: A Social History of Women's Scientific Interests 1520–1918* (New York: St Martin's Press, 1990), 85.

**11.** John Evelyn, 'Directions for the employment of your time [to Mary Evelyn]'; [early 1680s?]. British Library Add MS 78440, f38r. His underlinings.

**12.** Jacques du Bosc, for example, argued that reading was 'absolutely necessary to render both the wit and the humor [of women] acceptable', and Hannah Woolley stated that 'Reading furnisheth them [women] with agreeable discourse, and adopts them for the conversation of the most ingenious.' See Jacques du Bosc, *The Accomplish'd Woman. Written Originally in French, since made English, by the Honourable Walter Montague, Esq* (London: Printed for Gabriel Bedell and Tho. Collins, 1656), 67; Hannah Woolley, *The Gentlewomans Companion; Or, A Guide to the Female Sex: Containing Directions of Behaviour, in all Places, Companies, Relations, and Conditions, from their Childhood down to Old Age: Viz. As, Children to Parents. Scholars to Governours. Single to Servants. Virgins to Suitors. Married to Husbands. Huswifes to the House. Mistresses to the Servants. Mothers to Children. Widows to the World. Prudent to all. With Letters and Discourses upon all Occasions. Whereunto is added, A Guide for Cook-Maids, Dairy-Maids, Chamber-Maids, and all others that go to Service. The whole being an exact Rule for the Female Sex in General* (London: Printed by A. Maxwell for Dorman Nowman, 1673), 7.

**13.** Bathsua Makin, *An Essay to Revive the Antient Education of Gentlewomen in Religion, Manners, Arts & Tongues. With An Answer to the Objections against this Way of Education* (London: Printed by J. D., 1673), 35.

**14.** For the relationship between Makin and male contemporaries and predecessors, such as Milton and Poulain de la Barre, see James L. Helm, 'Bathsua Makin's *An Essay to Revive the Antient Education of Gentlewomen* in the Canon of Seventeenth-Century Educational Reform Tracts', *Cahiers Elisabéthains: A Journal of English Renaissance Studies* 44, no. 1 (1993): 45–51.

**15.** Mary Astell, *A Serious Proposal to the Ladies for the Advancement of their True and Greatest Interest* (New York: Source Book Press, 1970), 20. As will be seen later in this chapter, she enacted her prescriptions, being an avid reader of both Descartes and Malebranche.

**16.** Astell, *A Serious Proposal*, 129.

**17.** Melissa Reynolds has examined the importance of manuscripts in the fifteenth and sixteenth centuries to the spread and development of knowledge about the natural world – see Melissa Reynolds, *Reading Practice: The Pursuit of Natural Knowledge from Manuscript to Print* (Chicago, IL: University of Chicago Press, 2024).

**18.** This connection between scientific ideas and print culture is most clearly shown in Elizabeth Eisenstein's influential claim that the printing press was one of the key causes of the scientific revolution. Elizabeth L. Eisenstein, *The Printing Revolution in Early Modern Europe* (Cambridge: Cambridge University Press, 1986).

**19.** Graham Parry, 'The Great Picture of Lady Anne Clifford', in *Ashgate Critical Essays on Women Writers in England, 1550–1700: Volume 5: Anne Clifford and Lucy Hutchinson*, ed. Mihoko Suzuki and Mary Ellen Lamb (Abingdon: Routledge, 2016), 121–138.

**20.** For more information on early modern herbals, see Sarah Neville, *Early Modern Herbals and the Book Trade: English Stationers and the Commodification of Botany* (Cambridge: Cambridge University Press, 2022).

**21.** 'An Inventory of Bookes in the Lady Heaths closett', Egerton MS 2983 HEATH AND VERNEY PAPERS. Vol. VI, f79r. British Library. For more discussion of Heath's books, see Chapter 1.

22. Christof Wirsung, *The General Practise of Physicke. Conteyning all Inward and Outward parts of the body, with all the accidents and infirmities that are incident unto them, even from the crowne of the head to the sole of the foote* (London: Printed for Thomas Adams, 1617).

23. John H. Appleby, 'Woodall, John (1570–1643)', *Oxford Dictionary of National Biography*, 2008, accessed July 18, 2023, www-oxforddnb-com.libproxy.york.ac.uk /display/10.1093/ref:odnb/9780198614128.001.0001/odnb-9780198614128-e-29902 ?rskey=dxcH6R&result=1.

24. Appleby, 'Woodall, John'.

25. See, for example, Sarah Hutton, 'Alchemy and Cultures of Knowledge among Early Modern Women', *Early Modern Women: An Interdisciplinary Journal* 15, no. 2 (2021): 93–102; Penny Bayer, 'Women Alchemists and the Paracelsian Context in France and England, 1560–1616', *Early Modern Women* 15, no. 2 (2021): 103–112.

26. Jacques Guillemeau, *Child-birth or, The happy delivery of women: VVherein is set downe the government of women. In the time of their breeding childe: of their travaile, both naturall and contrary to nature: and of their lying in. Together with the diseases, which happen to women in those times, and the meanes to helpe them. With a treatise for the nursing of children. To which is added, a treatise of the diseases of infants, and young children: with the cure of them, and also of the small pox. Written in French by Iames Guillimeau the French Kings chirurgion* (London: Printed by A. Hatfield, 1612).

27. Raymond A. Anselment, ed., *The Remembrances of Elizabeth Freke, 1671–1714*, Camden Fifth Series, vol. 18 (Cambridge: Cambridge University Press, 2001), 173–175.

28. Anselment, *Remembrances*, 174.

29. James Hodder, *Hodder's Arithemetick: Or, that necessary Art made most easie. Being explained in a way familiar to the capacity of any that desire to learn it in a little time* (London, Printed by J. Darby, for Tho. Rooks, 1667). Z90 14, Beinecke Library, New Haven.

30. Ruth Wallis, 'Hodder, James (fl.1659–1673)', *Oxford Dictionary of National Biography*, 2004, accessed July 18, 2023, www-oxforddnb-com.libproxy.york.ac.uk /display/10.1093/ref:odnb/9780198614128.001.0001/odnb-9780198614128-e-13416 ?rskey=A70mMl&result=1.

31. Robert Fage, *Cosmography Or, A Description of the Whole World, Rpresented (by a more exact and certain Discovery) in the Excellencies of its Scituation, Commodities, Inhabitants, and History: Of Their Particular and Distinct Governments, Religions, Arms, and Degrees of Honour used amongst Them* (London, Printed by S. Griffin for John Overton, 1667). 2005 316, Beinecke Library.

32. Philip Barrough, *The Method of Phisicke, Containing the causes, signes, and cures of inward diseases in mans body from the head to the foote. Whereunto is added, the forme and rule of making remedies and medicines, which our Physitions commonly use at this day, with the proportion, quantitie, and names of each medicine* (Imprinted at London by Richard Field, 1596). RB 28188, Huntington Library, San Marino.

33. Jane Sharp, *The Midwives Book. Or the whole art of midwifery discovered. Directing childbearing women how to behave themselves* (London: Printed for *Simon Miller*, 1671). EPB/A/47965, Wellcome Library, London.

34. Catherine Sutherland has written about the discovery of Astell's library and its contents; see Catherine Sutherland, 'Books Owned by Mary Astell in the Old Library of Magdalene College, Cambridge', *The Library* 24, no. 3 (2023): 267–301.

35. Hilda L. Smith, *Reason's Disciples: Seventeenth-Century English Feminists* (Urbana, IL: University of Illinois Press, 1982); Ruth Perry, 'Radical Doubt and the Liberation of Women', *Eighteenth Century Studies* 18, no. 4 (1985): 472–493; Jacqueline Broad, 'Astell, Cartesian Ethics, and the Critique of Custom', in *Mary*

*Astell: Reason, Gender, Faith*, ed. William Kolbrener and Michal Michelson (London: Routledge, 2007), 165–180.

36. Jacqueline Broad, *The Philosophy of Mary Astell: An Early Modern Theory of Virtue* (Oxford: Oxford University Press, 2015), 27.

37. René Descartes, *Les Principes de la Philosophie* (A Paris: Chez Theodore Girard, 1681), 3. H.14.18, Magdalene College, Cambridge. Translation: 'that our senses are prone to deception, and that there is no certain truth in their testimony. The Life of Plato by Dacier, p76 . . . Sight and hearing have both some truth, and their testimony is faithful or the Poets would have reason to sing to us that we neither understand nor see anything truly'.

38. For more on Dacier, see Déborah Blocker, 'Servir le prince par la philologie: André Dacier (1651–1722), un érudit dans l'orbite du pouvoir royal', *Seventeenth-Century French Studies* 35, no. 1 (2013): 3–22. Dacier was married to Anne Le Fèvre Dacier, also a prominent translator and classicist – for information on her life, see Eliane Itti, *Madame Dacier, femme et savant du Grand Siècle: 1645–1720* (Paris: L'Harmattan, 2012).

39. André Dacier, *Les Oeuvres de Platon Traduites en Francois, avec des Remarques. Et la Vie de ce Philosophe, avec l'exposition des principaux dogmes de la Philosophie. Tome Première* (A Paris: Chez Jean Anisson Directeur de l'Imprimerie Royale, 1694), 75–76.

40. André Dacier, *Les Oeuvres de Platon Traduites en Francois, avec des Remarques. Et la Vie de ce Philosophe, avec l'exposition des principaux dogmes de la Philosophie. Tome Seconde* (A Paris: Chez Jean Anisson Directeur de l'Imprimerie Royale, 1694), 174.

41. Nicolas Malebranche, *De la recherche de la verité, où, L'on traitte de la nature de l'esprit de l'homme, & de l'usage qu'il en doit faire pour éviter l'erreur dans les sciences, Vol. 1* (A Amsterdam: Chez Henry Desbordes, 1688), 36. B.8.29, Magdalene College. For more on Astell and Malebranche, see Jacqueline Broad, 'Mary Astell's Malebranchean Concept of the Self', in *Early Modern Women on Metaphysics*, ed. Emily Thomas (Cambridge: Cambridge University Press, 2018), 211–226.

42. Malebranche, *De la recherche de la verité*. B.8.29, Magdalene College.

43. Lloyd Strickland, 'God's Creatures? Divine Nature and the Status of Animals in the Early Modern Beast–Machine Controversy', *International Journal of Philosophy and Theology* 74, no. 4 (2013): 291–309.

44. Strickland, 'God's Creatures?', 295.

45. José Manuel García Valverde, 'Gómez Pereira', *The Stanford Encyclopedia of Philosophy* (summer 2022 edition), Edward N. Zalta (ed.), accessed July 17, 2023, https://plato.stanford.edu/archives/sum2022/entries/gomez-pereira.

46. Stephen Gaukroger, *Descartes: An Intellectual Biography* (Oxford: Oxford University Press, 1997), 271.

47. Peter Harrison, 'Descartes on Animals', *The Philosophical Quarterly* 42, no. 167 (1992): 219–227.

48. Descartes, *Les Principes*. H.14.18, Magdalene College.

49. Edmund Halley, 'A Discourse Concerning Gravity, and Its Properties, Wherein the Descent of Heavy Bodies, and the Motion of Projects is briefly, but Fully Handled: Together with the Solution of a Problem of Great Use in Gunnery', *Philosophical Transactions (1683–1775)*, Vol. 16 (1686–1692), 3–4.

50. Nicolas Malebranche, *Meditations Chrestiennes, par L'Auteur de la Recherche de la Vérité* (A Cologne, Chez Balthasar D'Egmond & Compagnie, 1683). G.17.6, Magdalene College.

51. Sarah Hutton, *British Philosophy in the Seventeenth Century* (Oxford: Oxford University Press, 2015), 103. Sorana Corneanu and Koen Vermeir have argued that

Malebranche, Bacon, Descartes and other contemporary philosophers were all interested in the 'art of thinking', and that central to this was understanding the human mind – see Sorana Corneanu and Koen Vermeir, 'The Art of Thinking', in *The Cambridge History of the Philosophy of the Scientific Revolution*, ed. David Marshall Miller and Dana Jalobeanu (Cambridge: Cambridge University Press, 2022), 149–166.

52. Robert Boyle, *Some considerations about the reconcileableness of reason and religion by T.E., a lay-man; to which is annex'd by the publisher, a discourse of Mr. Boyle, about the possibility of the resurrection* (London: Printed by T. N. for H. Herringman, 1675), 30.

53. René Descartes, *Les Meditations Metaphysiques de René Descartes. Touchant la Première Philosophie* (A Paris: chez Theodore Girard, 1667). H.14.17, Magdalene College. Translation: 'Discourse on the method of rightly conducting one's reason and of seeking truth in the sciences. Then the Diotrique, the Meteors and the Geometry which are essays of this method.'

54. Malebranche, *De la recherche de la verité*. B.8.29, Magdalene College. Translation: 'it is more than 25 years since this work was composed'.

55. Pere Malebranche, *Traité de la Nature et de la Grace* (A Rotterdam: Chez Rainier Leers, 1701). D.6.52, Magdalene College.

56. Nicolas Malebranche, *Traité de Morale par l'Auteur de la Recherche de la Verité* (A Rotterdam, Chez Reinier Leers, 1684). D.6.53, Magdalene College.

57. Malebranche, *Meditations Chrestiennes*. G.17.6, Magdalene College.

58. Sara Pennell and Michelle DiMeo have argued that recipe books, like commonplace books, can be seen as a form of life-writing. See Michelle DiMeo and Sara Pennell, 'Introduction', in *Reading and Writing Recipe Books, 1550–1800*, ed. Michelle DiMeo and Sara Pennell (Manchester: Manchester University Press, 2013), 11.

59. Wall, *Recipes for Thought*, 4. Similarly, Pennell has argued, 'the alignment of women's intellectual practices with the prevailing educational parameters for the male population overshadows the extra-pedagogic ways in which women encountered, meditated and registered varieties of knowledge'. See Sara Pennell, 'Perfecting Practice? Women, Manuscript Recipes and Knowledge in Early Modern England', in *Early Modern Women's Manuscript Writing: Selected Papers from the Trinity/Trent Colloquium*, ed. Victoria E. Burke and Jonathan Gibson (Aldershot: Ashgate, 2004), 246.

60. Leong, *Recipes and Everyday Knowledge*, 3.

61. Leong, *Recipes and Everyday Knowledge*, 3.

62. Bisaker, Hannah, 1692, MS.1176, Wellcome Library.

63. Hudson, Sarah, 1678, MS.2954, Wellcome Library.

64. Wall, *Recipes for Thought*, 3.

65. Sara Pennell has argued for the centrality of relationships to the creation of manuscript recipe books, suggesting that these manuscripts were 'made possible by, and thrived upon, the circulation of recipes between mothers, sisters and daughters, friends and neighbours of all ranks'. See Pennell, 'Perfecting Practice?', 242.

66. Catchmay, Lady Frances, 1625, MS.184a, Wellcome Library.

67. There is not room here to discuss the implications of manuscript recipe books or other compilations being left in wills, but this would provide an interesting insight into the make-up of the recipients of such inheritances.

68. Elaine Leong, '"Herbals She Peruseth": Reading Medicine in Early Modern England', *Renaissance Studies* 28, no. 4 (2014): 556–578. Melissa Reynolds has made

a similar point regarding fifteenth- and sixteenth-century 'practical manuscripts'; that they 'excerpted, revised, and amended authoritative knowledge to suit the needs of the compilers and consumers'. Reynolds, *Reading Practice*, 4–5.

69. Amanda Herbert, *Female Alliances: Gender, Identity, and Friendship in Early Modern Britain* (New Haven, CT: Yale University Press, 2014).

70. Rebecca Winch, *Receipt Book of Rebeckah Winche, ca. 1666*. V.b.366, Folger Library, Washington, DC.

71. Lucatello's balsam was an early modern panacea, known to have been used by Isaac Newton and John Evelyn, among others. See Rob Iliffe, 'Isaac Newton: Lucatello Professor of Mathematics', in *Science Incarnate: Historical Embodiments of Natural Knowledge*, ed. Christopher Lawrence and Steven Shapin (Chicago, IL: University of Chicago Press, 1998), 135.

72. Michelle DiMeo, 'Authorship and Medical Networks: Reading Attributions in Early Modern Manuscript Recipe Books', in *Reading and Writing Recipe Books, 1550–1800*, ed. Michelle DiMeo and Sara Pennell (Manchester: Manchester University Press, 2013), 25–46.

73. Margaret Baker, *Receipt Book of Margaret Baker*, c.1675. V.a.619, Folger Library.

74. Woolley was a popular writer at the time, and *The Accomplish'd Lady's Delight* underwent nine print runs in the late seventeenth century (1670–1706). See Doreen Evenden Nagy, *Popular Medicine in Seventeenth-Century England* (Bowling Green, OH: Bowling Green State University Popular Press, 1988), 70.

75. V.a.619, f52r, Folger Library.

76. Hannah Woolley, *The Accomplish'd lady's delight in preserving, physick, beautifying, and cookery*, (London, Printed for B. Harris, 1675), 171. There have been many questions about the attribution of this work to Woolley, but as her name was on the printed edition in 1675, and thus was the name associated with the book by its readers, the authorship will not be contested here. For a recent discussion of Woolley's works and attribution, see Margaret J. M. Ezell, 'Cooking the Books, or, the Three Faces of Hannah Woolley', in *Reading and Writing Recipe Books, 1550–1800*, ed. Michelle DiMeo and Sara Pennell (Manchester: Manchester University Press, 2003), 159–178.

77. It is possibly significant that the lack of attribution here relates to the work of a female author, but there is no clear evidence that this was a gendered practice.

78. Leong has studied Elizabeth Freke's notes on Gerard's herbal, pointing out that Freke rarely copied word for word, but rephrased and paraphrased the printed text. Leong suggests that this indicates that Freke consulted other sources and listened to her own or her acquaintances' experience; that her 'reading for [medical] practice was not a hurried consultation of indices or a hunt for particular rare cures, rather it was a slow process of repeated readings, conversations and digestion'. Similarly, she uses the example of Margaret Boscawen, who took notes from Culpeper but imposed her own classification system. Elaine Leong, 'Herbals She Peruseth', 564, 567, 572. See earlier in this chapter for the mention of Freke's notes on the herbal in her book inventory.

79. Leong, 'Herbals She Peruseth', 572.

80. For a discussion of how the notebook form of the humanist commonplace developed during the scientific revolution, see Richard Yeo, *Notebooks, English Virtuosi, and Early Modern Science* (Chicago, IL: University of Chicago Press, 2014).

81. Anne Wentworth Watson, Baroness Rockingham, [Commonplace Book], [17th Century], Osborn b285, Beinecke Library.

82. Sarah Horsington, *Arcana, or, Mysteries in ye theory of physiology and chymistry: being authentick rules, for preparing spagyricall medicaments, for my own*

*observation and satisfaction. Also are manyfold private receipts, and remedies, prescriptions of T: H: M: D: Collected by ye Industry of the transcriber, of this manuscript, uxoris ejus S: H:*, 1666, MS.2009.015, Clark Library, Los Angeles.

83. Although there are no other records of Sarah, her husband Thomas (1616–1688) is recorded as a physician who trained in Leiden and practised in London. He was interested in iatrochemistry, an interest apparently shared with Sarah. See 'Dr [Thomas] Horsington (c.1618–1666)', *Early Modern Practitioners: Sample Data*, accessed April 25, 2019, http://practitioners.exeter.ac.uk/sample-data.

84. One of its only mentions comes from Lynette Hunter, who has discussed it in relation to scientific writings by women in the mid-seventeenth century, centred on Katherine Jones' circle. Hunter described Horsington's manuscript as a common-place book, whose 'effect is patterned on Boyle's and Willis's commentaries, yet is hard at work hammering out a distinctive vocabulary and syntax or discussion'. However, Hunter does not take this discussion any further, and the manuscript's significance for the history of reading and its relationship to the tradition of commonplacing has not been explored. Lynette Hunter, 'Sisters of the Royal Society: The Circle of Katherine Jones, Lady Ranelagh', in *Women, Science and Medicine 1500–1700: Mothers and Sisters of the Royal Society*, ed. Lynette Hunter and Sarah Hutton (Stroud: Sutton Publishing, 1997), 191.

85. MS.2009.015. f1v, Clark Library.

86. Robert Boyle, *Some Considerations Touching the Usefulness of Experimental Naturall Philosophy, Propos'd in a Familiar Discourse to a Friend, by way of Invitation to the Study of it* (Oxford: Printed by Hen: Hall Printer to the University, for Ric: Davis, 1663), 50.

87. Boyle, *Some Considerations*, 49.

88. MS.2009.015. f1v, Clark Library.

89. Boyle, *Some Considerations*, 16.

90. Referring to Boyle, *Some Considerations*, 262; 6–8; 17.

91. Boyle, *Some Considerations*, 38.

92. Michael Hunter, ed., *Robert Boyle Reconsidered* (Cambridge: Cambridge University Press, 1994); Lotte Mulligan, 'Robert Boyle, "The Christian Virtuoso" and the Rhetoric of "Reason"', in *Religion, Reason and Nature in Early Modern Europe*, ed. Robert Crocker (Dordrecht: Kluwer Academic Publishers, 2001), 97–116.

93. MS.2009.015. f1r, Clark Library.

## Chapter 5

# (Re-)reading and record-keeping

As we have seen throughout this book, the picture of women's reading habits is not complete without attention to manuscript reading. There has, of course, been a huge amount of attention paid to readers' manuscript interactions with print, but these often focus on the *writing* of these annotations rather than the experience of reading them or of re-reading the text after they have been made. Every intervention on or with the text will produce a new reading experience. When doing my research for this book, I used many modern library books that bore the marks of past readers, and noticed myself replicating their patterns. If a section of text was underlined, for example, my eye was drawn to it instinctually. The interventions of past readers had a tangible influence on my own reading practices. There is plenty of evidence from the early modern period that people were dedicated re-readers; they returned to texts multiple times and often record this in a variety of ways (some of which have already been covered in this book). This chapter will think beyond the act of reading a piece of print, to thinking about how readerly interventions – be that marginalia, commonplacing or excerpting – alter future reading experiences. This will add another dimension to the relationship between reading and identity, demonstrating the mutable and temporally specific nature of identity that is displayed and negotiated through reading acts.

The practice of re-reading has come up many times in this book so far, but in this chapter I want to reflect on what this specific process of re-engaging with a text multiple times, at different points in a life and in different ways, means for our understanding of how reading is a performance of identity. There have been few scholarly studies of re-reading. In studies of modern reading habits there are often two main reasons for re-reading posited: to better understand a text (usually, but not always, as part of an intellectual exercise or pastime); or to return to feelings one had on the first reading (perhaps particularly in the case of reading for pleasure).[1] Those motivations are certainly present here, but arguably there are innumerable reasons for re-reading, depending on the individual. One might re-read a list, for example, to check something or remind oneself of the contents. The same text might be read for multiple different reasons; for understanding, for pleasure, for the sake of argument.

If, as I have argued in this book, the process of reading is one of identity construction, then re-reading adds a layer of complexity to this – one is continually re-constructing and creating identity even in returning to the same text. As Pamela Mackenzie and Elisabeth Davies have argued, 're-reading requires both revisiting the text and encountering it anew, and that in re-reading a text, the reader is simultaneously revisiting and encountering him- or herself'.[2] This reveals both a reinforcement and a new construction of identity, and the fluidity of identity itself – each act creating it also alters it.

The best evidence we have of re-reading often comes from the marks made on the page. Marginalia frequently reveals multiple encounters with a text, either because the reader has specifically dated their reading (such as Anne Clifford in Chapter 2) or because there are different types of marginal annotation, which we can reasonably speculate were made at different times (such as Beckwith's annotations on her Bible in Chapter 1). Similarly, the writing of notes about reading, in the form of commonplace books or notebooks, can be assumed to be evidence of re-reading – it seems relatively unlikely that someone would take the trouble of compiling a commonplace book if they were not planning to ever return to it and read their excerpts.[3] This may well have happened in some cases, but ultimately the intention of a commonplace book is to encourage re-reading of specific passages of a text.

The practice of keeping commonplace books is often discussed in a similar way to the marginalia and 'active' reading habits that have been explored earlier in this book.[4] The culture of commonplacing and marginalia shows how a key part of the history of reading is the history of writing, particularly the process of creating records of reading, or of texts derived from reading. Moreover, the relationship between reading and events in an individual's lifetime, and the sociality of reading, as texts are edited or passed between different people, becomes clear. Writing about reading is a process of memorialisation, in which not only the text but also the events and relationships surrounding the reading experience are set down in manuscript or printed books. This then changes the reading experience for future readers of the book.

Writing about reading and reading itself, therefore, are both part of an extended practice of self-fashioning. Ella Ophir has made a similar argument about selfhood in her work on the notebooks of Evelyn Wilson, a London employment register clerk who died in 1934, and whose notebooks were discovered and published posthumously.[5] These included diary entries, extracts copied from texts and newspaper clippings. While Wilson was writing in a very different historical context, the approach Ophir has taken to the notebooks is useful here. Ophir suggests that we should look at these manuscripts as a practice, not a text, and that the work can therefore be seen as an 'extended, multifaceted work of periodic self-inscription'.[6] She elaborates: 'Wilson's practice of transcribing and collecting texts was continuous with the purposes and processes of diary writing with which it was interwoven: self-reflection, self-definition, and perhaps most fundamentally, the desire to wrest from the welter of life the clarity of articulate expression.'[7] Discussions of self-definition often come up in talking about writing, and thus could be linked to commonplacing as an act of writing rather than of reading. However, Ophir argues that the notebooks she is discussing are evidence of both, and that reading can be a tool for both self-recognition, and self-definition.[8] Steven Colclough has argued a similar point in relation to Elizabeth Freke's commonplace book, arguing that it demonstrates how Freke used reading to 'refashion her sense of self and history in her autobiographical writings'.[9] Both commonplacing and marginalia are then, in the same way as diary-writing, a way of understanding the world and the self, and of representing one's own identity (or aspects of that identity).[10]

This chapter will explore various forms of reading notes, both those left on the printed page and those made elsewhere, to think about how the process of writing can affect the reading experience, and how this can be a continual form of identity construction for an individual reader. This might be a reinforcement of an intellectual or political identity; it might be placing oneself within a sociable network; or it may simply be the act of claiming a text and altering it by adding one's own notes (which may or may not be related to the subject matter). Writing about reading is a process of memorialisation, in which not only the text but also the events and relationships surrounding the reading experience are set down in manuscript books. I will first consider how readers' note-taking and annotations reveal multiple levels of reading practice, and then move on to consider how more domestic annotations and notebooks show the way that women adapted reading practices for the household.

## Re-reading and reading notes

Marginalia in printed books not only reveal what people thought of their reading and what they read but can also show us the multiple ways in which they read – the practices associated with reading. Marginalia might be included to make sense of the text, to create shortcuts useful for skim reading or to add one's own ideas or cross-references. This is a particular form of marginalia, one which interacts directly with the text itself. However, it also alters the text. This might happen through a literal correcting or altering on the part of the reader (by correcting errors, for example), or it might be that annotations would create a different experience for future readers.

In Chapter 4, I looked at the scientific books owned by Mary Astell, who wrote extensive annotations on some select texts in her library. In this chapter, I want to think less about genre and more about how Astell used her annotations to shape her reading experience, and indeed herself as a reader. Astell frequently added explanatory or organisational notes to her books. One of her most common practices was to create contents pages or indexes for her books, sometimes even despite the fact that these already existed in printed form. Her copy of Descartes' *Les Principes de la Philosophie*, for example, which I discussed at length in Chapter 4, has extensive manuscript notes on the upper endpaper which acts as an index for Astell (see Figure 5.1).[11] For example, at the top of the page there is a line written by Astell that reads, 'The method of Learning Pref. p14.' This corresponds to the preface, where on page 14 there is a line that reads, 'en suitte dequoy, pour faire bien concevoir quell dessein j'ay eu en les publiant, je voudrois icy expliquer l'ordre qu'il me semble qu'on doit tenir pour s'instruire'.[12] Astell also used a shorthand system for referring to the different sections of the book (which was in four parts). For example, one item in the manuscript index is 'Gravity L.4.S.20'. The 'L' here probably stands for 'livre' (book) and the 'S' for 'sous-titre' (subtitle) – in the printed contents under 'la quatriesme partie', number 20 is 'l'explication de la seconde action, en laquelle consiste la pesanteur'.[13]

She added similar indexes or contents pages to several other of her books, although none are quite so detailed as the *Principes*. In her copy of Descartes' *Les Passions de l'Ame* she added her own contents page, listing the chapter number, a direct English translation of the chapter title, then the page number.[14] For example, she wrote, '11 How ye motion of ye muscles is made 16', which corresponds to Article XI on page 16, entitled 'Comment se sont les mouvements des muscles'. She did not finish the contents page, for reasons unclear: she only listed the articles up to number 132, whereas the book itself has 212 articles. This process of adding a

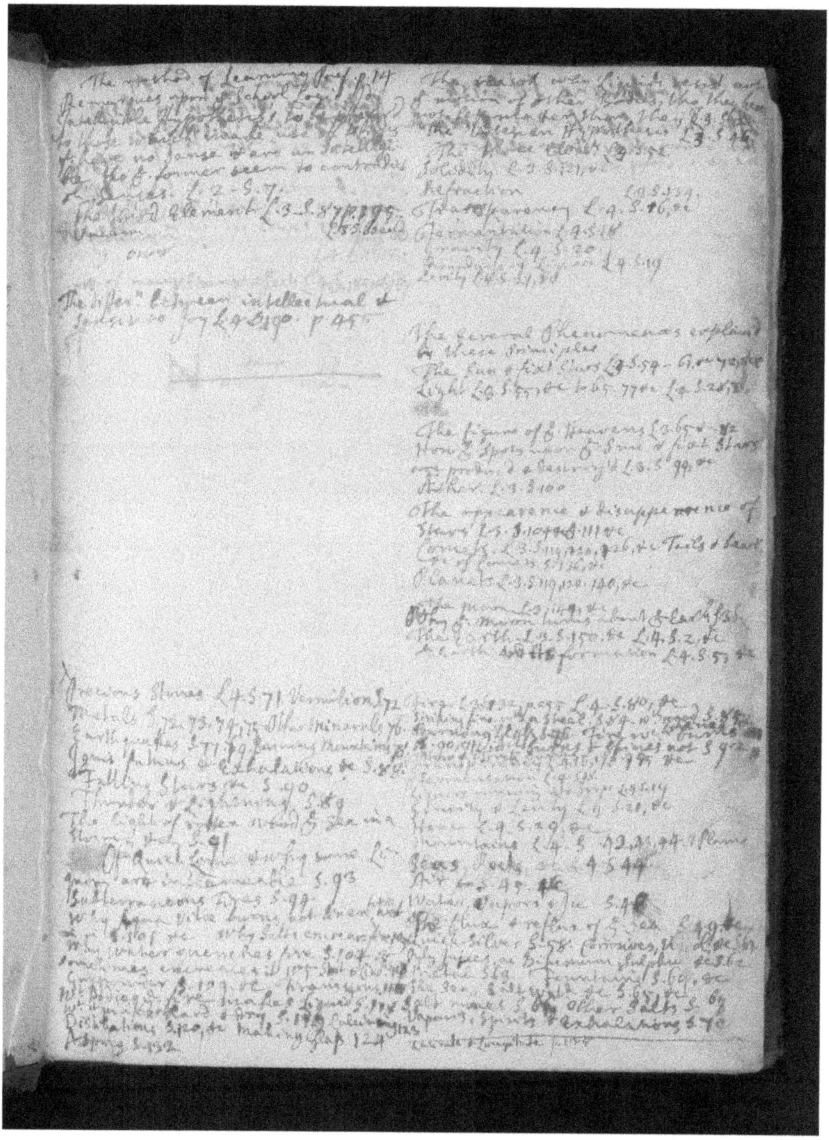

Figure 5.1: René Descartes, *Les Principes de la Philosophie*, H.14.18, Magdalene College, Cambridge.

contents or index to her books shows a clear desire for Astell to be able to navigate the book easily, and gives evidence for multiple readings. She must have wanted to be able to find the section she needed quickly. This may be a reason for adding a handwritten contents when there was already a printed version, as she was able to write it in English and therefore perhaps navigate it more easily. Astell made a definite imprint on her books;

by adding her own organisational notes, she was able to make her reading experience much easier and more effective for her needs.

There is also evidence of multiple re-readings in the way that Astell added marginal notes to her books. She annotated many of her texts in a mixture of pencil and pen; presumably this was not done at the same time, but shows different occasions on which Astell read the books. There is no clear distinction in the purpose of the pencil versus the pen annotations, but there are different annotations practices at play. In some instances, Astell added brief translation to the text: in the preface to Descartes' *Principes*, for example, she wrote in pencil, 'By means of w$^{ch}$' directly above 'Au moyen dequoy.'[15] This may have been one of the first readings, when she was trying to improve her French – this is not a complex phrase, so the fact that she translated that rather than some of the more technical language indicates that she was still getting to grips with the language. She also made corrections to the printed text on occasion. On her copy of William Sancroft's *Modern Policies*, she wrote 'ye' in the margins next to the word 'Bible', as no 'the' had been printed.[16] Finally, she changed the word 'ambiguous' to 'ambitious' by crossing out the 'gu' and writing 'ti' above the text.[17] Evidently there was one level of her reading which was largely concerned with understanding the text itself, either through translation or by making her own corrections.

There is also a level of reading that has a lot in common with the indexing Astell did on several of her texts. In many of her books she added short summaries of passages in the margins, acting as a reading guide. This usually took the form of a few words; on Descartes' *Principes*, she wrote short notes summarising the text, such as 'W$^{t}$ Wisdom is' next to a passage about philosophy and the nature of wisdom.[18] There were also the notes referring to other texts that I discussed in Chapter 4, which allowed her to develop and add to the ideas within the text itself. She did not only do this with philosophical texts, although these were the most common ones for her to annotate. She used x's to mark passages of interest in her copy of a Civil War pamphlet.[19] She also added some cross-referencing. This was a Royalist pamphlet, arguing that armed resistance to the king was illegitimate. Most of Astell's notes in this pamphlet were short summaries, but sometimes she referenced other reading. For example, she wrote, 'see in contradiction to ys M Lock of Gov viz p 33, 34' in the margins of page 3.[20] Dudley Diggs' Royalist ideas would be directly contrary to Locke's theory of the social contract between monarch and subjects; Astell was adding notes from her much more up-to-date reading, working to contextualise the text nearly half a century after its publication.

Each intervention that Astell made on the text added to and altered her own reading experience, whether they allowed her to improve her understanding of either the language or ideas, or to use the text more easily by being able to deconstruct it and find what she was looking for. This would then create a very different reading experience when she returned to the text – one altered by her own voice – and reinscribed her self-fashioning as an intellectual reader and participant in philosophical and political debates.

Anne Clifford's annotations also provide evidence of her re-reading and structured reading, as discussed in Chapter 2. She or her scribe recorded the dates of the readings or re-readings they made of her books in the front, providing a useful record of the time and sometimes place of her reading.[21] In her copy of Anthony Weldon's *The Court and Character of King James*, opposite the title page, a scribe has written, 'about the beginninge of June in 1669 I began to read this Booke my selfe in Appleby Castle and I & diverse of my men servants made an end of readinge of itt the 21st of ye same in 1669'.[22] The book was annotated with both Clifford's hand and that of a scribe, making multiple readings evident; it seems that Clifford would both read books herself and have them read to her. The annotations, such as the inscription above, are usually in Clifford's 'voice' if not her hand, indicating that she would direct the scribes to write in the margins. In some of her other extant books there has been a reasonably clear divide between the contents of the scribe's annotations and those of Clifford herself. Stephen Orgel, in studying Clifford's copy of *A Mirour for Magistrates*, notes the presence of three scribal hands, as well as numerous underlinings. *A Mirour* was a collection of poems, first published in 1559, from the perspective of various statesmen warning about the abuse of power.[23] He identifies the main hand as that of William Watkinson, Clifford's secretary throughout the 1660s and 1670s.[24] Watkinson's annotations provided most of the information about when and where reading took place, and adopted a variety of personas.[25] Clifford's annotations on the other hand, as with her copy of *Argenis*, are often more personal comments, particularly at points concerning her own family.

However, in *The Court and Character* this is not always the case. Some of Watkinson's annotations are quite prosaic, largely just noting the names of figures mentioned in the text. However, there is also a more subjective, political perspective shown. Next to a passage describing King James I, which reads, 'His Beard was very thin: His Tongue too large for his mouth, which ever made him speak full in the mouth, and made him drink very uncomely, as if eating his drink, which came out into the cup of each side of his mouth', the scribe has written, 'a righte description of Kinge James'.[26] James did not support Clifford's early attempts to regain her family estates, inherited by her uncle due to an entail, and was complicit in her disinheritance when he signed an order against her following her mother's death, allowing her husband to sign away his claim to her estates.[27] She recorded in her diary how 'sometimes he used fair means & persuasions, & sometimes foul means, but I was resolved before so as nothing would move me'.[28] Clifford's annotations hint towards their contentious relationship and a possible dislike on her part that continued years after his death.

Clifford's own spiky italic annotations are of a very similar tone to those in Watkinson's hand. She very evidently agreed with Weldon's unfavourable impression of King James.[29] Next to a few lines claiming, 'His sending Embassadours, were no lesse chargeable then dishonourable and unprofitable to him and his whole Kingdome; for he was ever abused in all Negotiations', Clifford wrote, 'True' in the margins.[30] Moreover, she wrote 'note' next to an underlined description of James as 'the wisest foole in Christendome'.[31] She also drew on her own experience, albeit not firsthand, by writing, 'this I have Herd' next to a passage about a supposed plot by Buckingham to kill James.[32] Clifford's annotations may not have structured her reading in the same way that Astell's did, but they would certainly have altered her re-reading experiences. Clifford backs up the text from her own experience and opinion, emphasising certain passages (usually about James' shortcomings) for subsequent readers. This may include herself – in re-reading the book, which she evidently did, either aurally or directly, she may have reaffirmed her own political position and her opposition to James, and perhaps even kept her grudge alive years after his death.

Manuscript notebooks similarly provide an invaluable insight into what and how women were reading in the early modern period. What women chose to copy into their notebooks, and the ways in which they structured the entries, allows us to consider their various and complex reading habits, and the temporality thereof. Extracts copied into books involved careful thought and selection, revealing a great deal about the compiler's own responses to the text, but also what they wanted to reveal to the world about their reading habits.

They were evidently books that were re-used and re-read beyond the initial compilation. They might pass through many hands and be read or written by many different authors. Elizabeth Lyttelton, daughter of Sir Thomas Browne, the physician and author of *Religio Medico*, kept a commonplace book that reveals some of the complexities of authorship in manuscript culture.[33] While the book is listed by Cambridge University's online catalogue as belonging to Elizabeth Lyttelton, it contains the signature of her sister, Mary Browne, on both the front and end flyleaves, and according to the catalogue notes was 'kept for the benefit of the daughters of Sir Thomas Browne, and was principally the property of his daughter Elizabeth. It contains pieces by and relating to Sir Thomas Browne, including a poem and piece of prose by him, although none of the writing is in Browne's hand'.[34] Victoria Burke has suggested that Elizabeth was the scribe, identifying two distinct phases of compilation probably dating to different times in her life, evidenced by slight handwriting differences. Burke suggests that the 'earlier entries consist primarily of religious verse, Englished extracts from the classics, proverbial couplets, and fragments from Sir Thomas Browne's writing. Sometimes filling in blank spaces left in her earlier transcriptions, Lyttelton returned, probably after 1687, to write a mixture of religious and secular poetry and prose'.[35] This very clearly attests to Elizabeth's re-reading habits – she returned to the text after several years and added to it, both showing a re-reading of the manuscript and a potential for it to be read again in the future.

One entry in particular gives a valuable insight into Elizabeth's early reading habits. It was written on behalf of Thomas Browne, and is entitled, 'The books which my daughter Elizabeth hath read unto me at nights till she read y$^{m}$ all out.'[36] The book list includes Plutarch, various histories (largely European rather than English), travel narratives and two mentions of religious texts, namely 'fox his book of Martyrs' and 'some hundreds of Sermons'.[37] This large, varied reading list is a relatively unusual curriculum for a young girl and the communal reading experience of father and daughter indicates that Thomas Browne was interested in his daughter's education. Margaret King has explored the influence of certain Renaissance men on their daughters' intellectualism, using examples of various Italian learned women whose fathers were instrumental in their early education.[38] Thomas Browne seems to have followed this path with Elizabeth, with whom he had a close relationship.[39] Lyttelton's intellectual interests were clearly heavily influenced by her father: for example, Burke has identified several extracts in the book that came from texts he is known to have owned. Browne himself kept many commonplace books, and he and his daughter shared a love of books.[40] The predominance of religious and devotional literature in the book list and the textual extracts is reflective of many women's reading habits at the time, at least those that they were willing to record.

Interventions by either men or women display aspects of gendered textual authority and the various uses of manuscripts that had multiple authors. An example of this gendered intervention can also be seen in the commonplace book written by Anne Ley and her husband, Roger Ley, now held in the William Andrews Clark Memorial Library. This book provides a useful source for looking at the interplay of gender and authorship in manuscript commonplace culture, and for thinking about reading notes as a process of memorialisation.[41] In this case, a woman, Anne Ley, was the primary compiler, with notes and extracts added later by her husband Roger, who was the curate of St Leonard's, Shoreditch. Anne wrote several poems, which appear to be her own works, but titles have been added in Roger's hand, suggesting he undertook, in Jill Seal Millman and Gillian Wright's words, a 'retrospective (re)ordering of his wife's writings'.[42] Presumably, the book was first compiled by Anne, with Roger adding material after her death. He included a short biography of Anne at the beginning, added titles to her entries, copied out some of her personal letters and her funeral sermon and finally included sermons of his own. Millman and Wright have also cautioned that he might have edited or manipulated Anne's works, although as it is presumed that it is her own hand, and not copied by a scribe, he could not have edited the poetry too drastically without leaving traces. His additions to the manuscript still represent an intervention, adding a layer of structure and order that Anne had not included. Her voice, therefore, is edited and structured through that of her husband, producing multiple identities depending on the point at which the reader interacted with the text.

Despite Roger's interventions, Anne's agency and self-fashioning in her compilation comes through. The first half of the book is taken up with Anne's writing, including extracts from Bishop Joseph Hall's *Meditations*, Anne's own poetry and copies of sermons. It is organised under thematic headings, just as in the humanist commonplace form. Many of the poems and original writings are commenting on items that Ley read and were often highly political, and their inclusion alongside the sermons makes a clear point about her religio-political position. For example, Ley wrote a poem that Roger later entitled, 'Upon a booke written at the beginning of the parliament 1640'. The poem sharply criticised the book, which may have been written by Stephen Marshall, part of the group who wrote, under the acronym Smectynmuus, a book outlining the Presbyterian theory of ministry in response to a publication by Joseph Hall.[43] Part of the poem reads:

> Our Ecclesiasticks those grave learned men
> Are vilifide and scornd by thy rude pen,
> As subtle shallow quite deprivd of wit,
> Good for no bussnesse but a hint or fit,
> Foule mouthd detraction thus to slander those,
> Because by them thy stile no higher rose,
> Is this the way to gaine the vulgars vote,
> Now made with preiudice against that coat,

On their desired ruins wilt thou raise
Thy forlorne hopes, and look for better daies.[44]

The Leys were Laudians, and Anne's scathing rebuttal shows her political insights and understanding of current events. Her suggestion that they were not going to the right to gain popular support is particularly interesting and a complex critique, rather than just dismissing the book. Despite her disgust with the publication, it is clear that she read it, and read it carefully enough to produce a poem criticising it in detail. Marie-Louise Coolahan has argued that '[Ley's] wife's texts are incorporated to his own royalist project to fashion a defiantly anti-Independent identity during the Interregnum'.[45] However, this diminishes Anne's role, and her own political beliefs. She clearly read widely, often contrary to her own views, and was well aware of the nuances of the political conflict at the beginning of the Civil War period.

The text clearly did function as a memorial, however. Alongside Roger's editorial interventions such as adding headings, he also transcribed several of Anne's letters in the second half of the volume, followed by her will and an extract from her funeral sermon. The will is headed, 'Part of that which she made in y$^{e}$ nature of a will June 7$^{th}$ 1636. When the plague began to breake forth more then before. She died of that sicknesse 5 yeeres and some moneths after.'[46] Roger's additions to Anne's text therefore move the manuscript from a set of reading and writing notes to a memorial to his wife. His choice of this particular manuscript to do so suggests that her reading notes and poems were an important part of her, and that he felt the need to preserve them as part of the memorial. This represents a more complicated construction of textual identity: Anne's own writing indicates that she wanted to communicate very firmly her political and religious beliefs, whereas Roger's additions altered this somewhat, bringing her personal life and her death into the picture. While we have no clear evidence for Anne re-reading this book (although, as with most commonplaces, I would argue that she probably did, not least through the process of compilation), clearly for future readers Roger's intervention would alter their experience and perception of the texts and of Anne herself.

All of these women used their reading notes to create a textual identity for themselves which was continually in formation; on each reading and re-reading, their identity was built. Therefore, it did not just happen in the act of writing, but in the act of reading; Clifford may have stated her hatred of King James in the act of writing the note, but in re-reading the text and its interplay with her own annotations, that identity was reaffirmed and contextualised. These identities may have been philosophical, intellectual or based on networks (such as with Astell and Lyttelton), or they may have been more political, as was the case with Clifford and Ley. Of course, it is, however, too simple to parcel these identities into neat categories; each act of annotation created another facet of the self.

This affective use of re-reading was perhaps most clearly expressed by Sarah Cowper, whose extensive commonplace books also bear notes from her explaining how she used them, beyond the initial compilation. At several points she explicitly recorded re-reading her miscellanies: in one, half of which contained many scriptural extracts, she wrote, 'This half of this Book is a Collection of Texts of Scripture w^c may be usefull to reveiw at any times 1^st Dec: 1684.'[47] In another miscellany, full of extracts from biblical commentaries, Cowper wrote on the first page, 'Sarah Cooper 1680', then underneath, 'I reccomend perticulerly the paraphrase upon the Book of Ecclesiastes.'[48] The latter note was written in a shakier hand, which was characteristic of her writing after 1705, thus indicating that she returned to the compilation several decades after initially creating it.[49] This is supported by an entry in the final volume of her diary, where she wrote on May 27, 1715, 'I am now reviewing a large manuscript which thirty-five years ago I collected from expositors of Scripture', referring to the 1680 manuscript.[50]

Cowper gave some indication of why she returned to her manuscripts in yet another religious miscellany, in which she included a preface about the compilation of the book. Reflecting on the process and her later use of the text, she wrote:

> I tasked my self to write one page every day, were it possible (as I hope it is not) that I shou'd never reape other Benefitt from the perusing of the best thoughts and Meditations of learned and Good Men, yet the present diversion from my own troubled thoughts may render it sufficiently worth my Time and Labour. In my reading I have mett with some great examples of this Method. One of Queen Elizabeth, who having a perticuler ffriendship for Henry the fourth of France, never laid any thing more to Heart than his Changing his Religion. This her Greif (says her Historian) she sought to allay by reading y^e sacred Scriptures, and the writings of the Fathers, and even the Books of Philosophers, translating about that time for an amusement Boethius de Consolatione philosophiae into Elegant English. It is recorded by Suetonius of Cesar Augustus, that in his reading all sort of Authors, he cheifly observ'd and transcrib'd such wholsome precepts, or Examples, as might serve him either for publick or private use which upon occasion he produc'd for instruction or admonitions he thought himself or any other had need.[51]

Cowper evidently found comfort in looking back over the religious extracts she had compiled, suggesting that they provided a 'diversion from my own troubled thoughts'. This may have been partly due to their subject matter as devotional extracts (Cowper's piety is well documented). However, the references she makes to Queen Elizabeth and Caesar Augustus, who found succour or use in non-devotional genres, indicate that she saw worth in any form of commonplacing.

In returning to her commonplace books, Cowper was able to remove herself from a situation she found difficult, and reaffirm her own religious piety and devotion that was so central to her concept of herself.[52] This is very similar to Clifford's practice; she was re-fashioning herself repeatedly in her reading of her commonplace books and reading notes. This was a different process to simply re-reading a text (even to re-reading scripture, which Cowper did avidly).[53] In returning to her own notes and organisation, her 'self' was much more clearly imprinted than if she had been reading an unannotated printed book.

## Marks of life

All of the examples so far have revealed women's self-fashioning in a way that was more or less directly related to the text they were reading, annotating or excerpting. Not all women made annotations that were directly related to the subject matter of the text, however, or that so clearly reveal their reading experiences in direct relation to the text. In Chapter 1, I looked at Susanna's Beckwith's annotations on her Bible, which revealed a great deal of annotations about her family life, acting as a memorandum for information such as her children's births. Beckwith's book holds an unusual number of annotations of different kinds but she is by no means the only woman to have used her book as a repository for domestic or familial notes. The writing of memoranda, whether in combination with other notes or not, was common.[54] It was common for this to be done in Bibles, as Beckwith did, but this was not the only genre used for such marginalia.[55] William Sherman in *Used Books* argued for the study of what he called the 'matriarchive', suggesting that we need to broaden our study of annotations to include women.[56] As he points out, 'there is some evidence (even if the surviving traces are now few and far between) that women used the printed books in their households not simply as guides to proper devotion or conduct but to store and circulate individual and collective records – in other words, in just the same way that they used manuscript compilations . . . readers used these blank but bounded spaces not only to register their reactions to the book but to turn the book itself into an *archive* – of culinary, spiritual, familial, financial, intellectual, medical, and even meteorological information'.[57] This section, therefore, will build on this idea and consider how annotations allowed women to create a sense of their self within the contexts of family life and sociability.[58]

One of the most common forms of annotation for women was inscribing their signatures, often with the formulation 'her book', which we have seen repeatedly throughout previous chapters. Familial and social relationships are visible in these autograph inscriptions. As Scott-Warren and Fleming have suggested, the flyleaves and endpapers of a book became a place where owners and readers could demonstrate their sociable and relational identity. These relationships were often, although not always, homosocial, revealing a book as a nexus in circles of female family and friends.[59] This is clearly important for a woman's identity: by advertising her place within such networks, she could lay claim to social standing, and advertise her political, social or intellectual allegiances.

Inscriptions attest to the fact that books were often given as gifts as part of these relationships between family and friends. On a copy of Francisco de Quintana's *The History of Don Fenise*, the front flyleaf is inscribed, 'Penelope Compton her Book g[e]uene hir by the Countes of Northapton May the 2: 1652.'[60] Below that is written 'An Compton' in a late seventeenth- or early eighteenth-century hand. The former inscription implies a level of ceremony with the gift-giving; this was not simply the lending of a book between two friends or acquaintances, but instead was a gesture significant enough for the recipient to mark it in ink. In this case, the book was originally given by Isabella Compton (née Sackville), the Countess of Northampton, to her sister-in-law, Penelope Compton, about five years after Isabella's marriage. The latter signature suggests that the book remained within the family, passed down to a daughter, sister or niece, or other female relative, who then felt the need to mark her own ownership. 'An' could have been Lady Anne Compton, who died in 1705. However, she married Hugh Cholmley in 1665/6, so if the hand is later, then she was either not using her married name or it was another Anne in the family.

A similar transaction is evident in Frances Wolfreston's copy of Cervantes' *The Travels of Persiles and Sigismunda*.[61] Wolfreston has written, 'Frances Wolfreston hor bouk geven hor by hor sister ursly medellmore' on the flyleaf. The fact of noting this down again gives some significance to the passing of the book between sisters; Wolfreston obviously wanted some record of the transaction. She often recorded the provenance of her books. In her copy of Chaucer held at the Folger Library, she noted that her mother-in-law, Mary Wolfreston, gave her the book.[62] This is revealing about familial relationships, and the ways in which book lending and giving formed part of a sociable transaction. Natalie Zemon Davis has discussed the role of the book as a gift in sixteenth-century France, arguing that books were 'part of systems of gift and obligation'.[63] Passing books between friends and family, then, was a marker of the relationship, a way of demonstrating closeness and possibly creating a shared experience through the act of reading.

Relationships between women are not the only ones revealed in inscriptions on books. There are several examples of men and women both signing books, for example in the case of the Kemp family. Their copy of Jean-Pierre Camus' *Admirable Events* is signed on the flyleaf, 'Robt Kemp: November 16: 1651', and then on the next page, undated but in a seventeenth-century hand, 'Mary Kemp her Book'.[64] It is unclear what relationship Robert and Mary Kemp bore to each other; whether husband and wife, brother and sister, or father and daughter, but the dual ownership claims are interesting. They may have signed it at different times, or possibly it was indicative of disputed book ownership.

Another example of this joint or contested ownership comes from the Folger Library's copy of Evelyn's *Publick Employment*. On the inside of the front cover is written, 'Elizabeth Herbert her Booke 1679', and on the opposite page, 'Nathanel Herbert his Booke 1679'.[65] Again, we cannot be certain of the exact relationship between these two, but the placement of their inscriptions, on pages facing each other, conjures an image of a (quite passive aggressive) contest over the book. Elizabeth has reiterated her claim by writing her name again, several times, on the back endpaper. These hints at familial relationships are rarely elaborated on, but such inscriptions give a partial insight into early modern intra- and inter-household connections. Books were used as part of the interaction between spouses, or other family members, in the early modern household, hinting at friendships or disagreements. Books clearly facilitated exchange in relationships, and these gifts were deemed noteworthy, either to the receiver or the giver. As evidenced by contemporary letters, lending books was very common, so it is hard to know whether these inscriptions are evidence of lending or donating the books, but either way the exchange hints at various familial and sociable relationships.

Books and notes on books could also be used to record other aspects of life, beyond demonstrating a sociable relationship. Text was at the heart of the household, and both women's annotations on printed books and their own manuscript compilations reveal this. Some domestic annotations reflected and were influenced by the genre of the book, as in the case of Frances Wolfreston's collection of almanacs.[66] Wolfreston included many familial notes, generally written alongside entries for the months in which the events took place.[67] For example, beside the entry for November 1666, Wolfreston wrote, 'my hosbond did the 5 day of this month was buried the 7 day'.[68] This is very unemotional, but there are several mentions of death in the almanacs, noting the dates of her mother, brother and other relatives' deaths. There is also information about family friends and acquaintances; on the page for September 1666, for example, Wolfreston wrote, 'Captin Atherly was maried this eare'.[69] She recorded the comings and goings of family members when they were visiting, and also added a list of 'Thes plais boucks i lend to cosen robart comarford in iun' at the end of the 1670 almanac, perhaps with the view to getting them back some day.[70] In each almanac, up until 1677, the year she died, Wolfreston included marginal annotations about the lives of family members and friends, noting births, marriages and deaths. Thus the almanac, already a way of organising the year, became a more personal tool with the addition of individual notes.[71]

Wolfreston's almanacs are the only ones that bear such practical, domestic notes, while her other books, if annotated at all, tend to include comments on the text itself. For example, in her copy of Shakerley Marmion's play *A Fine Companion*, held in the Huntington Library, she wrote at the end of the dramatis personae, 'a resnabell prity bouk of a usurer and his 2 daters and ther loves with other prity pasiges'.[72] Wolfreston's annotations were related to the text, but rarely appear to act as reading aids in the same way that Renaissance scholars may have used their marginalia. Her short comments on texts appear to act as personalised notes to enhance the reading experience, or record a personal response, but not necessarily as a way of aiding intellectual engagement.

Not all such annotations bore such a clear relation to the genre of the book, however, and reveal another facet of women's engagement with their books. For example, some household notes can be found in William Martyn's *The Historie, and Lives, of the Kings of England*, owned by the Egerton family and currently held in the Huntington Library.[73] The Egertons were a noble family, and John Egerton (1579–1649) was made the Earl of Bridgewater by James I. Alongside various signatures in both the front and back of the book, particularly the names Elizabeth and Frances, on the inside of the back cover someone (probably Frances Stanley Egerton, Countess of Bridgewater, and John's wife)[74] wrote, 'The yeare of our Lorde .1623. I did make at ashridge .3. of fine pelobeares .3. pare of a courcer sorte, and seuen pare of a corsser sort, all made at a time.'[75] Ashridge estate, in Hertfordshire, was owned by the Egerton family. 'Pelobeares' probably means pillowcases: Egerton was making a note of purchases of different types of pillowcases bought for the family estate.[76] The book was not simply used as a literary text; it also functioned as a place for noting domestic activities and making lists, the content of such notes far removed from the content of the book itself. It is unclear why Egerton chose to write this purchase list in this particular book: perhaps it was simply closest to hand. She may have been reading it at the time and made use of the available paper. The act of making such notes, however, changes the book's place within the household, making a historical/political work part of the more immediate world of domestic management.

This was not an uncommon practice. There is a similar list in Thomas Herbert's *A relation of some yeares trauaile, begunne anno 1626. Into Afrique and the greater Asia*, now held in Durham's Ushaw College Library.[77] This book was signed, 'Mary Lloyd her Booke 1684' on the title page. On the final page, above the printer's mark, there is a list in what appears to be Lloyd's hand, noting '9 shirts & shifts – 2 table cloths – 16 napkins – 1 wastcote – 2 crav$^{ts}$ – 2 aprons – 3 p$^{r}$[pair] ruffles – 3 night rails – 3 suits night clothes – 8 hand:'. As with Egerton's note above, there is no clear relationship between the list and the book it is in; Herbert's text is a travelogue, and the placing of the note on a blank endpage suggests that Lloyd was simply using it as a spare piece of paper. This would have an effect, however, on future readers of the book, whether Lloyd herself or others, and it changes the purpose of the book as an object, moving it far beyond the author's original intention.

This use of a book as a repository for domestic management was often done by numerous different readers. Another example of blank pages being used for accounting comes from a copy of Hugh Plat's *Delights for the Ladies*, now held in the Beinecke Library.[78] It is bound together with *A Closet for Ladies and Gentlewomen*, which is often also attributed to Plat – these texts were frequently sold together.[79] This book bears evidence of multiple ownership, with several women having written their names throughout the book. The majority of these are seventeenth- or early eighteenth-century hands. On the back flyleaf there is a page of notes that has been crossed out but is still legible; it reads, 'lad out for M$^{rs}$ Carter forten penc in letters', and underneath that, 'lad out for M$^{r}$ Carter to shaelings in leters'. It is difficult to determine, but this may well be the same hand as the inscription in the inside front flyleaf, which reads, 'Ellenor Hatcher her Booke 1666'. Perhaps some later reader – of which there were obviously several – crossed out the accounts. This may have been because it affected their own reading experience or they wanted to remove the mark of previous readers (although the other signatures had not been crossed out).

It was not only printed books that received this treatment. Francis Cholmondeley's commonplace book bears his signature on the back flyleaf ('Francis Cholmondeley His Booke'), but the manuscript also carries the signature of his wife, Elizabeth, on the same page: 'Elizabeth Cholmondeley her Booke Anno: Do: 1651'.[80] The majority of the manuscript, which contains various religious and philosophical reflections, is in Francis' hand. However, on the front flyleaf is a list of costs in what appears to be Elizabeth's hand, listing payments for fabrics, amongst other items.[81] There was obviously some shared ownership of the manuscript, even if it was written largely in a single hand. We can only speculate as to the reasons why Elizabeth may have signed the book, and it cannot be taken as proof of readership, but her intervention in the form of her signature and cost list shows some claim to the manuscript itself, and an active participation in the creation of the book as we see it now.

Books were therefore frequently used as repositories for accounts by women. This allowed them to exert some power over the text; by writing shopping lists and records of payments on books, they brought them into the domestic sphere and adapted them for their own purposes. Some examples given here are less radical than others – Hugh Plat's book was specifically about household management – but Egerton and Lloyd's inscriptions on history and travel texts respectively show a certain disregard for the genre of the book that demonstrates their authority as owners or readers, as in some ways does Elizabeth Cholmondeley's appropriation of her husband's commonplace book. These accounts (and indeed all the 'domestic' annotations collected here) would be read as well as written, and would potentially alter the reading experience. For the annotators, it may make future readings more personal, stamping a sense of their own identity on the book. For other readers, it may draw them out of the text itself – something which may have irritated a reader of Hatcher's book.

We rarely think about household accounts and lists as things that are read as well as written. However, there is clear evidence of re-reading in several women's notebooks from the seventeenth century. A common feature of women's manuscript notebooks is the inclusion of various different forms of extracts, such as household notes, recipes and diary entries, which do not simply reflect their literary activities but are evidence of wider reading beyond the print literary sphere. These were clearly read and re-read, both by their compilers and by others, and often had a sole female author. Their departure from the 'traditional' commonplace form and the lack of male intervention or authority has often led to them being overlooked in studies of active reading and note-taking, but in fact they provide valuable sources for a more comprehensive study of women's reading habits.

Elizabeth Lowther's commonplace book, held by the West Yorkshire Archive Service, provides a useful demonstration of this. The manuscript references the 'landes att Marton' and bears the name 'Lady Elizabeth Lowther'. Marton is a parish just south of Middlesborough, now called

Marton-in-Cleveland. According to the Victoria County History, the manor house there was sold by Thomas Layton in 1633 to Sir John Lowther.[82] This was Elizabeth's grandfather; her father, Ralph, died in 1696, at which point the manor passed to her brother John, who died without issue in 1729. Elizabeth herself was brought up at Ackworth Park in West Yorkshire, and married Robert Frank, Recorder of Pontefract. Given the name recorded on the notebook, she probably compiled it before her marriage. The manuscript contains a mixture of religious writings, letters, indentures, bills and other such documents.[83] It is easy to forget that the latter documents were a significant part of the everyday reading experience, particularly for women running their households. The manuscript is written in two hands, one neat secretary hand, presumably a scribe or a household clerk, and one messier italic, belonging to Lowther herself. The scribe's hand is the most common, but Lowther has added notes to the entries, created contents tables and written some sections herself.

It is difficult to get an overall sense of the reasons behind compiling the manuscript. It seems likely that it was intended as a record of the running of the family's property, an area for which many women of the gentry would have been responsible (although Elizabeth was unmarried at the time, which perhaps indicates she was taking on duties in preparation for marriage, or in the absence of another woman to run the household). However, there are also infrequent examples of other materials, for example the pages dedicated to 'A Brief Accompt of the Returne of the Israelites out of Egypt, of their passage in the Wildernesse of Arabia Petrea, of their Sacrifices during their stay in the wildernesse.'[84] This page of text is accompanied by a hand-drawn map showing the lands of Egypt and Palestine. This does not appear to have been directly excerpted from any specific text, but is rather a manuscript account relying on scripture and other religious writings about the persecution of the Israelites.[85] This is the only entry that does not appear to be directly linked to Lowther and her family, and the reasons for its inclusion and placement are unclear. It was written in the scribe's hand, with no accompanying notes by Lowther.

The book is structured by what Jonathan Gibson has called a 'reverse casting-off of blanks', which involves the compiler writing from both ends of the book, turning the volume upside down to start from the back of the manuscript.[86] He argues that 'compilers will use this method if a two-part structure is necessary and if they either (a) want to leave an equal amount of space for each type of entry, or (b) do not know how much space is required by each section'.[87] This implies a clear distinction in subject matter between the two sections, which can be seen only partially in Lowther's manuscript: the front section is largely taken up with copies of letters sent by and to her, which are also present in the end section, although there is a great deal of other material here as well. The deliberateness of the format and the way in which it was read is indicated in the heading for the contents page of the end section, written by Lowther, which reads, 'a catalogue of all things in this boock this way wrighten'. This implies that the two sections would be read independently, treated almost as two separate manuscripts.

There is very clear evidence for Lowther's reading of this manuscript as she wrote, at the end of the front section of the text, 'this boock loocked over the 27th of aprill 1689'.[88] She added the same inscription on the following page, at the end of the second section of the book, again implying that the two sections were treated as distinct (even though she 'loocked over' them on the same day). Lowther clearly read the book at least once, and it is possible (although there is admittedly no clear evidence for this) that this was when she added the notes to the scribe's text, annotating her manuscript in the same way as one would a printed book. Because of the dates on some of the bills entered in the manuscript, this could have been a few years after the composition, although not very many – the documents in the manuscript largely seem to have been created over the course of the 1680s. This is likely not, then, a re-reading from far in the future, motivated by a remembrance, but perhaps a more practical need to use the book to keep track of the family's affairs. It also served to signify Elizabeth's place in the household and her dedication to the running of the estate, displaying her power and competency within that space.

## Conclusion

In the discussion of annotating and commonplacing practices, it is often forgotten that these notes were themselves meant to be read and re-read. If we consider these practices as acts of reading as well as acts of writing, we can broaden our understanding of the reading experience itself. Throughout this book I have explored the connections between identity and reading: by looking at women's interventions in the text, we can gain a clearer understanding of that process. Identity construction is fluid: it does not happen just once but is formed and reformed continually as a person reads and re-reads the text, gaining different dimensions every time.

As with the last two chapters, this emphasises the need to look beyond print for a fuller understanding of women's reading habits. Women's reading notes and manuscript books demonstrate this process of identity construction very clearly; we can read them, as Ophir suggested, as forms of life-writing. This quite clearly is a form of autobiography that uses reading as a vector for understanding and negotiating identity. In recording their interactions with texts, whether by adding notes in margins or creating manuscript commonplace books, women were able to explore and communicate multiple facets of their selves, aligning themselves with political, religious, social or economic positions. In paying attention to re-reading practices, we can see the complexities of this identity construction; we can understand the temporality and fluidity of the practice much more clearly.

## Notes

1. Pamela Mackenzie and Elisabeth Davies, 'The Once and Future Self: (Re)Reading Personal Lists, Notes, and Calendars', in *Plotting the Reading Experience: Theory, Practice, Politics*, ed. Lynne McKechnie, Kjell Ivar Skjerdingstad, Knut Oterholm, Magnus Persson and Paulette M. Rothbauer (Waterloo, Ontario: Wilfrid Laurier University Press, 2016), 149–150.

2. Mackenzie and Davies, 'The Once and Future Self', 150.

3. Christopher Burlinson has challenged this in his chapter on student notebooks, arguing that they were not generally re-used beyond the period of study and/or examination. However, those notebooks can be tied to a particular point in time; the commonplace books in this chapter arguably had a longer life and were less associated with a specific, time-limited use. See Christopher Burlinson, 'The Use and Re-Use of Early Seventeenth-Century Student Notebooks: Inside and Outside the University', in *Material Readings of Early Modern Culture: Texts and Social Practices, 1580–1730*, ed. James Daybell and Peter Hinds (Basingstoke: Palgrave Macmillan, 2010), 229–245.

4. See, for example, Ann Moss, 'Commonplace-Rhetoric and Thought-Patterns in Early Modern Culture', in *The Recovery of Rhetoric: Persuasive Discourse and Disciplinarity in the Human Sciences*, edited by R. H. Roberts and J. M. M. Good (Charlottesville, VA: University Press of Virginia, 1993), 49–60; Moss, *Printed Commonplace-Books and the Structuring of Renaissance Thought* (Oxford: Clarendon, 1996). Elizabeth Griffiths and Jane Whittle produced a compelling study of women's manuscript notebooks, investigating the account books of the Norfolk-based Le Strange family, but they do not specifically connect this to reading practices. See Elizabeth Griffiths and Jane Whittle, *Consumption and Gender in the Early Seventeenth-Century Household: The World of Alice Le Strange* (Oxford: Oxford University Press, 2012). See also Jonathan Gibson, 'Casting Off Blanks: Hidden Structures in Early Modern Paper Books', in *Material Readings of Early Modern Culture: Texts and Social Practices, 1580–1730*, ed. James Daybell and Peter Hinds (Basingstoke: Palgrave Macmillan, 2010), 210. The boundaries between a commonplace book and other forms of manuscript compilation (such as a miscellany) are quite porous. See, for example, Fred Schurink, 'Manuscript Commonplace Books, Literature, and Reading in Early Modern England', *Huntington Library Quarterly* 73, no. 3 (2010): 453–469. See Victoria E. Burke, '"Memorial Books": Commonplaces, Gender, and Manuscript Compilation in Seventeenth-Century England', in *Ars Reminiscendi: Mind and Memory in Renaissance Culture*, ed. Donald Beecher and Grant Williams (Toronto: Centre for Reformation and Renaissance Studies, 2009), 121–138; Adam Smyth, 'Commonplace Book Culture: A List of Sixteen Traits', in

*Women and Writing c.1340–c.1650: The Domestication of Print Culture*, ed. Anne Lawrence-Mathers and Phillipa Hardman (York: York Medieval Press, 2010), 90–110.

5. Ella Ophir, 'The Diary and the Commonplace Book: Self-Inscription in *The Note Books of a Woman Alone*', *Biography* 38, no. 1 (2015): 41–55.

6. Ophir, 'The Diary and the Commonplace Book', 42.

7. Ophir, 'The Diary and the Commonplace Book', 42–43.

8. Ophir, 'The Diary and the Commonplace Book', 48.

9. Stephen Colclough, *Consuming Texts: Readers and Reading Communities 1695–1870* (Basingstoke: Palgrave Macmillan, 2007), 30.

10. This idea could be applied to the journals of seventeenth-century men such as Thomas Juxon, who wrote largely about political affairs, only rarely recording events from his own life. His identity in the journal was therefore intrinsically connected to the events he reported. See Keith Lindley and David Scott, ed., *The Journal of Thomas Juxon, 1644–1647*, Camden Fifth Series, vol. 13 (Cambridge: Cambridge University Press, 1999).

11. René Descartes, *Les Principes de la Philosophie* (A Paris: Chez Theodore Girard, 1681). H.14.18, Magdalene College, Cambridge.

12. Translation: 'Therefore, to better understand what I have published here, I would like here to explain the order which it seems to me necessary to follow to instruct oneself.'

13. Translation: 'the fourth part . . . the explanation of the second action, of which consists gravity'.

14. René Descartes, *Les Passions de l'Ame* (A Amsterdam: Chez Lovis Elzevier, 1650). H.9.19, Magdalene College.

15. Descartes, *Les Principes de la Philosophie*, 18.

16. William Sancroft, *Modern Policies, taken from Machiavel, Borgia, and other choice authors / by an eye-witnesse* (London: Printed for Tho. Dring, 1655), 6. G.10.77, Magdalene College.

17. Sancroft, *Modern Policies*, 16. It is not clear why she made this change, as having looked at several editions on Sancroft's work, this word is always printed as 'ambiguous', and it makes sense within the text.

18. Descartes, *Les Principes de la Philosophie*, 2.

19. Dudley Diggs, *The vnlawfulnesse of subjects taking up armes against their soveraigne, in what case soever: together with an answer to all objections scattered in their severall bookes. And a proofe that notwithstanding such resistance as they plead for, were not damnable, yet the present warre made upon the King is so, because those cases, in which onely some men have dared to excuse it, are evidently not now; His Majesty fighting onely to preserve himselfe, and the rights of the subjects / written by Dudley Diggs, Gentleman: late fellow of All-Soules Colledge in Oxford* ([London]: [s.n.], 1647). C.5.53, Magdalene College.

20. Diggs, *The vnlawfulnesse of subjects*, 3.

21. For more on reading and time, see Christina Lupton, *Reading and the Making of Time in the Eighteenth Century* (Baltimore, MD: Johns Hopkins University Press, 2018).

22. Anthony Weldon, *The Court and Character of King James. Whereunto is now added the Court of King Charles: Continued Unto the beginning of these unhappy Times. With some Observations upon Him instead of a Character. Collected and perfected by Sir A. W.* (Printed at London by R. I., 1651). WD/Hoth/A988/22, Cumbria Record Office, Kendal.

23. Harriet Archer and Andrew Hadfield, ed., *A Mirror for Magistrates in Context: Literature, History and Politics in Early Modern England* (Cambridge: Cambridge University Press, 2016).

24. Stephen Orgel, 'Reading Lady Anne Clifford's *A Mirovr for Magistrates*', in *Lady Anne Clifford: Culture, Patronage and Gender in 17th-Century Britain*, ed. Karen Hearn and Lyn Hulse (Leeds: Yorkshire Archaeological Society, 2009), 112.

25. Orgel, 'Reading Lady Anne Clifford's *A Mirovr for Magistrates*', 112.

26. Weldon, *The Court and Character of King James*, 165.

27. Anne Clifford, *The Diaries of Lady Anne Clifford*, ed. D. J. H. Clifford (Stroud: Sutton Publishing, 1990), 18.

28. Clifford, *The Diaries of Lady Anne Clifford*, 45.

29. Weldon had a minor position in James' household, but was dismissed by the king for writing a satire about the people of Scotland, and wrote *The Court and Character* as revenge (although this was not published until the 1650s). The venomous nature of the text has often been attributed to Weldon's anti-Scots views, and has been influential on subsequent portrayals of James I. See Jenny Wormald, 'James VI and I: Two Kings or One?', *History* 68, no. 223 (1983): 187–209; Pauline Croft, *King James* (Basingstoke: Palgrave Macmillan, 2003).

30. Weldon, *The Court and Character of King James*, 171.

31. Weldon, *The Court and Character of King James*, 173.

32. Weldon, *The Court and Character of King James*, 142.

33. Elizabeth Lyttelton, Commonplace Book, c.1680. MS Add 8460, Cambridge University Library, Cambridge.

34. 'Elizabeth Lyttleton: Commonplace Book', *ArchiveSearch*, Cambridge University Library, accessed September 27, 2023, collection: Elizabeth Lyttelton: Commonplace book, ArchiveSearch (cam.ac.uk).

35. Victoria E. Burke, 'Contexts for Women's Manuscript Miscellanies: The Case of Elizabeth Lyttelton and Sir Thomas Browne', *The Yearbook of English Studies* 33, Medieval and Early Modern Miscellanies and Anthologies (2003): 318.

36. MS Add 8460, f44v, Cambridge University Library.

37. MS Add 8460, f44v–f45r.

38. Margaret L. King, *Women of the Renaissance* (Chicago, IL: University of Chicago Press, 1991), 184.

39. Burke, 'Contexts for Women's Manuscript Miscellanies', 319.

40. Reid Barbour, *Sir Thomas Browne: A Life* (Oxford: Oxford University Press, 2013), 433.

41. Manuscript commonplace book of Anne and Roger Ley, c.1623–c.1667, MS.1952.003, Clark Library, Los Angeles.

42. Jill Seal Millman and Gillian Wright, ed., *Early Modern Women's Manuscript Poetry* (Manchester: Manchester University Press, 2005), 77.

43. Jane Stevenson and Peter Davidson, ed., *Early Modern Women Poets (1520–1700): An Anthology* (Oxford: Oxford University Press, 2001), 259.

44. MS.1952.003, f94v, Clark Library.

45. Marie-Louise Coolahan, 'Literary Memorialisation and the Posthumous Construction of Female Authorship', in *The Arts of Remembrance in Early Modern England: Memorial Cultures of the Post Reformation*, ed. Andrew Gordon and Thomas Rist (London: Routledge, 2016), 162.

46. MS.1952.003, f106r.

47. Sarah Cowper, *Miscellany*, c.1675–1705. D/EP F38, Hertfordshire Archives and Local Studies, Hertford.

48. Sarah Cowper, *Biblical Commentary*, c.1685. D/EP F39, Hertfordshire Archives and Local Studies.

49. 'Hertfordshire Archives and Local Studies: D/EP F39', *Perdita*, 2005, accessed September 26, 2023. Perdita: ms HRODEPF39: frames version (warwick.ac.uk).

50. Sarah Cowper, *Diary, Volume 7*, 1713–1716, 223. D/EP F35, Hertfordshire Archives and Local Studies.

51. Sarah Cowper, *Miscellany*, c.1690. D/EP F43, Hertfordshire Archives and Local Studies.

52. On Cowper's identity, see Anne Kugler, 'Constructing Wifely Identity: Prescription and Practice in the Life of Lady Sarah Cowper', *Journal of British Studies* 40, no. 3 (2001): 291–323.

53. Sarah Cowper, *Miscellany*, c.1700. D/EP F44, Hertfordshire Archives and Local Studies.

54. This has often been attributed to the limited availability of paper in the early modern world, but Helen Smith has recently argued, convincingly, that '[f]ar from being paper-short, early modern England was a society in which diverse kinds of paper circulated, and were used for a wealth of purposes'. See Helen Smith, '"A unique instance of art": The Proliferating Surfaces of Early Modern Paper', *Journal of the Northern Renaissance* 8 (2017): 18.

55. We can speculate that the use of the Bible for family memoranda could be due to the physicality of the book. As a large book, it not only had extensive space for notes but also would have occupied a definite physical space within the household. It, moreover, would have been a book that would have been treasured, very unlikely to be discarded, so there would be no danger of losing the notes.

56. William H. Sherman, *Used Books: Marking Readers in Renaissance England* (Philadelphia, PA: University of Pennsylvania Press, 2008).

57. Sherman, *Used Books*, 59.

58. Reading was often intertwined with seventeenth- and eighteenth-century sociability. Kate Loveman, for example, has examined information exchange, reading, book collecting and sociability in the late seventeenth century by looking at Samuel Pepys' library and reading habits. See Kate Loveman, *Samuel Pepys and his Books: Reading, News Gathering, and Sociability, 1660–1703* (Oxford: Oxford University Press, 2015). For an examination of Restoration sociability, see Susan E. Whyman, *Sociability and Power in Late-Stuart England: The Cultural World of the Verneys, 1660–1720* (Oxford: Oxford University Press, 1999); for the eighteenth-century French context and the role of the salon, see Antoine Lilti, *The World of the Salons: Sociability and Worldliness in Eighteenth-Century Paris*, trans. Lydia G. Cochrane (Oxford: Oxford University Press, 2005).

59. Victoria Burke has examined women's participation in heterosocial literary networks, examining both annotations and commonplace books. She argues, in relation to the Shakespeare first folio inscribed by Anne Denton, that 'Denton's positioning of herself as part of a circle is not something commonly seen on title pages of women's manuscripts; inscriptions declaring ownership are more typical'. This is certainly true for heterosocial interactions, but relationships between women were often inscribed on the pages of books, as will be demonstrated here. See Victoria E. Burke, 'Reading Friends: Women's Participation in "Masculine" Literary Culture', in *Early Modern Women's Manuscript Writing: Selected Papers from the Trinity/Trent Colloquium*, ed. Victoria E. Burke and Jonathan Gibson (Aldershot: Ashgate, 2004), 75.

60. Francisco de Quintana, *The History of Don Fenise. A New Romance, Written in Spanish by Francisco de las-Coveras. And now Englished by a Person of Honour* (London: Printed for Humphrey Moseley, 1651). He67 82, Beinecke Rare Book and Manuscript Library, New Haven.

61. Miguel de Cervantes, *The Travels of Persiles and Sigismunda. A Northern History. Wherein, amongst the variable Fortunes of the Prince of Thule, and this Princesse of Frisland, are interlaced many Witty Discourses, Morall, Politicall, and Delightfull. The first Copie, beeing written in Spanish; translated afterward into French; and now, last, into English* (London: Printed by *H. L.* for *M. L.*, 1619). PQ 6329.T77 1619, Clark Library.

62. Geoffrey Chaucer, *The Workes of Geffray Chaucer: newly printed with dyuers workes whiche were neuer in print before, as in the table more playnly dothe appere* (Imprynted at London, by Robart Toye, [1550?]), STC 5074 (copy 2), Folger Library, Washington, DC. For more on this acquisition, see Allison Wiggins, 'Frances Wolfreston's Chaucer', in *Women and Writing c.1340–c.1650: The Domestication of Print Culture*, ed. Anne Lawrence-Mathers and Phillipa Hardman (York: York Medieval Press, 2010), 77–89.

63. Natalie Zemon Davis, 'Beyond the Market: Books as Gifts in Sixteenth-Century France – The Prothero Lecture', *Transactions of the Royal Historical Society* 33 (1983): 69. For more work on the book as a gift, see Jason Scott-Warren, *Sir John Harington and the Book as Gift* (Oxford: Oxford University Press, 2001).

64. Jean-Pierre Camus, *Admirable Events: Selected out of Foure Bookes, Written in French by the Right Reverend, John Peter Camus, Bishop of Belley. Together with morall Relations, written by the same Author, and translated into English by S. Du Verger* (London: Printed by *Thomas Harper* for *William Brooks*, 1639). PQ1735 C3 E9E*, Clark Library.

65. John Evelyn, *Publick Employment and an Active Life with all it Appanages, Such as Fame, Command, Riches, Conversation, &c. Prefer'd to Solitude. In Reply to a late Ingenious Essay of a contrary Title* (London: Printed by J. M. for H. Herringman, 1667). E3511a, Folger Library.

66. Bound collection of Poor Robin and Dade almanacks annotated by Frances Wolfreston, 1666–1679, 1690, 1693, 1702–1705. MS. Don. e. 246, Bodleian Library, Oxford. The annotations continued after Wolfreston's last entry in 1677, and are in various hands, including that of her son, Stanford Wolfreston.

67. Many early modern owners of almanacs annotated their texts, notably John Evelyn. Adam Smyth has argued that Evelyn's notes served as the 'preparatory stage for his later diary writing', seeing almanac annotations as a form of life-writing. See Adam Smyth, 'Almanacs, Annotators and Life-Writing in Early Modern England', *English Literary Renaissance* 38, no. 2 (2008): 224. Smyth has also examined Isabella Twysden's 1647 almanac, which contained family notes as well as information about the progress of the Civil War. See Adam Smyth, *Autobiography in Early Modern England* (Cambridge: Cambridge University Press, 2010). Almanacs were popular books in the early modern household, and records of their purchase can be seen in many household account books. For example, Joyce Jeffreys recorded buying almanacs in her account book, as did Mary Gofton. See Judith M. Spicksley, ed., *The Business and Household Accounts of Joyce Jeffreys, Spinster of Hereford, 1638–1648* (London: British Academy, 2015); Mary Gofton, Account book of Mary Gofton (née Hanbury, afterwards Lady Sandys, afterwards Richardson), 1645–1649, MS. Eng. e. 3651, Bodleian Library.

68. MS. Don. e. 246, f15v, Bodleian Library.

69. MS. Don. e. 246, f14r, Bodleian Library.

70. MS. Don. e. 246, f122v, Bodleian Library.

71. For more on almanacs and time, see Laura Williamson Ambrose, 'Travel in Time: Local Travel Writing and Seventeenth-Century English Almanacs', *Journal of Medieval and Early Modern Studies* 43, no. 2 (2013): 419–443. Almanacs are often used as ways of exploring popular culture. See Bernard Capp, *Astrology and the Popular Press: English Almanacs, 1500–1800* (London: Faber, 1979); Louise Hill Curth, *English Almanacs, Astrology, and Popular Medicine, 1550–1700* (Manchester: Manchester University Press, 2007).

72. Shakerley Marmion, *A Fine Companion. Acted before the King and Queene at White-Hall, and sundrie times with great applause at the private House in Salisbury Court, By the Prince his Servants* (London: Printed by Aug. Mathewes for Richard Meighen, 1633), RB 62472 Huntington Library, San Marino. For more on reading plays, see Marta Straznicky, ed., *The Book of the Play: Playwrights, Stationers, and Readers in Early Modern England* (Amherst, MA: University of Massachusetts Press, 2006).

73. Stephen Tabor, curator of early printed books at the Huntington, explains the process of identifying the book as part of the Bridgewater library here: Stephen Tabor, 'Better Than Bacon', *Verso: The Blog of the Huntington Library, Art Collections, and Botanical Gardens*, July 6, 2016, accessed August 10, 2018, www.huntington.org/verso/2018/08/better-bacon.

74. France Egerton was a literary patron and keen book collector, and her 'Catalogue of my ladies books at London' has been studied by Heidi Brayman Hackel, among others. See Heidi Brayman Hackel, *Reading in Early Modern England: Print, Gender and Literacy* (Cambridge: Cambridge University Press, 2005).

75. William Martyn, *The Historie, and Lives, of the Kings of England; from William the Conqueror, unto the end of the Reigne of King Henrie the Eight* (London: Printed for John Bill, William Barret, and Henrie Fetherstone, 1615). RB 645687, Huntington Library.

76. Adam Smyth has examined records of finances and accounts as a form of autobiography, arguing that 'the financial record . . . was one of the most common forms of personal documentation, or self-accounting, in early modern England'. See Adam Smyth, 'Money, Accounting, and Life-Writing, 1600–1700: Balancing a Life', in *A History of English Autobiography*, ed. Adam Smyth (Cambridge: Cambridge University Press, 2016), 86. For a published edition of an early modern woman's account book, see Spicksley, ed., *The Business and Household Accounts of Joyce Jeffreys*.

77. Thomas Herbert, *A relation of some yeares trauaile, begunne anno 1626. Into Afrique and the greater Asia, especially the territories of the Persian monarchie: and some parts of the orientall Indies, and iles adiacent. Of their religion, language, habit, discent, ceremonies, and other matters concerning them. Together with the proceedings and death of the three late ambassadours: Sir D.C. Sir R.S. and the Persian Nogdi-Beg: as also the two great monarchs, the King of Persia, and the Great Mogol / By T. H. Esquier* 1634. Ushaw XIII.B.5.12, Ushaw College, Durham.

78. Hugh Plat, *Delights for the Ladies, to adorne their Persons, Tables, Closets, and Distillatories: With Beauties, Banquets, Perfumes, and Waters* (London, Printed by H. L., 1617), 2005 970, Beinecke Library.

79. Sarah Lindenbaum, 'A Closet for Ladies and Gentlewomen (1611)', *Early Modern Female Book Ownership*, 2022, accessed July 13, 2023, https://earlymodernfemalebookownership.wordpress.com/2022/07/05/a-closet-for-ladies-and-gentlewomen-1611.

80. Francis Cholmondeley, [Commonplace book], [ca. 1652]. Osborn b103, Beinecke Library.

81. Amanda Vickery has noted the importance of house-keeping in the lives of gentry women, albeit with reference to the Georgian period, challenging the

supposed separation of the domestic life of a genteel woman from the world of work that is often said to have begun in the Restoration era. See Amanda Vickery, *The Gentleman's Daughter: Women's Lives in Georgian England* (New Haven, CT: Yale University Press, 1999).

82. 'Parishes: Marton', in *A History of the County of York North Riding: Volume 2*, ed. William Page (London: Victoria County History, 1923), 264–268. *British History Online*, accessed June 20, 2019, www.british-history.ac.uk/vch/yorks/north/vol2/pp264-268.

83. Elizabeth Lowther, Commonplace Book, DD/RA/F/1, West Yorkshire Archive Service, Huddersfield.

84. DD/RA/F/1, 29.

85. The story of the Israelites was important for reformers in early modern England, in the century preceding Lowther's manuscript, who figured the English Protestants as God's chosen people. See Victoria Brownlee, *Biblical Readings and Literary Writings in Early Modern England, 1558–1625* (Oxford: Oxford University Press, 2018).

86. Gibson, 'Casting Off Blanks', 209.

87. Gibson, 'Casting Off Blanks', 209.

88. DD/RA/F/1, 420, West Yorkshire Archive Service.

# Conclusion

The woman reader presented in this book is a diverse one. In reading and writing about reading, women were continually engaged in a process of self-making that allowed them to negotiate their gender, religion, politics, intellectualism and social and sociable positions. In doing so, women entered into a discourse with contemporary gender norms. The prevailing cultural conversation about reading and gender, at least in the early seventeenth century, declared that devotional texts were key to ideal femininity, demonstrating piety and modesty. Romances, however, were largely seen as transgressive, encouraging the threateningly sexual side of female nature. This binary did of course change across the course of the century, and had variations according to age and social status, but it was broadly influential on both early modern and modern discourses about gender.

In writing about their reading of these two types of book, then, women revealed their reactions to these gender norms. Figures like Elizabeth Delaval could demonstrate their piety by showing their changed habits, drawing on advice literature tropes to present themselves as ideal feminine figures, consuming devotional literature and eschewing romances. However, they also moved far beyond this gendered binary. Margaret Hoby and Anne Sadleir read about theology and religious controversy, using texts to support and form their religious identity and to debate with others. Some women such as Dorothy Osborne also critically analysed romances and looked for role models within the genre, particularly by the later seventeenth century, and found profit in their emotional responses to the texts, dismantling the active/passive binary. Moreover, women such as Anne Pole, Judith Barrington, Mary Astell and many others advertised their interest in political events and scientific theories, mathematics, medicine and international current affairs, often working to place themselves in intellectual, social, political, religious and economic networks.

Their representations of this reading in diaries, memoirs and letters, or in their annotations and manuscript notebooks, allowed them to negotiate their identity. This was sometimes an effort to construct an identity for oneself in a text retrospectively or to manipulate the self into a certain figure, informed by contemporary gender norms, such as in the cases of Grace Mildmay and Delaval. Or it could be a continual process of self-fashioning, with identity being formed in the process of both reading and writing about reading, and in the process of re-reading, as we saw in the final chapter.[1]

Reading and writing about text were therefore performative. In making marginal notes, inscribing names and dedications, excerpting passages, making book lists or discussing reading in personal writings, women were able to express aspects of their identity. This identity, however, should not be solely reduced to their gender. It is possible to question the category of the 'woman reader' itself. While I have used sex as a primary method of selection, there are many other issues at play. They almost certainly would have all considered themselves women, but this does not mean that they can be taken as representative of all women readers in the seventeenth century. The women explored here were all from wealthy families, largely classed as gentry or, in some cases, nobility. They had the ability to read and, perhaps more importantly, to write about their reading. They also had the financial resources to buy books and paper, and the time in which to read and write. They were also almost certainly white.[2] Race was as performative as class or gender, therefore women were engaging in a representation of their whiteness and socio-economic status alongside their femininity.[3] This may not have always been conscious, but, as demonstrated in this book, reading was a marker of identity. In paying attention to the different and overlapping forms this identity could take, we can gain a more complex picture of how early modern readers used their reading habits and understood themselves.

Throughout this book, the multiplicity of ways in which women responded to cultural norms has been demonstrated. They adopted and adapted humanist reading practices based on their own personal needs and circumstances. They read the news in a variety of forms, using it as a way of engaging with events, people and places from which they were physically removed. Moreover, they used reading as a way of constructing a character for themselves in text, often influenced by, but not necessarily directly based on, contemporary gender norms. Class identity, politics and sectarianism all played significant roles in the identity construction seen in early modern women's personal writing. Anne Clifford is perhaps the most obvious example of this, using her reading to signify her aristocratic position, influenced by her long battle to reclaim her inheritance. However, she was not the only one. Even the women who made an effort to conform to a particular idealised image of early modern womanhood did so in a way that influenced their (often politically infused) religious identity alongside their femininity.

This idea of reading as performative, as the action of constructing identity, follows the argument put forward by Judith Butler that '*Gender* is not a noun, but neither is it a set of free-floating attributes, for we have seen that the substantive effect of gender is performatively produced and compelled by the regulatory practices of gender coherence . . . in this sense, gender is always a doing.'[4] Reading is therefore one action by which people can perform gender. This is not to put the agency of the experience on to the text; rather, the reaction to and use of the culturally constructed gender of the text by the reader in any given moment is what constitutes the experience of gender. Gender is thus located in the gap in between the reader and the text: in the act or event of reading itself. If we take this approach, the reader becomes more of an imaginative construct, detached from the sex of the individual. Gender could be determined by cultural norms, with the 'feminine' embodying a specific set of characteristics and behaviours, but this would be separate from the actions of women. The 'woman reader' as a category is destabilised. As has been shown throughout this book, the 'woman reader' cannot be seen as a single entity, but instead should be nuanced by intersections with other categories such as wealth, social status, religion and political position.

Further studies in the history of women's reading could draw on feminist, postcolonial and queer historiography to complicate our analytical categories of gender and sex. It has been demonstrated by many scholars, particularly from postcolonial and queer studies, that the tendency to see 'women' as a uniform group (often united in being subject to patriarchal oppression) obscures the many and varied other forms of oppression that operated along class and race lines.[5] If another cross-section of source material had been used, perhaps highlighting the reading experiences of lower-class women, or that of Catholic women either within Britain or on the continent, the results would be different again. This is not to render the category of woman irrelevant but to argue that we need to recognise the many, multifaceted aspects of identity. Moreover, when we talk about narratives of reading, we need to be aware of the many social and cultural factors that influenced the practice of reading.

The history of women's reading therefore needs to be more nuanced and to move beyond the chronologies and questions that have held sway for so long. In doing so, we can better understand the experience of reading in early modern England and open up our studies to groups that have so often been overlooked. This book has demonstrated how we can move away from the active/passive reading binary, seeing all uses of reading, whether for pleasure, education or devotion, as part of a process of identity formation. Texts provided many uses for people, often at the same time – one could, for example, as Osborne did, both read romances for pleasure and critique their writing style – but they were always, consciously or not, implicated in the process of representing and creating a 'self' for the reader. Moreover, this shows the important opportunity that books and reading presented women. They were able, through their reading, to construct themselves as figures of learning, scientists, political observers and theologians. This allowed them to participate in worlds that were often closed to them, perhaps through their exclusion from institutions or through their physical distance from places of politics. By reading about these topics, and crucially by representing that reading to the world, they were able to claim a place in the spheres of politics, science and religion. This is not just a story of print: in order to properly understand women's participation in the world, we have to look at manuscript reading as well, as the continued importance of manuscript newsletters, for example, demonstrates. Participation through text should be recognised as just as important as other forms of participation in these worlds, otherwise we severely restrict our understanding of early modern politics, science and religion.

This emphasises the importance that reading and books have for understanding identity in the early modern period; it allows us to move beyond actions and instead see how individuals wanted to represent themselves, giving a much greater insight into concepts of gender and the self. In doing so, we can also create a more nuanced understanding of gender, by demonstrating the many ways in which one could act as a 'woman' by seeing it as a category that every individual constructs for themselves. At the heart of my argument is the close, almost inextricable connection between reading and identity. This was an ongoing process, and one which involved many layers of influences, be they social or cultural. I have shown the range and breadth of women's reading habits across the seventeenth century, and argued that although cultural conversations about gender may have been preoccupied with controlling reading, this was only partially influential on women readers themselves. They may have sometimes used the language of conduct literature to present themselves as an ideal feminine reader (as in the case of Delaval, for example, or Hoby), but this was rarely one-dimensional; there were almost always other facets of identity demonstrated through their choice of text. They were, moreover, certainly not constrained or limited by contemporary gender ideology. Instead, they created a much more individualised representation of their identities, just as often rejecting gender norms as replicating them, and showing the ways in which their political, economic, social and religious identities existed alongside and as part of their femininity. This identity was not static, often changing with each reading and/or writing act or experience, and was frequently informed by interactions beyond the page and the interior self. The sociality of women's identities has been recognised by feminist scholars, but there has been less attention paid to the temporally fluid and changeable nature of that identity. Women in the early modern period used their reading and the experiences, relationships and actions that were linked to that reading to engage in an ongoing process of identity construction, one which could change based on time and circumstance, and paying attention to this can help us to understand early modern gender and selfhood much more clearly.

## Notes

1. This follows Kate Flint's suggestion, mentioned in the Introduction. See Kate Flint, *The Woman Reader 1837–1914* (Oxford: Oxford University Press, 1993), 40–41.

2. The study of whiteness in the early modern period is only beginning to be discussed, often in the context of Shakespeare or early modern theatre studies. See, for example, Ian Smith, 'We Are Othello: Speaking of Race in Early Modern Studies', *Shakespeare Quarterly* 67, no. 1 (2016): 104–124; Smith, 'White Skin, Black Masks: Racial Cross-Dressing on the Early Modern Stage', *Renaissance Drama* 32 (2003): 33–67.

3. Whiteness has historically been under-theorised; in the 1990s Ruth Frankenberg argued that '"whiteness" refers to a set of cultural practices that are usually unmarked and unnamed'. Ruth Frankenberg, *White Women, Race Matters: The Social Construction of Whiteness* (Minneapolis, MN: University of Minnesota Press, 1993), 1. Increasingly, however, scholars are beginning to explore the performativity of race in the early modern period. Kimberly Poitevin, for example, has argued that whiteness could be assumed through the use of cosmetics. She has suggested that through their use of cosmetics to make their skin appear white, 'early modern women reproduced long standing associations of beauty with whiteness and helped solidify associations between racial difference and skin color'. Arthur Little has also seen whiteness as performative, this time focusing on representations of race on the early modern stage. He points out that whiteness was not an overarching category, but that 'in early modern England whiteness belonged to the elite, not to the "people"'. Finally, Cheryl Harris wrote that whiteness was both 'public reputation and personal property' (property meaning both the ownership of whiteness and whiteness as the ability to own property). See Kimberly Poitevin, 'Inventing Whiteness: Cosmetics, Race, and Women in Early Modern England', *Journal for Early Modern Cultural Studies* 11, no. 1 (2011): 72; Arthur L. Little, Jr., 'Introduction: Assembling an Aristocracy of Skin', in *White People in Shakespeare: Essays on Race, Culture and the Elite*, ed. Arthur L. Little, Jr. (London: The Arden Shakespeare, 2022), 4; Cheryl I. Harris, 'Whiteness as Property', in *Critical Race Theory: The Key*

*Writings That Formed the Movement*, ed. Kimberlé Crenshaw, Neil Gotanda, Garry Peller and Kendall Thomas (New York: The New Press, 1995), 282.

4. Judith Butler, *Gender Trouble: Feminism and the Subversion of Identity* (London: Routledge, 1990), 34.

5. Ania Loomba and Melissa E. Sanchez, 'Introduction: Why "Feminism"? Why Now?', in *Rethinking Feminism in Early Modern Studies: Gender, Race, and Sexuality*, ed. Ania Loomba and Melissa E. Sanchez (London: Routledge, 2016), 2.

# Select bibliography

## Online resources


*Annotated Books Online: A Digital Archive of Early Modern Books.* Accessed June 23, 2023. www.annotatedbooksonline.com.

'Early Modern Annotated Books from UCLA's Clark Library'. *Calisphere: University of California.* Accessed June 23, 2023. https://calisphere.org/collections/26771.

*Early Modern Female Book Ownership: #HerBook.* Accessed June 23, 2023. https://earlymodernfemalebookownership.wordpress.com.

*Early Modern Women's Marginalia.* Accessed August 12, 2024. https://earlymodernwomensmarginalia.cems.anu.edu.au.

Isham, Elizabeth. *Book of Rememberance.* Accessed August 30, 2023. http://web.warwick.ac.uk/english/perdita/Isham/bor_p26r.htm.


## Printed primary sources


Ainsworth, Samuel. *A Sermon Preached at the Funerall of that religious Gentle-woman M*^is^ Dorothy Hanbury, *Wife to* Edward Hanbury *Esq. living at Kelmarsh in Northampton-shire: Who dyed the 12. day of* June, *and was buried at Navesby in Northampton-shire* July *13. Anno Dom.* 1642. London: Printed by Richard Cotes, for Stephen Bowtell, 1645.

Ambrose, Isaac. *Redeeming the Time. A Sermon Preached at Preston in Lansashire, January 4*^th^ *1657, at the Funeral of the Honourable Lady, the Lady Margaret Houghton. Revised, and, somewhat Enlarged; and, at the importunity of some Friends, now published.* London: Printed for Rowland Reynolds, 1674.

Astell, Mary. *A Serious Proposal to the Ladies for the Advancement of their True and Greatest Interest.* New York: Source Book Press, 1970.

Barclay, John. *Barclay his Argenis: Or, The Loves of Poliarchus and Argenis: Faithfully translated out of Latine into English, By Kingesmill Long, Gent.* London: Printed by G. P. for Henry Seile, 1625.

Baxter, Richard. *A Treatise on Conversion Preached, and now published for the use of those that are strangers to a true conversion, especially the grosly ignorant and ungodly.* London: Printed for R. W. for Nevil Simmons, 1657.

Baxter, Richard. *A Breviate of the Life of Margaret, The Daughter of* Francis Charlton, *of* Apply *in* Shropshire, *Esq; And Wife of* Richard Baxter. London: Printed for *B. Simmons*, 1681.

*The Bible. That is, the Holy Scriptures Conteined in the Olde and New Testament. Translated according to the Ebrew and Greeke, and conferred with the best transla-ons in diuers languages. With most profitable annotations vpon all the hard places, and other things of great importance, as may appeare in the Epistle to the Reader.* Imprinted at London by the Deputies of Christopher Barker, Printer to the Queenes most excellent Maiestie, 1597.

*The Bible translated according to the Ebrew and Greeke, and conferred with the best translations in diuers languages; with most profitable annotationsvpon all the hard places, and other things of great importance, as may appeare in the epistle to the reader; and also a most profitable concordance for the readie finding out of any thing in the same conteined.* Imprinted at London by the Deputies of Christopher Barker, 1599.

Birchall, John. *The Non-Pareil, Or, the Vertuous Daughter Surmounting all her Sisters: Described, In a Funerall Sermon upon the Death of that vertuous Lady,* Elizabeth Hoyle, *late wife of the Worshipfull* Thomas Hoyle, *Alderman of the City of* Yorke. York: Printed by *Tho: Bro[. . .]*,1644.

Bosc, Jacques du. *The Accomplish'd Woman. Written Originally in French, since made English, by the Honourable Walter Montague, Esq.* London: Printed for Gabriel Bedell and Tho. Collins, 1656.

Boyle, Robert. *Some Considerations Touching the Usefulness of Experimental Naturall Philosophy, Propos'd in a Familiar Discourse to a Friend, by way of Invitation to the Study of it.* Oxford: Printed by Hen: Hall Printer to the University, for Ric: Davis, 1663.

Boyle, Robert. *Some considerations about the reconcileableness of reason and religion by T.E., a lay-man; to which is annex'd by the publisher, a discourse of Mr. Boyle, about the possibility of the resurrection.* London: Printed by T. N. for H. Herringman, 1675.

Brathwaite, Richard. *The English Gentlewoman, drawne out to the full body: Expressing What Habilliments doe best attire her, What Ornaments doe best adorne her, What Complements doe best accomplish her.* London: Printed by B. Alsop and T Fawcet, for Michael Sparke, 1631.

Brathwaite, Richard. *Ar't asleepe Husband? A Boulster Lecture; Stored with all variety of witty jeasts, merry Tales, and other pleasant passages; Extracted, From the choicest flowers of Philosophy, Poesy, antient and moderne History. Illustrated with Examples of incomparable constancy, in the excellent History of Philocles and Doriclea*. London: Printed by R. Bishop, for *R.B.*, 1640.

Breton, Nicholas. *The Good and the Badde, Or Descriptions of the Worthies, and Unworthies of this Age. Where the Best may see their Graces, and the Worst discerne their Baseness*. London: Printed by George Purslowe for Iohn Budge, 1616.

Bryan, John. *The Vertuous Daughter. A Sermon Preached at Saint Maries in Warwicke at the Funerall of the most vertuous and truely religious young Gentlewoman, Mistresse Cicely Puckering, Daughter and Co-heire to the right Worshipfull, Sir Thomas Puckering, Knight and Baronet, the fourteenth day of Aprill, 1636*. London: Printed by *Thomas Harper*, for *Lawrence Chapman*, 1636.

Camus, Jean-Pierre. *Admirable Events: Selected out of Foure Bookes, Written in French by the Right Reverend, John Peter Camus, Bishop of Belley. Together with morall Relations, written by the same Author, and translated into English by S. Du Verger*. London: Printed by *Thomas Harper* for *William Brooks*, 1639.

Cervantes, Miguel de. *The Travels of Persiles and Sigismunda. A Northern History. Wherein, amongst the variable Fortunes of the Prince of Thule, and this Princesse of Frisland, are interlaced many Witty Discourses, Morall, Politicall, and Delightfull. The first Copie, beeing written in Spanish; translated afterward into French; and now, last, into English*. London: Printed by *H. L.* for *M. L.*, 1619.

Chaucer, Geoffrey. *The Workes of Geffray Chaucer: newly printed with dyuers workes whiche were neuer in print before, as in the table more playnly dothe appere*. Imprynted at London, by Robart Toye, [1550?].

Clifford, Anne. *The Diaries of Lady Anne Clifford*. Edited by D. J. H. Clifford. Stroud: Sutton Publishing, 1990.

Clifford, Anne. *Anne Clifford's Autobiographical Writing, 1590–1676*. Edited by Jessica Malay. Manchester: Manchester University Press, 2018.

Coate, Mary, ed. *The Letter-Book of John Viscount Mordaunt 1658–1660*. Camden Third Series, Vol. 66. London: Offices of the Royal Historical Society, 1945.

Collinges, John. *Par Nobile. Two Treatises. The one, concerning the Excellent Woman, Evincing a person Fearing the Lord, to be the most Excellent Person: Discoursed more privately upon the Death of the Right Honourable, the Lady Frances Hobart, late of Norwich, from Pro.31.29,30,31. The other, Discovering a Fountain of Comfort and Satisfaction, to persons walking with God, yet living and dying without sensible Consolations: discovered, from Psal. 17. 15. at the Funerals of the Right Honourable, the Lady Katharine Courten, preached at Blicklin, in the County of Norfolk, March 27. 1652. With the Narratives of the holy Lives and Deaths of those two Noble Sisters.* London: 1669.

Culpeper, Nicholas. *Culpeper's Directory for Mid Wives: Or, a Guide for Women. The Second Part.* London: Printed by *Peter Cole*, 1662.

Dacier, André. *Les Oeuvres de Platon Traduites en Francois, avec des Remarques. Et la Vie de ce Philosophe, avec l'exposition des principaux dogmes de la Philosophie. Tome Première.* A Paris: Chez Jean Anisson Directeur de l'Imprimerie Royale, 1694.

Dacier, André. *Les Oeuvres de Platon Traduites en Francois, avec des Remarques. Et la Vie de ce Philosophe, avec l'exposition des principaux dogmes de la Philosophie. Tome Seconde.* A Paris: Chez Jean Anisson Directeur de l'Imprimerie Royale, 1694.

D'Audiguier, Vital. *A Tragi-Comicall History of Our Times, Under the Borrowed Names of Lisander and Calista.* London: Printed by R. Y. for G. Lathum, 1635.

Delaval, Elizabeth. *The Meditations of Lady Elizabeth Delaval, Written Between 1662 and 1671.* Edited by Douglas G. Greene. Gateshead: Printed for the Surtees Society by Northumberland Press, 1978.

Descartes, René. *Les Passions de l'Ame.* A Amsterdam: Chez Lovis Elzevier, 1650.

Descartes, René. *Les Meditations Metaphysiques de René Descartes. Touchant la Première Philosophie.* A Paris: chez Theodore Girard, 1667.

Descartes, René. *Les Principes de la Philosophie.* A Paris: Chez Theodore Girard, 1681.

Diggs, Dudley. *The vnlawfulnesse of subjects taking up armes against their soveraigne, in what case soever: together with an answer to all objections scattered in their severall bookes. And a proofe that notwithstanding such resistance as they plead for, were not damnable, yet the present warre made upon the King is so, because those cases, in which onely some men have dared to excuse it, are evidently not now; His Majesty fighting onely to preserve himselfe, and the rights of the subjects / written by Dudley Diggs, Gentleman: late fellow of All-Soules Colledge in Oxford.* [London]: [s.n.], 1647.

Donne, John. *Pseudo-Martyr. Wherein Out of Certaine Propositions and Gradations, This Conclusion is Evicted. That Those Which Are of the Romane Religion in This Kingdome, May and Ought to Take the Oath of Allegiance.* London: Printed by *W. Stansby* for *Walter Burre*, 1610.

[Drake, Judith]. *An Essay in Defence of the Female Sex. In which are inserted the Characters of A Pedant, A Squire, A Beau, A Vertuoso, A Poetaster, A City-Critick &c. In a Letter to a Lady, Written by a Lady.* London: Printed for A. Roper and E. Wilkinson, and R. Clavel, 1696.

Evelyn, John. *Publick Employment and an Active Life with all it Appanages, Such as Fame, Command, Riches, Conversation, &c. Prefer'd to Solitude. In Reply to a late Ingenious Essay of a contrary Title*. London: Printed by J. M. for H. Herringman, 1667.

Freke, Elizabeth. *The Remembrances of Elizabeth Freke, 1671–1714*. Edited by Raymond A. Anselment. Camden Fifth Series, Volume 18, Cambridge: Cambridge University Press, 2001.

Gouge, William. *Of Domesticall Duties Eight Treatises*. London: Printed by Iohn Haviland for William Bladen, 1622.

Guillemeau, Jacques. *Child-birth or, The happy delivery of women: VVherein is set downe the government of women. In the time of their breeding childe: of their travaile, both naturall and contrary to nature: and of their lying in. Together with the diseases, which happen to women in those times, and the meanes to helpe them. With a treatise for the nursing of children. To which is added, a treatise of the diseases of infants, and young children: with the cure of them, and also of the small pox. Written in French by Iames Guillimeau the French Kings chirurgion*. London: Printed by A. Hatfield, 1612.

Halley, Edmund. 'A Discourse Concerning Gravity, and Its Properties, Wherein the Descent of Heavy Bodies, and the Motion of Projects is briefly, but Fully Handled: Together with the Solution of a Problem of Great Use in Gunnery'. *Philosophical Transactions (1683–1775)*, Vol. 16 (1686–1692).

Hammond, Henry. *A Paraphrase, and Annotations Upon all the Books of the New Testament: Briefly explaining all the difficult places thereof.* London: Printed by *J. Flesher* for *Richard Royston*, 1653.

Hammond, Henry. *A Paraphrase and Annotations Upon the Books of the Psalms: Briefly Explaining the Difficulties thereof.* London: Printed by *R. Norton*, for *Richard Royston*, 1659.

Herbert, Thomas. *A relation of some yeares trauaile, begunne anno 1626. Into Afrique and the greater Asia, especially the territories of the Persian monarchie: and some parts of the orientall Indies, and iles adiacent. Of their religion, language, habit, discent, ceremonies, and other matters concerning them. Together with the proceedings and death of the three late ambassadours: Sir D.C. Sir R.S. and the Persian Nogdi-Beg: as also the two great monarchs, the King of Persia, and the Great Mogol / By T. H. Esquier* 1634.

Hoby, Margaret. *The Diary of Lady Margaret Hoby*. Edited by Dorothy M. Meads. London: George Routledge & Sons, 1930.

Hodder, James. *Hodder's Arithemetick: Or, that necessary Art made most easie. Being explained in a way familiar to the capacity of any that desire to learn it in a little time*. London, Printed by J. Darby, for Tho. Rooks, 1667.

Hunter, Lynette, ed. *The Letters of Dorothy Moore, 1612–64: The Friendships, Marriage and Intellectual Life of a Seventeenth-Century Woman*. Aldershot: Ashgate, 2004.

Hutchinson, Lucy. *Memoirs of the Life of Colonel Hutchinson, with the fragment of an autobiography of Mrs Hutchinson*. Edited by James Sutherland. London: Oxford University Press, 1973.

Jeffreys, Joyce. *The Business and Household Accounts of Joyce Jeffreys, Spinster of Hereford, 1638–1648*. Edited by Judith M. Spicksley. London: British Academy, 2015.

Jocelin, Elizabeth. *The Mothers Legacie, to her unborne childe*. London: Printed by Iohn Haviland, for William Barret, 1624.

Juxon, Thomas. *The Journal of Thomas Juxon, 1644–1647*. Edited by Keith Lindley and David Scott. Camden Fifth Series, Vol. 13. Cambridge: Cambridge University Press, 1999.

*The last words of Coll. Richard Rumbold, Mad. Alicia Lisle, Alderman Henry Cornish, and Mr. Richard Nelthrop who were executed in England and Scotland for high treason in the year 1685*. London: s.n., 1685.

Leigh, Dorothy. *The Mothers Blessing. Or the Godly Counsaile of a Gentle-woman not long since deceased, left behind for her Children: Containing many good exhortations, and godly admonitions, profitable for all Parents to leaue as a Legacy to their Children, but especially for those, who by reason of their young yeeres stand most in need of Instruction*. Printed at London for Iohn Budge, 1616.

Leigh, Dorothy. *The Mother's Blessing. Or, The godly Counsell of a Gentle-woman, not long since deceased, left behinde her for her Children. Containing many good exhortations, and good admonitions profitable for all Parents to leave as a Legacy for their Children*. Printed at London by Tho. Cotes, for Andrew Crooke, 1640.

Lewis, Thomas Taylor, ed. *Letters of the Lady Brilliana Harley, Wife of Sir Robert Harley, of Brampton Bryan, Knight of the Bath*. London: Printed for the Camden Society, 1854.

Loftis, John, ed. *The Memoirs of Anne, Lady Halkett and Ann, Lady Fanshawe*. Oxford: Clarendon Press, 1979.

Lupton, Thomas. *A Thousand Notable Things of Sundry sorts, enlarged. Whereof some are Wonderful, some Strange, some Pleasant, divers Necessary, a great sort Profitable, and many very Precious. Whereunto is now added, many Excellent New Conceits never before Printed, very Witty, Useful and Delightful*. London: Printed for *M. Wotton* and *G. Conyers*, 1686.

Makin, Bathsua. *An Essay to Revive the Antient Education of Gentlewomen in Religion, Manners, Arts & Tongues. With An Answer to the Objections against this Way of Education.* London: Printed by J. D. to be sold by Tho. Parkhurst, 1673.

Malebranche, Nicolas. *Meditations Chrestiennes, par L'Auteur de la Recherche de la Vérité.* A Cologne, Chez Balthasar D'Egmond & Compagnie, 1683.

Malebranche, Nicolas. *Traité de Morale par l'Auteur de la Recherche de la Verité.* A Rotterdam: Chez Reinier Leers, 1684.

Malebranche, Nicolas. *De la recherche de la verité, où, L'on traitte de la nature de l'esprit de l'homme, & de l'usage qu'il en doit faire pour éviter l'erreur dans les sciences, Vol. 1.* A Amsterdam: Chez Henry Desbordes, 1688.

Malebranche, Pere. *Traité de la Nature et de la Grace.* A Rotterdam: Chez Rainier Leers, 1701.

Markham, Gervase. *Countrey contentments, or The English Huswife Containing the Inward and Outward Vertues Which Ought to Be in a Compleate Woman.* Printed at London by *I.B*, for *R. Jackson*, 1623.

Marmion, Shakerley. *A Fine Companion. Acted before the King and Queene at White-Hall, and sundrie times with great applause at the private House in Salisbury Court, By the Prince his Servants.* London: Printed by Aug. Mathewes for Richard Meighen, 1633.

Martyn, William. *The Historie, and Lives, of the Kings of England; from William the Conqueror, unto the end of the Reigne of King Henrie the Eight.* London: Printed for John Bill, William Barret, and Henrie Fetherstone, 1615.

Milton, John. *The Tenure of Kings and Magistrates: Proving, that is it Lawfull, and hath been held so through all Ages, for any, who have the Power, to call to account a Tyrant, or wicked King, and after due conviction, to depose, and put him to death; if the ordinary Magistrate have neglected, or deny'd to doe it.* London: Printed by Matthew Simmons, 1649.

Milton, John. *Eikonoklastes. In answer to a book intitl'd Eikon basilike, the portrature of His Sacred Majesty in his solitudes and sufferings.* London: Printed by T. N., 1650.

Moody, Joanna, ed. *The Private Correspondence of Jane Lady Cornwallis Bacon, 1613–1644.* London: Associated University Presses, 2003.

Mornai, Philip of. *Fowre Bookes, of the Institution, Use and Doctrine of the Holy Sacrament of the Eucharist in the Old Church. As Likewise, How, When, And by what Degrees the Masse if Brought in, in place thereof.* London: Printed by Iohn Windet, for I. B. T. M. and W. P., 1600.

Mornai, Philip of. *A Treatise of the Church, Wherein are Handled the Principall Questions Mooued in our Time Concerning that Matter.* Imprinted at London by L.S. for George Potter, 1606.

Norden, John. *A Pensive Mans Practise verie profitable for all persons.* London: Printed by William Hall for Richard Bradocke, 1610.

Osborne, Dorothy. *Dorothy Osborne: Letters to Sir William Temple*. Edited by Kenneth Parker. London: Penguin Books, 1987.

Overbury, Thomas. *A Wife Now the Widdow of Sir Thomas Overburye. Being a most exquisite and singular poem of the choice of a Wife. Whereunto are added many witty Characters, and conceited Newes, written by himselfe and other learned Gentlemen his friends.* London: Printed for Lawrence Lisle, 1614.

Patin, Charles. *Travels Thro' Germany, Swisserland, Bohemia, Holland; and other Parts of Europe: Describing the most Considerable Citys, and the Palaces of Princes: Together, with Historical Relations, and Critical Observations upon Ancient Medals and Inscriptions.* London: Printed for *A. Swall* and *T. Child*, 1697.

Penney, Norman, ed. *The Household Account Book of Sarah Fell of Swarthmoor Hall.* S.I.: Bibliolife, 2011.

Pollock, Linda, ed. *With Faith and Physic: The Life of a Tudor Gentlewoman, Lady Grace Mildmay, 1552–1620*. London: Collins & Brown, 1993.

Porter, Jerome. *The Flowers of the Liues of the Most Renowned Saincts of the Three Kingdoms England Scotland, and Ireland Written and collected out of the best authours and manuscripts of our nation, and distributed according to their feasts in the calendar.* Printed at Doway, 1632.

Quintana, Francisco de. *The History of Don Fenise. A New Romance, Written in Spanish by Francisco de las-Coveras. And now Englished by a Person of Honour.* London, Printed for Humphrey Moseley, 1651.

Rainbowe, Edwarrd. [Lord Bishop of Carlisle]. *A Sermon Preached At the Funeral of the Right Honorable Anne Countess of* Pembroke, Dorset, *and* Montgomery, *Who died* March *22. 1675/6, and was Interred* April *the 14th following at* Appleby in Westmoreland. *With Some Remarks on the Life of that Eminent Lady.* London: Printed for *R. Royston*, 1677.

Richardson, Elizabeth. *A Ladies Legacie to her Daughters. In three books. Composed of prayers and meditations, fitted for severall times, and upon severall occasions. As also several prayers for each day in the weeke.* London: Printed by *Tho. Harper*, 1645.

Rogers, Timothy. *The Character of a Good Woman, Both in a Single and Marry'd State. In a Funeral Discourse on Prov. 31. 10. Who can find a vertuous Woman? For her Price is far above Rubies. Occasion'd by the*

*Decease of Mrs. Elizabeth Dunton, Who Died May 28. 1697. With an Account of Her Life and Death; and part of the Diary writ with her own Hand: With a Preface, containing a Brief History of several Excellent Women.* London: Printed for John Harris, 1697.

Sancroft, William. *Modern policies, taken from Machiavel, Borgia, and other choice authors / by an eye-witnesse.* London: Printed for Tho. Dring, 1655.

Savile, George, Marquis of Halifax. *The Lady's New-year's Gift: Or, Advice to a Daughter, Under these following Heads: Viz. Religion, Husband, House, Family and Children, Behaviour and Conversation, Friendships, Censure, Vanity and Affectation, Pride, Diversions.* London: Printed for Matth. Gilliflower, and James Partridge, 1692.

Scudéry, Madeleine de. *Ibrahim, or, the Illustrious Bassa. An Excellent New Romance. The Whole Work, In Foure Parts. Written in French by Monsieur de Scudery, and Now Englished by Henry Cogan, Gent.* London: Printed for Humphry Moseley, *William Bentley,* and *Thomas Heath,* 1652.

Searle, Arthur, ed. *Barrington Family Letters, 1628–1632.* Camden Fourth Series Volume 28. London: The Royal Historical Society, 1983.

Shakespeare, William. *Mr. VVilliam Shakespeares comedies, histories, & tragedies: published according to the true originall copies.* London: Imprinted by Isaac Iaggard, and Ed. Blount, 1623.

Sharp, Jane. *The Midwives Book. Or the whole art of midwifery discovered. Directing childbearing women how to behave themselves.* London: Printed for *Simon Miller,* 1671.

Spenser, Edmund. *Calendarium pastorale, sive Æglogæ duodecim, totidem anni mensibus accommodatæ. Anglicè olim scriptæ ab Edmundo Spensero anglorum poetarum principe: nunc autem eleganti Latino carmine donatæ a Theodoro Bathurst, aulæ Pembrokianæ apud Cantabrigienses aliquando socio.* Londini: impensis M[ercy]. M[eighen]. T[homas]. C[ollins]. & G. Bedell, 1653.

Taylor, Jeremy. *Theologia eklektike. A Discourse of the Liberty of Prophesying. Shewing the unreasonableness of prescribing to other mens faith, and the iniquity of persecuting differing opinions.* London: Printed for R. Royston, 1647.

Thornton, Alice. *My First Booke of my Life.* Edited by Raymond A. Anselment. Lincoln, NE: University of Nebraska Press, 2014.

Tipper, Elizabeth. *The Pilgrim's Viaticum: Or, the Destitute, but not Forlorn. Being a Divine Poem, Digested from Meditations upon the Holy Scripture.* London: Printed by J. Wilkins, 1698.

Vives, Juan Luis. *The Education of a Christian Woman: A Sixteenth-Century Manual*. Edited and translated by Charles Fantazzi. Chicago, IL: University of Chicago Press, 2000.

Walker, Clement. *Anarchia Anglicana: Or, the History of Independency. With observations historicall and politicque upon this present Parliament, begun Anno 16. Caroli Primi*. [London, s.n.], 1648.

Wallington, Nehemiah. *The Notebooks of Nehemiah Wallington, 1618–1654: A Selection*. Edited by David Booy. Aldershot: Ashgate, 2007.

Weldon, Anthony. *The Court and Character of King James. Whereunto is now added the Court of King Charles: Continued Unto the beginning of these unhappy Times. With some Observations upon Him instead of a Character. Collected and perfected by Sir A. W.* Printed at London by R. I., 1651.

Whately, William. *A Bride-Bush, Or A Wedding Sermon: Compendiously Describing the Duties of Married Persons: By performing whereof, Marriage shall be to them a great Helpe, which now finde it a little Hell.* Printed at London by William Iaggard, for Nicholas Bourne, 1617.

Wirsung, Christof. *The General Practise of Physicke. Conteyning all Inward and Outward parts of the body, with all the accidents and infirmities that are incident unto them, even from the crowne of the head to the sole of the foote*. London: Printed for Thomas Adams, 1617.

Woolley, Hannah. *The Gentlewomans Companion; O, A Guide to the Female Sex: Containing Directions of Behaviour, in all Places, Companies, Relations, and Conditions, from their Childhood down to Old Age: Viz. As, Children to Parents. Scholars to Governours. Single to Servants. Virgins to Suitors. Married to Husbands. Huswifes to the House. Mistresses to the Servants. Mothers to Children. Widows to the World. Prudent to all. With Letters and Discourses upon all Occasions. Whereunto is added, A Guide for Cook-Maids, Dairy-Maids, Chamber-Maids, and all others that go to Service. The whole being an exact Rule for the Female Sex in General*. London: Printed by A. Maxwell for Dorman Nowman, 1673.

Woolley, Hannah. *The Accomplish'd lady's delight in preserving, physick, beautifying, and cookery*. London, Printed for B. Harris, 1675.

Woolley, Hannah. *The Compleat Servant-Maid; Or, the Young Maidens Tutor. Directing them how they may fit, and qualifie themselves for any of these Employments. Viz. Waiting-Woman, House-keeper, Chamber-Maid, Cook-Maid, Under Cook-Maid, Nursery-Maid, Dairy-Maid, Laundry-Maid, House-Maid, Scullery-Maid. Composed for the great benefit and advantage of all young Maidens*. London: Printed for T. Passinger, 1677.

## Manuscript sources


### Beinecke Rare Book and Manuscript Library, New Haven, CT

| | |
|---|---|
| Osborn fb210 | 25 letters of news relative to the abdication of K. James 2 to Lady Clopton, from Mr. Hamon, 1688–1689. |
| Osborn b103 | Cholmondeley, Francis. [Commonplace book]. [ca. 1652]. |
| Osborn b435 | Fitzherbert, Frances. Frances Fitzherbert manuscript miscellany: dedicated to Lady Elizabeth Cromwell, circa 1693–1703. |
| 1971 + 62 | Luttrell, Narcissus. Broadsides, single sheets, and pamphlets reporting affairs in Ireland during the war of 1689–1691, collected and dated in manuscript by Narcissus Luttrell. 1689–1698. |
| Osborn b49 | Newell, Elizabeth. [A Collection of devotional verse]. [ca. 1655–1668]. |
| OSB MSS 60 | Newsletters addressed to Madam Pole, James Marshall and Marie-Louise Osborn Collection. |
| Osborn b285 | Watson, Anne Wentworth, Baroness Rockingham. [Commonplace Book]. [17th century]. |
| Osborn b202 | Webber, Mary. [Commonplace Book]. 1694. |

### Bodleian Library, Oxford

| | |
|---|---|
| MS. Don. e. 246 | Bound collection of Poor Robin and Dade almanacks annotated by Frances Wolfreston, 1666–1679, 1690, 1693, 1702–1705. |
| MS. Eng. e. 3651 | Gofton, Mary. Account book of Mary Gofton (née Hanbury, afterwards Lady Sandys, afterwards Richardson). 1645–1649. |
| MS. Eng. c. 6812 | Grey Family Correspondence. 1691–1788. |

### British Library

| | |
|---|---|
| Add MS 29596 | Correspondence and papers of the Hatton and Finch families, 1514–1779. |
| Add MS 46942 | Egmont Papers Vol. XXIII. Correspondence etc. |
| Add MS 78309 | Evelyn Papers Vol. CXLII. Correspondence and papers. |
| Add MS 78436 | Evelyn Papers Vol. CCLXIX. Correspondence and papers. |
| Add MS 78440 | Evelyn Papers Vol. CCLXXIII. Correspondence and papers. [1675]–1685. |

| | |
|---|---|
| Egerton MS 2983 | Heath and Verney Papers Vol. VI. Miscellaneous inventories and accompts 1599–1799. |
| Add Ch 44538 | Pawley, Francis. Inventory of her goods. 1681. |

### Cambridge University Library

| | |
|---|---|
| MS Add 8460 | Lyttelton, Elizabeth. Commonplace Book. C.1680. |

### Cumbria Record Office, Kendal

| | |
|---|---|
| WD/HOTH/1/10 | Clifford, Lady Anne. *Great Books of Record.* |

### Derbyshire Record Office, Matlock

| | |
|---|---|
| D258/38/1 | Inventory of Elizabeth Gell's goods. 1705. |
| D5557.2 | Correspondence: German Pole (1626–1683). |
| D5557.3 | Correspondence: Samuel Pole (d.1731). |

### Folger Shakespeare Library

| | |
|---|---|
| V.a.619 | Baker, Margaret. *Receipt Book of Margaret Baker.* c.1675. |
| X.d.493 | Helsby, Mary Hatton. *Autograph letters signed from Mary Hatton Helsby to various recipients [manuscript], 1651–1668.* |
| V.b.366 | Winch, Rebecca. *Receipt Book of Rebeckah Winche, ca. 1666.* |

### Henry E. Huntington Library

| | |
|---|---|
| mssHM 15369 | Hastings, Elizabeth, Countess of Huntingdon. *Certaine Collections of the right Hon. Elizabeth late Countess of Huntingdon for her own private use*, 1633. |

### Hertfordshire Archives and Local Studies, Hertford

| | |
|---|---|
| D/EP F35 | Cowper, Sarah. *Diary, Volume 7*, 1713–1716. |
| D/EP F37 | Cowper, Sarah. *Commonplace Book.* |
| D/EP F38 | Cowper, Sarah. *Miscellany.* |
| D/EP F39 | Cowper, Sarah. *Biblical Commentary.* |
| D/EP F43 | Cowper, Sarah. *Miscellany.* |
| D/EP F44 | Cowper, Sarah. *Miscellany.* |

### Trinity College, Cambridge

R.5.5 Sadleir, Anne. Collection of Letters, Drafts, and Other Papers.
R.16.2 The Trinity Apocalypse.

### Wellcome Library

MS.1176 Bisaker, Hannah. 1692.
MS.184a Catchmay, Lady Frances. 1625.
MS.2954 Hudson, Sarah, 1678.
MS 751/54–55. Sleigh, Elizabeth, and Felicia Whitfeld. 'An Inventory of the Lady Sleighs bookes May 12 1647'.

### West Yorkshire Archive Service, Huddersfield

DD/RA/F/1 Lowther, Elizabeth. Commonplace Book.

### William Andrews Clark Memorial Library

Misc Mss Grant, Arthur. Autograph Letters signed to Elizabeth Tollemache. 1615–1619.
MS.2009.015 Horsington, Sarah. *Arcana, or, Mysteries in ye theory of physiology and chymistry: being authentick rules, for preparing spagyricall medicaments, for my own observation and satisfaction. Also are manyfold private receipts, and remedies, prescriptions of T: H: M: D: Collected by ye Industry of the transcriber, of this manuscript, uxoris ejus S: H:*, 1666.
MS.1952.003 Manuscript commonplace book of Anne and Roger Ley. c.1623–c.1667.
MS.1951.021 Pole Newsletter Collection.

## Newspapers

*The Flying Post, or the Post-Master*
*The London Gazette*

## Secondary sources

'#HerBook'. Twitter. Accessed June 23, 2023. https://twitter.com/search?q=%23herbook&src=typed_query.

Acheson, Katherine, ed. *Early Modern English Marginalia*. Abingdon: Routledge, 2019.

Acheson, Katherine. 'The Occupations of the Margins: Writing, Space, and Early Modern Women'. In Acheson, *Early Modern English Marginalia*, 70–90.

Achinstein, Sharon. *Milton and the Revolutionary Reader.* Princeton, NJ: Princeton University Press, 1994.

Akkerman, Nadine. *Invisible Agents: Women and Espionage in Seventeenth-Century Britain*. Oxford: Oxford University Press, 2018.

Alexander, Gavin. 'Sir Philip Sidney's *Arcadia*'. In *The Oxford Handbook of English Prose, 1500–1640*, edited by Andrew Hadfield, 219–234. Oxford: Oxford University Press, 2023.

Allan, David. *Commonplace Books and Reading in Georgian England.* Cambridge: Cambridge University Press, 2010.

Allison, C. FitzSimons. *The Rise of Moralism: The Proclamation of the Gospel from Hooker to Baxter.* London: SPCK, 1966.

Ambrose, Laura Williamson. 'Travel in Time: Local Travel Writing and Seventeenth-Century English Almanacs'. *Journal of Medieval and Early Modern Studies* 43, no. 2 (2013): 419–443.

Amussen, Susan D. *An Ordered Society: Gender and Class in Early Modern England*. New York: Columbia University Press, 1988.

Anderson, Jennifer, and Elizabeth Sauer, eds. *Books and Readers in Early Modern England: Material Studies*. Philadelphia, PA: University of Pennsylvania Press, 2002.

Anselment, Raymond. 'Feminine Self-Reflection and the Seventeenth-Century Occasional Meditation'. *The Seventeenth Century* 26, no. 1 (2011): 69–93.

Apple, Rima D., Gregory J. Downey and Stephen L. Vaughn, eds. *Science in Print: Essays on the History of Science and the Culture of Print.* Madison, WI: University of Wisconsin Press, 2012.

Appleby, John H. 'Woodall, John (1570–1643)'. *Oxford Dictionary of National Biography*, 2008. Accessed July 18, 2023, www-oxforddnb-com.libproxy.york.ac.uk/display/10.1093/ref:odnb/9780198614128.001.0001/odnb-9780198614128-e-29902?rskey=dxcH6R&result=1.

Arblaster, Paul. 'Posts, Newsletters, Newspapers: England in a European System of Communications'. In *News Networks in Seventeenth Britain and Europe*, edited by Joad Raymond, 19–34. Abingdon: Routledge, 2006.

Archer, Harriet, and Andrew Hadfield, eds. *A Mirror for Magistrates in Context: Literature, History and Politics in Early Modern England.* Cambridge: Cambridge University Press, 2016.

Atherton, Ian. '"The Itch grown a Disease": Manuscript Transmission of News in the Seventeenth Century'. In Raymond, *News, Newspapers, and Society*, 39–65.

Aughterson, Kate, ed. *Renaissance Women: A Sourcebook: Constructions of Femininity in England*. London: Routledge, 1995.

Baker, Nicholson. *The Size of Thoughts: Essays and Other Lumber*. London: Vintage, 1997.

Ballaster, Ros. *Seductive Forms: Women's Amatory Fiction from 1684 to 1740*. Oxford: Clarendon Press, 1992.

Barber, Alex W. '"It is Not Easy What to Say of our Condition, Much Less to Write It": The Continued Importance of Scribal News in the Early 18th Century'. *Parliamentary History* 32, no. 2 (2013): 293–316.

Barbour, Reid. *Sir Thomas Browne: A Life*. Oxford: Oxford University Press, 2013.

Barnard, John, D. F. McKenzie and Maureen Bell, eds. *The Cambridge History of the Book in Britain. Volume 4: 1557–1695*. Cambridge: Cambridge University Press, 2002.

Baron, Sabrina A. 'The Guises of Dissemination in Early Seventeenth-Century England: News in Manuscript and Print'. In Dooley and Baron, *The Politics of Information in Early Modern Europe*, 41–56.

Baron, Sabrina A. 'Licensing Readers, Licensing Authorities in Seventeenth-Century England'. In Anderson and Sauer, *Books and Readers in Early Modern England*, 217–242.

Bayer, Penny. 'Women Alchemists and the Paracelsian Context in France and England, 1560–1616'. *Early Modern Women* 15, no. 2 (2021): 103–112.

Beal, Peter. 'Notions in Garrison: The Seventeenth-Century Commonplace Book'. In *New Ways of Looking at Old Texts: Papers of the Renaissance English Text Society, 1985–1991*, edited by W. Speed Hill, 131–147. Binghamton, NY: Renaissance English Text Society, 1993.

Beilin, Elaine V. *Redeeming Eve: Women Writers of the English Renaissance*. Princeton, NJ: Princeton University Press, 1987.

Bell, Maureen. 'Hannah Allen and the Development of a Puritan Publishing Business, 1646–51'. *Publishing History* 26 (1989): 5–66.

Bell, Maureen. 'Women in the English Book Trade 1557–1700'. *Leipziger Jahrbuch zur Buchgeschichte* 6 (1996): 13–45.

Bell, Maureen. 'Reading in Seventeenth-Century Derbyshire: The Wheatcrofts and Their Books'. In *The Moving Market: Continuity and Change in the Book Trade*, edited by Peter Isaac and Barry MacKay, 161–168. New Castle, DE: Oak Knoll Press, 2001.

Bell, Maureen. 'Women and the Production of Texts: The Impact of the History of the Book'. In *The Book Trade in Early Modern England: Practices, Perceptions, Connections*, edited by John Hinks and Victoria E. M. Gardner, 107–131. London: British Library, 2013.

Bellingradt, Daniel, Paul Nelles and Jeroen Salman, eds. *Books in Motion in Early Modern Europe: Beyond Production, Circulation and Consumption*. London: Palgrave Macmillan, 2017.

Bennet, H. S. *English Books and Readers, 1475–1557: Being a Study in the History of the Book Trade from Caxton to the Incorporation of the Stationers' Company*. Cambridge: Cambridge University Press, 1952.

Bennet, H. S. *English Books and Readers, 1558–1603: Being a Study in the History of the Book Trade in the Reign of Elizabeth I*. Cambridge: Cambridge University Press, 1965.

Bennet, H. S. *English Books and Readers, 1693–1640: Being a Study in the History of the Book Trade in the Reigns of James I and Charles I*. Cambridge: Cambridge University Press, 1970.

Berry, Helen. *Gender, Society and Print Culture in Late-Stuart England*. Aldershot: Ashgate, 2003.

Berry, Helen. '"Nice and Curious Questions": Coffee Houses and the Representation of Women in John Dunton's *Athenian Mercury*'. *The Seventeenth Century* 12, no. 2 (1997): 257–276.

Betteridge, Maurice S. 'The Bitter Notes: The Geneva Bible and its Annotators'. *The Sixteenth Century Journal* 14, no. 1 (1983): 41–62.

Birrell, T. A. 'Reading as a Pastime: The Place of Light Literature in Some Gentlemen's Libraries of the 17th Century'. In *Property of a Gentleman: The Formation, Organisation and Dispersal of the Private Library 1620–1920*, edited by Robin Myers and Michael Harris, 113–131. Winchester: St Paul's Bibliographies, 1991.

Blair, Ann M. *Too Much to Know: Managing Scholarly Information before the Modern Age*. New Haven, CT: Yale University Press, 2010.

Bleichmar, Daniela, and Peter C. Mancall, eds. *Collecting across Cultures: Material Exchanges in the Early Modern Atlantic World*. Philadelphia, PA: University of Pennsylvania Press, 2011.

Blocker, Déborah. 'Servir le prince par la philologie: André Dacier (1651–1722), un érudit dans l'orbite du pouvoir royal'. *Seventeenth-Century French Studies* 35, no. 1 (2013): 3–22.

Boran, Elizabethanne, and Mordechai Feingold, eds. *Reading Newton in Early Modern Europe*. Leiden: Brill, 2017.

Botonaki, Effie. 'Seventeenth-Century Englishwomen's Spiritual Diaries: Self-Examination, Covenanting, and Account Keeping'. *The Sixteenth Century Journal* 30, no. 1 (1999): 3–21.

Bowden, Caroline. 'The Library of Mildred Cooke Cecil, Lady Burghley'. *The Library* 6 (2005): 3–29.

Bowden, Caroline. 'Women in Educational Spaces'. In Knoppers, *The Cambridge Companion to Early Modern Women's Writing*, 86–96.

Bowden, Caroline. 'Books and Reading at Syon Abbey, Lisbon, in the Seventeenth Century'. In *Syon Abbey and Its Books: Reading, Writing, and Religion, c.1400–1700*, edited by E. A. Jones and Alexandra Walsham, 177–202. Woodbridge: Boydell, 2010.

Brandtzæg, Siv Gøril, Paul Goring and Christine Watson, eds. *Travelling Chronicles: News and Newspapers from the Early Modern Period to the Eighteenth Century*. Leiden: Brill, 2018.

Brink, Jean R. 'Bathsua Reginald Makin: "Most Learned Matron"'. *Huntington Library Quarterly* 54, no. 4 (1991): 313–326.

Broad, Jacqueline. 'Astell, Cartesian Ethics, and the Critique of Custom'. In *Mary Astell: Reason, Gender, Faith*, edited by William Kolbrener and Michal Michelson, 165–180. London: Routledge, 2007.

Broad, Jacqueline. *The Philosophy of Mary Astell: An Early Modern Theory of Virtue*. Oxford: Oxford University Press, 2015.

Broad, Jacqueline. 'Mary Astell's Malebranchean Concept of the Self'. In *Early Modern Women on Metaphysics*, edited by Emily Thomas, 211–226. Cambridge: Cambridge University Press, 2018.

Brod, Manfred. 'Politics and Prophecy in Seventeenth-Century England: The Case of Elizabeth Poole'. *Albion* 31, no. 3 (1999): 395–412.

Broomhall, Susan. 'Destroying Order, Structuring Disorder: Gender and Emotions'. In *Gender and Emotions in Medieval and Early Modern Europe: Destroying Order, Structuring Disorder*, edited by Susan Broomhall, 1–16. Abingdon: Routledge, 2015.

Brown, Sylvia, ed. *Women's Writing in Stuart England: The Mothers' Legacies of Dorothy Leigh, Elizabeth Joscelin and Elizabeth Richardson*. Stroud: Sutton Publishing, 1999.

Brownlee, Victoria. *Biblical Readings and Literary Writings in Early Modern England, 1558–1625*. Oxford: Oxford University Press, 2018.

Bryson, Anna. *From Courtesy to Civility: Changing Codes of Conduct in Early Modern England*. Oxford: Clarendon Press, 1998.

Buelow, George J. *A History of Baroque Music*. Bloomington, IN: Indiana University Press, 2004.

Burke, Peter. 'A Civil Tongue: Language and Politeness in Early Modern Europe'. In Burke et al., *Civil Histories*, 31–48.

Burke, Peter, Brian Harrison and Paul Slack, eds. *Civil Histories: Essays Presented to Sir Keith Thomas*. Oxford: Oxford University Press, 2000.

Burke, Victoria E. 'Ann Bowyer's Commonplace Book (Bodleian Library Ashmole MS 51): Reading and Writing among the "Middling Sort"'. *Early Modern Literary Studies* 6, no. 3 (2001): 1–28.

Burke, Victoria E. 'Contexts for Women's Manuscript Miscellanies: The Case of Elizabeth Lyttelton and Sir Thomas Browne'. *The Yearbook of English Studies* 33, Medieval and Early Modern Miscellanies and Anthologies (2003): 316–328.

Burke, Victoria E. 'Reading Friends: Women's Participation in "Masculine" Literary Culture'. In Burke and Gibson, *Early Modern Women's Manuscript Writing*, 75–90.

Burke, Victoria E. '"Memorial Books": Commonplaces, Gender, and Manuscript Compilation in Seventeenth-Century England'. In *Ars Reminiscendi: Mind and Memory in Renaissance Culture*, edited by Donald Beecher and Grant Williams, 121–138. Toronto: Centre for Reformation and Renaissance Studies, 2009.

Burke, Victoria E., and Jonathan Gibson, eds. *Early Modern Women's Manuscript Writing: Selected Papers from the Trinity/Trent Colloquium*. Aldershot: Ashgate, 2004.

Burlinson, Christopher. 'The Use and Re-Use of Early Seventeenth-Century Student Notebooks: Inside and Outside the University'. In *Material Readings of Early Modern Culture: Texts and Social Practices, 1580–1730*, edited by James Daybell and Peter Hinds, 229–245. Basingstoke: Palgrave Macmillan, 2010.

Burton, Antoinette. *Dwelling in the Archive: Women Writing House, Home, and History in Late Colonial India*. Oxford: Oxford University Press, 2003.

Butler, Judith. *Gender Trouble: Feminism and the Subversion of Identity*. London: Routledge, 1990.

Calis, Richard, Frederick Clark, Christian Flow, Anthony Grafton, Madeline McMahon, and Jennifer M. Rampling. 'Passing the Book: Cultures of Reading in the Winthrop Family, 1587–1730'. *Past & Present* 241, no. 1 (2018): 60–141.

Cambers, Andrew. 'Readers' Marks and Religious Practice: Margaret Hoby's Marginalia'. In King, *Tudor Books and Readers*, 211–231.

Cambers, Andrew. *Godly Reading: Print, Manuscript and Puritanism in England, 1580–1720*. Cambridge: Cambridge University Press, 2011.

Cambers, Andrew. 'Reading, The Godly, and Self-Writing in England, circa 1580–1720'. *Journal of British Studies* 46, no. 4 (2012): 796–825.

Cambers, Andrew, and Michelle Wolfe. 'Reading, Family Religion, and Evangelical Identity in Late Stuart England'. *The Historical Journal* 47, no. 4 (2004): 875–896.

Campbell, Jill. 'Domestic Intelligence: Newspaper Advertising and the Eighteenth-Century Novel'. *The Yale Journal of Criticism* 15, no. 2 (2002): 251–291.

Capp, Bernard. *Astrology and the Popular Press: English Almanacs, 1500–1800*. London: Faber, 1979.

Capp, Bernard. *When Gossips Meet: Women, Family and Neighbourhood in Early Modern England*. Oxford: Oxford University Press, 2003.

Capp, Bernard. '"Jesus Wept" but Did the Englishman? Masculinity and Emotion in Early Modern England'. *Past & Present* 224, no. 1 (2014): 75–108.

Carré, Jacques. 'Communication et Rapports Sociaux dans les Traités de Savoir-Vivre Britanniques (XVIIe–XVIIIe siècle)'. In *Pour une Histoire des Traités de Savoir-Vivre en Europe*, edited by Alain Montandon, 269–300. Clermont-Ferrand: Associations des Publications de la Faculté des Lettres et Sciences Humaines de Clermont-Ferrand, 1994.

Carter, Rodney G. S. 'Of Things Said and Unsaid: Power, Archival Silences, and Power in Silence'. *Archivaria* 61 (2006): 215–233.

Cavallo, Guglielmo, and Roger Chartier, eds. *A History of Reading in the West*. Translated by Lydia G. Cochrane. Cambridge: Polity Press, 1999.

Cavallo, Sandra, and Lyndan Warner, eds. *Widowhood in Medieval and Early Modern Europe*. Abingdon: Routledge, 2014.

Chalmers, Hero. '"The Person I Am, or What They Made Me to Be": The Construction of the Feminine Subject in the Autobiographies of Mary Carlton'. In *Women, Texts and Histories 1575–1760*, edited by Clare Brant and Diane Purkiss, 164–194. London: Routledge, 1992.

Chalus, Elaine. *Elite Women in English Political Life, c.1754–1790*. Oxford: Oxford University Press, 2005.

Chambers, Douglas D. C., and David Galbraith, eds. *The Letterbooks of John Evelyn*. Toronto: University of Toronto Press, 2014.

Chapple, J. A. V. 'Christopher Codrington's Verses to Elizabeth Cromwell'. *The Journal of English and German Philology* 60, no. 1 (1961): 75–78.

Chartier, Roger. 'Leisure and Sociability: Reading Aloud in Early Modern Europe'. In *Urban Life in the Renaissance*, edited by Susan Zimmerman and Ronald F. E. Weissman, 103–120. Newark, DE: University of Delaware Press, 1989.

Chartier, Roger. *The Order of Books: Readers, Authors and Libraries in Europe between the Fourteenth and the Eighteenth Centuries*. Translated by Lydia G. Cochrane. Cambridge: Polity Press, 1994.

Chavura, Stephen A. 'Mixed Constitutionalism and Parliamentarianism in Elizabethan England: The Case of Thomas Cartwright'. *History of European Ideas* 41, no. 3 (2015): 318–337.

Chedgzoy, Kate, Melanie Hansen and Suzanne Trill, eds. *Voicing Women: Gender and Sexuality in Early Modern Writing*. Keele: Keele University Press, 1996.

Chorpenning, Joseph F. 'Santa Teresa's *Libro de la Vida* as Romance: Narrative Movements and Heroic Quest'. *Revista Canadiense de Estudios Hispánicos* 14, no. 1 (1989): 51–64.

Clark, Peter. 'The Ownership of Books in England, 1560–1640: The Example of Some Kentish Townfolk'. In *Schooling and Society: Studies in the History of Education*, edited by Lawrence Stone, 95–111. Baltimore, MD: Johns Hopkins University Press, 1976.

Clark, Sandra. 'The Broadside Ballad and the Woman's Voice'. In *Debating Gender in Early Modern England 1500–1700*, edited by Cristina Malcolmson and Mihoko Suzuki, 103–120. Basingstoke: Palgrave Macmillan, 2002.

Clarke, Elizabeth. 'Elizabeth Jekyll's Spiritual Diary: Private Manuscript or Political Document?' In *English Manuscript Studies 1100–1700, Vol. 9: Writings by Early Modern Women*, edited by Peter Beal and Margaret J. M. Ezell, 218–237. London: The British Library, 2000.

Clarke, Elizabeth. 'Beyond Microhistory: The Use of Women's Manuscripts in a Widening Political Arena'. In *Women and Politics in Early Modern England, 1450–1700*, edited by James Daybell, 205–221. Aldershot: Ashgate, 2004.

Clarke, Elizabeth. 'Women in Church and in Devotional Spaces'. In Knoppers, *The Cambridge Companion to Early Modern Women's Writing*, 110–123.

Clymer, Lorna, ed. *Ritual, Routine, and Regime: Repetition in Early Modern British and European Cultures*. Toronto: University of Toronto Press in association with the UCLA Center for Seventeenth- and Eighteenth-Century Studies and the William Andrews Clark Memorial Library, 2006.

Cohen, Ralph. 'History and Genre'. In *Genre Theory and Historical Change: Theoretical Essays of Ralph Cohen*, edited by John L. Rowlett, 85–104. Charlottesville, VA: University of Virginia Press, 2017.

Colclough, Stephen. *Consuming Texts: Readers and Reading Communities 1695–1870*. Basingstoke: Palgrave Macmillan, 2007.

Collinson, Patrick. 'The Role of Women in the English Reformation illustrated by the Life and Friendships of Anne Locke'. *Studies in Church History* 2 (1965): 258–272.

Collinson, Patrick. *Godly People: Essays on English Protestantism and Puritanism*. London: Hambledon Press, 1983.

Collinson, Patrick. 'Cartwright, Thomas'. *Oxford Dictionary of National Biography*. 2004. Accessed September 12, 2023. www.oxforddnb .comview/article/4820?docPos=1.

Condren, Conal. *Argument and Authority in Early Modern England: The Presupposition of Oaths and Offices*. Cambridge: Cambridge University Press, 2006.

Connors, Richard. 'The Nature of Stability in the Augustan Age'. *Parliamentary History* 28, no. 1 (2009): 27–40.

Coolahan, Marie-Louise. 'Literary Memorialisation and the Posthumous Construction of Female Authorship'. In *The Arts of Remembrance in Early Modern England: Memorial Cultures of the Post Reformation*, edited by Andrew Gordon and Thomas Rist, 161–178. London: Routledge, 2016.

Corneanu, Sorana, and Koen Vermeir. 'The Art of Thinking'. In *The Cambridge History of the Philosophy of the Scientific Revolution*, edited by David Marshall Miller and Dana Jalobeanu, 149–166. Cambridge: Cambridge University Press, 2022.

Cotterill, Anne. 'Fit Words at the "pitts brinke": The Achievement of Elizabeth Isham'. *Huntington Library Quarterly* 73, no. 2 (2010): 225–248.

Coulton, Richard, Matthew Mauger, and Christopher Reid, eds. *Stealing Books in Eighteenth-Century London*. Basingstoke: Palgrave Macmillan, 2016.

Cowan, Brian. 'What Was Masculine about the Public Sphere? Gender and the Coffeehouse Milieu in Post-Restoration England'. *History Workshop Journal* 51, no. 1 (2001): 127–157.

Cowan, Brian. 'Mr. Spectator and the Coffeehouse Public Sphere'. *Eighteenth-Century Studies* 37, no. 3, Critical Networks (2004): 345–366.

Crawford, Julie. 'Reconsidering Early Modern Women's Reading, or, How Margaret Hoby Read Her De Mornay'. *The Huntington Library Quarterly* 73, no. 2 (2010): 193–223.

Crawford, Julie. *Mediatrix: Women, Politics, and Literary Production in Early Modern England*. Oxford: Oxford University Press, 2014.

Cressy, David. *Literacy and the Social Order: Reading and Writing in Tudor and Stuart England*. Cambridge: Cambridge University Press, 1980.

Cressy, David. 'Books as Totems in Seventeenth-Century England and New England'. *Journal of Library History* 21 (1986): 92–106.

Croft, Pauline. *King James*. Basingstoke: Palgrave Macmillan, 2003.

Cross, Claire. 'The Religious Life of Women in Sixteenth-Century Yorkshire'. *Studies in Church* History 27, Women in the Church (1990): 307–324.

Curth, Louise Hill. *English Almanacs, Astrology, and Popular Medicine, 1550–1700*. Manchester: Manchester University Press, 2007.

Cust, Richard. 'News and Politics in Early Seventeenth-Century England'. *Past & Present* 112, no. 1 (1986): 60–90.

Dackerman, Susan, ed. *Prints and the Pursuit of Knowledge in Early Modern Europe*. Cambridge, MA: Harvard Art Museums, 2011.

Danner, Dan G. 'The Contribution of the Geneva Bible of 1560 to the English Protestant Tradition'. *The Sixteenth Century Journal* 12, no. 3 (1981): 5–18.

Darley, Gillian. *John Evelyn: Living for Ingenuity*. New Haven, CT: Yale University Press, 2006.

Darnton, Robert. 'What Is the History of Books?' *Daedalus* 111, no. 3 Representations and Realities (1982): 65–83.

Darnton, Robert. 'First Steps towards a History of Reading'. *Australian Journal of French Studies* 23 (1986): 5–30.

Darnton, Robert. 'First Steps towards a History of Reading'. *Australian Journal of French Studies* 51, no. 2–3 (2014): 152–177.

Davidoff, Leonore, and Catherine Hall. *Family Fortunes: Men and Women of the English Middle Class, 1780–1850*. London: Hutchinson, 1987.

Davies, Simon F., and Puck Fletcher, eds. *News in Early Modern Europe: Currents and Connections*. Leiden: Brill, 2014.

Davis, Natalie Zemon. 'Beyond the Market: Books as Gifts in Sixteenth-Century France: The Prothero Lecture'. *Transactions of the Royal Historical Society* 33 (1983): 69–88.

Daybell, James. *Women Letter-Writers in Tudor England*. Oxford: Oxford University Press, 2006.

Daybell, James. *The Material Letter in Early Modern England: Manuscript Letters and the Cultures and Practices of Letter-Writing, 1512–1635*. Basingstoke: Palgrave Macmillan, 2012.

Daybell, James. 'Gendered Archival Practices and the Future Lives of Letters'. In *Cultures of Correspondence in Early Modern Britain*, edited by James Daybell and Andrew Gordon, 210–236. Philadelphia, PA: University of Pennsylvania Press, 2016.

Daybell, James. 'The Scribal Circulation of Early Modern Letters'. *Huntington Library Quarterly* 79, no. 3 (2016): 365–385.

DeGroff, Hannah Jane. 'Textual Networks and the Country House: The 3rd Earl of Carlisle at Castle Howard'. PhD thesis, University of York, 2012.

Detlefsen, Karen. 'The Rise of a Public Science? Women and Natural Philosophy in the Early Modern Period'. In *The Cambridge History of Philosophy of the Scientific Revolution*, edited by David Marshall Miller and Dana Jalobeanu, 128–145. Cambridge: Cambridge University Press, 2022.

DiMeo, Michelle. 'Authorship and Medical Networks: Reading Attributions in Early Modern Manuscript Recipe Books'. In DiMeo and Pennell, *Reading and Writing Recipe Books*, 25–46.

DiMeo, Michelle, and Sara Pennell. 'Introduction'. In DiMeo and Pennell, *Reading and Writing Recipe Books*, 1–22.

DiMeo, Michelle, and Sara Pennell, eds. *Reading and Writing Recipe Books, 1550–1800*. Manchester: Manchester University Press, 2013.

Dobranski, Stephen B. *Readers and Authorship in Early Modern England*. Cambridge: Cambridge University Press, 2005.

Dodds, Lara. 'Margaret Cavendish's Domestic Experiment'. In *Genre and Women's Life Writing in Early Modern England*, edited by Michelle M. Dowd and Julie A. Eckerle, 151–168. London: Routledge, 2007.

Dolan, Frances. 'Reading, Writing, and Other Crimes'. In *Feminist Reading of Early Modern Culture: Emerging Subjects*, edited by Valerie Traub, Lindsay M. Kaplan and Dympna Callaghan, 142–167. Cambridge: Cambridge University Press, 1996.

Donagan, Barbara. 'Downing, Calybute'. *Oxford Dictionary of National Biography*. 2010. Accessed May 26, 2019, www.oxforddnb.comview/10.1093/ref:odnb/9780198614128.001.0001/odnb-9780198614128-e-7980?rskey=45ypi8&result=1.

Donawerth, Jane, ed. *Rhetorical Theory by Women before 1900: An Anthology*. Lanham, MD: Rowman and Littlefield, 2002.

Donawerth, Jane. 'Women's Reading Practices in Seventeenth-Century England: Margaret Fell's "Women's Speaking Justified"'. *The Sixteenth Century Journal* 37, no. 4 (Winter 2006): 985–1005.

Doody, Margaret Anne. *The True Story of the Novel*. New Brunswick, NJ: Rutgers University Press, 1997.

Dooley, Brendan. *Angelica's Book and the World of Reading in Late Renaissance Italy*. London: Bloomsbury, 2016.

Dooley, Brendan, and Sabrina A. Baron. *The Politics of Information in Early Modern Europe*. London: Routledge, 2001.

'Dr [Thomas] Horsington (c.1618–1666)'. *Early Modern Practitioners: Sample Data*. Accessed April 25, 2019. http://practitioners.exeter.ac.uk/sample-data.

Dragstra, Henk, Sheila Otway and Helen Wilcox, eds. *Betraying Our Selves: Forms of Self-Representation in Early Modern English Texts*. Basingstoke: Macmillan, 2000.

Durston, Christopher, and Jacqueline Eales, eds. *The Culture of English Puritanism, 1560–1700*. London: Palgrave Macmillan, 1996.

Eagleton, Mary. 'Genre and Gender'. In *Modern Genre Theory*, edited by David Duff, 250–262. London: Routledge, 2000.

Eales, Jacqueline. *Puritans and Roundheads: The Harleys of Brampton Bryan and the Outbreak of the English Civil War*. Cambridge: Cambridge University Press, 1990.

Eales, Jacqueline. 'Gender Construction in Early Modern England and the Conduct Books of William Whately (1583–1639)'. *Studies in Church History* 34 (1998): 163–174.

Eardley, Alice. 'Marketing Aspiration: Fact, Fiction, and the Publication of French Romance in Mid-Seventeenth-Century England'. In *Seventeenth-Century Fiction: Text and Transmission*, edited by Jacqueline Gomski and Isabelle Moreau, 131–142. Oxford: Oxford University Press, 2016.

Eckerle, Julie A. 'Coming to Knowledge: Elizabeth Isham's Autobiography and the Self-Construction of an Intellectual Woman'. *a/b: Auto/Biography Studies* 25, no. 1 (2010): 97–121.

Eckerle, Julie A. *Romancing the Self in Early Modern Englishwomen's Life Writing*. Farnham: Ashgate, 2013.

Eijnatten, Joris van, ed. *Preaching, Sermon and Cultural Change in the Long Eighteenth Century*. Leiden: Brill, 2009.

Eisenstein, Elizabeth L. *The Printing Revolution in Early Modern Europe*. Cambridge: Cambridge University Press, 1986.

'Elizabeth Lyttleton: Commonplace Book'. *Janus*. Cambridge University Library. Accessed September 27, 2023. Collection: Elizabeth Lyttelton: Commonplace book, ArchiveSearch (cam.ac.uk).

Ezell, Margaret J. M. 'The Myth of Judith Shakespeare: Creating the Canon of Women's Literature'. *New Literary History* 21, no. 3, New Historicisms, New Histories, and Others (1990): 579–592.

Ezell, Margaret J. M. 'Elizabeth Delaval's Spiritual Heroine: Thoughts on Redefining Manuscript Texts by Early Women Writers'. In *English Manuscript Studies, Volume 3*, edited by Peter Beal and Jeremy Griffiths, 216–237. London: The British Library, 1992.

Ezell, Margaret J. M. 'The Politics of the Past: Restoration Women Writers on Women Reading History'. In *Pilgrimage for Love: Essays in Early Modern Literature in Honour of Josephine A. Roberts*, edited by Sigrid King, 19–40. Tempe, AZ: Arizona Center for Medieval and Renaissance Studies, 1999.

Ezell, Margaret J. M. 'Cooking the Books, or, the Three Faces of Hannah Woolley'. In DiMeo and Pennell, *Reading and Writing Recipe Books*, 159–178.

Ferdinand, Christine. 'Constructing the Frameworks of Desire: How Newspapers Sold Books in the Seventeenth and Eighteenth Centuries'. *Prose Studies* 21, no. 2 (1998): 157–175.

Feroli, Teresa. "*Infelix Simulacrum*': The Rewriting of Loss in Elizabeth Jocelin's *The Mothers Legacie*'. *ELH* 61, no. 1 (1994): 89–102.

Ferrell, Lori Anne. 'Preaching and the English Parliaments in the 1620s'. *Parliamentary History* 34, no. 1 (2015): 142–154.

Ferriss, Suzanne, and Mallory Young, eds. *Chick Lit: The New Woman's Fiction*. London: Routledge, 2006.

Field, Catherine. '"Many hands hands": Writing the Self in Early Modern Women's Recipe Books'. In *Genre and Women's Life Writing in Early Modern England*, edited by Michelle M. Dowd and Julie A. Eckerle, 49–64. Aldershot: Ashgate, 2007.

Fitzgerald, Colleen. 'To Educate or Instruct? Du Bosc and Fénelon on Women'. In *Women's Education in Early Modern Europe: A History, 1500–1800*, edited by Barbara J. Whitehead, 159–192. New York: Garland, 1999.

Fitzmaurice, James, Josephine A. Roberts, Carol L. Barash, Eugene R. Cunnar, and Nancy A. Gutierrez, eds. *Major Women Writers of Seventeenth-Century England*. Ann Arbor, MI: University of Michigan Press, 1997.

Fleming, Juliet. *Graffiti and the Writing Arts of Early Modern England*. Philadelphia, PA: University of Pennsylvania Press, 2001.

Fletcher, Anthony. 'The Protestant Idea of Marriage in Early Modern England'. In *Religion, Culture and Society in Early Modern Britain: Essays in Honour of Patrick Collinson*, edited by Anthony Fletcher and Peter Roberts, 161–181. Cambridge: Cambridge University Press, 1994.

Fletcher, Anthony. *Gender, Sex and Subordination in England, 1500–1800*. New Haven, CT: Yale University Press, 1995.

Flint, Kate. *The Woman Reader 1837–1914*. Oxford: Oxford University Press, 1993.

Forster, G. C. F. 'Faction and County Government in Early Stuart Yorkshire'. *Northern History* 11, no. 1 (1976): 70–86.

Foster, Joseph. *The Register of Admissions to Gray's Inn, 1521–1889, together with the register of marriages in Gray's Inn Chapel, 165–1754*. London: Hansard Publishing Union, 1889.

Fox, Adam. *Oral and Literate Culture in England, 1500–1700*. Oxford: Oxford University Press, 2000.

Frankenberg, Ruth. *White Women, Race Matters: The Social Construction of Whiteness*. Minneapolis, MN: University of Minnesota Press, 1993.

Frearson, Michael. 'The Distribution and Readership of London Corantos in the 1620s'. In *Serials and Their Readers, 1620–1914*, edited by Robin Myers and Michael Harris, 1–25. Winchester: St Paul's Bibliographies, 1993.

Friedman, Alice T. 'Constructing an Identity in Prose, Plaster and Print: Lady Anne Clifford as Writer and Patron of the Arts'. In *Ashgate Critical Essays on Women Writers, 1550–1700, Volume Five: Anne Clifford and Lucy Hutchinson*, edited by Mihoko Suzuki, 103–120. Farnham: Ashgate, 2009.

Friedrich, Markus. *The Birth of the Archive: A History of Knowledge*. Translated by John Noel Dillon. Ann Arbor, MI: University of Michigan Press, 2018.

Fries, Udo. 'Newspapers from 1665 to 1765'. In *News as Changing Texts: Corpora, Methodologies and Analysis*, edited by Roberta Facchinetti, Nicholas Brownlees, Birte Bös and Udo Fries, 49–89. Newcastle upon Tyne: Cambridge Scholars Publishing, 2015.

Fuentes, Marisa J. *Dispossessed Lives: Enslaved Women, Violence, and the Archive*. Philadelphia, PA: University of Pennsylvania Press, 2016.

Fulton, Thomas. *Historical Milton: Manuscript, Print, and Political Culture in Revolutionary England*. Amherst, MA: University of Massachusetts Press, 2010.

Furniss, Tom. 'Reading the Geneva Bible: Notes towards an English Revolution?' *Prose Studies* 31, no. 1 (2009): 1–21.

Gaukroger, Stephen. *Descartes: An Intellectual Biography*. Oxford: Oxford University Press, 1997.

Gerson, Carole. 'Locating Female Subjects in the Archives'. In *Working in Women's Archives: Researching Women's Private literature and Archival Documents*, edited by Helen M. Buss and Marlene Kadar, 7–22. Waterloo, Ontario: Wilfrid Laurier University Press, 2001.

Gheeraert-Graffeuille, Claire. 'Genre et Histoire: le Cas des Mémoires Féminins de la Révolution Anglaise'. *Dix-Septième Siècle* 257, no. 4 (2012): 651–663.

Gibson, Jonathan. 'Casting off Blanks: Hidden Structures in Early Modern Paper Books'. In *Material Readings of Early Modern Culture: Texts and Social Practices, 1580–1730*, edited by James Daybell and Peter Hinds, 208–228. Basingstoke: Palgrave Macmillan, 2010.

Gill, Catie. *Women in the Seventeenth-Century Quaker Community: A Literary Study of Political Identities, 1650–1700*. Aldershot: Ashgate, 2005.

Gillespie, Katharine. *Domesticity and Dissent in the Seventeenth Century: English Women's Writing and the Public Sphere*. Cambridge: Cambridge University Press, 2004.

Glaisyer, Natasha. '"The Most Universal Intelligencers": The Circulation of the *London Gazette* in the 1690s'. *Media History* 23, no. 2 (2017): 256–280.

Glaisyer, Natasha, and Sara Pennell, eds. *Didactic Literature in England 1500–1800: Expertise Constructed.* Aldershot: Ashgate, 2003.

Goodman, Jennifer R. '"That wommen holde in ful greet reverence": Mothers and Daughters Reading Chivalric Romances'. In *Women, the Book and the Worldly: Selected Proceedings of the St Hilda's Conference, 1993, Volume II*, edited by Lesley Smith and Jane H. M. Taylor, 25–30. Cambridge: D. S. Brewer, 1995.

Goodrich, Jaime. *Faithful Translators: Authorship, Gender and Religion in Early Modern England.* Evanston, IL: Northwestern University Press, 2014.

Gowing, Laura. *Gender Relations in Early Modern England.* Harlow: Pearson, 2012.

Gowing, Laura. 'Girls on Forms: Apprenticing Young Women in Seventeenth-Century London'. *Journal of British Studies* 55 (2016): 447–473.

Grafton, Anthony, and Joanna Weinburg. *'I have always loved the Holy Tongue': Isaac Casaubon, the Jews, and a Forgotten Chapter in Renaissance Scholarship.* Cambridge, MA: The Belknap Press of Harvard University Press, 2011.

Graham, Elspeth, Hilary Hinds, Elaine Hobby and Helen Wilcox, eds. *Her Own Life: Autobiographical Writings by Seventeenth-Century Englishwomen.* London: Routledge, 1989.

Graham, Elspeth, Hilary Hinds, Elaine Hobby and Helen Wilcox. 'Introduction'. In Graham et al., *Her Own Life*, 1–26.

Grande, Nathalie. 'Quand le Roman Oeuvre en Moraliste: Madeleine de Scudéry et Clélie'. *Dalhousie French Studies* 27: Réflexions sur le genre moraliste au dix-septième siècle (1994): 31–49.

Gray, Catherine. 'Feeding on the Seed of Woman: Dorothy Leigh and the Figure of Maternal Dissent'. *ELH* 68, no. 3 (2001): 563–592.

Greaves, Richard L. 'The Nature and Intellectual Milieu of the Political Principles in the Geneva Bible Marginalia'. *Journal of Church and State* 22, no. 2 (1980): 233–249.

Greengrass, Mark. 'Philippe Duplessis-Mornay, Jacques VI et Ier, et la reunion de christianisme 1603–1619'. *Albineana* 18 (2006): 423–461.

Griffiths, Elizabeth, and Jane Whittle. *Consumption and Gender in the Early Seventeenth-Century Household: The World of Alice Le Strange.* Oxford: Oxford University Press, 2012.

Groot, Jerome de. 'John Denham and Lucy Hutchinson's Commonplace Book'. *Studies in English Literature, 1500–1900* 48, no. 1, the English Renaissance (2008): 147–163.

Gusdorf, Georges. 'Conditions and Limits of Autobiography'. In *Autobiography: Essays Theoretical and Critical*, edited by James Olney, 28–48. Princeton, NJ: Princeton University Press, 1980.

Gwynn, Lucy. 'The Design of the English Domestic Library in the Seventeenth Century: Readers and Their Book Rooms'. *Library Trends* 60 (2011): 43–53.

Hackel, Heidi Brayman. 'The Countess of Bridgewater's London Library'. In Anderson and Sauer, *Books and Readers in Early Modern England*, 138–159.

Hackel, Heidi Brayman. '"Boasting of Silence": Women Readers in a Patriarchal State'. In Sharpe and Zwicker, *Reading, Society and Politics in Early Modern England*, 101–121.

Hackel, Heidi Brayman. *Reading in Early Modern England: Print, Gender and Literacy*. Cambridge: Cambridge University Press, 2005.

Hackel, Heidi Brayman. 'Turning to Her "Best Companion[s]": Lady Anne Clifford as Reader, Annotator and Book Collector'. In Hearn and Hulse, *Lady Anne Clifford: Culture, Patronage and Gender in 17th-Century Britain*, 99–108.

Hackel, Heidi Brayman, and Catherine E. Kelly, eds. *Reading Women: Literacy, Authorship, and Culture in the Atlantic World, 1500–1800*. Philadelphia, PA: University of Pennsylvania Press, 2008.

Hackett, Helen. *Women and Romance Fiction in the English Renaissance*. Cambridge: Cambridge University Press, 2000.

Hadfield, Andrew, Matthew Dimmock and Abigail Shinn, eds. *The Ashgate Research Companion to Popular Culture in Early Modern England*. Farnham: Ashgate Publishing, 2014.

Hall, Timothy L. *Separating Church and State: Roger Williams and Religious Liberty*. Urbana, IL: University of Illinois Press, 1998.

Hamling, Tara and Catherine Richardson. *A Day at Home in Early Modern England: Material Culture and Domestic Life, 1500–1700*. New Haven, CT: Yale University Press, 2017.

Hampson Patterson, Mary. *Domesticating the Reformation: Protestant Best Sellers, Private Devotion, and the Revolution of English Piety*. Madison, WI: Fairleigh Dickinson University Press, 2007.

Hardy, Mary. 'The Seventeenth-Century English and Scottish Reception of Francis de Sales' *An Introduction to a Devout Life*'. *British Catholic History* 33, no. 2 (2016): 228–258.

Harris, Cheryl I. 'Whiteness as Property'. In *Critical Race Theory: The Key Writings That Formed the Movement*, edited by Kimberlé

Crenshaw, Neil Gotanda, Garry Peller and Kendall Thomas, 276–291. New York: The New Press, 1995.

Harris, Francis. 'A Revolution Correspondence: Elizabeth Packer Geddes and Elizabeth Burnet'. In *Women, Identities and Communities in Early Modern Europe*, edited by Stephanie Tarbin and Susan Broomhall, 165–180. Aldershot: Ashgate, 2008.

Harris, Johanna, and Elizabeth Scott-Baumann, eds. *The Intellectual Culture of Puritan Women, 1558–1680*. Basingstoke: Palgrave Macmillan, 2011.

Harrison, Peter. 'Descartes on Animals'. *The Philosophical Quarterly* 42, no. 167 (1992): 219–227.

Heal, Felicity. 'Reputation and Honour in Court and Country: Lady Elizabeth Russell and Sir Thomas Hoby'. *Transactions of the Royal Historical Society* 6 (1996): 161–178.

Hearn, Karen, and Lynn Hulse, eds. *Lady Anne Clifford: Culture, Patronage and Gender in 17th-Century Britain*. Leeds: Yorkshire Archaeological Society, 2009.

Heller, Jennifer. 'The Legacy and Rhetorics of Maternal Zeal'. *ELH* 75, no. 3 (2003): 603–623.

Heller, Jennifer. *The Mother's Legacy in Early Modern England*. Farnham: Ashgate, 2011.

Helm, James L. 'Bathsua Makin's *An Essay to Revive the Antient Education of Gentlewomen* in the Canon of Seventeenth-Century Educational Reform Tracts'. *Cahiers Elisabéthains: A Journal of English Renaissance Studies* 44, no. 1 (1993): 45–51.

Herbert, Amanda. *Female Alliances: Gender, Identity, and Friendship in Early Modern Britain*. New Haven, CT: Yale University Press, 2014.

Herman, Arthur L. 'Protestant Churches in a Catholic Kingdom: Political Assemblies in the Thought of Philippe Duplessis-Mornay'. *The Sixteenth-Century Journal* 21, no. 4 (1990): 543–557.

Herman, Ruth. *The Business of a Woman: The Political Writings of Delarivier Manley*. Newark, DE: University of Delaware Press, 2003.

'Hertfordshire Archives and Local Studies: D/EP F39'. *Perdita*, 2005. Accessed September 26, 2023. Perdita: ms HRODEPF39: frames version (warwick.ac.uk).

Heyd, Michael. *'Be Sober and Reasonable': The Critique of Enthusiasm in the Seventeenth and Early Eighteenth Centuries*. Leiden: Brill, 1995.

Hill, Christopher. *Society and Puritanism in Pre-Revolutionary England*. London: Secker and Warburg, 1964.

Hill, Christopher. 'Foreword'. In Raymond, *Making the News*, ix–xi.

Hindle, Steve. 'Below Stairs at Arbury Hall: Sir Richard Newdigate and his Household Staff, c.1670–1710'. *Historical Research* 85, no. 227 (2012): 71–88.

Hindmarsh, D. Bruce. *The Evangelical Conversion Narrative: Spiritual Autobiography in Early Modern England*. Oxford: Oxford University Press, 2005.

Hintz, Carrie. *An Audience of One: Dorothy Osborne's Letters to Sir William Temple, 1652–1654*. Toronto: University of Toronto Press, 2005.

Hiscock, Andrew. *Reading Memory in Early Modern Literature*. Cambridge: Cambridge University Press, 2011.

Hobby, Elaine. *Virtue of Necessity: English Women's Writing, 1646–1688*. London: Virago, 1988.

Hobby, Elaine. 'A Woman's Best Setting Out Is Silence: The Writings of Hannah Woolley'. In *Culture and Society in the Stuart Restoration*, edited by Gerald MacLean, 179–200. Cambridge: Cambridge University Press, 1995.

Hodgkin, Katherine, ed. *Women, Madness and Sin in Early Modern England: The Autobiographical Writings of Dionys Fitzherbert*. Farnham: Ashgate, 2010.

Hodgson-Wright, Stephanie, ed. *Women's Writing of the Early Modern Period, 1588–1688: An Anthology*. Edinburgh: Edinburgh University Press, 2002.

Horowitz, Louise K. 'Pastoral Fiction'. In *A New History of French Literature*, edited by Denis Hollier, 258–261. Cambridge, MA: Harvard University Press, 1994.

Houlbrooke, Ralph. *Death, Religion and the Family in England, 1480–1750*. Oxford: Clarendon Press, 1998.

Houston, R. A. *Literacy in Early Modern Europe: Culture and Education 1500–1800*. London: Routledge, 2002.

How, James. *Epistolary Spaces: English Letter Writing from the Foundation of the Post Office to Richardson's* Clarissa. Aldershot: Ashgate, 2003.

Howsam, Leslie. 'In My View: Women and Book History'. *SHARP News* 7, no. 4 (1998): 1–2.

Hubbard, Eleanor. 'Reading, Writing, and Initialing: Female Literacy in Early Modern London'. *Journal of British Studies* 54, no. 3 (2015): 564–576.

Hughes, Ann. 'Men, the "Public" and the "Private" in the English Revolution'. In Lake and Pincus, *The Politics of the Public Sphere in Early Modern England*, 191–212.

Hughes, Ann. *Gender and the English Revolution*. Abingdon: Routledge, 2012.

Hughes, Derek, and Janet Todd, eds. *The Cambridge Companion to Aphra Behn*. Cambridge: Cambridge University Press, 2004.

Hull, Suzanne W. *Chaste, Silent and Obedient: English Books for Women, 1477–1640*. San Marino, CA: Huntington Library, 1988.

Hunt, Arnold. 'The Books, Manuscripts and Literary Patronage of Mrs Anne Sadleir (1585–1670)'. In Burke and Gibson, *Early Modern Women's Manuscript Writing*, 205–236.

Hunt, Arnold. 'Libraries in the Archives: Researching Provenance in the British Library'. In *Libraries within the Library: The Origins of the British Library's Printed Collections*, edited by Giles Mandelbrote and Barry Taylor, 363–384. London: The British Library. 2009.

Hunter, Lynette. 'Sisters of the Royal Society: The Circle of Katherine Jones, Lady Ranelagh'. In *Women, Science and Medicine 1500–1700: Mothers and Sisters of the Royal Society*, edited by Lynette Hunter and Sarah Hutton, 178–197. Stroud: Sutton Publishing, 1997.

Hutton, Sarah. 'Thomas Jackson, Oxford Platonist, and William Twisse, Aristotelian'. *Journal of the History of Ideas* 39, no. 4 (1978): 635–652.

Hutton, Sarah. *British Philosophy in the Seventeenth Century*. Oxford: Oxford University Press, 2015.

Hutton, Sarah. 'Alchemy and Cultures of Knowledge among Early Modern Women'. *Early Modern Women: An Interdisciplinary Journal* 15, no. 2 (2021): 93–102.

Iliffe, Robert. 'Author-Mongering: The "Editor" between Producer and Consumer'. In *The Consumption of Culture 1600–1800: Image, Object, Text*. Edited by Ann Bermingham and John Brewer, 166–192. London: Routledge, 1995.

Iliffe, Robert. 'Isaac Newton: Lucatello Professor of Mathematics'. In *Science Incarnate: Historical Embodiments of Natural Knowledge*, edited by Christopher Lawrence and Steven Shapin, 121–155. Chicago, IL: University of Chicago Press, 1998.

Ingram, Randall. 'Seventeenth-Century Didactic Readers, Their Literature, and Ours'. In Glaisyer and Pennell, *Didactic Literature in England, 1500–1800*, 63–78.

Isaacs, Tina. 'The Anglican Hierarchy and the Reformation of Manners, 1688–1738'. *The Journal of Ecclesiastical History* 33, no. 3 (1982): 391–411.

Itti, Eliane. *Madame Dacier, femme et savant du Grand Siècle: 1645–1720*. Paris: L'Harmattan, 2012.

Jack, Belinda. *The Woman Reader*. New Haven, CT: Yale University Press, 2013.

Jackson, Ian. 'Approaches to the History of Readers and Reading in Eighteenth-Century Britain'. *The Historical Journal* 47, no. 4 (2004): 1041–1054.

Jaggar, Alison M. 'Love and Knowledge: Emotion in Feminist Epistemology'. In *Gender/Body/Knowledge: Feminist Reconstructions of Being and Knowing*, edited by Alison M. Jaggar and Susan Bordo, 145–171. New Brunswick, NJ: Rutgers University Press, 1990.

Jagodzinski, Cecile M. *Privacy and Print: Reading and Writing in Seventeenth-Century England*. Charlottesville, VA: University Press of Virginia, 1999.

Jardine, Lisa, and Anthony Grafton. '"Studied for Action": How Gabriel Harvey Read His Livy'. *Past & Present* 129 (1990): 30–78.

Jensen, Michael. '"Simply" Reading the Geneva Bible: The Geneva Bible and Its Readers'. *Literature and Theology* 9, no. 1 (1995): 30–45.

Jimerson, Randall C. *Archives Power: Memory, Accountability, and Social Justice*. Chicago, IL: Society of American Archivists, 2009.

Johns, Adrian. *The Nature of the Book: Print and Knowledge in the Making*. Chicago, IL: University of Chicago Press, 1998.

Jones, Emily Griffiths. 'Romance, Narrative Vision, and Elect Community in Seventeenth-Century England'. PhD thesis, Boston University, 2014.

Jones, Vivian. *Women in the Eighteenth Century: Constructions of Femininity*. London: Routledge, 1990.

Karant-Nunn, Susan. *The Reformation of Feeling: Shaping the Religious Emotions in Early Modern Germany*. Oxford: Oxford University Press, 2010.

Kaufman, Gloria. 'Juan Luis Vives on the Education of Women'. *Signs* 3, no. 4 (1978): 891–896.

Keating, Erin M. 'The Role of Manuscript Newsletters in Charles II's Performance of Power'. *Restoration: Studies in English Literary Culture, 1660–1700* 41, no. 2 (2017): 33–51.

Keeble, N. H. *Richard Baxter: Puritan Man of Letters*. Oxford: Clarendon Press, 1982.

Keeble, N. H., ed. *The Cultural Identity of Seventeenth-Century Woman: A Reader*. London: Routledge, 1994.

Keeble, N. H., ed. *The Cambridge Companion to Writing of the English Revolution*. Cambridge: Cambridge University Press, 2001.

Kelly, Joan. 'Early Feminist Theory and the *Querelle des Femmes*, 1400–1789'. *Signs* 8, no. 1 (1982): 4–28.

Kelly, Joan. *Women, History and Theory: The Essays of Joan Kelly*. Chicago, IL: University of Chicago Press, 1984.

Kennedy, A. 'Rebellion, Government and the Scottish Response to Argyll's Rising of 1685'. *Journal of Scottish Historical Studies* 36, no. 1 (2016): 40–59.

Kenny, Amy. *Humoral Wombs on the Shakespearean Stage*. London: Palgrave Macmillan, 2019.

Kent, Susan Kingsley. *Gender and Power in Britain, 1640–1990*. New York: Routledge, 1999.

Kerr, Heather, and Claire Walker, eds. *Fama and Her Sisters: Gossip and Rumour in Early Modern Europe*. Turnhout: Brepols, 2015.

Killeen, Kevin, Helen Smith and Rachel Willie, eds. *The Oxford Handbook of the Bible in Early Modern England, c. 1530–1700*. Oxford: Oxford University Press, 2015.

King, John N., ed. *Tudor Books and Readers: Materiality and the Construction of Meaning*. Cambridge: Cambridge University Press, 2010.

King, Margaret L. *Women of the Renaissance*. Chicago, IL: University of Chicago Press, 1991.

King, Rachael Scarborough. 'The Manuscript Newsletter and the Rise of the Newspaper, 1665–1715'. *Huntington Library Quarterly* 79, no. 3 (2016): 411–437.

King, Rachael Scarborough. 'All the News That's Fit to Write: The Eighteenth-Century Manuscript Newsletter'. In Brandtzæg et al., *Travelling Chronicles*, 95–118.

King, Rachael Scarborough. *Writing to the World: Letters and the Origins of Modern Print Genres*. Baltimore, MD: Johns Hopkins University Press, 2018.

King, Rachael Scarborough. '"~~Sir~~ Madam": Female Consumers of Parliamentary News in Manuscript Newsletters'. *Parliamentary History* 41, no. 1 (2022): 119–134.

Kintgen, Eugene R. *Reading in Tudor England*. Pittsburgh, PA: University of Pittsburgh Press, 1996.

Kishlansky, Mark. 'Charles I: A Case of Mistaken Identity'. *Past & Present* 189 (2005): 41–80.

Knight, Leah, Micheline White and Elizabeth Sauer, eds. *Women's Bookscapes in Early Modern England: Reading, Ownership, Circulation*. Ann Arbor, MI: University of Michigan Press, 2018.

Knights, Mark. 'Politics after the Glorious Revolution'. In *A Companion to Stuart Britain*, edited by Barry Coward, 455–473. Oxford: Blackwell Publishing, 2003.

Knights, Mark. *Representation and Misrepresentation in Later Stuart Culture: Partisanship and Political Culture*. Oxford: Oxford University Press, 2005.

Knoppers, Laura Lunger. *The Cambridge Companion to Early Modern Women's Writing*. Cambridge: Cambridge University Press, 2009.

Knoppers, Laura Lunger. 'Introduction: Critical Framework and Issues'. In Knoppers, *The Cambridge Companion to Early Modern Women's Writing*, 1–18.

Knoppers, Laura Lunger, ed. *The Oxford Handbook of Literature and the English Revolution*. Oxford: Oxford University Press, 2012.

Kolbrener, William, and Michal Michelson, eds. *Mary Astell: Reason, Gender, Faith*. Aldershot: Ashgate, 2007.

Koopmans, Joop W. *Early Modern Media and the News in Europe: Perspectives from the Dutch Angle*. Leiden: Brill, 2018.

Kopperman, Paul E. *Sir Robert Heath, 1575–1649: Window on an Age*. Woodbridge: Boydell Press for the Royal Historical Society, 1989.

Kugler, Anne. 'Constructing Wifely Identity: Prescription and Practice in the Life of Lady Sarah Cowper'. *Journal of British Studies* 40, no. 3 (2001): 291–323.

Kugler, Anne. *Errant Plagiary: The Writing Life of Lady Sarah Cowper*. Stanford, CA: Stanford University Press, 2002.

Lake, Peter. 'Feminine Piety and Personal Potency: The "Emancipation" of Mrs Jane Ratcliffe'. *The Seventeenth Century* 2, no. 2 (1987): 143–165.

Lake, Peter. 'Business as Usual? The Immediate Reception of Hooker's *Ecclesiastical Polity*'. *The Journal of Ecclesiastical History* 52, no. 3 (2001): 456–486.

Lake, Peter, and Steven Pincus, eds. *The Politics of the Public Sphere in Early Modern England*. Manchester: Manchester University Press, 2007.

Lamb, Mary Ellen. *Gender and Authorship in the Sidney Circle*. Madison, WI: University of Wisconsin Press, 1990.

Lamb, Mary Ellen. 'The Agency of the Split Subject: Lady Anne Clifford and the Uses of Reading'. *English Literary Renaissance* 22 (1992): 347–368.

Lamb, Mary Ellen. 'Constructions of Women Readers'. In Woods and Hannay, *Teaching Tudor and Stuart Women Writers*, 23–34.

Lamb, Mary Ellen. 'The Sociality of Margaret Hoby's Reading Practices and the Representation of Reformation Interiority'. *Critical Survey* 12, no. 2 (2000): 17–32.

Larminie, Vivienne. 'Marriage and the Family: The Example of the Seventeenth-Century Newdigates'. *Midlands History* 9, no. 1 (1984): 1–22.

Larminie, Vivienne. 'Fighting for Family in a Patronage Society: The Epistolary Armoury of Anne Newdigate (1574–1618)'. In *Early Modern Women's Letter-Writing, 1450–1700*, edited by James Daybell, 94–108. London: Palgrave Macmillan, 2001.

Laroche, Rebecca. '"To take in hand the practice of phisick": Early Modern Women's Signatures in Print Medical Texts'. In *New Ways of Looking at Old Texts, IV*, edited by Michael Denbo, 269–278. Tempe, AZ: Arizona Center for Medieval and Renaissance Studies, 2008.

Laroche, Rebecca. *Medical Authority and Englishwomen's Herbal Texts, 1550–1650*. Farnham: Ashgate, 2009.

Larson, Katherine. *Early Modern Women in Conversation*. Basingstoke: Palgrave Macmillan, 2011.

Laurence, Anne. *Women in England 1500–1760: A Social History*. New York: St. Martin's Press, 1994.

Lawrence-Mathers, Anne, and Phillipa Hardman, eds. *Women and Writing c.1340–c.1650: The Domestication of Print Culture*. York: York Medieval Press, 2010.

Lee, Jongsook. 'Who Is Cecilia, What Was She? Cecilia Bulstrode and Jonson's Epideictics'. *Journal of English and Germanic Philology* 85, no. 1 (1986): 20–34.

Leong, Elaine. '"Herbals She Peruseth": Reading Medicine in Early Modern England'. *Renaissance Studies* 28, no. 4 (2014): 556–578.

Leong, Elaine. *Recipes and Everyday Knowledge: Medicine, Science and the Household in Early Modern England*. Chicago, IL: University of Chicago Press, 2018.

Lettinga, Neil. 'Covenant Theory Turned Upside Down: Henry Hammond and Caroline Anglican Moralism: 1643–1660'. *Sixteenth-Century Journal* 24, no. 3 (1993): 653–669.

Levelt, Sjoerd. 'Early Modern Marginalia and #earlymoderntwitter'. In Acheson, *Early Modern English Marginalia*, 234–256.

Lewalski, Barbara Kiefer. 'Re-Writing Patriarchy and Patronage: Margaret Clifford, Anne Clifford, and Aemilia Lanyer'. *The Yearbook of English Studies* 21 (1991): 87–106.

Lewalski, Barbara Kiefer. *Writing Women in Jacobean England*. Cambridge, MA: Harvard University Press, 1993.

Liapi, Lena. '"The Talke of the Towne": News, Crime and the Public Sphere in Seventeenth-Century London'. *Cultural and Social History* 14, no. 5 (2017): 549–564.

Lilti, Antoine. *The World of the Salons: Sociability and Worldliness in Eighteenth-Century Paris*. Translated by Lydia G. Cochrane. Oxford: Oxford University Press, 2005.

Lindenbaum, Sarah. 'Hiding in Plain Sight: How Electronic Records Can Lead Us to Early Modern Women Readers'. In Knight et al., *Women's Bookscapes in Early Modern Britain*, 193–213.

Lindenbaum, Sarah. 'About'. *Frances Wolfreston Hor Bouks*. December 2, 2018. Accessed May 4, 2019. https://franceswolfrestonhorbouks.com.

Lindenbaum, Sarah. 'Memorializing the Everyday: The Evidence of the Final Decade of Frances Wolfreston's Life'. *The Seventeenth Century* 37, no. 3 (2022): 449–476.

Lindenbaum, Sarah. 'A Closet for Ladies and Gentlewomen (1611)'. *Early Modern Female Book Ownership*. 2022. Accessed July 13, 2023. https://earlymodernfemalebookownership.wordpress.com2022/07/05/a-closet-for-ladies-and-gentlewomen-1611.

Lindley, David. *The Trials of Frances Howard: Fact and Fiction at the Court of King James*. Abingdon: Routledge, 1993.

Little, Jr., Arthur L., ed. *White People in Shakespeare: Essays on Race, Culture and the Elite*. London: The Arden Shakespeare, 2022.

Lockyer, Roger. *Buckingham: The Life and Political Career of George Villiers, First Duke of Buckingham, 1592–1628*. London: Routledge, 1981.

Longfellow, Erica. *Women and Religious Writing in Early Modern England*. Cambridge: Cambridge University Press, 2004.

Longfellow, Erica. '"Take unto ye words": Elizabeth Isham's "Booke of Rememberance" and Puritan Cultural Forms'. In Harris and Scott-Baumann, *The Intellectual Culture of Puritan Women*, 122–134.

Loomba, Ania, and Melissa E. Sanchez. 'Introduction: Why "Feminism"? Why Now?' In *Rethinking Feminism in Early Modern Studies: Gender, Race, and Sexuality*, edited by Ania Loomba and Melissa E. Sanchez, 1–14. London: Routledge, 2016.

Love, Harold. 'Scribal Publication in Seventeenth-Century England'. *Transactions of the Cambridge Bibliographical Society* 9, no. 2 (1987): 130–154.

Love, Harold. 'How Personal Is a Personal Miscellany? Sarah Cowper, Martin Clifford and the "Buckingham Commonplace Book"'. In *Order and Connexion: Studies in Bibliography and Book History*, edited by R. C. Alston, 111–126. Cambridge: D. S. Brewer, 1997.

Loveman, Kate. *Samuel Pepys and his Books: Reading, News Gathering, and Sociability, 1660–1703*. Oxford: Oxford University Press, 2015.

Lucas, Caroline. *Writing for Women: The Example of Woman as Reader in Elizabethan Romance*. Milton Keynes: Open University Press, 1989.

Lupton, Christina. *Reading and the Making of Time in the Eighteenth Century*. Baltimore, MD: Johns Hopkins University Press, 2018.

Lynch, Kathleen. *Protestant Autobiography in the Seventeenth-Century Anglophone World*. Oxford: Oxford University Press, 2012.

MacGillivray, Royce. *Restoration Historians and the English Civil War*. The Hague: Martinus Nijhoff, 1974.

Mack, Phyllis. *Visionary Women: Ecstatic Prophecy in Seventeenth-Century England*. Berkeley, CA: University of California Press, 1992.

Mackenzie, Pamela, and Elisabeth Davies. 'The Once and Future Self: (Re)Reading Personal Lists, Notes, and Calendars'. In *Plotting the Reading Experience: Theory, Practice, Politics*, edited by Lynne

McKechnie, Kjell Ivar Skjerdingstad, Knut Oterholm, Magnus Persson and Paulette M. Rothbauer, 149–166. Waterloo, Ontario: Wilfrid Laurier University Press, 2016.

MacLean, Gerald. 'Literacy, Class, and Gender in Restoration England'. *Text* 7 (1994): 307–335.

Mancall, Peter, ed. *Bringing the World to Early Modern Europe: Travel Accounts and Their Audiences*. Leiden: Brill, 2007.

Mandelbrote, Giles, and K. A. Manley, eds. *The Cambridge History of Libraries in Britain and Ireland. Volume 2: 1640–1850*. Cambridge: Cambridge University Press, 2006.

Manguel, Alberto. *A History of Reading*. London: Flamingo, 1997.

Manoff, Marlene. 'Mapping Archival Silence: Technology and the Historical Record'. In *Engaging with Records and Archives: Histories and Theories*, edited by Fiorella Foscarini, Heather MacNeil, Bonnie Mac and Gillian Oliver, 63–82. London: Facet Publishing, 2016.

Marshall Miller, David and Dana Jalobeanu. 'The Disciplinary Revolutions of Early Modern Philosophy and Science'. In *The Cambridge History of Philosophy of the Scientific Revolution*, edited by David Marshall Miller and Dana Jalobeanu, 1–12. Cambridge: Cambridge University Press, 2022.

Mayer, Jean-Christophe. *Shakespeare's Early Readers: A Cultural History from 1590 to 1800*. Cambridge: Cambridge University Press, 2018.

McColley, Diane K. 'Milton and the Sexes'. In *The Cambridge Companion to Milton*, edited by Dennis Danielson, 175–192. Cambridge: Cambridge University Press, 1999.

McDowell, Paula. *The Women of Grub Street: Press, Politics and Gender in the London Literary Marketplace, 1678–1730*. Oxford: Clarendon, 1998.

McElligott, Jason. 'Ownership Inscriptions and Life Writing in the Books of Early Modern Women'. In *Women's Life Writing and Early Modern Ireland*, edited by Julie A. Eckerle and Naomi McAreavey, 229–252. Lincoln, NE: University of Nebraska Press, 2019.

McGiffert, Michael. 'Henry Hammond and Covenant Theology'. *Church History* 74, no. 2 (2005): 255–285.

McGovern, Jonathan. 'The Political Sermons of Lancelot Andrewes'. *The Seventeenth Century* 34, no. 1 (2019): 3–25.

McIver, Bruce. '"A Wife Now the Widdow": Lawrence Lisle and the Popularity of the Overburian Characters'. *South Atlantic Review* 59, no. 1 (1994): 27–44.

McKitterick, David. 'Women and Their Books in Seventeenth-Century England: The Case of Elizabeth Puckering'. *The Library* 1, Seventh Series (2000): 359–380.

Meale, Carol M., and Julia Boffey. 'Gentlewomen's Reading'. In *The Cambridge History of the Book in Britain. Volume 3: 1400–1557*, edited by Lotte Hellinga and J. B. Trapp, 526–540. Cambridge: Cambridge University Press, 1999.

Mendelson, Sara Heller. 'The Weightiest Business: Marriage in an Upper-Gentry Family in Seventeenth-Century England'. *Past & Present* 85 (1979): 126–135.

Mendelson, Sara Heller. 'The Civility of Women in Seventeenth-Century England'. In Burke et al., *Civil Histories*, 111–126.

Mendle, Michael. 'Preserving the Ephemeral: Reading, Collecting, and the Pamphlet Culture of Seventeenth-Century England'. In Anderson and Sauer, *Books and Readers in Early Modern England*, 201–216.

Mentz, Steve. *Romance for Sale in Early Modern England: The Rise of Prose Fiction*. Aldershot: Ashgate, 2006.

Meredith, Rosamond. 'A Derbyshire Family in the Seventeenth Century: The Eyres of Hassop and Their Forfeited Estates'. *British Catholic History* 8, no. 1 (1965): 12–77.

Millar, Laura A. *Archives: Principles and Practices*. London: Facet Publishing 2017.

Millman, Jill Seal, and Gillian Wright, eds. *Early Modern Women's Manuscript Poetry*. Manchester: Manchester University Press, 2005.

Millstone, Noah. 'Designed for Collection: Early Modern News and the Production of History'. *Media History* 23, no. 2 (2017): 177–198.

Molekamp, Femke. 'Using a Collection to Discover Reading Practices: The British Library Geneva Bibles and a History of Their Early Modern Readers'. *Electronic British Library Journal* (2006): 1–13.

Molekamp, Femke. '"Of the Incomparable treasure of the Holy Scriptures": The Geneva Bible in the Early Modern Household'. In *Literature and Popular Culture in Early Modern England*, edited by Matthew Dimmock and Andrew Hadfield, 121–137. Farnham: Ashgate, 2009.

Molekamp, Femke. 'Seventeenth-Century Funeral Sermons and Exemplary Female Devotion: Gendered Spaces and Histories'. *Renaissance and Reformation / Renaissance et Réforme* 35, no. 1 Special issue: Gendering Time and Space in Early Modern England (2012): 43–63.

Molekamp, Femke. *Women and the Bible in Early Modern England: Religious Reading and Writing*. Oxford: Oxford University Press, 2013.

Molekamp, Femke. 'Therapies for Melancholy and Inordinate Passion in the Letters of Dorothy Osborne to Sir William Temple (1652–1654)'. *The Seventeenth Century* 29, no. 3 (2014): 255–276.

Molekamp, Femke. 'The Making of the Geneva Bible: Histories of Translation and Reading'. *AHRC Translating Cultures*. Accessed

June 24, 2019. http://translatingcultures.org.uk/awards/fellowship-awards/the-making-of-the-geneva-bible-histories-of-translation-and-reading.

Moore, Helen. 'Romance: *Amadis de Gaule* and John Barclay's *Argenis*'. In *The Oxford Handbook of English Prose, 1500–1640*, edited by Andrew Hadfield, 59–76. Oxford: Oxford University Press, 2013.

Morgan, Paul. 'Frances Wolfreston and "Hor Bouks": A Seventeenth-Century Woman Book Collector'. *The Library* 6th Series, 11, no. 3 (1989): 197–219.

Moss, Ann. 'Commonplace-Rhetoric and Thought-Patterns in Early Modern Culture'. In *The Recovery of Rhetoric: Persuasive Discourse and Disciplinarity in the Human Sciences*, edited by R. H. Roberts and J. M. M. Good, 49–60. Charlottesville, VA: University Press of Virginia, 1993.

Moss, Ann. *Printed Commonplace-Books and the Structuring of Renaissance Thought*. Oxford: Clarendon, 1996.

Moxham, Noah, and Joad Raymond, eds. *News Networks in Early Modern Europe*. Leiden: Brill, 2016.

Mulligan, Lotte. 'Robert Boyle: "The Christian Virtuoso" and the Rhetoric of "Reason"'. In *Religion, Reason and Nature in Early Modern Europe*, edited by Robert Crocker, 97–116. Dordrecht: Kluwer Academic Publishers, 2001.

Murphy, Jessica C. *Virtuous Necessity: Conduct Literature and the Making of the Virtuous Woman in Early Modern England*. Ann Arbor, MI: University of Michigan Press, 2015.

Nagy, Doreen Evenden. *Popular Medicine in Seventeenth-Century England*. Bowling Green, OH: Bowling Green State University Popular Press, 1988.

Narveson, Kate. *Bible Readers and Lay Writers in Early Modern England: Gender and Self-Definition in an Emergent Writing Culture*. Aldershot: Ashgate, 2012.

Neville, Sarah. *Early Modern Herbals and the Book Trade: English Stationers and the Commodification of Botany*. Cambridge: Cambridge University Press, 2022.

Nevitt, Marcus. *Women and the Pamphlet Culture of Revolutionary England, 1640–1660*. Aldershot: Ashgate, 2006.

Nevitt, Marcus. 'Women in the Business of Revolutionary News: Elizabeth Alkin, "Parliament Joan," and the Commonwealth Newsbook'. In Raymond, *News, Newspapers, and Society*, 84–108.

Newcomb, Lori Humphrey. 'Gendering Prose Romance in Renaissance England'. In Saunders, *A Companion to Romance*, 121–139.

Newcomb, Lori Humphrey. 'Frances Wolfreston's Annotations as Labours of Love'. In *Women's Labour and the History of the Book in*

*Early Modern England*, edited by Valerie Wayne, 243–266. London: The Arden Shakespeare, 2020.

'Newdigate Family Collection of Newsletters'. *Folger Finding Aids*. Accessed January 20, 2019. https://findingaids.folger.edu /dfonewdigate.xml.

Norbrook, David. 'Lucy Hutchinson: Theology, Gender and Translation'. *The Seventeenth Century* 30, no. 2 (2015): 139–162.

North, Marcy L. 'Anonymity's Subject: James I and the Debate over the Oath of Allegiance'. *New Literary History* 33, no. 2, Anonymity (2002): 215–232.

Oates, Rosamund. *Moderate Radical: Tobie Matthew and the English Reformation*. Oxford: Oxford University Press, 2018.

Ophir, Ella. 'The Diary and the Commonplace Book: Self-Inscription in *The Note Books of a Woman Alone*'. *Biography* 38, no. 1 (2015): 41–55.

Orgel, Stephen. 'Marginal Maternity: Reading Lady Anne Clifford's A Mirror for Magistrates'. In *Printing and Parenting in Early Modern England*, edited by Douglas A. Brooks, 267–289. Aldershot: Ashgate, 2003.

Orgel, Stephen. 'Reading Lady Anne Clifford's *A Mirovr for Magistrates*'. In Hearn and Hulse, *Lady Anne Clifford: Culture, Patronage and Gender in 17th-Century Britain*, 109–116.

Ostovich, Helen, and Elizabeth Sauer, eds. *Reading Early Modern Women: An Anthology of Texts in Manuscript and Print, 1550–1700*. London: Routledge, 2004.

Ottway, Sheila. 'Dorothy Osborne's Love Letters: Novelistic Glimmerings and the Ovidian Self'. *Prose Studies* 19, no. 2 (1996): 149–159.

Outram, Dorinda. *The Enlightenment*. Cambridge: Cambridge University Press, 2005.

Parageau, Sandrine. 'Auto Didacticism and the Construction of Scientific Discourse in Early Modern England: Margaret Cavendish's and Anne Conway's "Intellectual Bricolage"'. In *Women and Science, 17th Century to Present: Pioneers, Activists and Protagonists*, edited by Donna Spalding Andréolle and Véronique Molinari, 3–18. Newcastle: Cambridge Scholars Publishing, 2011.

'Parishes: Marton'. In *A History of the County of York North Riding: Volume 2*, edited by William Page, 264–268. London: Victoria County History, 1923. *British History Online*. Accessed June 20, 2019. www .british-history.ac.uk/vch/yorks/north/vol2/pp264-268.

Paster, Gail Kern, Katherine Rowe and Mary Floyd-Wilson, eds. *Reading the Early Modern Passions: Essays in the Cultural History of Emotion*. Philadelphia, PA: University of Pennsylvania Press, 2004.

Patterson, Annabel. 'Dryden and Political Allegiance'. In Zwicker, *The Cambridge Companion to John Dryden*, 221–236.

Paulson, Ronald. 'Dryden and the Energies of Satire'. In Zwicker, *The Cambridge Companion to John Dryden*, 37–58.

Peacey, Jason. 'Sir Thomas Cotton's Consumption of News'. *The Library* 7th series, 7 (2006): 3–24.

Peacey, Jason. *Print and Public Politics in the English Revolution*. Cambridge: Cambridge University Press, 2013.

Peacey, Jason. 'The Revolution in Print'. In *The Oxford Handbook of the English Revolution*, edited by Michael J. Braddick, 276–293. Oxford: Oxford University Press, 2015.

Peacey, Jason. 'A Royalist Reads the News: Sir Edward Hyde and Civil War Journalism'. In *Clarendon Reconsidered: Law, Loyalty and Literature, 1640–1674*, edited by P. Major, 16–36. London: Routledge, 2018.

Pearce, Lynne. *Feminism and the Politics of Reading*. London: Arnold, 1997.

Pearce, Lynne. 'Popular Romance and Its Readers'. In Saunders, *A Companion to Romance*, 521–538.

Pearson, Jacqueline. 'Women Reading, Reading Women'. In *Women and Literature in Britain, 1500–1700*, edited by Helen Wilcox, 80–99. Cambridge: Cambridge University Press, 1996.

Pender, Patricia, and Rosalind Smith, eds. *Material Cultures of Early Modern Women's Writing*. Houndmills: Palgrave Macmillan, 2014.

Pennell, Sara. 'Perfecting Practice? Women, Manuscript Recipes and Knowledge in Early Modern England'. In Burke and Gibson, *Early Modern Women's Manuscript Writing*, 237–258.

Perry, Ruth. 'Radical Doubt and the Liberation of Women'. *Eighteenth Century Studies* 18, no. 4 (1985): 472–493.

Peters, Kate. *Print Culture and Early Quakers*. Cambridge: Cambridge University Press, 2005.

Pettegree, Andrew. *The Invention of News: How the World Came to Know about Itself*. New Haven, CT: Yale University Press, 2014.

Phillips, Patricia. *The Scientific Lady: A Social History of Women's Scientific Interests 1520–1918*. New York: St. Martin's Press, 1990.

Phillips, Susan E. *Transforming Talk: The Problem with Gossip in Late Medieval England*. University Park, PA: The Pennsylvania State University Press, 2007.

Pincus, Steve. '"Coffee Does Politicians Create": Coffeehouses and Restoration Political Culture'. *Journal of Modern History* 67, no. 4 (1995): 807–834.

Pohl, Nicole. *Women, Space and Utopia, 1600–1800*. Aldershot: Ashgate, 2006.
Poitevin, Kimberly. 'Inventing Whiteness: Cosmetics, Race, and Women in Early Modern England'. *Journal for Early Modern Cultural Studies* 11, no. 1 (2011): 59–89.
Pollnitz, Aysha. *Princely Education in Early Modern Britian*. Cambridge: Cambridge University Press, 2015.
Pollock, Linda. '"Teach her to Live Under Obedience": The Making of Women in the Upper Ranks of Early Modern England'. *Continuity and Change* 4, no. 2 (1989): 231–258.
Pollock, Linda, ed. *With Faith and Physic: The Life of a Tudor Gentlewoman, Lady Grace Mildmay, 1552–1620*. London: Collins & Brown, 1993.
Poole, Kristen. '"The Fittest Closet for All Goodness": Authorial Strategies of Jacobean Mothers' Manuals'. *Studies in English Literature, 1500–1900* 35, no. 1 The English Renaissance (1995): 69–88.
Potter, Ursula. 'Elizabeth Drama and *The Instruction of a Christian Woman by Juan Luis Vives*'. In *What Nature Does Not Teach: Didactic Literature in the Medieval and Early Modern Periods*, edited by Juanita Feros Ruys, 261–286. Turnhout: Brepols Publishers, 2008.
Radway, Janice A. *Reading the Romance: Women, Patriarchy, and Popular Literature*. London: Verso, 1987.
Raven, James, Helen Small and Naomi Tadmor. 'Introduction: The Practice and Representation of Reading in England'. In *The Practice and Representation of Reading in England*, edited by Raven, Small and Tadmor, 1–21. Cambridge: Cambridge University Press, 2010.
Raymond, Joad. 'Introduction'. In Raymond, *Making the News*, 1–25.
Raymond, Joad, ed. *Making the News: An Anthology of the Newsbooks of Revolutionary England 1641–1660*. Gloucester: The Windrush Press, 1993.
Raymond, Joad, ed. *News, Newspapers, and Society in Early Modern Britain*. London: Frank Cass, 1999.
Raymond, Joad. 'The Newspaper, Public Opinion, and the Public Sphere in the Seventeenth Century'. In Raymond, *News, Newspapers, and Society*, 109–140.
Raymond, Joad. *The Invention of the Newspaper: English Newsbooks, 1641–1649*. Oxford: Clarendon Press, 2005.
Raymond, Joad. 'Irrational, Impractical and Unprofitable: Reading the News in Seventeenth-Century Britain'. In Sharpe and Zwicker, *Reading, Society and Politics in Early Modern England*, 185–212.

Raymond, Joad, ed. *The Oxford History of Popular Print Culture, Volume 1: Cheap Print in Britain and Ireland to 1660*. Oxford: Oxford University Press, 2011.

Reid, Kirsty, and Fiona Paisley, eds. *Sources and Methods in Histories of Colonialism: Approaching the Imperial Archive*. Abingdon: Routledge, 2017.

Rendall, Jane. 'Women and the Public Sphere'. *Gender & History* 11, no. 3 (1999): 475–488.

Reynolds, Melissa. *Reading Practice: The Pursuit of Natural Knowledge from Manuscript to Print*. Chicago, IL: University of Chicago Press, 2024.

Richards, Jennifer. *Voices and Books in the English Renaissance: A New History of Reading*. Oxford: Oxford University Press, 2019.

Richards, Jennifer, and Fred Schurink. 'Introduction: The Textuality and Materiality of Reading in Early Modern England'. *Huntington Library Quarterly* 73, no. 3 (2010): 345–361.

Richardson, Sarah. '"Well-neighboured Houses": The Political Networks of Elite Women, 1780–1860'. In *Women in British Politics, 1760–1860: The Power of the Petticoat*, edited by Kathryn Gleadle and Sarah Richardson, 56–73. London: Palgrave Macmillan, 2000.

Richter, David H. *Reading the Eighteenth-Century Novel*. Oxford: Wiley, 2017.

Roberts, Josephine A. 'Extracts from *Arcadia* in the Manuscript Notebook of Lady Katherine Manners'. *Notes and Queries* 28, no. 1 (1981): 35–36.

Roberts, Sasha. 'Reading in Early Modern England: Contexts and Problems'. *Critical Survey* 12, no. 2 (2000): 1–16.

Roberts, Sasha. *Reading Shakespeare's Poems in Early Modern England*. Basingstoke: Palgrave Macmillan, 2003.

Romkins, Renée, and Antia Wiersma, eds. *Gender and Archiving: Past, Present, Future*. Amsterdam: Verloren, 2017.

Rosenwein, Barbara H. *Emotional Communities in the Early Middle Ages*. Ithaca, NY: Cornell University Press, 2006.

Ross, Sarah C. E. 'Epic, Meditation, or Sacred History? Women and Biblical Verse Paraphrase in Seventeenth-Century England'. In Killeen et al., *The Oxford Handbook of the Bible in Early Modern England*, 484–498.

Ross, Sarah C. E., and Elizabeth Scott-Baumann, eds. *Women Poets of the English Civil War*. Manchester: Manchester University Press, 2018.

Ryrie, Alec. *Being Protestant in Reformation Britain*. Oxford: Oxford University Press, 2013.

Salmon, Vivian. 'Women and the Study of Language in Sixteenth and Seventeenth-Century England'. *Histoire Epistémologie Langage* 16, no. 2 (1994): 95–119.

Salzman, Paul, ed. *An Anthology of Elizabethan Prose Fiction*. Oxford: Oxford University Press, 1987.

Salzman, Paul, ed. *Early Modern Women's Writing: An Anthology, 1560–1700*. Oxford: Oxford University Press, 2000.

Salzman, Paul. 'Royalist Epic and Romance'. In Keeble, *The Cambridge Companion to Writing of the English Revolution*, 215–232.

Salzman, Paul. *Reading Early Modern Women's Writing*. Oxford: Oxford University Press, 2006.

Salzman, Paul. 'Anne Clifford's Annotated Copy of Sidney's *Arcadia*'. *Notes and Queries* 56, no. 4 (2009): 554–555.

Salzman, Paul, ed. *Expanding the Canon of Early Modern Women's Writing*. Newcastle upon Tyne: Cambridge Scholars Publishing, 2010.

Saunders, Corinne. 'Introduction'. In Saunders, *A Companion to Romance*, 1–9.

Saunders, Corinne, ed. *A Companion to Romance: From Classical to Contemporary*. Oxford: Blackwell Publishing, 2004.

Schaeffer, John D. 'Tropical Latitude: Prophecy, Orality, and the Rhetoric of Tolerance in Jeremy Taylor's *The Liberty of Prophesying*'. *Studies in Philology* 101, no. 4 (2004): 454–470.

Schneider, Gary. *The Culture of Epistolarity: Vernacular Letters and Letter Writing in Early Modern England, 1500–1700*. Newark, DE: University of Delaware Press, 2005.

Schochet, Gordon J. *The Authoritarian Family and Political Attitudes in Seventeenth-Century England: Patriarchalism in Political Thought*. London: Transaction Books, 1988.

Schurink, Fred. '"Like a Hand in the Margine of a Booke": William Blount's Marginalia and the Politics of Sidney's *Arcadia*'. *Review of English Studies* 59, no. 238 (2008): 1–24.

Schurink, Fred. 'Manuscript Commonplace Books, Literature, and Reading in Early Modern England'. *Huntington Library Quarterly* 73, no. 3 (2010): 453–469.

Scott-Baumann, Elizabeth. 'Lucy Hutchinson, the Bible and *Order and Disorder*'. In Harris and Scott-Baumann, *The Intellectual Culture of Puritan Women, 1558–1680*, 176–189.

Scott-Baumann, Elizabeth. *Forms of Engagement: Women, Poetry and Culture 1640–1680*. Oxford: Oxford University Press, 2013.

Scott-Warren, Jason. 'News, Sociability, and Bookbuying in Early Modern England: The Letters of Sir Thomas Cornwallis'. *The Library* 7th series, 1 (2000): 377–398.

Wittman, Reinhard. 'Was There a Reading Revolution at the End of the Eighteenth Century?' In Cavallo and Chartier, *A History of Reading in the West*, 284–312.

Wolfe, Heather. 'Reading Bells and Loose Paper: Reading and Writing Practice of the English Benedictine Nuns of Cambrai and Paris'. In Burke and Gibson, *Early Modern Women's Manuscript Writing*, 135–156.

Wolfgang, Aurora, and Sharon Diane Nell. 'The Theory and Practice of Honnêteté in Jacques Du Bosc's *L'Honnête femme* (1632–36) and *Nouveau recueil de lettres des dames de ce temps* (1635)'. *Cahiers du Dix-Septième: An Interdisciplinary Journal* 13, no. 2 (2011): 56–91.

Woods, Susanne, and Margaret P. Hannay, eds. *Teaching Tudor and Stuart Women Writers*. New York: The Modern Language Association of America, 2000.

Woolf, Daniel. 'News, History, and the Construction of the Present in Early Modern England'. In Dooley and Baron, *The Politics of Information in Early Modern Europe*, 80–118.

Woolf, D. R. *Reading History in Early Modern England*. Cambridge: Cambridge University Press, 2000.

Wormald, Jenny. 'James VI and I: Two Kings or One?' *History* 68, no. 223 (1983): 187–209.

Wray, Ramona. 'Recovering the Reading of Renaissance Englishwomen: Deployments of Autobiography'. *Critical Survey* 12, no. 2 (2000): 33–48.

Wray, Ramona. 'Autobiography'. In Knoppers, *The Cambridge Companion to Early Modern Women's Writing*, 194–207.

Wrightson, Keith. 'The Politics of the Parish in Early Modern England'. In *The Experience of Authority in Early Modern England*, edited by Paul Griffiths, Adam Fox and Steve Hindle, 10–46. London: Palgrave Macmillan, 1996.

Yeo, Richard. *Notebooks, English Virtuosi, and Early Modern Science*. Chicago, IL: University of Chicago Press, 2014.

Ziegler, Georgianna. 'Lost in the Archives? Searching for Records of Early Modern Women'. In Woods and Hannay, *Teaching Tudor and Stuart Women Writers*, 315–347.

Ziegler, Georgianna. 'Lady Anne Clifford Reads John Selden'. In Acheson, *Early Modern English Marginalia*, 134–154.

Zwicker, Steven N. 'The Constitution of Opinion and the Pacification of Reading'. In Sharpe and Zwicker, *Reading, Society and Politics in Early Modern England*, 295–316.

Zwicker, Steven N., ed. *The Cambridge Companion to John Dryden*. Cambridge: Cambridge University Press, 2004.

# Index

www.ingramcontent.com/pod-product-compliance
Lightning Source LLC
LaVergne TN
LVHW052015300826
846742LV00019B/68
* 9 7 8 1 9 1 5 2 4 9 4 1 8 *